PROSECUTORIAL DISCRETION AT THE INTERNATIONAL CRIMINAL COURT

This timely book provides a comprehensive guide to, and rigorous analysis of, prosecutorial discretion at the International Criminal Court. This is the first study of its kind to take the reader through all the key stages of the Prosecutor's decision-making process. Starting from preliminary examinations and the decision to investigate, the book also explores case selection processes and plea agreements, culminating in the question of how to end engagement in specific situations. The book serves as a guide to the Rome Statute through the lens of the Prosecutor's activities. With its unique combination of legal theory and specific policy analysis, it addresses broader questions that will be relevant to other international and hybrid criminal courts and tribunals. The book will be of interest to students, practitioners of law, academics, and the wider public concerned with international law, criminal justice and international relations.

Volume 77 in the series Studies in International Law

Studies in International Law

Recent titles in this series

Arctic Law and Governance: The Role of China and Finland
Edited by Timo Koivurova, Qin Tianbao, Tapio Nykänen and Sébastien Duyck

States, the Law and Access to Refugee Protection: Fortresses and Fairness
Edited by Maria O'Sullivan and Dallal Stevens

Revisiting the Concept of Defence in the Jus ad Bellum:
The Dual Face of Defence
Johanna Friman

The International Legal Protection of Persons in Humanitarian Crises
Dug Cubie

The International Committee of the Red Cross and its Mandate to Protect and Assist: Law and Practice
Christy Shucksmith

The Impact of Investment Treaty Law on Host States:
Enabling Good Governance
Mavluda Sattorova

Allocating International Responsibility Between Member States and International Organisations
Nikolaos Voulgaris

Predictability and Flexibility in the Law of Maritime Delimitation, 2nd edition
Yoshifumi Tanaka

Feminist Engagement with International Criminal Law: Norm Transfer, Complementarity, Rape and Consent
Eithne Dowds

Asylum Control and Access to Protection: Admission, Readmission and Human Rights
Mariagiulia Giuffré

Intertemporal Linguistics in International Law: Beyond Contemporaneous and Evolutionary Treaty Interpretation
Julian Wyatt

The Responsibility to Protect and the Failures of the United Nations Security Council
P M Butchard

The Role of Multilateral Environmental Agreements: A Reconciliatory Approach to Environmental Protection in Armed Conflict
Britta Sjostedt

For a complete list of titles in this series, see www.bloomsburyprofessional.com/uk/series/studies-in-international-law

Prosecutorial Discretion at the International Criminal Court

Anni Pues

• HART •
OXFORD • LONDON • NEW YORK • NEW DELHI • SYDNEY

HART PUBLISHING

Bloomsbury Publishing Plc

Kemp House, Chawley Park, Cumnor Hill, Oxford, OX2 9PH, UK

1385 Broadway, New York, NY 10018, USA

HART PUBLISHING, the Hart/Stag logo, BLOOMSBURY and the Diana logo are trademarks of Bloomsbury Publishing Plc

First published in Great Britain 2020

A catalogue record for this book is available from the British Library.

Library of Congress Cataloging-in-Publication data

Names: Pues, Anni Henriette author.

Title: Prosecutorial discretion at the International Criminal Court / Anni Pues.

Description: Oxford ; New York : Hart, 2020. | Series: Studies in international law ; volume 77 | Based on author's thesis (doctoral - University of Glasgow, 2017) issued under title: A critical legal analysis of prosecutorial discretion at the International Criminal Court : towards more transparency, accountability, and legitimacy. | Includes bibliographical references and index.

Identifiers: LCCN 2020005179 (print) | LCCN 2020005180 (ebook) | ISBN 9781509928682 (hardcover) | ISBN 9781509928699 (Epub)

Subjects: LCSH: Prosecution (International law)—Decision making. | International Criminal Court

Classification: LCC KZ7332 .P84 2020 (print) | LCC KZ7332 (ebook) | DDC 345/.05042—dc23

LC record available at https://lccn.loc.gov/2020005179

LC ebook record available at https://lccn.loc.gov/2020005180

ISBN: HB: 978-1-50992-868-2
ePDF: 978-1-50992-870-5
ePub: 978-1-50992-869-9

Typeset by Compuscript Ltd, Shannon

Acknowledgements

Writing this book was only possible through the tremendous support I have experienced from different sides. At various stages, James Sloan, Robin Geiss, Lindsey Farmer, Robert Cryer and Christian Tams had some important input into this project. Some of the initial research for this book was supported through a University of Glasgow College of Social Sciences PhD Scholarship. The School of Law at the University of Glasgow has been a great home to write this book. This work has benefited greatly from discussions of my work with various inspiring academics. I want to highlight the participants of the 2015 ASIL workshop of the International Criminal Law Interest Group, who provided a very helpful sounding board for my work in progress. The PluriCourts Centre for the Study of the Legitimate Roles of the Judiciary in the Global Order at the University of Oslo supported my visit to Oslo, where I had the chance to present my work. The discussion there has greatly refined my thinking. I also want to thank many wonderful women in the postgraduate and academic community in Scotland. Nina Westoby, Lenneke Sprik, Caterine Ward, Clare Frances Moran, Joanna Dingwall, Mo Hume and many others have been crucial to getting this book done through the shared hours of writing, discussions and words of advice. Lastly, I want to say thank you to my family for their wholehearted support for this project. My partner, Andy Cumbers, has been the most important source of support and encouragement, and David and Anna have both in their own ways contributed to the journey that has resulted in this thesis.

Contents

Abbreviations

AC	Appeal Chamber
ASP	Assembly of States Parties
CAR	Central African Republic
DCC	Document containing the charges
DRC	Democratic Republic of the Congo
FARC	Revolutionary Armed Forces of Colombia
HRW	Human Rights Watch
ICC	International Criminal Court
ICCSt	Rome Statute of the International Criminal Court
ICD	International Crimes Division
ICTR	International Criminal Tribunal for Rwanda
ICTY	International Criminal Tribunal for the former Yugoslavia
LRA	Lord's Resistance Army
OTP	Office of the Prosecutor
PTC	Pre-Trial Chamber
RPE	Rules of Procedure and Evidence of the International Criminal Court
SC	Security Council
SCSL	Special Court for Sierra Leone
STL	Special Tribunal for Lebanon
TC	Trial Chamber

Table of Cases

European Court of Human Rights

Domestic Courts

Inter-American Court of Human Rights

International Criminal Court

International Criminal Tribunal for the former Yugoslavia

International Criminal Tribunal for Rwanda

Introduction

IN JULY 1998, at the end of a five-week, intensely negotiated conference in Rome, 120 states voted decisively to establish the first ever permanent international criminal court. It was widely celebrated as a success in the fight against impunity. Within four years, 60 states had signed and ratified the Rome Statute of the International Criminal Court and the International Criminal Court (ICC) was established. In 2003, the Court started its operations, the first ICC Prosecutor, Luis Moreno Ocampo, was appointed, and a year later the first investigation launched.

Twenty years on, the Court finds itself under immense pressure. With the cases against Kenyan President Kenyatta and the Sudanese (ex-)President Al-Bashir, the Prosecutor started prosecutions against then two sitting heads of African states. Although the Court has, under the lead of the current Prosecutor Fatou Bensouda, moved out of Africa with its decision to investigate in Georgia, at the time of writing (in September 2019), all cases pending before the Court still only feature defendants from African countries. The exercise of prosecutorial discretion was heavily implicated in these investigation and case selection decisions. They triggered severe criticism and led to allegations of 'anti-African bias' and Western hegemony over developing countries.[1] The African Union openly lobbied for African states to withdraw from the ICC and South Africa, the Gambia, and Burundi duly withdrew from the Rome Statute.[2] Subsequently, the Gambia saw a change in government and rescinded its withdrawal, and in South Africa the judiciary put a halt to the move.[3] Yet, the Court's legitimacy has been severely damaged. When the ICC is perceived as biased, it cannot 'guarantee lasting respect for and the enforcement of international justice'.[4] Therefore, the Prosecutor has a crucial task in using her discretionary powers to contribute

[1] C Jalloh, 'Regionalizing International Criminal Law?' (2009) 9 *International Criminal Law Review* 445, 462–63 with further references; he provides a good overview over the shift of perception of the ICC in African countries, quoting Ugandan scholar Mamdani: '[The] ICC is rapidly turning into a Western court to try African crimes against humanity'.

[2] See UN Treaty Collection, 'Rome Statute of the International Criminal Court', endnote 2, listing the dates of withdrawal notices and depositary notification numbers of South Africa (withdrawal notification withdrawn on 7 March 2017), Burundi, and Gambia (withdrawal notification withdrawn on 10 February 2017), available at: treaties.un.org/doc/Publication/MTDSG/Volume%20II/Chapter%20XVIII/XVIII-10.en.pdf.

[3] *Democratic Alliance v Minister of International Relations and Cooperation & Others*, High Court of South Africa, Judgment, Case No 83145/2016, 22 February 2017 declared the withdrawal notice as invalid because of the lack of parliamentary approval in South Africa.

[4] The drafters expressed this as one of the motivations to establish the ICC in the Preamble of the ICCSt.

to enhanced perceptions of the legitimacy of the Court, and to persuade its constituencies of the importance of its purpose and mission.

Against this background, this book investigates the Prosecutor's discretionary powers as the core of an evolving system of international criminal justice that aspires to achieve universal jurisdiction. This book offers a comprehensive guide to and a rigorous analysis of discretion in the Rome Statute. It is the first study that takes the reader through all the key stages of the Prosecutor's decision-making processes. Starting from preliminary examinations and the decision to investigate, the book undertakes a detailed and systematic exploration of case selection processes that entail fundamental questions on the choices of defendants and charging processes as well as negotiating justice through plea agreements. It also revisits the interests of justice and outlines the space that potentially exists to move beyond Western conceptions of justice to make the ICC a genuinely international justice mechanism that can take into account local culture and perceptions. This culminates in the question of how to end engagement in specific country situations.

The discussion merges some of the fundamental questions of international criminal law with the unique challenges triggered through the Court's *sui generis* nature which melds common and civil law features together. The Prosecutor is the ICC's chief strategist and gatekeeper.[5] In contrast to all other international criminal tribunals that had specifically defined mandates and jurisdictional bounds, the ICC has a unique jurisdiction that allows it under specific conditions to operate worldwide.[6] An additional difficulty is that the Rome Statute of the International Criminal Court is in parts vague leaving many gaps to be filled through the Court's practice.[7] It is an international criminal justice system that is still under construction. The exercise of prosecutorial discretion is critical to make the Court work, and, ultimately, to safeguard the Court's legitimacy.

But 'what is discretion, or what is the exercise of discretion?'[8] HLA Hart started his enquiry into 'discretion' in 1956 with this question as part of a Legal Philosophy Discussion Group at Harvard, which consisted of more than 20 professors interested in examining discretion. The meetings of this group turned out to be enormously popular. Harvard's discussion group was fully aware how much the context of discretion mattered, dependent on which legal tradition the system was placed in, and which type of law was concerned. It was in this period that HLA Hart wrote his recently discovered essay on discretion. This essay is a small part of a larger body of theoretical scholarship in the

[5] L Reydams, J Wouters and C Ryngaert (eds), *International Prosecutors* (Oxford, Oxford University Press, 2012) 2.

[6] A Security Council referral can trigger ICC investigations in states that are not Parties to the Rome Statute.

[7] Also referred to as the 'Statute' or the 'Rome Statute' in the main body throughout this book, whereas footnotes contain the abbreviation 'ICCSt'.

[8] HLA Hart, 'Discretion' (2013) 127 *Harvard Law Review* 652, 652.

post-war setting to rethink the concepts of law in opposition to tyranny and fascism.[9] These issues are once again sadly pressing in the current geopolitical order. The discourse on discretion within this scholarship offers the foundation for the conceptualisation of prosecutorial discretion in this book.[10]

Prosecutorial discretion is often seen as a threat to the integrity of the law, entailing the danger of opening the door to a politicised Prosecutor. Yet, discretion is pivotal to making the system work. Instead of perceiving discretion as beyond the law, the study of discretion in this book seeks to promote an understanding of discretion that is firmly embedded in, and limited through law, and guided by key aims and values in international criminal law. Inspired by the work of Harvard's discussion group, the book sets out to answer what the nature of prosecutorial discretion at the ICC is and asks a series of sub-questions: how is the Prosecutor equipped with discretionary powers, and how does she currently exercise them? What are the legal limits of these discretionary powers? Which values and principles should guide the exercise of discretion? And lastly, what mechanisms of accountability and review exist?[11]

The book argues for a structured and principled exercise of prosecutorial discretion.[12] It opposes the suggestion that detailed guidelines should be developed for its exercise, because this would hamper the flexibility of the ICC system.[13] The ICC requires a high level of flexibility to fulfil its mandate of addressing 'the most serious crimes of concern to the international community'.[14] The decisions that the Prosecutor makes are by their nature highly selective: she must ensure that she explains these decisions in an adequate manner so that they are not perceived as arbitrary. At the same time, the Prosecutor must work on the basis of an international treaty-based framework that contains compromises and ambiguities.

Ambiguities are nothing new for international law; the discipline might to a certain extent always contain an aspect of 'muddling through'.[15] This is

[9] GC Shaw, 'HLA Hart's Lost Essay: Discretion and the Legal Process School' (2013) 127 *Harvard Law Review* 666, 691.

[10] Another key work this book draws on in its reflections on discretion is R Dworkin, *Taking Rights Seriously* (London, Duckworth, 1977).

[11] Hart, 'Discretion' (n 8) 652 poses a similar set of questions eloquently ending: 'What can be done to maximize the beneficial operation of the use of discretion and to minimize any harm that it does?' Ultimately, the harms and benefits are, transferred to the ICC, its impact on the legitimacy of the Court.

[12] KC Davis, *Discretionary Justice, A Preliminary Inquiry* (Baton Rouge, LA, Louisiana State University Press, 1969) 97–98 explains that the purpose of structuring discretion is to control the manner of its exercise. For a more structured exercise of discretion, open policies and decisions that are made based on these policies and that deliberate on the reasons (open reasons) are important. 'Openness is the natural enemy of arbitrariness and a natural ally in the fight against injustice'.

[13] For a key contribution see A Marston Danner, 'Enhancing the Legitimacy and Accountability of Prosecutorial Discretion at the International Criminal Court' (2003) 97 *The American Journal of International Law* 510, 541, who argues that such guidelines would contribute to consistency and impartiality. This would assist the Court in achieving legitimacy and the perception of legitimacy.

[14] Preamble ICCSt.

[15] J Klabbers, 'Friedrich Kratochwil. The Status of Law in World Society: Meditations on the Role and Rule of Law' (2015) 25 *European Journal of International Law* 1195, 1199.

particularly pronounced in the work of the Prosecutor – not because of the very dedicated and hard-working staff who work in the Office of the Prosecutor (OTP), but because of the task at hand: the nature of the often ambiguous legal framework, the high expectations, the lack of enforcement powers and the multitude of practical constraints. Yet, the criminal law aspect of the Court's work, with its potential impact on people's lives, requires coherence in the procedures of the Court. Such procedural coherence is a key element in protecting against arbitrariness. The contribution I seek to make with this book is to provide a better understanding of the legal core, of discretionary processes at work. The analysis makes visible the scope of discretion at the different stages of the proceedings and delineates the boundaries of that discretion. The book pinpoints the general principles that the Prosecutor should aim for within the legal and practical constraints and demonstrates what a structured and principled exercise of procedural discretion should entail. It argues for a principled approach that is more transparent regarding individual decisions, which in turn would contribute to the Prosecutor becoming more accountable and responsive.

The proposals made in this book are informed by the idea that the ICC must aim to be a responsive institution. The notion of responsive law has been developed as opposed to repressive systems of law which build on submissive compliance, and to autonomous understandings of law that perceive law as independent of politics and focus strongly on the right process.[16] Responsiveness in the legal order perceives social pressures as sources of knowledge strongly focusing on the purpose of the system.[17] Law needs to respond to the social context in which it operates. The Prosecutor can only operate within the framework of the Rome Statute, the rules and principles of international law, and human rights law.[18] Responsiveness to social pressures, and developments in the

[16] P Nonet and P Selznick, *Law & Society in Transition: Towards Responsive Law* (New Brunswick, Transaction Publishers, 2001) 16.

[17] ibid, 77.

[18] Art 21 ICCSt: Applicable Law

'1. The Court shall apply:

(a) In the first place, this Statute, Elements of Crimes and its Rules of Procedure and Evidence;
(b) In the second place, where appropriate, applicable treaties and the principles and rules of international law, including the established principles of the international law of armed conflict;
(c) Failing that, general principles of law derived by the Court from national laws of legal systems of the world including, as appropriate, the national laws of States that would normally exercise jurisdiction over the crime, provided that those principles are not inconsistent with this Statute and with international law and internationally recognized norms and standards.

2. The Court may apply principles and rules of law as interpreted in its previous decisions.
3. The application and interpretation of law pursuant to this article must be consistent with internationally recognized human rights, and be without any adverse distinction founded on grounds such as gender as defined in article 7, paragraph 3, age, race, colour, language, religion or belief, political or other opinion, national, ethnic or social origin, wealth, birth or other status'.

international community, are therefore only possible within the scope of discretion contained in the legal framework of the ICC system. In the first instance, it is the Prosecutor – as the public face of the Court – who is equipped with discretion that allows flexible answers. Persuading the Court's constituents and the wider international community of its purpose requires strict observance of the rule of law but also a principled use of discretion in a transparent way.[19] Ultimately, adoption of such an approach would have a positive effect on the legitimacy of the Court.

In some areas of prosecutorial discretion, the practice is only gradually emerging. From 2013 onwards, the Prosecutor published a series of relevant policy papers.[20] One conviction at the ICC was based on a plea agreement between the OTP and the defence. At the time of finishing the work on this book in September 2019, no strategy has been developed regarding how to end investigations into situations of conflict. Outlining the role of prosecutorial discretion in the completion processes enters entirely new legal territory. The analysis in this book draws on the broad scholarship in the field and surrounding disciplines, as well as the Court's decisions, OTP reports, submissions, policy papers, public statements made by the Prosecutor, NGO reports, and other similar sources. The research has benefited greatly from the wealth of literature concerning the ICC and the practice of prosecutorial discretion in specific areas of the Court's operations.[21]

I. OUTLINE OF THE BOOK

To set the scene for what follows, chapter one provides a theoretical framework for analysis. It analyses the nature of discretion in the ICC system as a system *sui generis* and identifies two different dimensions of discretion operable in the Prosecutor's powers: a procedural dimension of discretion, in legal theoretical discourses often referred to as 'strong' discretion; and an interpretative

[19] Nonet and Selznick (n 16) 77: '[Only] when an institution is truly purposive can there be a combination of integrity and openness, rule and discretion'.

[20] ICC/OTP: Policy on Children, November 2016; Policy Paper on Case Selection and Prioritisation, 15 September 2016; Policy Paper on Sexual and Gender-Based Crimes, June 2014; Policy Paper on Preliminary Exminations, November 2013.

[21] Key contributions include Marston Danner (n 13); M Brubacher, 'Prosecutorial Discretion within the International Criminal Court' (2004) 2 *Journal of International Criminal Justice* 71; A Greenawalt, 'Justice without Politics? Prosecutorial Discretion and the International Criminal Court' (2007) 39 *New York University Journal of International Law & Politics* 584; B Lepard, 'How Should the ICC Prosecutor Exercise His or Her Discretion: The Role of Fundamental Ethical Principles' (2009) 43 *John Marshall Law Review* 553; J Goldston, 'More Candour about Criteria: The Exercise of Discretion by the Prosecutor of the International Criminal Court' (2010) 8 *Journal of International Criminal Justice* 383; K Ambos and I Stegmiller, 'Prosecuting International Crimes at the International Criminal Court: Is there a Coherent and Comprehensive Prosecution Strategy?' (2013) 59 *Crime, Law and Social Change* 415; M deGuzman, 'Choosing to Prosecute: Expressive Selection at the International Criminal Court' (2012) 33 *Michigan Journal of International Law* 265.

discretionary dimension, also conceptualised as 'weak' discretion.[22] Procedural discretion affords the Prosecutor with the flexibility regarding procedural courses of action, whereas the interpretative discretionary dimension gives flexibility in the application of the law, adjusting broad notions such as gravity, or the interests of justice, to the specific factual circumstances that confront the ICC in the diverse situations and cases before it. The chapter explains how the legality of decisions is pivotal to, but not sufficient for, the aim of ensuring a discretionary decision-making process that safeguards and enhances the legitimacy of the Court. Legitimacy is a multilayered concept that requires the Prosecutor to gear her discretion towards the guiding aims and principles expressed in the Rome Statute: namely, the prevention and deterrence of international crimes; closure of the gap of impunity; and the protection of victims' interests. Lastly, this chapter sets out how accountability can be achieved through formal and pragmatic mechanisms in which transparency of the discretionary decisions is a key element. Based on this framework for analysis, the subsequent chapters evaluate discretionary decisions that are critical for the Prosecutor's function as the gatekeeper to and chief strategist of the ICC.

Chapter two addresses the exercise of discretion throughout the preliminary examination stage. At this widely unregulated stage, discretion is most pronounced. This chapter explores the conduct of preliminary examinations and explicitly addresses their hugely diverging length. It argues that the Prosecutor is limited in the exercise of discretion through obligations such as the duty to ensure effective investigations in article 54(1)(b) of the Statute. The chapter also evaluates how the exercise of prosecutorial discretion can better serve the aims of prevention, deterrence and victims' interests at this stage. A structured exercise of discretion is warranted during the preliminary examination phase that distinguishes more clearly between situations where realistic prospects of positive complementarity emerge from those where swift action is warranted. Against this background, this chapter demonstrates how an increased level of transparency can provide for pragmatic accountability through public scrutiny where formal review mechanisms are absent.

Chapter three then undertakes an analysis of discretionary choices regarding whether to initiate an investigation as the end point of preliminary examinations. It deconstructs the claim of the Prosecutor that she is duty-bound to exercise her *proprio motu* powers. Negating the scope of discretion, where there is some, bears the danger of arbitrary choices because the Prosecutor fails to consider and balance competing interests such as the need to investigate other possible situations that are under preliminary examination. The ICC system, working at full capacity, reveals a structural deficit because it has no clear mechanism assigned for necessary prioritisation processes. It is argued that it would be absurd if the Prosecutor is only free to consider resource constraints

[22] See for the distinction of strong and weak discretion Dworkin (n 10) 31.

so long as the OTP delays completing a preliminary examination, whereas, once a reasonable basis to proceed was established, the Office had a duty to initiate an investigation. This chapter argues for a change of the OTP practice, openly acknowledging the need for the investigation of specific situations and the limits of the ICC's capacities. This would provide the opportunity to raise alarm bells and alert the international community about the need for alternative ways to secure accountability. In this way, the ICC, as the only permanent international criminal court, could set standards and be one (albeit critical) layer in a multi-dimensional system of international criminal law. This would also recognise explicitly that the Court does not have the capacity to secure that justice is done in all those situations of conflict and mass atrocity that would warrant it.

Chapter four turns to the case selection process, focusing on the selection of defendants and the choice of charges. The chapter demonstrates how legal limitations to prosecutorial discretion derive from rules such as the right to a fair trial for the defendant and the principle of equality. Within these limitations, the scope of discretion in the case selection process must be geared towards realising the Court's aims. The OTP should do so through decisions that, taking constraints such as resource pressures into account, aim to maximise the impact of the deterrence and prevention potential of the Court. A critical guiding aim for case selection processes is that the OTP ought to represent all areas of victimisation through case selection within a specific situation. Only a fair and balanced choice of cases and charges, that does not distort the roles of different sides in a conflict, but fairly represents what has happened, can secure the legitimacy of the Court.

Moving on to the trial stage of the proceedings, chapter five analyses the scope for, and emerging practice of, plea agreements at the ICC. Negotiating justice in the face of the most serious crimes such as genocide and crimes against humanity is highly contentious. The clash in legal cultures and approaches to negotiated justice led to the compromise in the Rome Statute that provided the Prosecutor with the ability to enter into discussions with the defence while not being able to strike binding agreements. Analysing the scope of discretion, it is argued that plea agreements have some potential for the ICC despite the tensions created in relation to some of the broader aims of the Court and international criminal law more generally. However, the OTP is bound to address informational asymmetry and ensure that due process requirements are met from the outset. Although any plea agreement will entail some compromise, agreements on charges run counter to the spirit of the Rome Statute if the result would distort a genuine account of what happened and is merely driven by efficiency gains. The ICC is presented with a chance to use plea agreements to construct a restorative justice approach,[23] counterbalancing the compromise entailed in any

[23] N Combs, *Guilty Pleas in International Criminal Law* (Stanford, CA, Stanford University Press, 2007).

agreement through genuine chances for victims to uncover the truth and secure a contribution to reconciliation.

Moving on from those procedural dimensions of discretion, chapter six focuses on the conceptual analysis of the interests of justice in article 53(1)(c) and (2)(c) of the Statute. The interests of justice are one of those open concepts in the Rome Statute that contain scope for some interpretative discretion. This interpretative dimension provides the Prosecutor with some freedom to determine the constitutive elements of the interests of justice. A key argument advanced in this chapter is that the interpretative dimension does not allow any space for managerial considerations such as budgetary concerns, political pressures or the potential availability of evidence. In contrast, peace considerations are firmly within one of the elements that ought to be considered as part of the interests of justice because of the interrelationship between both. Beyond the interpretative dimension, the interests of justice contain direct procedural consequences. Indeed, the chapter argues that the Prosecutor should use the interests of justice more flexibly than the current policy implies. A contextual interpretation of the Rome Statute would allow the Prosecutor to react more flexibly to emerging transitional arrangements and peace negotiations in a country through a preliminary halt of investigations or the withdrawal of charges. It will be important to listen to the voices of victims and communities in conflict to ensure that the ICC contributes to genuine international justice in a way that provides space for legal pluralism.

The last chapter, chapter seven, contains an assessment of the role for prosecutorial discretion in the development of completion strategies for the Court's activities in a situation. This is an unprecedented challenge for an international criminal court because of the ICC's unique jurisdictional scope, and the Prosecutor will have a key role to play in it. The discussion addresses the end of preliminary examinations as well as that of investigations of situations through the lens of Colombia and Uganda. The Prosecutor is tasked with dynamic complementarity assessments during preliminary examinations and investigations, as countries develop domestic justice responses. The principle of complementarity impacts directly on prosecutorial discretion beyond the threshold of admissibility. The respect for state sovereignty requires adjusted prosecutorial strategies at the ICC level, whenever countries develop the ability and show the willingness to live up to their responsibility of addressing international crimes within their jurisdiction. The interests of justice should play a central role, critically inserting an additional dimension beyond state sovereignty and the international perspective through victims' voices. The state has failed to prevent and punish international crimes within its jurisdiction or might even have been complicit in them. Victim voices are those that are best able to determine whether state efforts will realise their rights to truth and justice.

Negotiating the tensions between state sovereignty and the need to enforce international criminal law will require the Prosecutor and the Court to be in dialogue with, and responsive to, its constituents. These tensions, the future prospects for international criminal law more broadly, and the ICC in particular, will also be addressed in the conclusion to the book. Ultimately, only if the Court can successfully negotiate these tensions for the benefit of those who suffered from crime and atrocity, can it achieve its mission of creating respect for international justice.

Lastly, on a more technical note, a couple of remarks on the use of language in this book. The book uses the terms 'situation' and 'cases' as broadly distinguished within the ICC. Situation, refers to the more general context of a situation of crisis that is generally 'defined in terms of temporal, territorial and in some cases personal parameters'; cases, refer to more specific incidents within a situation and entail proceedings starting with the issuance of an arrest warrant or a summons to appear.[24] The strict divide between the two, however, might not always be possible in practice and should perhaps be rethought for future investigations.

Regarding the use of personal pronouns, generally this book refers to the Prosecutor as 'she', reflecting the fact that with Fatou Bensouda, it is currently a woman that fills this role. Having said that, the personal pronoun 'he' is used whenever specific reference is made to decisions or actions of the previous Prosecutor at the ICC, Luis Moreno Ocampo. Reference to the defendant is made using the male personal pronoun. Currently every defendant, except one, at the ICC has been male. Using only one pronoun contributes to better readability. Any 'good/evil' gender narrative that could be read into these choices is entirely unintentional.

[24] *Situation in the Democratic Republic of the Congo*, Decision on Applications for Participation in the Proceedings of VPRS-1, VPRS-2, VPRS-3, VPRS-4, VPRS-5, VPRS-6, ICC-01/01-101-tEN-Corr, 17 January 2006, para 65.

1

A Theoretical Framework for the Analysis of Prosecutorial Discretion at the ICC

I. INTRODUCTION

> The real challenge posed to a Prosecutor is to choose from many meritorious complaints the appropriate ones for international intervention.[1]

AFTER 15 YEARS of operations, the Office of the Prosecutor (OTP) at the International Criminal Court (ICC) is conducting 10 preliminary examinations in countries that have experienced complex and prolonged conflicts such as Afghanistan and Colombia as well as 11 investigations in 10 different countries.[2] Each investigation addresses situations that contain dozens of potential cases; however, the ICC is limited in its capacity to pursue those and, to date, these investigations have resulted in the prosecution of 27 cases.[3] The figures demonstrate the high degree of selectivity that is necessary at the early stages of the proceedings. Selectivity in this context is understood as the 'discretionary power to do nothing about a case in which enforcement would be clearly justified, the result [being] … selective enforcement'.[4] The challenge for the Prosecutor is the appropriate selection, through the exercise of prosecutorial discretion, in such way that it is not perceived as arbitrary and optimises the impact of the cases that are chosen. Nevertheless, the choices

[1] L Arbour cited in J Goldston, 'More Candour about Criteria: The Exercise of Discretion by the Prosecutor of the International Criminal Court' (2010) 8 *Journal of International Criminal Justice* 383, 389.

[2] Preliminary examinations are conducted in Afghanistan, Colombia, Guinea, Iraq/UK, Nigeria, Palestine, The Philippines, Bangladesh/Myanmar, Ukraine and Venezuela. Investigations in the Democratic Republic of the Congo, Uganda, two distinct investigations in the Central African Republic, Darfur/Sudan, Kenya, Libya, Côte d'Ivoire, Mali, Georgia, and Burundi. See for an overview: www.icc-cpi.int.

[3] The cases feature one or two defendants.

[4] KC Davis, *Discretionary Justice, A Preliminary Inquiry* (Baton Rouge, LA, Louisiana State University Press, 1969) 163. R Cryer, *Prosecuting International Crimes* (Cambridge, Cambridge University Press, 2005) provides an excellent analysis of other selective effects in international criminal law. It addresses selectivity in the jurisdiction *rationae personae* of different international courts and tribunals and demonstrates how the definitions of the crimes included in the Rome Statute entail selective effects.

made will inevitably disappoint many who hope that the ICC will deliver justice for them.

The Prosecutor's decisions also have the potential to undermine the Court's legitimacy through perceptions of bias. Why has the Prosecutor, to date, only prosecuted cases from Africa? Why do most prosecutions focus on non-state actors and not address the alleged crimes committed by government forces as is so far the case in the situation in Côte d'Ivoire? These are the kinds of questions that indicate how strongly the selective, discretionary decisions of the Prosecutor influence perceptions of the Court's legitimacy. Therefore, it is crucial that the exercise of discretion aims at safeguarding and enhancing the legitimacy of the Court.

This chapter outlines a framework for the analysis of prosecutorial discretion that is focused on those elements that are crucial for the legitimacy of the Court. As such, its focus is more theoretical in nature than those that follow. Because the ICC is unique in its design and aims, the nature of prosecutorial discretion differs from other international and domestic systems. It entails highly symbolic decisions, contains policy and procedural decisions, and requires the use of indeterminate notions such as gravity and the interests of justice. As I will explain in this chapter in more detail, it is crucial to determine the legal limits to the scope of discretion at the different stages of the proceedings, as well as those aims and principles that should guide them. A further layer of analysis includes accountability mechanisms, and the degree of transparency of the discretionary decisions as well as their reasons. Accountability and transparency are crucial elements to safeguard and enhance the legitimacy, as well as the quality, of prosecutorial decision-making.

II. UNDERSTANDING PROSECUTORIAL DISCRETION IN ITS SYSTEMIC CONTEXT

Prosecutorial discretion at the ICC is distinct from prosecutorial discretion in domestic systems, because it is located in a system combining elements from different legal traditions as well as unique features.[5] The trial at the ICC is, for example, structured as a party process resembling common law structures. But in contrast to prosecutors in some common law systems, the Prosecutor at the ICC is obliged to investigate incriminating as well as exonerating circumstances equally,[6] which is more akin to the procedure in civil law systems.[7] Unique to

[5] It is therefore sometimes qualified as a system *sui generis*; see, eg, C Safferling, *International Criminal Procedure* (Oxford, Oxford University Press, 2012) 280.

[6] Art 54(1) ICCSt: 'The Prosecutor shall: (a) In order to establish the truth … investigate incriminating and exonerating circumstances equally'.

[7] C Buisman, 'The Prosecutor's Obligation to Investigate Incriminating and Exonerating Circumstances Equally: Illusion or Reality?' (2014) 27 *Leiden Journal of International Law* 205, 206

the ICC system is the relationship between the Prosecutor and the Pre-Trial Chambers, whereby the latter must authorise or confirm certain prosecutorial decisions.[8] These mechanisms allow control[9] and supervision of prosecutorial decisions and shape its form, although the precise boundaries of this control can be contentious.

The ICC is also different from domestic systems because its legal authority is located in international law with its horizontal nature. Unlike domestic systems, the legal system governing the ICC does not feature 'the state' in the central role holding the monopoly of force and supreme authority.[10] The Prosecutor can formulate her own policies to guide her exercise of discretionary powers. The Assembly of States Parties (ASP) to the Rome Statute has only a limited role in this through its management oversight over the Prosecutor, the budgetary competences, and its possibilities to establish control mechanisms in order to enhance efficiency and economy at the Court.[11] Furthermore, the Prosecutor cannot rely on stringent enforcement of discretionary decisions, because of the lack of direct enforcement power and the OTP's reliance on voluntary compliance by states with the decisions of the Court. Because of all these differences, the meaning of prosecutorial discretion within a specific domestic system cannot simply be transferred to the ICC. Furthermore, as will be shown subsequently, this absence of the state and the difficulties arising therefrom make it essential that the Prosecutor pay specific attention to safeguarding the Court's legitimacy. Although the legitimacy of the Court matters, beyond being instrumental for the functioning of the Court, only a legitimate Court is able to contribute to international justice.

Prosecutorial discretion at the ICC is also different from discretion at other international courts and tribunals. The ICC is the only international criminal tribunal with potentially universal territorial jurisdiction.[12] All other international tribunals are designed to deal with one country or conflict alone.[13]

explains that this provision, based on a German proposal, attempts to strike a balance between civil and common law traditions.

[8] Art 15(4) and art 53(3)(b) ICCSt.

[9] One example of control is the disclosure regime at the pre-trial stage of the proceedings; see for an overview of the procedure and further references, V Nerlich, 'The Confirmation of Charges Procedure at the International Criminal Court: Advance or Failure?' (2012) 10 *Journal of International Criminal Justice* 1339, 1343–44.

[10] D Robinson, 'A Cosmopolitan Liberal Account of International Criminal Law' (2013) 26 *Leiden Journal of International Law* 127, 146–47.

[11] Art 112(2)(b), (4) ICCSt. Although more recently, calls have become louder that the ASP take on a leading role in reforming the ICC. See, eg, D Guilfoyle, 'Reforming the International Criminal Court: Is it Time for the Assembly of State Parties to be the adults in the room?' 8 May 2019, available at: ejiltalk.org.

[12] The exercise of jurisdiction is depending on the conditions set out in art 12 ff ICCSt and covers all State Parties as well as non-Member States in case of a referral by the Security Council (art 13(b) ICCSt) or acceptance of the jurisdiction of the Court in case of a non-party state (art 12(3) ICCSt).

[13] As examples: the International Criminal Tribunal for the former Yugoslavia (ICTY); the International Criminal Tribunal for Rwanda (ICTR); the Special Court for Sierra Leone (SCSL); and the Special Tribunal for Lebanon (STL).

Only the ICC Prosecutor has the competence to trigger the jurisdiction of the Court and can initiate investigations into specific situations on her own initiative.[14] Another distinguishing feature is the relationship between the Court and domestic jurisdictions. In contrast to the primary jurisdiction of the *ad hoc* tribunals, the ICC's jurisdiction is complementary to the jurisdiction of the State Parties.[15] This means that the State Parties have the primary responsibility to investigate and prosecute international crimes; at the ICC, cases are only admissible if 'the State is unwilling or unable … to carry out the investigation or prosecution'.[16] This changes the dynamics of interaction between the Prosecutor and State Parties; the principle of complementarity provides states with a tool to challenge prosecutorial decisions, which, in contrast, was not the case at the *ad hoc* tribunals.[17] At the same time, the vast territorial reach of the ICC restricts the OTP in the number of cases it can bring in each situation under investigation. This makes it necessary for the Prosecutor to make much more drastic selection decisions than her counterparts.[18] Because of these differences, the evaluation of prosecutorial discretion at the ICC is not based on a comparative approach, but within its own unique context.

III. DIMENSIONS OF DISCRETION

To understand the notion of prosecutorial discretion, the ordinary meaning of discretion in the English language serves as the starting point of this enquiry. Discretion is defined as 'the freedom to decide what should be done in a particular situation'.[19] The Rome Statute provides the Prosecutor with the 'freedom to decide what should be done' whenever the Prosecutor is provided with procedural discretion[20] as the freedom to decide on procedural action or legal consequences. Procedural discretion can be clearly identified in the Rome Statute: 'The Prosecutor may' is one of its indicators.[21] Another is the absence of any regulation in those areas that are primarily within the competence of the Prosecutor. Procedural discretion derives from the legal process and contains the freedom to decide between different procedural options after applying the facts

[14] Art 15(1) ICCSt.
[15] Preamble ICCSt.
[16] Art 17(1)(a) ICCSt.
[17] Art 17 ICCSt equips states with the possibility to challenge the admissibility of cases.
[18] Number of individuals indicted by the ICTY 161, by the ICTR 93.
[19] See 'Discretion' in Oxford Dictionaries, available at: www.oxforddictionaries.com/definition/english/discretion.
[20] Procedural discretion is not a novel notion. See, eg, R Bone, 'Who Decides? A Critical Look at Procedural Discretion' (2007) 28 *Cardozo Law Review* 1962. He refers to interpretive and procedural discretion reflecting on judicial powers granted to judges in the US American Federal system of civil procedure.
[21] See, eg, art 15(1) ICCSt.

to the legal framework. This form of discretion provides the Prosecutor with flexibility in the type of action or inaction that she chooses.

A. Procedural Discretion

Mapping the most important areas of procedural discretion shows that they are mainly located at the periphery of Court proceedings, or, in other words, outside the courtroom. This includes the preliminary examination stage, in which article 15(2) of the Statute allows the Prosecutor flexibility regarding how she wants to conduct a preliminary examination.[22] Once an investigation is under way, case selection is another area with considerable scope for procedural choices such as the choice of incidents and charges. Also, the Rome Statute is entirely silent on the question of completing the investigation in a situation. This provides the Prosecutor with some freedom to choose how to master this task, because she is equipped with the competence to decide about the beginning of an investigation and should therefore also be in charge of the end.[23] Beyond those big decisions with a direct effect on the workload of the Court, the Prosecutor is vested with procedural discretion in various other areas. Throughout investigations, the Prosecutor and the OTP staff need to take discretionary decisions on a day-to-day basis over the course and direction of an investigation. At the trial stage, for example, it is within the discretion of the OTP how to present her case[24] or whether to appeal a judicial decision, provided the legal grounds for an appeal are met.[25] However, the discretionary power of the Prosecutor shrinks drastically inside the courtroom during the pre-trial and trial stage, because her role is reduced to that of a party, on a par with the defence.

The procedural discretionary dimension is constrained by a variety of legal limitations. Dworkin used a very helpful metaphor in that regard: discretion is the hole in a doughnut, with the dough being the legal framework limiting and determining the hole – the space for discretionary powers in a system.[26] In this conception, even 'strong' discretion is not totally unbound as it is all located within the hole; certain standards of fairness, rationality and effectiveness, for example, always apply.[27] Similarly, HLA Hart suggests that 'avowed' discretion is constrained by institutional aims or accountability mechanisms within

[22] Art 15(2) ICCSt: 'The Prosecutor shall analyse the seriousness of the information received. For this purpose he or she *may* seek additional information' (emphasis added).

[23] R Hamilton, 'The ICC's Exit Problem' (2015) 47 *New York University Journal of International Law and Politics* 1, 26 similarly identifies the Prosecutor as mainly responsible for the development of ICC exit strategies.

[24] Art 69(3) ICCSt: 'The parties may submit evidence relevant to the case'.

[25] Art 82(1) ICCSt: 'Either party may appeal'.

[26] R Dworkin, *Taking Rights Seriously* (London, Duckworth, 1977) 31.

[27] ibid, 33.

a system.[28] His positivist approach was linked to a 'broad postwar liberal project' attempting to promote an understanding of law that would bolster liberal values and distinguish liberal democracy from Nazism and fascism, an aim also shared by Dworkin.[29] Promoting the rule of law from a positivist angle requires a system of positively determined norms. Within this determined set of rules, flexibility of the system is provided through discretion. This allows a system to respond to the unforeseen. The key to securing the rule of law within this flexible system is to constrain the exercise of discretion.[30] Of key importance is therefore that we develop an accurate understanding for the different dimensions of prosecutorial discretion at the ICC and its legal constraints. Ultimately, this is important for the promotion of the rule of law and for safeguarding the legitimacy of the Court – themes that are at the heart of the book.

B. Interpretative Discretion

Procedural discretionary decisions most often also contain a component of interpretative discretion. Decisions on whether to start an investigation into a specific situation or case are based on a legal framework that contains the application of indeterminate or open notions like 'gravity'[31] or 'interests of justice' in articles 17 and 53 of the Statute. These provisions regulate access to the Court and are crucial for the Prosecutor's function as a gatekeeper to the Court; as the organ deciding which situations will be investigated and which cases will potentially reach ICC courtrooms. The indeterminacy of both notions is in part the product of treaty negotiations, but also reflects the fact that it is very difficult to find precise descriptions for those extraordinary situations where international crimes are committed.[32] Article 17 of the Statute regulates the admissibility of cases and demands 'sufficient gravity' as well as the unwillingness or inability of a state to genuinely carry out an investigation or prosecution in a case.[33]

[28] HLA Hart, 'Discretion' (2013) 127 *Harvard Law Review* 652, 653.

[29] GC Shaw, 'HLA Hart's Lost Essay: Discretion and the Legal Process School' (2013) 127 *Harvard Law Review* 666, 673.

[30] Similarly see DJ Galligan, *Discretionary Powers: A Legal Study of Official Discretion* (Oxford, Clarendon Press, 1986) 108–63. He offers an extensive analysis of constraints on the exercise of discretion, which he distinguishes between practical and value-based. CE Schneider, 'Discretion and Rules, A Lawyer's View' in K Hawkins (ed), *The Uses of Discretion* (Oxford, Clarendon Press, 1994) 79–87 also emphasises the importance of constraints on different types of discretion. He highlights that those constraints cannot just be found in the legal system itself but extend far into the social context of the decision-making process, for example, to the training decision-makers have received.

[31] See for a discussion of interpretative discretion in the notion of gravity A Pues, 'Discretion and the Gravity of Situations at the International Criminal Court' (2017) 17 *International Criminal Law Review* 960.

[32] M deGuzman, 'Gravity and the Legitimacy of the International Criminal Court' (2008) 32 *Fordham International Law Journal* 1400, 1416.

[33] Art 17(1)(a), (b), (d) ICCSt.

Article 53(1) and (2) of the Statute govern the initiation of an investigation and prosecution requiring the Prosecutor to take into account the gravity of a crime as well as the interests of justice. What the 'interests of justice' might demand can depend on various factors; the only factors specifically mentioned in the Rome Statute are victims' interests, which might be diverse in themselves, and the gravity of the crimes.[34] Using such indeterminate notions initially provides some freedom for the Prosecutor to decide which facts she should consider and which elements to use to determine the meaning of these notions in the specific context of a situation or a case. This freedom entails a discretionary dimension because it requires complex subjective judgement beyond mere norm interpretation as to how to identify and weigh the abstract and factual elements that should be used to determine, for example, the interests of justice. While the degree of the interpretative discretionary dimension might vary, it is an act of legal interpretation and legal reasoning combined with a choice of and a balancing act between the factual circumstances that constitutes the exercise of interpretative discretion. Hence, some scope of interpretative discretion is contained in the procedural decisions particularly at the start of proceedings. Once proceedings in a case are under way, any interpretative discretionary scope shifts to the Chambers. It is therefore only at the initial stages of the proceedings and also at the stage of completing an investigation into a situation that the Prosecutor has some interpretative discretion.

This interpretative discretionary dimension[35] is intertwined with and cannot always be separated from the procedural dimension. For example, any decision to select a case for prosecution entails an assessment of the gravity of the crime. It is important to acknowledge these different dimensions because 'discretion is heavily implicated in the use of rules: interpretative behaviour is involved in making sense of rules'.[36] Yet, the identification of an interpretative discretionary dimension is not uncontroversial because it questions the possibility to determine the application of an indeterminate notion to exacting legal requirements. The Pre-Trial Chamber (PTC) required the latter in its review of the Prosecutor's decision not to initiate an investigation regarding a referral brought by the Union of Comoros, the Hellenic Republic and Cambodia regarding the Israeli raid of the so-called Gaza Flotilla.[37] Awareness that these interpretative and procedural interpretative dimensions exist will help to better understand the discretionary

[34] Art 53(1)(c) ICCSt.

[35] As similarly done by Galligan (n 30) 109; N Lockhart and E Sheargold, 'In Search of Relevant Discretion: The Role of the Mandatory/Discretionary Distinction in WTO Law' (2010) 13 *Journal of International Economic Law* 379, 410 identify 'interpretive discretion' in the power to interpret indeterminate or vague notions in WTO law and in distinction to the discretion to adopt or not to apply rules.

[36] K Hawkins, *The Uses of Discretion* (Oxford, Clarendon Press, 1994) 1.

[37] *Situation on the Registered Vessels of the Union of Comoros, the Hellenic Republic and the Kingdom of Cambodia*, Decision on the request of the Union of Comoros to review the Prosecutor's decision not to initiate an investigation, PTC I, ICC-01/13/34, 16 July 2015, para 14.

decision-making process. It aids in identifying how far review processes ought to go and what should limit and guide the discretionary decision-making process.[38]

Distinguishing different types, or dimensions, of discretion is common in legal theoretical discourses. Hart as an important scholar in the positivist tradition refers to 'avowed' discretion whenever the lawmaker explicitly grants the power of making alternative legal choices, whereas 'concealed' discretion features whenever dispositive rules do not 'yield a determinate result' and includes the interpretation of statutes.[39] Hart's concept of 'avowed discretion' corresponds in part with Dworkin's concept of 'strong discretion' whenever 'someone is charged with making decisions'[40] but is not bound by particular standards set by the authority in question. Dworkin contrasts this strong discretion to 'weak' discretion, whenever, beyond legal reasoning, applicable standards demand specific judgement as to their interpretation.[41] Yet other scholars develop other, slightly diverging categories of discretion depending on the systems they work within. Kenneth Culp Davis as the author of one of the foundational texts on the study of discretion broadened the jurisprudential discourse on the subject beyond judicial discretion and acknowledged different types of discretion in the public law and administrative sphere.[42] Galligan acknowledges interpretive discretion wherever rules or standards are indeterminate.[43] Ultimately, all these scholars acknowledge the different dimensions of a procedural or interpretative nature that are subject to different limitations in the system.

Through distinguishing between these dimensions of discretion, I offer a novel perspective that can sharpen our understanding of the discretionary processes at work. In the day-to-day practice of the Court, procedural decisions make up the vast majority of decisions; they are the oil that makes the ICC engine run. Yet, the interpretative dimension is one that has triggered considerable conflict between the PTCs and the OTP. The dispute around the question of whether the OTP ought to investigate the *Gaza Flotilla* case is at the core of this dispute. In an earlier article, I argued that the gravity notion contains an element of interpretative discretion. This observation matters for the delineation of the competences on who would have the last say on the gravity of a situation.

> [T]he assessment of gravity involves … the evaluation of numerous factors and information relating thereto, which the Prosecutor has to balance in reaching her decision.

[38] See as an example of the importance of delineating the different elements constituting the discretionary decision-making process for judicial review: *Situation on the Registered Vessels of the Union of the Comoros, the Hellenic Republic and the Kingdom of Cambodia*, Judgment on the appeal of the Prosecutor against Pre-Trial Chamber I's Decision on the Application for Judicial Review by the Government of the Union of the Comoros, ICC-01/13-98, 2 September 2019, paras 78–81.

[39] Hart (n 28) 656; Shaw (n 29); N Lacey, 'The Path Not Taken: HLA Hart's Harvard Essay on Discretion' (2013) 127 *Harvard Law Review* 636.

[40] Dworkin (n 26) 31.

[41] ibid, 31–32.

[42] Davis (n 4).

[43] Galligan (n 30) 109.

> In this regard, the Appeals Chamber, … considers that the Prosecutor enjoys a *margin of appreciation*, which the pre-trial chamber has to respect when reviewing the Prosecutor's decision. Accordingly, the Appeals Chamber, by majority, finds that it is not the role of the pre-trial chamber to direct the Prosecutor as to what result she should reach in the gravity assessment or what weight she should assign to the individual factors. The pre-trial chamber may, however, oblige the Prosecutor to take into account certain factors and/or information relating thereto when reconsidering her decision not to initiate an investigation.[44]

The Appeals Chamber issued a decision[45] on the conflict between the OTP and PTC regarding whether the Prosecutor's final decision not to investigate the Gaza Flotilla incident could be subject to judicial review. The Appeals Chamber has now found that the judges have the final say over the legal interpretation of all those elements that make up the gravity notion,[46] or, in a more abstract sense that can be part of the open legal concepts contained in the Rome Statute. The OTP, however, has the last say on the factual assessment. The PTC guards the consistency in the development of the law, whereas the OTP is closer to the facts at these early pre-investigative stages and has the last say on the factual considerations.[47] This way, the reviewability of interpretative discretionary processes becomes more clear-cut.

IV. PROSECUTORIAL DISCRETION AGAINST THE BACKDROP OF PERCEPTIONS OF LEGITIMACY

The Court cannot contribute to the 'respect for and the enforcement of international justice'[48] if its work creates perceptions of bias among its stakeholders. Respect and enforcement exist in a mutually reinforcing relationship to one another, and both require that the Court and its actions are perceived as legitimate. While legitimacy matters as a value in its own right, another key aspect of its importance is that perceptions of rules or decisions as legitimate contribute to enhanced compliance with them.[49] Legitimacy, as the perception of rightfulness, has different layers to it that will be addressed in the following discussion. It is not sufficient for the Prosecutor to stick to the rules of the Rome Statute, to act within the set framework of legality. Whenever rules do

[44] AC Judgment *Comoros* (n 38) para 81.

[45] AC Judgment *Comoros* (n 38).

[46] ibid, para 78.

[47] ibid, para 80.

[48] Preamble ICCSt.

[49] T Franck, 'Legitimacy in the International System' (1988) 82 *American Journal of International Law* 705, 712 has analysed this compliance-pull at the international level; T Tyler and J Jackson, 'Future Challenges in the Study of Legitimacy and Criminal Justice' in J Tankebe and A Liebling (eds), *Legitimacy and Criminal Justice: An International Exploration* (Oxford, Oxford University Press, 2013) 89 confirm from a general criminal justice perspective the compliance-inducing effect of legitimacy.

not prescribe a specific result, when they leave scope for discretion, this requires further efforts on the part of the Prosecutor to be perceived as acting in a legitimate way. Therefore, the Prosecutor needs to focus efforts in such way that the exercise of prosecutorial discretion actively contributes to those aims and principles expressed in the Rome Statute, as they are those that connect the different constituents such as victim groups, State Parties, third states and the international community with the ICC.

The discourse on compliance in international law or on why states obey the law is a big and complex question for which no simple answer is available.[50] The Prosecutor is not equipped with any independent enforcement mechanisms and therefore heavily relies on state compliance and assistance to enforce her decisions.[51] It is her task to be persuasive in her decisions. The establishment of the ICC as such has never been described as lacking in legitimacy;[52] indeed, it was broadly celebrated as a success. Of key importance for the analysis of prosecutorial discretion is the fair and coherent application[53] of the rules in the ICC system. Fairly applied rules bear more persuasive power. Where rule application is necessarily selective because a regime such as the ICC cannot address all situations to the same extent, it requires great efforts to safeguard some form of coherence and fairness in the process. Ensuring that ICC action is perceived as legitimate requires a discourse between the Court, the State Parties and the wider community that must include deliberation on the if and how of discretionary decision-making processes.[54] A further piece in this jigsaw of achieving compliance is the need to trigger processes of internalisation of international rules in domestic orders.[55] All of these different factors are linked to decisions perceived as legitimate, which in turn can provide a stronger power to garner support for and compliance with the Court's decisions. Part of compliance with

[50] HH Koh, 'Why Do Nations Obey International Law?' (1997) 106 *Yale Law Journal* 2599, 2659 with an excellent overview of the history of the discourse.

[51] K Raustiala and A-M Slaughter, 'International Law, International Relations and Compliance' in W Carlsnaes, T Risse and B Simmons (eds), *The Handbook of International Relations* (Thousand Oaks, CA, Sage Publications, 2002) represent a school of thought that highlights the importance of enforcement mechanisms for compliance in international law. This approach, however, is less relevant for this book, because the ICC lacks independent enforcement power.

[52] T Franck, *Fairness in International Law and Institutions* (Oxford, Clarendon Press, 1995) 26 ff identifies norm creation processes as one essential component for perceptions of legitimacy. Norms need to be created based on the 'right process'.

[53] Franck, *Fairness in International Law and Institutions* (n 52), demonstrates that the interpretation and application of rules needs to appear as fair and coherently applied to contribute to perceptions of legitimacy; see also Koh (n 50) 2601.

[54] A Chayes and A Handler Chayes, *The New Sovereignty: Compliance with International Regulatory Agreements* (Cambridge, Cambridge University Press, 1995) 25 argue that a managerial approach of persuasion by the treaty institution combined with efforts that facilitate internalisation of treaty regimes at the domestic level achieve the best results of compliance. Koh (n 50) 2646 and 2655 develops a mediating position between Franck's emphasis on fairness and Chayes' approach that describes compliance-induction with international norms as 'a repeated cycle of interaction, interpretation, and internalization through which international law acquires its "stickiness"'.

[55] Chayes and Chayes Handler (n 54).

the ICC regime is to facilitate a process of internalisation of the Rome Statute through the principle of complementarity, which demands that State Parties ensure the investigation and prosecution of international crimes at the national level. Fairness, communication and internalisation therefore are all parts of compliance-inducing processes.

Beyond the compliance-inducing component, legitimacy as such is critical for international criminal justice; it must be perceived as the right thing to do. For those reasons the Prosecutor is required to facilitate a persuasive discourse through the exercise of prosecutorial discretion. It requires the Prosecutor to actively communicate, but also to listen and respond to critique. Therefore, the legal analysis of the exercise of prosecutorial discretion in this book will focus on those elements that are seen as key to achieving legitimacy and that trigger debate.

A. The Importance of Legality

For the Prosecutor's task to safeguard the Court's legitimacy, the legality of decisions is crucial[56] but not sufficient.[57] The legality of all those decisions that have led to the sole focus on investigations in African countries during the first decade of the Court's work has never been challenged, yet these decisions have contributed vastly to perceptions of bias[58] and thus undermined the legitimacy of the Court.[59] Legality in the context of this book is the exercise of prosecutorial discretion according to established rules that can be determined by reference to the legal framework of the Court and its case law.[60] But when it comes to the exercise of discretion, where the law is not linear in its application, legitimacy requires more than legality. A decision might be within the legal scope of prosecutorial discretion yet not very persuasive, as the critique of the

[56] L Moreno Ocampo, 'Prologue: The Prosecutor's Use of Legal Policies' in M Minow, C True-Frost and A Whiting (eds), *The First Global Prosecutor: Promise and Constraints* (Ann Arbor, MI, University of Michigan Press, 2015) 5 as the first Prosecutor at the ICC emphasised the need for legality to the OTP's decisions. 'If the Prosecutor were not perceived as respecting the law, the entire Rome Statute's legitimacy might be undermined'.

[57] M Varaki, 'Effectiveness Considerations Between Legitimacy and Prosecutorial Discretion' (2014) 108 *Proceedings of the Annual Meeting (ASIL)* 304, 308 critiques this stance as too narrowly focused on legality only without engaging with and addressing the perceptions of the relevant constituents like State Parties, victim communities and others.

[58] C Jalloh, 'Regionalizing International Criminal Law?' (2009) 9 *International Criminal Law Review* 445, 462–63 with further references; he provides a good overview over the shift of perception of the ICC in African countries.

[59] A Franceschet, 'The International Criminal Court's Authority Crisis and Kant's Political Ethics' (2016) 16 *International Criminal Law Review* 201, 204 links the 'legitimacy crisis' to the design of the Court as a purely legal actor which clashes with the inevitable role the Court has to play in politics.

[60] See A Cassese, 'The Legitimacy of International Criminal Tribunals and the Current Prospects of International Criminal Justice' (2012) 25 *Leiden Journal of International Law* 491, 492 for the understanding of legality.

Court's focus on Africa has shown. The relationship between legality and legitimacy is not linear; not every legal discretionary decision is necessarily perceived as legitimate. Popovski and Turner remark in this context:

> An action is always either legal or illegal; it cannot be partly legal. In contrast, legitimacy is fluid and changing – it depends on perceptions and outcomes. As a subjective interpretation of what is desirable and appropriate, legitimacy can be maintained by a constant effort to ensure conformity with the normative expectations of the affected constituents.[61]

It does not necessarily follow that when the Prosecutor acts according to the law that this safeguards the legitimacy of the Court, because legality is only one – albeit crucial – component of legitimate action. However, the legality of a discretionary decision is at the core of its legitimacy.[62] Therefore, the first step of the analysis will focus on the precise scope of prosecutorial discretion provided in the Rome Statute. To use Dworkin's metaphor: how big is the hole in the doughnut? What precisely are the legal boundaries and limitations applicable to the different dimensions of discretion?

The legal constraints have to be reconciled with the practical constraints in the work of the Prosecutor. The ICC Prosecutor is as much a judicial institution as a manager of a big international organisation. In scholarly debates, managerial discretion is sometimes seen as beyond 'the legal paradigm'.[63] Lacey locates discretion entirely within a judicial context and governed by the rule of law, whereas managerial discretion seems to be unconstrained by the rule of law.[64] However, in the exercise of prosecutorial discretion at the ICC, the demands of the rule of law, and of a neutral, impartial and independent institution, meet with the task of managing highly politicised cases and practical constraints. The Prosecutor has to face challenges such as budgetary constraints, limitations on the enforcement of possible decisions, or security issues. Similarly, the ICC is placed in a politically loaded sphere; navigating a still relatively young institution through the muddy waters of international relations,[65] again, is a managerial task. The analysis will therefore address where there is any scope for such managerial considerations in the exercise of prosecutorial discretion and how their impact can be reconciled with the rule of law.

[61] V Popovski and N Turner, 'Legality and Legitimacy in the International Order' *Policy Brief* No 5 (United Nations University, 2008) 3.

[62] Franck, 'Legitimacy in the International System' (n 49) 738–41; M Kumm, 'The Legitimacy of International Law: A Constitutionalist Framework of Analysis' (2004) 15 *European Journal of International Law* 907, 917 establishing a 'principle of international legality'; D Beetham, 'Revisiting Legitimacy, Twenty Years on' in J Tankebe and A Liebling (eds), *Legitimacy and Criminal Justice: An International Exploration* (Oxford, Oxford University Press, 2013) 20.

[63] Lacey (n 39) 369.

[64] ibid.

[65] D Bosco, *Rough Justice: The International Criminal Court in a World of Power Politics* (New York, Oxford University Press USA, 2014) gives a detailed account of the prosecutorial strategy at the ICC and its approach to negotiate the ICC's position from an international relations perspective.

B. A Principled Exercise of Discretion

Legitimacy is broader than the legality of a decision in that it consists of different layers and perceptions.[66] One core element is the rightful exercise of power, which demands the legality of its exercise. However, the legal framework applicable can be flawed and therefore the legal exercise of power can still lack or lose legitimacy. In order to constitute the legitimate exercise of power, it must additionally be based on principles and purposes that connect the constituents of the Court.[67] Criminological research has shown that the exercise of power in a fair and just way, reflective of moral values, makes it easier for individual actors to accept that power and to identify with it, because it has a different persuasive dynamic.[68] The ICC Prosecutor has to connect with very different audiences, which makes it more difficult to identify shared values. The OTP must appeal to and persuade individuals, victim communities and civil society, as well as State Parties, third states and international organisations. So far, little empirical research has attempted to unravel whether a parallel persuasive dynamic can be pursued regarding multiple communities as diverse as those the ICC deals with, from individual victims to the Security Council (SC). The Prosecutor is therefore in unchartered waters. The one common denominator is expressed in the aims that are included in the Rome Statute: deterrence and prevention, closing the gap of impunity, safeguarding victims' interests, and protecting human rights. Positively connecting to these values is important in order to persuade actors to accept the Prosecutor's authority and comply with her decisions.

Responding to the task of sustaining the legitimacy of the Court, the exercise of prosecutorial discretion also needs to be coherent and effective in order to achieve the persuasive power that creates a pull towards acceptance and compliance. Coherence can be achieved through treating like cases alike (the principle of equality before the law) and through consistency in the application of the law.[69] But this alone is not necessarily sufficient in order to persuade state actors at the international level. State actors have an expectation that the authority exercising a power granted should perform effectively in fulfilling the common purposes and principles for which it was established.[70] At the ICC, the efficiency of the Court is an ongoing concern of the State Parties and has repeatedly been discussed in the ASP.[71] In summary, the task of sustaining the legitimacy of the

[66] Popovski and Turner (n 61) 3.

[67] Beetham (n 62) 19; J-M Coicaud, 'Crime, Justice, and Legitimacy: A Brief Theoretical Inquiry' in J Tankebe and A Liebling (eds), *Legitimacy and Criminal Justice: An International Exploration* (Oxford, Oxford University Press, 2013) 40 refers to power being exercised in order to 'satisfy key needs and expectations of non-power holders'.

[68] Tyler and Jackson (n 49) 89–91.

[69] Franck, 'Legitimacy in the International System' (n 49) 742.

[70] Beetham (n 62) 31.

[71] See as examples ICC/ASP/14/Res.1, adopted on 26 November 2015, para J.5(c): 'Finding appropriate ways to preserve the Court's long-term ability to deliver on its mandate effectively and efficiently, while being mindful of the financial constraints of States Parties'; similarly ICC/ASP/13/Res.1, 17 December 2014, para I.3 specifically requesting efficient strategic planning from the OTP.

Court can best be achieved through a principled[72] and purposeful exercise of the Prosecutor's power, geared towards achieving those aims that the ICC was created for and responding to those values that hold its constituents together. The analysis will therefore trace those applicable principles and purposes that should guide the Prosecutor in the exercise of the different types of prosecutorial discretion.

Ultimately, the legitimacy of the ICC depends on the approval of its decisions by its stakeholders and, foremost, those states the Court interacts with: the relevant agents must acknowledge power as rightful.[73] The acknowledgement of and the consent to power are in the case of the ICC in the first instance expressed through the act of joining the Rome Statute, a process that has stalled more recently.[74] However, this initial approval is not sufficient to sustain the legitimacy of the Court in the long run. Indeed, while many African states signed and ratified the Rome Statute early on in the process, the Court has faced a backlash by some of those states through their sustained non-compliance with ICC decisions regarding the arrest of long-time Sudanese President Omar Al Bashir, against whom the ICC has issued an arrest warrant. Uganda is a good example: it was the first to refer a situation to the Court but failed to comply with the ICC arrest warrant for al Bashir during a visit to the country.[75] While the referral of a situation to the Court was an active acknowledgement of the ICC's authority, non-compliance with Court orders has the reverse effect of de-legitimisation through the refusal of the Court's authority that is contained in the act of non-compliance. This supports the observation that legitimacy is not static but a dynamic process, based on forms of interaction and discourse between institutional actors and the subjects of this institution.[76] It is therefore important to analyse where improvements in an institution or practice are desirable to safeguard the legitimacy of the Court and sustain the Prosecutor's ability to guarantee respect for international justice and to enforce it.

Central to the analysis is to identify which principles represent common values and should guide the exercise of prosecutorial discretion at the ICC. Some general principles such as equality before the law and fairness have already been mentioned in the above discussion as indispensable parts of justice. Article 21(3) of the Rome Statute further sets out the principles applicable to the Court such

[72] The term 'principled discretion' features in some of the Anglo-American legal theory contributions on the topic of exercising discretion: T O'Malley, *Principled Discretion: Developing a Coherent Sentencing Policy* (Newbridge, Irish Academic Press, 2010); KC Kennedy, 'Equitable Remedies and Principled Discretion: The Michigan Experience' (1997) 74 *University of Detroit Mercy Law Review* 609, 614; PC Hoffer, 'Principled Discretion: Concealment, Conscience, and Chancellors' (1991) 3 *Yale Journal of Law & the Humanities* 53.

[73] Beetham (n 62) 19; Cassese (n 60) 492.

[74] Between 2012 and 2019, only Guatemala, Côte d'Ivoire, Palestine and El Salvador joined the ICC.

[75] *Prosecutor v Al Bashir*, Decision requesting the Republic of Uganda to provide submissions on its failure to arrest and surrender Omar Al-Bashir to the Court, PTC II, ICC-02/15-01/09-262, 16 May 2016.

[76] See Beetham (n 62) 32 with examples on the dynamic relationship.

as internationally recognised human rights and non-discrimination. This provision is applicable because, according to article 34 of the Statute, the Prosecutor is one of the organs of the Court. Whether adherence to these, or other identified principles, is visible in the practice of the Prosecutor will also be part of the analysis.

The analysis will be further informed by Shklar's critique of legalist positions. In her study on legalism, Shklar demonstrates that a legal act as such does not necessarily produce justice. For a legal act to be just it must conform to the applicable rules, and the application of these rules must further be clearly geared towards greater principles like fairness and impartiality.[77] This corresponds to a great extent with the view advanced above on the importance of linking legality with principles and purposes. Shklar argues, however, that the evolution of legalist positions has led to a growing distinction between law and non-law and to 'ever more refined and rigid systems of formal definitions'.[78] Law, as a discipline, has become isolated from the social context in which it operates:

> Law is endowed with its own values, which are all treated as a single 'block' sealed off from general social history, from general social theory, from politics, and from morality … [I]t aims at preserving law from irrelevant considerations, but it has ended by fencing legal thinking off from all contact with the rest of historical thought and experience.[79]

One of the contentious issues in this context is, for example, the question whether peace considerations are within the scope of elements that can determine the interests of justice. Is it a convincing outcome not to consider peace within the interests of justice? The analysis of prosecutorial discretion will consider how the Prosecutor can be responsive to the different constituents of the Court (the State Parties, the conflicted communities and wider civil society) and the realities on the ground so as to avoid being stuck in a legalist bubble in The Hague.

V. ACCOUNTABILITY MECHANISMS FOR PROSECUTORIAL DISCRETION

The last pillar of the analysis addresses accountability mechanisms for prosecutorial discretion in the Rome Statute. Intertwined with accountability is transparency, and both play key roles in the process of safeguarding and enhancing legitimacy because both components ensure that decision-makers are in fact responsive to constituents' concerns.[80] The legality of decisions as well as their principled exercise can only be ascertained through a framework

[77] JN Shklar, *Legalism, Law, Morals, and Political Trials*, Reprint (Cambridge, MA, Harvard University Press, 1986) 113–14.

[78] ibid, 2.

[79] ibid, 3.

[80] Kumm (n 62) 926; Coicaud (n 67) 40.

of accountability. At the same time, only a transparent exercise of prosecutorial discretion can demonstrate to the different stakeholders involved that the Prosecutor responds to key principles and promotes those values of concern to the broader international community. The Rome Statute provides for a range of different mechanisms of judicial review at the different stages of the proceedings. However, at certain points such as during preliminary examinations, the Rome Statute currently lacks any formal accountability mechanisms. As Stiglitz pointed out, where direct accountability of an agency is missing, this increases the importance for its actions to be open and transparent to facilitate some form of control.[81] The structure of accountability mechanisms and the degree of transparency in the practice of the Court must therefore form part of the analysis.

Accountability is understood as a multidimensional concept. Generally, it is defined as the relationship between an actor and a forum, in which the actor has an obligation to explain and to justify his or her conduct; the forum can pose questions and pass judgement, while the actor may face consequences.[82] Regarding the ICC, accountability is a concept with different dimensions, because the Prosecutor interacts with a number of different stakeholders in very different ways.[83] Most importantly, she interacts with State Parties and the conflicted communities (communities whose members might have been involved in the perpetration of crimes or have suffered as victims), but she also engages at different levels with other communities such as NGOs, academics and wider civil society. It is important to carve out those features that allow for interaction between the Prosecutor and the different stakeholders. These provide possibilities for the Prosecutor to justify her actions and for the stakeholders to challenge prosecutorial discretionary decisions. These mechanisms include formal review structures as well as pragmatic or informal accountability mechanisms.

[81] J Stiglitz, 'On Liberty, the Right to Know, and Public Discourse: The Role of Transparency in Public Life' in MJ Gibney (ed), *Globalizing Rights, The Oxford Amnesty Lectures* (Oxford, Oxford University Press, 1999) 155.

[82] M Bovens, 'Analysing and Assessing Accountability: A Conceptual Framework' (2007) 13 *European Journal of International Law* 447, 450.

[83] One possibility for the Chambers of the Court to hold the Prosecutor to account in case of a lack of compliance with Court orders is the implementation of sanctions for misconduct against the OTP based on art 71(1) ICCSt which allows the Court to implement disciplinary measures against an OTP member of staff who represents the Prosecutor throughout specific proceedings. The Appeal Court (AC) clarified that this possibility exists in the proceedings against Lubanga in which the OTP repeatedly refused to comply with a Court order to disclose information that was of relevance for the defence. *Prosecutor v Lubanga*, Judgment on the Appeal of the Prosecutor against the Decision of Trial Chamber I of 8 July 2010 entitled 'Decision on the Prosecution's Urgent Request for Variation of the Time-Limit to Disclose the Identity of Intermediary 143 or Alternatively to Stay Proceedings Pending Further Consultation with the VWU', ICC-01/04-01/06-2582, 8 October 2010, para 59.

A. The Role of Judicial Review

At the different stages of the proceedings, the Rome Statute provides for varying degrees of judicial supervision of prosecutorial decisions. For example, at the preliminary stage of the proceedings, the Rome Statute does not provide any judicial review mechanisms. Only once the point has been reached where a decision on the initiation of an investigation or prosecution has been taken, does the Rome Statute (at article 53(3)) allow for judicial review of decisions under specific conditions based on requests of the referring State Party, the SC, or on the PTC's own motion. However, victims are excluded from requesting judicial review. Without delving into detail here (this will be done in the subsequent chapters), this example shows that formal judicial review does not necessarily provide for the possibility for all stakeholders of the Court to challenge prosecutorial decisions. Legitimisation, however, is linked to the communication and justification of actions by a variety of stakeholders. The nature of judicial review of prosecutorial discretionary decisions at the ICC therefore needs to be considered in view of these different layers of legitimacy.

Two crucial questions arise: who holds the Prosecutor to account, and to whom does the Prosecutor need to respond? These are relevant because the different stakeholders of the Court will be motivated by very different interests when pursuing communication with the Prosecutor. The interests of victim communities might strongly diverge from those of a State Party; this might especially be the case when the State Party itself is allegedly involved in crimes subject to investigation at the ICC. In the context of safeguarding or enhancing the legitimacy of the Court, it is crucial to understand who has access to formal accountability mechanisms and who is excluded from the formal judicial review process.

Formal review mechanisms are paradoxically 'often at [their] best when … limited to correction of arbitrariness or illegality, and [they] may be relatively ineffective when [they] include de novo review'.[84] Kenneth Culp Davis made this important observation in his foundational work on discretion; the ineffectiveness stemming from the fact that one exercise of discretion is replaced against another.[85] The contentious PTC decision[86] not to authorise an investigation in Afghanistan is a case in point. The PTC exercised discretion in such a way that it denied the request for the authorisation of an investigation on the grounds that such an investigation would not be in the interests of justice. This decision illustrates the importance of analysing how broad the scope of judicial review

[84] Davis (n 4) 142.

[85] ibid.

[86] *Situation in the Islamic Republic of Afghanistan*, Decision pursuant to Article 15 of the Rome Statute on the Authorisation of an Investigation into the Situation in the Islamic Republic of Afghanistan, ICC-02/17-33, 12 April 2019.

in the Rome Statute is. If the system was designed in such a way that it simply replaces prosecutorial discretion with judicial discretion, this allows no effective control over that exercise of discretion and does not ensure that the judiciary is guided by the right principles and values in their decisions. The inherent difficulties with the exercise of discretion remain. These forms of accountability can only effectively contribute to the broader legitimacy of the Court if the system of judicial review controls the legality and principled exercise of prosecutorial discretion without interfering with the Prosecutor's core mandate.

B. Transparency as a Tool of Accountability and Effectiveness

Transparency fosters 'the integrity, efficiency, effectiveness and accountability of public authorities, so helping affirm their legitimacy'.[87] Transparency is crucial in order to allow communication and control between the Prosecutor and other stakeholders at the ICC. It has a variety of functions: it is a tool for pragmatic accountability beyond the access to formal accountability mechanisms; it allows the Prosecutor to explain and justify her decisions, reach out to a variety of audiences, and promote the principles she is guided by (integrity and effectiveness); and lastly, through the need for deliberation transparency contributes to more rational decision-making on the part of the Prosecutor (effectiveness). For those reasons, the analysis will pay particular attention to the current degree of transparency in the practice of the Prosecutor and explore avenues to increase the level of transparency so as to make full use of its benefits.

The focus on transparency is important because it fosters pragmatic or informal accountability. While the Rome Statute might not feature a legal obligation for the Prosecutor to explain the decisions to non-State Parties or wider civil society, she will have to do so if she wants positive interaction with these stakeholders. Through their reactions to the Prosecutor's discretionary decisions, especially when choosing whether to cooperate with the Prosecutor, these entities have the ability to call her to account for her discretionary acts.[88] The downside of this can be undue politically motivated pressure and contradictory

[87] Preamble of the Council of Europe Convention on Access to Official Documents, Council of Europe Treaty Series – No 205, 18 June 2009 (not entered into force yet, one more ratification required).

[88] A Marston Danner, 'Enhancing the Legitimacy and Accountability of Prosecutorial Discretion at the International Criminal Court' (2003) 97 *American Journal of International Law* 510, 530 f demonstrates this dynamic using the case of *Prosecutor v Barayagwiza*, ICTR–97–19: prosecutorial misconduct led to an AC decision to release the defendant, which in turn triggered strong reactions by various actors, the Rwandan state, NGOs, and the EU that again spurred the Prosecutor to submit a motion asking for reconsideration of the decision and presenting new facts. This successful motion helped avoiding release of the accused. While, from a fair trial perspective, the Prosecutor and the Court have many questions to answer, the important point here is the dynamic of pragmatic accountability, which allowed Rwanda to hold the Prosecutor to account for his failed performance in the prosecution of one of the major figures in the Rwandan genocide.

initiatives trying to influence the Prosecutor.[89] However, such attempts to influence the Prosecutor are inevitable and independent of a transparent approach. Building on the insights into the dynamic of pragmatic accountability through transparency, Marston Danner developed her call for prosecutorial guidelines.[90] Diverging from this approach, the analysis here focuses on the question of how far transparency of individual decisions is important to create space for enhanced forms of pragmatic accountability.

Beyond providing for some form of accountability, the communicative function of transparency provides another advantage in itself. The Court is in a position of responsibility towards conflicted communities in that it can, and must, express a collective normative system of values.[91] A 'communicative court' could provide emancipation for the marginalised through its expressive power,[92] if it allows those affected by crimes and conflict to use this force to create pressure that leads towards the internalisation of the norms embodied in the Rome Statute. But beyond this effect of communication and transparency, that the Court could achieve greater legitimacy in its 'dealings with populations affected by legal interventions' through 'a communicative relationship [that] would entail (a) accessibility, (b) self-justification, and (c) encouragement of debate':[93]

> A communicative court would justify decisions by the court and its officials. Naturally, judgments are all about reason-giving, but officials of a communicative court should also be prepared to give reasons for not opening a particular investigation or not prosecuting a particular person, and should give reasons in a language and through media accessible to the population, not just to their peers. Examples of existing practices are the ICC prosecutor's reasoned decisions not to open investigations in Iraq or Venezuela, or the ICTY prosecutor's defence of plea bargaining. In both these cases, however, the communication appears to have been directed towards global more than specifically affected local audiences.[94]

The sub-functions of accessibility, self-justification and encouragement of debate can all be tied back to the integrity of the Court and its effectiveness. As much as the Prosecutor not only needs to act impartially, but also be seen to act impartially, justice needs to be seen as being done by the different audiences of the Court and, most importantly, those affected by the crimes. Transparent communication is therefore key.

Lastly, the transparent exercise of prosecutorial discretion requires deliberation by the Prosecutor. She needs to provide explanations and reveal the reasons for her decisions. This contributes to a more rational and structured decision-making process on the part of the Prosecutor.[95] It compels an awareness of the

[89] ibid, 534.
[90] ibid.
[91] M Glasius, 'Do International Criminal Courts Require Democratic Legitimacy?' (2012) 23 *European Journal of International Law* 43.
[92] ibid, 64.
[93] ibid.
[94] ibid, 65.
[95] Davis (n 4) 98.

boundaries of the discretionary powers as well as control over the manner of its exercise. In order to improve the quality of these decisions, a first stage at the individual decision-making level is to indicate that discretion is being exercised.[96] It is only possible to be guided by rational and legally circumscribed principles in the decision-making process if the decision-maker is made aware of the fact that she has to exercise discretion. By openly explaining the guiding principles and motives for a decision, active consideration of these principles is enforced. Combined with the pressure of public scrutiny of the decision, this is most likely to ensure a stronger pull to even-handed justice. As Davis remarked: 'Reasoned opinions pull towards even-handed justice but the pull is stronger if the opinions are out in the open'.[97] For all those reasons, the current degree of transparency in the practice of the Prosecutor will be analysed and further avenues to increase it, in order to make full use of its benefits, will be explored. The focus on transparency supports the overall aim that prosecutorial discretion at the ICC must contribute to turning the Court into a responsive institution.

VI. CONCLUDING REMARKS

Wherever the rules are clear, the exercise of power is less contentious than in the discretionary areas of prosecutorial powers where the Rome Statute provides scope for flexibility in the application of the law. In order to achieve more accountability and legitimacy, prosecutorial discretion warrants systematic analysis focusing in particular on those elements that help in achieving and safeguarding legitimacy. The different dimensions of discretion – ranging from procedural (or strong) discretionary decisions to the scope of interpretative (or weak) discretion contained in indeterminate notions – will be helpful in enabling a more precise debate about how discretion should be exercised. This is linked to the second step of analysing the distinct legal constraints on the scope of discretion. The Prosecutor can only demonstrate the legality of her decisions if and when the boundaries are clear. Nevertheless, this alone is not sufficient to ensure an even-handed approach to justice that is not only legal but also perceived as a legitimate exercise of power. The Prosecutor needs to actively respond to key values and principles that ought to guide her exercise of discretion. This positive connection to key values and aims, the principled exercise of discretion, requires communication with the different stakeholders of the Court to allow for different layers of accountability. Accountability through transparency can help push the Prosecutor to act in ways that increase the legitimacy of the Court. Ultimately, the Prosecutor and the Court are dependent on their actions being acknowledged as legitimate; otherwise the Court will not be able to succeed in its mission to close the gap of impunity and to promote international justice.

[96] M Feldmann, 'Social Limits to Discretion: An Organizational Perspective' in K Hawkins (ed), *The Uses of Discretion* (Oxford, Clarendon Press, 1992) 167 who explains the rational actor model, in which at first a problem has to be recognised.

[97] Davis (n 4) 98.

2

Prosecutorial Discretion During Preliminary Examinations

I. INTRODUCTION

THE PRELIMINARY EXAMINATION is the initial stage of the proceedings at the International Criminal Court (ICC), commencing with the receipt of information, comprising of an examination of available information, and concluding with a decision on whether to initiate an investigation. In the first instance, the conduct of preliminary examinations serves to determine whether a reasonable basis to proceed with an investigation exists.[1] Beyond this function, preliminary examinations have gained importance as a strategic tool for the Prosecutor. The Office of the Prosecutor (OTP) regards them as a cost-effective way of fulfilling the Court's mandate by contributing to the closure of the gap of impunity through the strategy of positive complementarity,[2] ideally obviating the need for the Court's intervention through the activation of national proceedings in the countries under preliminary examination. Furthermore, the OTP uses preliminary examinations to aid investigations and to create networks of cooperating partners.[3] To that effect, the Prosecutor actively uses her discretion; she makes discretionary choices as to which situations should be moved swiftly towards investigation and which are to remain at the preliminary stage. Making these choices entails the prioritisation of one examination over another. Prioritising some situations, however, amounts to a selection process, because the Prosecutor can only pursue a limited number of investigations. Once this limit has been reached, this will effectively exclude the possibility of ICC investigations in the immediate future because the potential resources of the Office will already be committed.

At present, this process of prioritisation and selection is not transparent in the practice of the OTP. The only visible element is the huge disparity in the

[1] It has also been portrayed as an institutional 'green light' process. M Gawronski, 'The Legalistic Function of Preliminary Examinations: Quality Control as a Two-Way Street' in M Bergsmo and C Stahn (eds), *Quality Control in Preliminary Examinations, Volume 1* (Brussels, Torkel Opsahl, 2018) 180.

[2] See ICC/OTP, Report on Preliminary Examination Activities 2015, 12 November 2015, para 16.

[3] Gawronski (n 1) 620.

length of preliminary examinations, ranging between one week for the situation in Libya and more than a decade for preliminary examinations of the conflicts in Colombia and Afghanistan. A key critique in this chapter is that a hidden prioritisation and selection process feeds into perceptions of bias that the Court is struggling with and risks spawning frustrations on the part of victim groups, both aspects jeopardising its legitimacy. Another contentious point is the impact of lengthy examinations on the availability of evidence, which was, among others, one of the reasons why the Pre-Trial Chamber (PTC) concluded that an investigation in Afghanistan was not in the interests of justice.[4] Against this background, this chapter takes stock of the legal framework and the practice of the Prosecutor. The Prosecutor's discretion at this stage is not entirely unfettered but limited through the duty to ensure effective investigations.[5] In this chapter, I argue that a structured exercise of discretion is warranted during the preliminary examination phase that distinguishes more clearly between situations where realistic prospects of positive complementarity emerge from those where swift action is warranted. The absence of any formal accountability mechanisms at the preliminary stage lead me to make a case for greater transparency of discretionary decisions beyond the annual preliminary examination reports, forming part of a plea for radical transparency of the exercise of prosecutorial discretion at the ICC.

II. THE LAW AND PRACTICE OF PRELIMINARY EXAMINATIONS

The Rome Statute provides for a broad scope for discretion throughout the preliminary stage because of the absence of any specific provisions. After the approach to preliminary examinations was largely opaque during the first years, the OTP clarified its policies in the 2013 Policy Paper on Preliminary Examinations. This paper is not legally binding but a statement of intent as to how the OTP would exercise its discretion in conducting preliminary examinations. Part of this policy and the stated commitment to transparency is the annual publication of preliminary examinations reports.[6] These feature a phased approach: the first phase comprises an initial assessment of the information received for the decision regarding whether to open a preliminary examination.[7] If a preliminary examination is opened, it is conducted in three further phases

[4] *Situation in the Islamic Republic of Afghanistan*, Decision pursuant to Article 15 of the Rome Statute on the Authorisation of an Investigation into the Situation in the Islamic Republic of Afghanistan, ICC-02/17, 12 April 2019, para 93: 'The very availability of evidence for crimes dating back so long in time is also far from being likely'.

[5] For a more in-depth discussion and proposals on time limits on preliminary examinations, see A Pues, 'Towards the "Golden Hour"? A Critical Exploration of the Length of Preliminary Examinations' (2017) 15 *Journal of International Criminal Justice* 435.

[6] The OTP has released annual reports on its preliminary examinations since 2011.

[7] ICC/OTP, Policy Paper on Preliminary Examinations 2013, November 2013, para 77.

examining the jurisdiction of the Court, admissibility issues, and the interests of justice, mirroring the requirements of article 53(1) of the Statute. The process ends with a decision on whether to initiate an investigation, a question that I will return to in the next chapter.

A. Discretion in the Filter Process in Phase One

The first phase comprises an initial assessment of the information that the OTP receives from multiple sources such as individuals, NGOs, or state actors. It serves to determine whether the information is manifestly outside the jurisdiction of the Court, if it relates to any ongoing proceedings, or if it relates to a new matter warranting further analysis.[8] At this point, the Prosecutor has a duty to consider all information the Court receives, because article 15(2) of the Statute demands that the Prosecutor shall analyse the seriousness of the information received. In total, the OTP has received over 13,000 communications since 2002; in the reporting period of 2018 alone, the OTP assessed 443 of the communications as manifestly outside the Court's jurisdiction.[9] Although technically speaking this is already the start of a preliminary examination, these communications are not labelled as such and are not included in the annual preliminary examination reports. In general, this is a sensible approach for managing the flood of information that the OTP must deal with.

A caveat, however, has to be made for one form of exercising discretion during this initial phase. The OTP uses phase one to exclude communications on incidents not manifestly outside the Court's jurisdiction, but where the jurisdictional links are not very pronounced. The OTP described the discretionary component as follows:

> In practice, the Office may occasionally encounter situations where alleged crimes are not manifestly outside the jurisdiction of the Court, but do not clearly fall within its subject-matter jurisdiction. In such situations, the Office will first consider whether the lack of clarity applies to most, or a limited set of allegations, and in the case of the latter, whether they are nevertheless of such gravity to justify further analysis. The Office will then consider whether the exercise of the Court's jurisdiction may be restricted due to factors such as a narrow geographic and/or personal scope of jurisdiction and/or the existence of national proceedings relating to the relevant conduct. In such limited situations, the Office will also take into account its prosecutorial strategy of focusing on those most responsible for the most serious crimes under the Court's jurisdiction, and as a general rule, will follow a conservative approach in terms of deciding whether to open a preliminary examination. It will, however, endeavour to give a more detailed response to the senders of such communications outlining the Office's reasoning for its decisions.[10]

[8] ibid, para 78. This approach is also outlined in Reg 27 RegOTP.
[9] ICC/OTP, Report on Preliminary Examination Activities 2018, 5 December 2018, para 18.
[10] ibid, para 15.

This approach contains a considerable degree of discretion with selection based on the degree of responsibility of potential perpetrators.

The OTP pursued this approach in the context of communications related to Da'esh, also known as ISIS. Between June 2014 and December 2017, Da'esh captured, controlled and operated with impunity over large swathes of territory in Iraq, committing grave violations of international human rights law and international humanitarian law – acts that may amount to war crimes, crimes against humanity and genocide.[11] In a press release, the Prosecutor explained that she had been reviewing information regarding allegations of 'widespread atrocities' and 'crimes of unspeakable cruelty', but that she would not open a preliminary examination because the jurisdictional basis, only provided via the nationality of some foreign fighters in the ranks of Da'esh, would be too narrow.[12] The OTP went well beyond the initial filter function of phase one, filtering out information related to incidents manifestly outside the Court's jurisdiction, and exercised a considerable degree of discretion with its procedural decision not to examine any more closely whether the criteria for opening an investigation might be met.

The jurisdictional link, provided through the nationality of some Da'esh fighters, might have been narrow and hence would have resulted in very selective investigations and prosecutions. Zakerhossein critiqued the decision succinctly when contending that 'selective justice that puts an end to the culture of impunity in the context of a situation is a justifiable selective justice. When selectivity is inevitable, selective justice is better than no justice'.[13] Yet, years on from the Prosecutor's decision not even to begin a preliminary examination, a glaring gap of impunity exists in relation to crimes committed by Da'esh. With few exceptions,[14] hardly any states that are parties to the Rome Statute have to date initiated any proceedings against their own nationals who allegedly committed international crimes in Syria or Iraq as members of Da'esh. Perhaps there would have been a greater willingness if the OTP had used a preliminary examination to stimulate such proceedings. The OTP missed a chance here to use preliminary examinations to stimulate national proceedings through the policy of positive complementarity, a policy that I will discuss further in the following section. It has been argued that the exercise of discretion during this phase is necessary

[11] United Nations, 'Letter dated 15 November 2018 from the Special Adviser and Head of the United Nations Investigative Team to Promote Accountability for Crimes Committed by Da'esh/ Islamic State in Iraq and the Levant addressed to the President of the Security Council', S/2018/1031, 16 November 2018, 5.

[12] ICC/OTP, 'Statement of the Prosecutor of the International Criminal Court, Fatou Bensouda, on the Alleged Crimes Committed by ISIS', 8 April 2015, available at: www.icc-cpi.int. Based on art 12(2)(b) ICCSt, the Court has jurisdiction over accused that are nationals of State Parties.

[13] MH Zakerhossein, 'To Bury a Situation Alive: A Critical Reading of the ICC Prosecutor's Statement on the ISIS Situation' (2016) 16 *International Criminal Law Review* 613, 618.

[14] A Shubert and N Schmidt, 'German ISIS member faces war crime trial over Yazidi girl's murder' (CNN, 9 April 2019), available at: edition.cnn.com.

to avoid that the OTP spreads its resources too thinly.[15] The need to carefully plan workload and resource distribution, however, is an overarching concern that does not just apply to phase one but to the entire preliminary examination phase. It is argued that it is of key importance to make such discretionary prioritisation and selection decisions transparent. The Da'esh example provides a good illustration of how the initial filtering phase is ill-suited to the exercise of prosecutorial discretion and should be reduced to its key function, separating those situations manifestly outside the scope of the Court's jurisdiction from those that warrant further examination.

B. The Conduct of Preliminary Examinations

When the Prosecutor decides to commence a preliminary examination, the in-depth analysis begins with the Court's jurisdiction in phase two, the admissibility of potential cases within the broader situation of crisis (phase three), and the interests of justice (phase four). The policy decision to approach preliminary decisions in this way is ultimately a discretionary choice given the absence of any specific provisions in the Rome Statute. There is some merit in the legalistic step-by-step (or phase-by-phase) approach shaped by the criteria of article 53(1) of the Rome Statute to prepare the decision to investigate. After all, only if the OTP has positively determined that it would potentially have jurisdiction regarding the potential crimes reported to the ICC, does further action seem justified. However, a rigid phased approach also bears the danger of rendering the proceedings very cumbersome, particularly given that the length of some preliminary examinations lasting a decade or more is hardly justifiable.[16] The exercise of discretion to date at this stage therefore urgently requires some revision.

i. The Length of Preliminary Examinations

During the leadership of the first two Prosecutors, Luis Moreno Ocampo and Fatou Bensouda, preliminary examinations were conducted within time frames that differed by 12 or more years. With a view to the length of a preliminary examination, the OTP has repeatedly argued that the absence of any provision was a deliberate choice of the drafters of the Rome Statute to provide the Prosecutor with the necessary flexibility to adjust to the specific circumstances

[15] A Khojasteh, 'The Preliminary Examination Stage: Theory and Practice of the OTP's Phase 1 Activities' in M Bergsmo and C Stahn (eds), *Quality Control in Preliminary Examinations, Volume I* (Brussels, Torkel Opsahl, 2018) 241.

[16] In the more recent practice, the OTP appears to move towards a more holistic approach, albeit only mentioned in passing. See ICC/OTP, Report on Preliminary Examination Activities 2018, 5 December 2018, para 284.

in the different situations.[17] As I have argued elsewhere,[18] this argument is not convincing. The drafting history does not support the claim of a deliberate decision. Indeed, given that preliminary examinations as such are barely mentioned in the Rome Statute, the exception being the reference in article 15(6), it seems more likely that the relevance of preliminary examinations has been underestimated throughout the drafting process. This gap in the regulatory framework does de facto provide scope for prosecutorial discretion at this stage. This scope, however, is not unfettered but legally limited through other provisions as I will demonstrate in the next section of the chapter.

A set timetable might not be workable for the Prosecutor, because information flows that feed into the analysis will differ greatly from country to country. This alone, however, cannot explain the vast differences in the different preliminary examinations. The broad scope of discretion through the absence of any regulation throughout the preliminary examination is also used as a management tool. '[T]he limited resources of the Office mean that not every situation can be immediately investigated, but some prioritization … is necessary'.[19] It is the Prosecutor's responsibility to manage the workload of the OTP and its resources.[20] Currently, the Office exceeds its own capacities and therefore has had to postpone necessary investigations.[21] Given the multitude of conflicts and atrocities, this workload is not going to reduce any time soon. Prioritisation and, ultimately, selection through the exercise of discretion at the preliminary examination stage is therefore inevitable. However, no preliminary examination report touches on these issues. The Policy Paper on Preliminary Examinations itself does not address this point either. A key critique is that these prioritisation and selection processes are hidden.

ii. Complementarity Issues

Complementarity issues have considerable impact on the length of preliminary examinations. The OTP needs to evaluate domestic proceedings,[22] which can be a difficult process if information is not readily available. In cases of situations referred by the affected states, these self-referring states express their inability

[17] Policy Paper Preliminary Examinations 2013 (n 7) para 89; *Situation in the Central African Republic*, Prosecution's Report Pursuant to Pre-Trial Chamber's II 30 November 2006 Decision Requesting Information on the Status of the Preliminary Examination of the Situation in the Central African Republic, ICC-01/05-7, 15 December 2006, paras 9, 10.

[18] Pues (n 5) 442.

[19] ICC/OTP Paper on some policy issues before the Office of the Prosecutor, Annex: Referrals and Communications, September 2003, section I.C.

[20] Art 42(2) ICCSt.

[21] ICC/OTP, Strategic Plan 2016–2018, 6 July 2015, para 5 in which the OTP admits that this has 'negatively influenced perceptions of the Office'.

[22] F Guariglia and E Rogier, 'The Selection of Situations and Cases by the OTP of the ICC' in C Stahn (ed), *The Law and Practice of the International Criminal Court* (Oxford, Oxford University Press, 2015) 356.

or unwillingness to investigate and prosecute[23] obviating the need for a lengthy analysis of national proceedings for this group of preliminary examinations. By contrast, in non-referred situations it will be necessary to pay close attention to the existence and nature of any domestic proceedings, and the Prosecutor's intervention may itself serve as a stimulus. In Guinea, for example, the announcement of the ICC preliminary examination triggered the start of slow but steady domestic investigations that eventually led to prosecutions and included the indictment of the former head of state.[24] Equally, the evaluation of ongoing domestic proceedings in Georgia and Russia appears to have accounted for the duration of the preliminary examination in Georgia, at least to some extent. Yet, on the other hand, the Prosecutor commenced phase three in Afghanistan only in 2013 – after the examination had already been ongoing for six years.[25] The considerable delays until that date were attributed to the security situation in the country and reluctant cooperation from various governments.[26] In such circumstances, it appears that the phased approach seems to have slowed proceedings down, supporting the point made earlier about the need for revisions to the practice of the preliminary examination stage.

iii. The Policy of Positive Complementarity

The Guinea example connects to the prosecutorial policy of positive complementarity. In the Rome Statute the primary responsibility of parties for the prosecution of international crimes rests with the states, expressed in the statutory principle of complementarity.[27] The policy of positive complementarity builds on this principle and aims at encouraging and promoting domestic prosecutions, wherever feasible.[28] The preliminary examination in Colombia is a key example of this policy.[29] Colombia was one of the first and still ongoing preliminary examinations pending in the OTP. Over the years, the OTP has not only monitored developments in Colombia but engaged in a dialogue with various stakeholders, in particular regarding judicial proceedings against those who appear to be most responsible for alleged crimes.[30] It remains unknown whether

[23] H van der Wilt 'Self-Referrals as an Indication of the Inability of States to cope with Non-State Actors' in C Stahn (ed), *The Law and Practice of the International Criminal Court* (Oxford, Oxford University Press, 2015) 212–13 describes the 'air of helplessness' that the different self-referrals seem to share.

[24] ICC/OTP, Report on Preliminary Examination Activities 2016, 14 November 2016, paras 271–76.

[25] ICC/OTP, Report on Preliminary Examination Activities 2013, November 2013, para 56.

[26] ICC/OTP, Report on Preliminary Examination Activities 2012, November 2012, para 37.

[27] Preamble and art 17 ICCSt.

[28] ICC/OTP, Report on the Activities Performed during the First Three Years, June 2003–June 2006, 12 September 2006, para 58; Policy Paper on Preliminary Examinations (n 7) paras 100–03.

[29] ICC/OTP, Situation in Colombia Interim Report, November 2012, providing an overview of the preliminary examination.

[30] For a description of the activities, see ICC/OTP, Report on Preliminary Examination Activities, 2 December 2014, para 114.

developments in Colombia would have been different – either positively, in the sense that effective national proceedings would have been stimulated faster, or negatively, disrupting peace talks – if the ICC had started investigations in Colombia at some point in the past 12 years.[31] Seils highlights the difficulty with the OTP approach, using the example of cases of extra-judicial executions carried out by the military.[32] While the OTP has emphasised that it wants to see those most responsible brought to justice for these crimes, so far almost no cases have been brought in Colombia targeting this group.[33] '[I]t is unclear what explains the OTP's continued patience on this matter'.[34] This remark goes to the heart of the matter: how long does the Statute allow the Prosecutor to wait and see?

III. LEGAL LIMITS THROUGH THE DUTY TO ENSURE EFFECTIVE INVESTIGATION

The lack of any legal provisions in the ICC legal framework provides the Prosecutor with a wide discretionary scope on how to conduct preliminary examinations. Having said that, the absence of any specific rules does not mean that this discretion is entirely unfettered. Other legal provisions in the framework of the ICC form boundaries that require the Prosecutor to actively consider how the management needs of the Office can be reconciled with those boundaries.[35] A key provision in this context is the duty to act efficiently, based on the obligation of the Prosecutor in article 54(1)(b) of the Rome Statute to 'take appropriate measures to ensure effective investigation and prosecution of crimes within the jurisdiction of the Court'. The provision is ambiguous as to whether this provision only applies once an investigation is under way or would extend to the preliminary stage of the proceedings. It would defeat the object and purpose of this provision, aimed at efficacy in the process of truth finding, if this duty did not extend to the preliminary examination that determines the start of, and prepares the ground for, an investigation. This argument is also supported by rule 47(2) of the Rules of Procedure and Evidence. The Prosecutor may 'request the Pre-Trial Chamber to take such measures as may be necessary to ensure the efficiency and integrity of the proceedings'. The rule applies at the preliminary examination stage and enables the Prosecutor, for example, to secure witness testimony. It demonstrates that the efficiency of

[31] See P Seils, 'Putting Complementarity in its Place' in C Stahn (ed), *The Law and Practice of the International Criminal Court* (Oxford, Oxford University Press, 2015) 326 for a comprehensive and critical discussion of the OTP's strategy in Colombia.

[32] ibid.

[33] ibid.

[34] ibid, 323.

[35] See also Pues (n 5) 446, arguing that the principle of impartiality has an additional limiting effect.

any subsequent investigative proceedings at the preliminary examination stage matters. Therefore, the Prosecutor needs to actively consider that the flexibility in the scope of preliminary examinations is always reconciled with the duty to secure effective investigations.

At this point, it should be emphasised that the legal model developed here, delineating the scope of discretion and its legal constraints, often contrasts with reality. The work of the OTP is factually limited by a multitude of factors such as the need to secure state support for its interventions and different socio-historic factors that come into play in situations of crisis such as mistrust in any official actors or the need to interact with isolated communities, where no communication channels exist. If states, international organisations, or other stakeholders such as affected communities or NGOs do not provide the OTP with high-quality information,[36] this poses serious obstacles to the Prosecutor's work at the preliminary examination stage, because the Prosecutor does not actively investigate but needs to rely on external information. Any discussion of the limitations has to be mindful of these practical constraints. The approach in this book seeks to ensure that legal limitations become visible, stripping discretionary processes down to the bones of the legal framework. Doing so then allows for a more accurate understanding of what are legal and what are political or practical constraints that influence the work of the ICC Prosecutor.

A. Features of the Duty to Ensure Effective Investigations

The duty to ensure effective investigations is the core legal limitation to prosecutorial discretion at the preliminary examination stage. But what does this duty require? Generally, swift action is warranted for criminal investigations to be successful as the probability of a strong evidentiary base is highest very soon after the commission of a crime.[37] International human rights law provides only limited guidance as it does not establish a general minimum standard for 'good investigation'.[38] But it does require investigative authorities to act as promptly as possible.[39] An additional aspect in interpreting the 'duty to take

[36] Gawronski (n 1) 200.

[37] Pues (n 5) 444: 'Evidence tends to vanish over time: witnesses' memories fade, and forensic evidence is less readily available'.

[38] See J Chevalier-Watts, 'Effective Investigations under Article 2 of the European Convention on Human Rights: Securing the Right to Life or an Onerous Burden on a State?' (2010) 21 *European Journal of International Law* 701, 712 with further references.

[39] *Case of Vargas-Areco v Paraguay*, Judgment of 26 September 2006, § 77; *Case of Ximenes-Lopes*, Judgment of 4 July 2006, Series C No 149, para 148; *Case of the Ituango Massacres*, Judgment of 1 July 2006, Series C No 148, para 296; *Case of the Pueblo Bello Massacre*, Judgment of 31 January 2006, Series C No 140, para 143; *Case of the Mapiripán Massacre*, Judgment of 15 September 2005, Series C No 134, paras 219, 223. See also *Nachova and others v Bulgaria* [GC], Application Nos 43577/98 and 43579/98, Judgment of 6 July 2005, para 111; *Alpar v Turkey*, Application No 22643/07, Judgment of 26 January 2016, paras 46 ff finding that the state has a duty to

appropriate measures to ensure effective investigation' is that the Rome Statute links this obligation to the 'respect [for] the interests and personal circumstances of victims and witnesses ... tak[ing] into account the nature of the crime'.[40] Similar to the notion of 'interests of justice', victims' interests take centre stage. For the Prosecutor, this therefore requires that information gathering and analysis at the preliminary stage is focused on securing pathways for effective investigation as well as understanding victims' interests.

An example for the effects of a prolonged preliminary examination is the Afghanistan situation. The preliminary examination was made public in 2007, but the OTP only sought the authorisation to investigate the situation in 2017. Security issues and reluctant state cooperation had impacted on the length of the examination.[41] How this preliminary examination was conducted illustrates the point made earlier very well. Security issues and the lack of state cooperation are factual constraints that limit the OTP; however, little consideration seems to have been given to the duty to ensure effective investigations.[42] While I disagree with many aspects of the PTC decision not to authorise an ICC investigation in Afghanistan and will return to this decision in the following chapters, I do agree with one point made by the PTC: 'The very availability of evidence for crimes dating back so long in time is also far from being likely'.[43] The decision provides a valuable lesson to learn for the conduct of preliminary examinations. If a swift investigation does not appear feasible then measures must be taken or in place – either through the ICC or through another competent investigatory body – to secure evidence in order to ensure that effective investigation remains possible at a later stage.

B. A Structured Approach to Balancing Constraints

In practice, the OTP has to deliver a difficult balancing act between factual and legal constraints that impact on the scope of discretion. The Prosecutor as a legal organ has to exercise discretion according to the rule of law and yet ensure a managerial approach that takes account of the budget, the staff's security and wellbeing, and political pressures. Squaring this circle requires a structured approach to ensure consistency in the exercise of discretion.

investigate allegations of torture effectively and reasonably expeditiously, which was not the case for an investigation lasting five years and six months; *CAS and CS v Romania*, Application No 26692/05, Judgment of 20 March 2012, para 74 ff finding that an investigation of grave sexual violence against a seven-year-old child was neither prompt nor effective when it took five years, including a three-week delay in securing the initial medical examination of the victim and the lapse of two months before the main suspect was interviewed.

[40] Art 54(1)(b) ICCSt.

[41] Preliminary Examination Report 2016 (n 24) para 230.

[42] See Pues (n 5) 449 for the critique that politically contentious preliminary examinations such as Afghanistan or Palestine appear to have been conducted incomprehensively slowly.

[43] *Afghanistan* Decision (n 4) para 93.

A structured approach to discretion[44] has to be based on consistent criteria. The need for such consistent criteria is also anchored in the Rome Statute through the principle of impartiality. The 2013 Policy Paper sets out that the 'principle of impartiality, which flows from article 21(3) of the Statute, means that the Office will apply consistent methods and criteria, irrespective of the States or parties involved or the person(s) or group(s) concerned'.[45] The need for structured decision-making processes, however, needs to go beyond the phased approach based on article 53(1) of the Statute, outlined above, and actively consider and weigh legal constraints and factual obstacles. Regarding the prioritisation or selection of specific preliminary examinations, any more specific criteria are lacking in the existing policy. Concerning the length of preliminary examinations, which de facto has a prioritising and selective effect, the policy paper states only that 'analysis is adjusted to the specific features of each particular situation, which may include, inter alia, the availability of information, the nature, scale and frequency of the crimes, and the existence of national responses in respect of alleged crimes'.[46] Yet, in practice it is not clear how the Prosecutor applies those criteria. The situation concerning the deportation of Rohingya people from Myanmar to Bangladesh is a rare example in which the Prosecutor seems time-conscious. The OTP reports that it will 'seek to ensure completion of this preliminary examination within a reasonable time'.[47] Despite the desperate situation that the Rohingya find themselves in, from a legal perspective the question remains open regarding why it seems more important in this situation than in others to conclude the examination.

A key point missing from the prosecutorial criteria in how to exercise discretion at the preliminary examination stage is the duty to ensure effective investigations. When the chance of effective investigations might be jeopardised, the flexibility through discretion ends. For a structured exercise of discretion, the OTP ought to actively consider how it can ensure at the preliminary examination stage that effective investigations can take place, either through the ICC or in other jurisdictions.

IV. GUIDING AIMS AND PRINCIPLES

The exercise of discretion does not only need to adhere to the applicable legal limitations such as the duty to ensure effective investigations but must also be exercised in a principled way in order to safeguard the legitimacy of the ICC. These discretionary processes and the results must be persuasive and perceived

[44] See KC Davis, *Discretionary Justice, A Preliminary Inquiry* (Baton Rouge, LA, Lousiana State University Press, 1969); seminal work on the study of discretion and the need for structure.
[45] Policy Paper Preliminary Examinations 2013 (n 7) para 28.
[46] ibid, para 89.
[47] Preliminary Examination Report 2018 (n 16) para 41.

as lawful even if they will often leave some constituents disappointed. To achieve this, it is crucial that the exercise of discretion is actively and visibly geared towards the aims and principles expressed in the Rome Statute, ending impunity and 'thus contributing to the prevention of such crimes'.[48] Another key aspect in the Rome Statute is victims' interests. They have a prominent place in the ICC system and the Prosecutor needs to ensure that victims' interests guide the exercise of discretion from the start of any preliminary examination. All these notions – ending impunity, prevention, victims' interests – are only very broad-brush and to some extent fluid concepts. Nevertheless, they have to be the starting point for the task of achieving a more principled exercise of discretion.

However, some scholars doubt the deterrence potential and hence the preventative effect of international criminal justice mechanisms.[49] These voices make an important contribution through their fundamental challenge of general assumptions. However, the Prosecutor ought to fulfil the task assigned to her by the drafters of the Rome Statute, which is to end impunity and achieve crime prevention through investigation and prosecution.[50] The introduction to this chapter has highlighted the OTP's rather optimistic stance that the preliminary examinations were a cost-effective way of achieving deterrence and prevention. The critical voices have a point in that it is not a straightforward undertaking to achieve deterrence and prevention through ICC intervention. For this difficult task, it is important that the Prosecutor carefully evaluates, where a research- and evidence-lead approach backs up the conduct of preliminary examinations, to ensure that effective measures are taken towards investigation, either through domestic proceedings or at the international level.

A. Deterrence and the Strategy of Positive Complementarity

A key element of the Prosecutor's strategy at the preliminary examination stage is the policy of positive complementarity. This strategy goes beyond the mere evaluation of information for the sake of preparing whether or not to launch a full investigation. The policy of positive complementarity, in a nutshell, aims at activating domestic proceedings through the pressure of preliminary examinations. A key justification for this strategy is the point that the OTP is not able

[48] Preamble ICCSt.

[49] See, eg, M Drumbl, 'Collective Violence and Individual Punishment: The Criminality of Mass Atrocity' (2005) 99 *Northwestern University Law Review* 101, who questions whether *genocidaires* can be impressed through prosecution while those on the ground who support mass atrocities will not have to fear trial at the international level; equally doubtful, I Tallgren, 'The Sensibility and Sense of International Criminal Law' (2002) 13 *European Journal of International Law* 561.

[50] S Nouwen, 'The International Criminal Court and Conflict Prevention in Africa' in T Karbo and K Virk (eds), *The Palgrave Handbook of Peacebuilding in Africa* (Cham, Springer, 2018) 90 describes the ICC's mandate as deontological in that it requires crime prevention through ending impunity by investigation and prosecution.

to investigate all the situations before it. For that reason, it seems a sensible approach to attempt to activate other jurisdictions to trigger investigations and prosecutions and indeed, to use the OTP's own words, is a cost-effective way to fulfil the ICC's mandate. In practice, the strategy requires considerable fine-tuning. Currently, it is not clear in which preliminary examination the Prosecutor actively works towards the activation of domestic proceedings, and it is not clear whether it only pursues this strategy with regard to those jurisdictions that have a territorial jurisdictional link or whether it is a more all-encompassing strategy. Also, a key question and concern is whether lengthy proceedings can contribute to the stimulation of domestic prosecutions or risk at some point losing their potential to stimulate domestic proceedings. Preliminary examinations are a unique feature at the ICC. Hence, the ICC and the international community are in a learning process on how to create an effective international criminal justice system. Fine-tuning the conduct of preliminary examinations according to emerging and future research is critical to maximise their potential as a trigger of active domestic investigations and prosecutions that can contribute to the task of ending impunity and through this contribute to the prevention of crime.

To date, very little is known about the deterrence potential and the dynamics of preliminary examinations. The studies that are emerging on the deterrence potential of the ICC mostly do not distinguish between different forms of ICC interventions (preliminary examinations, investigations and the prosecution of different actors in the conflict).[51] It is suggested that the ICC can deter human rights abuses of ratifying countries by inflicting three types of costs on potential perpetrators: '(1) domestic costs, (2) international audience costs, and (3) prosecution costs'.[52] The Court can influence these directly through, for example, the prosecution of specific perpetrators and by the international community of increasing the audience costs.[53] This connects with Jo and Simmons' findings that the ICC can have some influence on the behaviour of state actors and on those non-state actors, who seek legitimacy.[54] Jo and Simmons view prosecutorial deterrence as deterrence of unlawful behaviour because of fear of consequences, together with social deterrence, the social pressure towards law-abiding behaviour because of its informal consequences.[55] They suggest that prosecutorial deterrence is enhanced by any condition that makes prosecution more likely in

[51] H Jo and B Simmons, 'Can the International Criminal Court Deter Atrocity?' (2016) 70 *International Organization* 443 who suggest a deterrent effect on those actors that strife for legitimacy; B Appel, 'In the Shadow of the International Criminal Court: Does the ICC Deter Human Rights Violations ?' (2018) 62 *Journal of Conflict Resolution* 3; G Dancy and E Wiebelhaus-Brahm, 'The Impact of Criminal Prosecutions during Intrastate Conflict' (2018) 55 *Journal of Peace Research* 47, 58 who suggest that international prosecutions are 'not causally related to the probablity of conflict termination', hence at least seem to have no damaging effect.

[52] Appel (n 51) 8.

[53] ibid, 22.

[54] Jo and Simmons (n 51).

[55] ibid, 444.

a given domestic jurisdiction, such as ratification of the Rome Statute, passage of ICC-implementing legislation, national trials, or court reforms that make trials more probable and credible.[56] The study, however, does not consider whether and under what circumstances a preliminary examination can already contribute to such pressure. Dancy and Montal show in their study that ICC investigations trigger increased domestic prosecution activities not only regarding the issues targeted by the ICC but by creating a spill-over effect in prompting national proceedings,[57] whereas the same statistical evidence is not available for preliminary examinations.

Some key points seem to emerge: the Court seems to have some deterrence potential but this is very context-specific. Deterrence effects are not only generated through the direct threat of investigation and prosecution. The dynamic seems to be more complex in that deterrence effects are stronger when they are combined with the stimulation of domestic and international demands for reform and accountability mechanisms.[58] It seems to work best in those countries that have ratified the Rome Statute and are also receiving other international aid. And crucially, the prosecutorial efforts are most effective in fostering a deterrence effect as 'part of a package' with broad international and local support.[59]

One key concern regarding the current prosecutorial strategy is the length of preliminary examinations. Human rights activists warn that the strategy bears a danger of desensitising actors because it creates a perception that the ICC will be less likely to intervene.[60] Scholars observed similarly that if the Court wants to preserve any deterrence effect, 'then it must be able to provide a modicum of certainty that it can and will intervene in at least some cogently selected cases'.[61] These concerns are to some extent supported by a recent case study into the situation in Kenya. Only after the Prosecutor moved to a full investigation and decided to launch cases against six Kenyans, did observers detect some deterrent potential.[62] The preliminary examination triggered only some reforms on

[56] ibid, 449.

[57] G Dancy and F Montal, 'Unintended Positive Complementarity: Why International Criminal Court Investigations May Increase Domestic Human Rights Prosecutions' (2017) 111 *American Journal of International Law* 689, 690.

[58] Jo and Simmons (n 51) 469. K Sikkink, *The Justice Cascade: How Human Rights Prosecutions are Changing World Politics* (New York, Norton, 2011) 169 proposes that prosecutions lead to improvements in human rights practices, both through punishment (deterrence) and by communication of norms (socialisation); her research, however, is mainly based on developments in Latin America and not on the evaluation of countries under ICC investigation or examination.

[59] Jo and Simmons (n 51) 470.

[60] Human Rights Watch (HRW), *Pressure Point: The ICC's Impact on National Justice* (2018) 15–16 suggests that waiting for too long decreases the certainty among domestic actors that the ICC would act. In Colombia, the study found, domestic actors were fairly certain that the ICC would not start an investigation.

[61] F Mégret and N Jurdi, 'The International Criminal Court, the "Arab Spring" and its Aftermath' (2016) *Diritto umani e diritto internazionale* 1, 24, available at: papers.ssrn.com/sol3/papers.cfm?abstract_id=2793884.

[62] Y Dutton and T Alleblas, 'Unpacking the Deterrent Effect of the International Criminal Court: Lessons From Kenya' (2017) 91 *St John's Law Review* 105, 109–10.

paper but never led to any real attempts at prosecuting those responsible for the post-election violence at the heart of the ICC proceedings.[63] 'Nevertheless, the evidence also indicates that during that time period the increased costs associated with the ICC's interventions may have influenced state leaders to commit abuses to help them hold on to or gain power in order to thwart the ICC'.[64]

The preliminary examination in Colombia, the longest of the Court so far, is a showcase for the strategy of positive complementarity. The Prosecutor kept the developments in Colombia under examination and engaged in a series of meetings and consultations with the Colombian government and non-state actors to promote domestic proceedings.[65] To summarise the developments in a nutshell: in 2016, the Colombian government announced a peace agreement with one of the largest rebel groups, the Revolutionary Armed Forces of Colombia (FARC). The Prosecutor welcomed the peace agreement and emphasised the importance of accountability mechanisms for crimes committed during the 52-year-long armed conflict in Colombia.[66] But throughout the whole process, critical voices raised the alarm that the various legislative efforts, as part of the attempts to negotiate peace, were not designed to ensure effective justice for victims.[67] Nevertheless, the Prosecutor praised the 2016 peace agreement as an important step and announced that the OTP will 'continue to support' the efforts to implement it to ensure accountability under the 'Special jurisdiction for Peace' in Colombia.[68] Whether Colombia turns out to become a success story for the policy of positive complementarity remains to be seen. It remains unknown whether the process in Colombia could have developed differently if the Prosecutor had moved from a preliminary examination to the start of an investigation more quickly. It is of particular importance that lessons are learned from the developments in Colombia to understand in what way the exercise of discretion at the preliminary stage can most effectively contribute to an increase of prosecutions domestically, how it can facilitate the internalisation of norms, and ultimately contribute to the prevention of future crimes.

The important message from existing research is that the strategy of positive complementarity can contribute to deterrence if it is 'part of a package' that includes international efforts in the country as well as local support for the ICC.[69] In order to guide prosecutorial discretion at the preliminary stage,

[63] ibid.

[64] ibid, 110.

[65] See for details on the activities ICC/OTP, 'Situation in Colombia Interim Report', November 2012.

[66] ICC/OTP, 'Statement of ICC Prosecutor, Fatouh Bensouda, on the Conclusion of the Peace Negotitations between the Government of Colombia and the Revolutionary Armed Forces of Colombia – People's Army' (1 September 2016), available at: www.icc-cpi.int//Pages/item.aspx?name=160901-otp-stat-colombia.

[67] As a recent example HRW's analysis 'Agreeing to Impunity', 22 December 2015, available at: www.hrw.org.

[68] Bensouda on the Conclusion of the Peace Negotitations (n 66).

[69] See also Human Rights Watch, *Pressure Point* (n 60) 16.

this will have to include building support for the ICC efforts locally as well as acting in concert with other international agencies. The OTP will have to assess carefully how it seeks to implement deterrence through a successful strategy of positive complementarity. During the terms of Prosecutors Moreno-Ocampo and Bensouda, the strategy of positive complementary appears as an opaque concept leaving the impression that the strategy of positive complementarity seemed perhaps a convenient avoidance strategy to stay clear of the investigation of politically contentious situations. Did the OTP genuinely believe that Afghanistan would develop the capacity to prosecute some of the crimes at the heart of the situations such as the CIA rendition programme?

As a start towards a more visible distinction between the preliminary examinations as such in the sense of the legal analysis towards a decision whether to investigate and those in which a justified policy of positive complementarity seems feasible, it is proposed to introduce different categories of examinations. A situation like Colombia is not 'preliminarily examined' as such; in reality, it is a monitoring process within the strategy of positive complementarity. Wherever this strategy can justifiably be employed at the preliminary stage, the OTP might do so but should make this clear. Perceived non-action might impact on the legitimacy of the Court in two ways: on the one hand indirectly through undermining the deterrence effect of the Court, and on the other more directly through raised but unfulfilled expectations. While the aim of prevention and deterrence should guide the exercise of prosecutorial discretion, the current slow-motion approach fails to convince in its claim to contribute to deterrence.

B. Victims' Interests as Guidance Throughout the Preliminary Stage

Beyond prevention and deterrence, victims' interests are key for a principled exercise of procedural discretion at the preliminary stage.[70] The drafters of the Rome Statute explicitly embedded victims' interests at different points in the Rome Statute: through article 53(1)(c), which obliges the Prosecutor to consider victims' interests as part of the interests of justice at the point of deciding whether to initiate an investigation; in article 54(1)(b), which demands that the Prosecutor ensures effective investigation and prosecution of crimes and in doing so respects the interests of victims; and article 68(3), which provides victims with formal participation mechanisms throughout the pre-trial and trial proceedings to present their views and concerns. However, none of these provisions applies directly at the preliminary stage. Therefore, the Prosecutor

[70] Sikkink (n 58) 163 outlined how prevention, deterrence and victims' interests are interconnected. As part of her qualitative research, she spoke to many victims of torture and their families in different countries and contexts and all expressed the wish to prevent future international crimes like torture.

has no legal obligation to respond to victims' interests at this early point. But these provisions do confirm the importance of victims' interests for the ICC. Additionally, victims are one of the key constituents of the Court, which is why discretion that aims at enhancing legitimacy should respond to these interests. Victims have internationally acknowledged rights to truth and justice.[71] These rights include the right to gain clarity of what happened and to the prosecution of identified perpetrators.[72] Victims are ultimately the group to whom justice matters most. For these reasons, it is proposed that victims' interests must be a leading consideration for the Prosecutor even throughout the preliminary examination stage as part of a more principled way of exercising discretion.[73]

The OTP acknowledges the importance of the interests of victims at the preliminary stage; according to its policy papers, the OTP actively seeks to engage with victim groups and their representatives.[74] Additionally, the Court provides for formal participatory rights from the point of judicial authorisation proceedings based on article 15(4) of the Statute, indicating the importance of victims' interests for the decision.[75] The legal framework of the Court and the prosecutorial policies confirm the importance of victims' interests. Gearing the exercise of prosecutorial discretion in every examination towards exploring and responding to victims' interests is therefore a key task for the Prosecutor.

One caveat with a view to victims' interests as a guiding aim is that they can be diverse and contradictory in settings of large-scale conflicts with often opposing sides involved in committing international crimes.[76] For victims, investigation can come either too early, because a conflict is under way and ICC investigation hinders peace agreements.[77] Or it might come too late.[78] Or only the voices of

[71] *Prosecutor v Katanga and Chui*, Decision on the Set of Procedural Rights Attached to Procedural Status of Victim at the Pre-Trial Stage of the Case, ICC-01/04-01/07-474, 13 May 2008, paras 31–39 with extensive references to international human rights law.

[72] ibid.

[73] S Kendall and S Nouwen, 'Representational Practices at the International Criminal Court: The Gap between Juridified and Abstract Victimhood' (2013) 76 *Law & Contemporary Problems* 235, 239 provide a range of references to actors inside and outside the Court, who identify victims' interests as a telos of the Court.

[74] Policy Paper Preliminary Examinations 2013 (n 7) para 68; ICC/OTP, Policy Paper on Sexual and Gender-Based Crimes, June 2014, 22; ICC/OTP, Policy Paper on Victims' Participation, April 2010, 3.

[75] *Situation in the Republic of Kenya*, Order to the Victims Participation and Reparations Section Concerning Vitcims' Representations Pursuant to Article 15(3) of the Statute, PTC II, ICC-01/09-4, 10 December 2009, para 9.

[76] D Robinson, 'Inescapable Dyads: Why the ICC Cannot Win' (2015) 28 *Leiden Journal of International Law* 323, 333 sees the consideration of victims' interests as one of these inescapable dyads of the ICC in which the Court cannot win.

[77] K Hanlon, 'Peace or Justice: Now That Peace is Being Negotiated in Uganda, Will the ICC Still Pursue Justice?' (2007) 14 *Tulsa Journal of Comparative & International Law* 295, 306 with the example of Ugandan peace talks with the Lord Resistance Army in which local communities demanded that the ICC case against their leaders would need to be dropped before concluding any peace agreement.

[78] Robinson (n 76) with further examples.

sufferers from physical violence are heard while those who suffered merely from the conditions of two decades of violence remain unheard.[79] Because of the diversity of victims' interests, it is not a linear exercise to consider these interests in the discretionary decision-making process. The diverse nature makes it more difficult for the OTP to be responsive to victims' interests.

Beyond the OTP policy, the prosecutorial practice at the preliminary stage does not make the active consideration of victims' interests visible. In the Central African Republic (CAR), the OTP had received clear confirmation that victims 'were awaiting the involvement of the ICC in order to see justice done and to recover their dignity' during their mission to Bangui in November 2005.[80] However, it took another 18 months before the Prosecutor opened an investigation in the CAR.[81] In the report, the OTP submitted to the PTC on the progress regarding the decision-making process, there is no mention of victims' interests.[82] Although victims were awaiting ICC involvement, this did not lead to a swift decision on opening an investigation. Another example in which it is difficult to see how the OTP has actively taken victims' interests into account is the preliminary examination in Afghanistan. The number of victims has dramatically risen throughout the examination since 2007. In none of the preliminary examination reports does the OTP explain whether they have assessed victims' interests and how they have taken those into account.[83] While the policies state a commitment of the OTP to victims' interests, the practice in individual situations does not sufficiently reflect this. Being stuck in The Hague, far removed from the country in question, ICC activities can quickly appear as 'nothing more than an expensive foreign judicial exercise'.[84] Exercising discretion in such a way that it is guided by victims' interests, and remains responsive to these, is the only way to ensure that the ICC can genuinely connect to the people on the ground.

V. ACCOUNTABILITY

Another important aspect for the exercise of discretion that is not just seen as legal but also as legitimate, is the possibility to hold the Prosecutor to account

[79] Kendall and Nouwen (n 73) 242.

[80] 'Situation in the Central African Republic', Background Factsheet ICC-OTP-BN-20070522-220-A_EN, 22 May 2007, 3.

[81] ibid.

[82] Prosecution's Report Pursuant to Pre-Trial Chamber's II 30 November 2006 Decision Requesting Information on the Status of the Preliminary Examination of the Situation in the Central African Republic (n 17).

[83] ICC/OTP, Report on Preliminary Examination Activities 2011, 13 December 2011, paras 20–30; Preliminary Examination Report 2012 (n 26) paras 20–39; Preliminary Examination Report 2013 (n 25) paras 19–56; Preliminary Examination Report 2014 (n 30) paras 75–102; Preliminary Examination Report 2015 (n 2) paras 111–35.

[84] This is the stark verdict given by the International Federation for Human Rights (FIDH), 'Enhancing Victims' Rights Before the ICC: A View from Situation Countries on Victims' Rights Before the ICC' (2013) www.fidh.org/IMG/pdf/fidh_victimsrights_621a_nov2013_ld.pdf, 8.

for her actions. Because only some form of accountability can help to assure that the Prosecutor exercises discretion only within the legal limits outlined above and acts in a principled way. The Rome Statute itself contains no provisions that would allow any judicial review of the conduct of preliminary examinations. Equally, regulation 46 of the Regulations of the Court contains no suitable avenue for a substantial increase in accountability for the exercise of prosecutorial discretion at the preliminary stage. Introducing forms of judicial review throughout the preliminary examination stage would require change *de lege ferenda*. Accountability through transparency therefore plays a key role at this preliminary stage in the process of safeguarding and enhancing the legitimacy of the ICC.

A. Formal Accountability Through Regulation 46 of the Regulations of the Court?

Regulation 46 is the one provision in the broader legal framework of the Court that has been used in attempts to hold the Prosecutor to account for the conduct of a preliminary examination. The provision provides for the responsibility of the PTC for 'any matter' arising in a situation that has been assigned to it by the Presidency.[85] It had first been used by the CAR in the attempt to request a progress report on the preliminary examination that had been pending at the preliminary stage for 31 months.[86] In response to that request, PTC III used regulation 46(2) of the Regulations of the Court to formally demand the Prosecutor to report on the progress of the examination.[87] The PTC noted that the Prosecutor was obligated to 'promptly' inform, in writing, the state that referred the situation, when she decides not to initiate an investigation.[88] This suggested that the prolonged non-decision was comparable to the decision not to investigate. The Prosecutor

[85] Reg 46:

> 2. The Presidency shall assign a situation to a PTC as soon as the Prosecutor has informed the Presidency in accordance with regulation 45. The Pre-Trial Chamber shall be responsible for any matter, request or information arising out of the situation assigned to it, save that, at the request of a Presiding Judge of a Pre- Trial Chamber, the President of the Pre-Trial Division may decide to assign a matter, request or information arising out of that situation to another PTC in the interests of the administration of justice.
>
> 3. Any matter, request or information not arising out of a situation assigned to a Pre-Trial Chamber in accordance with sub-regulation 2, shall be directed by the President of the Pre-Trial Division to a PTC according to a roster established by the President of that Division.

[86] Prosecution's Report pursuant to Pre-Trial Chamber's II 30 November 2006 Decision Requesting Information on the Status of the Preliminary Examination of the Situation in the Central African Republic (n 17).

[87] ibid.

[88] ibid, 3.

rejected the PTC's supervisory role stating that 'no decision under Article 53(1) has been made, and that accordingly there is no exercise of prosecutorial discretion susceptible to judicial review by the Chamber'.[89] This submission reveals some flawed thinking because no decision or no activity is a form of exercising prosecutorial discretion. Though not accepting a legal obligation, the OTP nevertheless submitted a report to the PTC in 'the interests of transparency', reporting on the state of the examination and expressing the hope to complete the examination as 'expeditiously as possible'.[90] This preliminary examination was exceptionally long for a referred situation, and the OTP has since dealt with all other referred situations much more quickly, although it never acknowledged the possibility of accountability under regulation 46. Effectively, the tug-of-war over accountability at the preliminary examination stage ended with a draw in this case.

But was the PTC right in requesting the report, or did it infringe on the Prosecutor's discretion? The regulation is ambiguous in its scope as it refers to 'any matter, request or information' arising from an assigned situation. The PTC has a point in equating a non-decision about an investigation with a negative decision, which would trigger the right of the state to be informed. Not starting with an investigation swiftly can lead to the loss of evidence and can violate the duty to ensure effective investigations. Having said that, these judge-made regulations of the Court do not belong to the canon of applicable sources of law for the Court.[91] The Regulations only secure the routine functioning of the Court.[92] The interpretation of regulation 46 in the CAR decision would effectively widen the scope of PTC competences and stand in contradiction to the functions and powers of the PTC as set out in article 57 of the Statute. While the CAR examination illustrates the need for accountability, the PTC's interpretation of regulation 46 as providing access to judicial supervision beyond provisions in the Rome Statute fails to convince. Any formal accountability would need to be introduced *de lege ferenda*.

A more recent decision confirms the proposition made here that regulation 46 is not a sufficient basis to introduce judicial review over the exercise of prosecutorial discretion at the preliminary stage.[93] Ousted Egyptian ex-President Morsi and his Freedom and Justice Party launched a complaint based on regulation 46(3) after the Prosecutor had dismissed their communication of alleged international crimes

[89] Prosecution's Report Pursuant to Pre-Trial Chamber's II 30 November 2006 Decision Requesting Information on the Status of the Preliminary Examination of the Situation in the Central African Republic (n 17) para 1.

[90] ibid, paras 11, 20.

[91] Art 21 ICCSt.

[92] Art 52(1) ICCSt.

[93] Request under Regulation 46(3) of the Regulations of the Court, Decision on the Request for Review of the Prosecutor's Decision of 23 April 2014 Not to Open a Preliminary Examination Concerning Alleged Crimes Committed in the Arab Republic of Egypt, and the Registrar's Decision of 25 April 2015, PTC II, ICC-RoC46(3)-01/14-3, 12 September 2014.

committed in Egypt and acceptance of the Court's jurisdiction. Egypt is not a State Party to the Rome Statute, and Morsi lacked the legal standing to accept the jurisdiction of the Court at the time of the declaration, as he was not acting president any more.[94] The OTP therefore considered the communication to be manifestly outside the Court's jurisdiction and did not formally open a preliminary examination.[95] In contrast to the previous decision, PTC II interpreted regulation 46(3) of the Regulations as a merely administrative regulation, which would not provide judicial review mechanisms beyond those in the Rome Statute.[96] While the decision in the CAR was based on regulation 46(2), the request here was based on paragraph 3. However, no substantial difference exists between both paragraphs: it is merely a formal distinction between situations in which a PTC has already been assigned and where this is not the case. The PTC in the 'Egyptian decision' argued that articles 15 and 53 of the Statute were exhaustive and clarified that judicial review of a decision not to initiate an investigation in non-referred situations is only possible if that decision is based on the interests of justice.[97] According to this decision, regulation 46 does not fill the gap of formal accountability that exists at the preliminary stage. While the 2006 decision seemed to suggest a proactive stance of the PTC to provide far-reaching judicial supervision beyond the limited mechanisms provided in the Rome Statute, this development has not continued. Any move towards more formal accountability demands amendment of the legal framework of the Court. Regulation 46 cannot fill the void.

B. Pragmatic Accountability Through Transparency

The shift in the OTP practice towards a more transparent approach throughout the preliminary examination stage provides possibilities to hold the Prosecutor to account in a pragmatic way through debate and public scrutiny. Pragmatic accountability is crucial because of the gap in formal mechanisms that exists during this stage. The move to more transparency includes the release of annual reports that summarise the preliminary examination activities of the OTP and more country-specific reports at the end of a preliminary examination.[98] Despite these efforts, crucial parts of the jigsaw are missing. The exercise of

[94] ICC Press Release, 'The determination of the Office of the Prosecutor on the communication received in relation to Egypt', ICC-OTP-20140508-PR1003, 8 May 2014, available at: www.icc-cpi.int/Pages/item.aspx?name=pr1003.

[95] Egypt is therefore not listed on the ICC web page as a preliminary examination, nor included in the 2014 OTP Report on Preliminary Activities.

[96] PTC II Decision Egypt Request (n 93) para 5.

[97] ibid, paras 7–8.

[98] The move to more structured forms of transparency can be observed since 2011, when the OTP published its first preliminary examination report. See for the general policy commitment, Policy Paper Preliminary Examinations (n 7) paras 94–97. Since, the OTP has published annual reports on its preliminary examinations as well as country-specific reports (Korea, Honduras, Nigeria) that provide an in-depth analysis of the statutory criteria in the specific situation.

prosecutorial discretion as such at this stage is not transparent. Discretionary decisions, such as the one taken not even to examine communications related to Da'esh any further, because of the lack of a focus on more senior perpetrators, are not included in the regular reports. Instead these were left to the far more informal and less structured form of a press release, while the important prioritisation processes among possible investigations – decisions that can make a key difference for if and when victims might see justice done – are not visible. Uneven practices are difficult to comprehend and can easily undermine the perceptions of the Court. It is therefore important to increase the level of transparency further to make the exercise of prosecutorial discretion visible at this stage.

i. Transparency Through Guidelines

One medium to provide more transparency and accountability for the Prosecutor can be the development of specific prosecutorial guidelines. This approach has been particularly dominant in the debate throughout the first years of the Court.[99] While, to date, no complex catalogue of guidelines for the Prosecutor has been developed, the Prosecutor has moved to the adoption of specific policy papers such as the 2013 Policy Paper on Preliminary Examination Activities that provide an insight into the thinking and working methods of the OTP.[100] The publication of such policy papers is a halfway response to the demand for guidelines. The Policy Paper on Preliminary Examinations, however, does not address one of the key issues – *how* the Prosecutor exercises her discretion and balances managerial demands through resource constraints with the obligation to fulfil its mandate. There is still a gap to be filled with regard to the specific exercise of discretion in the ongoing work of the OTP. This gap could not be filled by more detailed guidelines, because guidelines are schematic. Instead, what is required is the transparent balancing exercise between different possibilities that explains why the OTP prioritises one examination over another and allows scrutiny of these reasons.

Any call for more transparency, however, should be tempered with caution because of security issues and the need to secure the effectiveness of any investigation. Transparency can be a double-edged sword as it forces the Prosecutor

[99] See A Marston Danner, 'Enhancing the Legitimacy and Accountability of Prosecutorial Discretion at the International Criminal Court' (2003) 97 *The American Journal of International Law* 510, 541 ff suggesting a 'Canadian-style' collection of guidelines with commentary. See similarly A Mcdonald and R Haveman, 'Prosecutorial Discretion: Some Thoughts on "Objectifying" the Exercise of Prosecutorial Discretion by the Prosecutor of the ICC' [Expert Consultation Process on General Issues Relevant to the ICC Office of the Prosecutor] (2003), available at: www.issafrica.org/anicj/uploads/McDonald-Haveman_issues_relevant.pdf.

[100] R Hamilton, 'The ICC's Exit Problem' (2015) 47 *New York University Journal of International Law and Politics* 1, 29 argues that the publication of specific policies has not shielded the Prosecutor from public criticism for her discretionary decisions.

to deliberate on the direction of future investigations. Transparency means that information is out in the open. Social media allows the communication of this information at great speed and beyond borders. Academics, journalists and NGOs use this for ongoing public debate about the development of international criminal justice issues. However, social media activities can also pose security challenges for witnesses and persons cooperating with the ICC.[101] The need for pragmatic accountability therefore demands that transparency should always be balanced against the need for protection of the individuals working with the Court and for the need to secure potential success for an investigation.

Regarding the exclusion of those potential situations that had been filtered out at the first phase – not because they were manifestly outside the jurisdiction of the Court but because the jurisdictional link seemed too weak such as regarding Da'esh – the level of pragmatic accountability could be increased if the Prosecutor included such discretionary decisions in the annual examination reports. A press release can provide an additional vehicle to reach a broader lay public. However, it does not replace a more structured and professional account that explains in detail the reasons for a decision. Such an approach to more openness in the annual reporting system could broadly provide two benefits: it would increase the quality of decision-making processes, because the decision-maker structures and rationalises why she or he has taken a specific decision. Open and structured discretionary decisions show a more reasoned approach. But it could also provide for a system of communication between the ICC, State Parties and the wider public about situations of crisis that require a justice response but do not squarely fall within the ICC's jurisdiction. Taking the Da'esh example, a more structured inclusion of such information into the annual reports could serve the function of alarming the wider public that some State Parties might not fully live up to their duty to investigate and prosecute its nationals who commit international crimes as part of Da'esh. Such forms of two-way communication between the Court and its stakeholders could prove beneficial. This would more effectively serve a strategy of ensuring that State Parties live up to their primary responsibility to investigate and prosecute, while also holding the Prosecutor to account for her own decisions through public scrutiny and debate.

ii. Making Selection Processes Visible

Another key aspect that requires more transparency is the prioritisation and selection process throughout the preliminary examination stage. In some situations, domestic developments and the pursuit of positive complementarity

[101] The ICC/OTP, Strategic Plan 2012–2015, 11 October 2013, para 49 explains: 'The level of sophistication with regard to interference with witnesses has increased. Blogs and social media also create new protection challenges, particularly with names of persons allegedly interacting with the Court being published. All of this results in a general climate of fear and in reduced cooperation of witnesses which impacts on the ability of the Office to investigate and prosecute'.

might justify not to move towards an investigation. These situations, however, should be distinguished from those that do not show considerable potential for effective investigations and prosecutions at other, domestic or regional, jurisdictional levels. Such differentiated reporting provides scope for a more precise debate, better helps victims to know what to expect of the Court, and might even provide an incentive for actors that strive for legitimacy to minimise 'international audience costs' or even benefit from being identified as a country that makes visible efforts to address impunity gaps and could attract additional aid. The deterrence dynamics discussed above are based on the assumptions of rational choices. These might work both ways, negatively and positively. It demonstrates the multiple benefits of greater transparency in the discretionary decision-making processes at the preliminary examination stage.

Transparency requires explanation of why the different treatment of different states is justified, and how the OTP seeks to ensure effective investigations. It can help to avoid scenarios like that in Côte d'Ivoire. In 2003, Côte d'Ivoire had accepted the jurisdiction of the ICC and reconfirmed this acceptance in 2010 and May 2011 in the light of an ongoing situation of crisis and violence that confronted the country. Nevertheless, the OTP remained inactive for years and it took a Security Council request to trigger the ICC to take action. Finally, in October 2011, a full investigation into the situation could commence.[102] Connected to this point, I have called elsewhere[103] for the introduction of timelines within which preliminary examinations should be concluded. While rigid timelines might not be feasible, the need for more explicit justifications seems warranted to ensure that the decisions with prioritising effects are justified.

VI. CONCLUDING REMARKS

The preliminary examination stage, with its prioritisation and selection process of situations for investigation or for those which merit a strategy of positive complementarity, is widely unregulated and provides great scope for the exercise of procedural discretion. The OTP has moved considerably over the first decade of practice towards a more transparent approach with the introduction of specific reporting mechanisms. Despite these efforts, the exercise of prosecutorial discretion in specific situations remains opaque. Prolonged preliminary examinations such as the Afghanistan examination have failed terribly, resulting in the PTC's decision not to authorise an investigation.

[102] *Situation in the Republic of Côte d'Ivoire*, Decision Pursuant to Article 15 of the Rome Statute on the Authorisation of an Investigation into the Situation in the Republic of Côte d'Ivoire, PTC III, ICC-02/11-14, 3 October 2011.

[103] Pues (n 5). See for a critical discussion D Bosco, 'Putting the Prosecutor on a Clock? Responding to Variance in the Length of Preliminary Examinations' (2018) 112 *AJIL Unbound* 158.

The Prosecutor needs to ensure and demonstrate that she exercises discretion firmly aimed at prevention and deterrence and based on a responsive approach to victims' interests in a situation. This requires a swift analysis of available information and a clear distinction between those situations that provide potential for a successful strategy of positive complementarity and those that warrant swift investigation at the international level. Additionally, victims' interests in the specific situation and the local context need to be key in guiding the exercise of prosecutorial discretion. Radical transparency and responsiveness to its key constituents, victim communities and State Parties are vital for a principled exercise of prosecutorial discretion at the preliminary examination stage, a stage that has become so vital in the practice of the Prosecutor.

3

A Duty to Investigate?

I. INTRODUCTION

THE POST-ELECTION VIOLENCE in Kenya in 2007 was at the heart of the first situation in which the Prosecutor decided to use his *propio motu* powers to initiate an investigation. The Prosecutor informed the Kenyan government that it was the Office of the Prosecutor's 'duty to open an investigation' after attempts to encourage national judicial proceedings had failed.[1] But was the Prosecutor duty bound to move to an investigation? If so, how can the delay of a decision in Afghanistan be justified? This chapter deconstructs the Prosecutor's assertion of a duty to investigate. The analysis of the International Criminal Court (ICC) system in action and working at full capacity reveals a structural deficit, because it has no clear mechanism assigned for necessary prioritisation processes. It would be absurd if the Prosecutor could only address resource constraints so long as the Office of the Prosecutor (OTP) delays completing a preliminary examination, whereas, once a 'reasonable basis to proceed' was established, the Office had a duty to initiate an investigation. As argued in the previous chapter, hiding necessary prioritisation away in a lengthy preliminary examination process is not a viable tool.

This chapter addresses the appropriate discretionary decision-making processes for necessary selection decisions when the system faces more situations that would merit investigation than it can pursue. Article 53(1)(c) of the Statute provides some scope for discretion '[t]aking into account the gravity of the crime and the interests of victims, there are nonetheless substantial reasons to believe that an investigation would not serve the interests of justice'. However, because of the very limited role that this provision can play in managing a system that reaches the limits of its capacities, the Prosecutor is required to openly exercise discretion and acknowledge that investigations into specific situations would be warranted but are not prioritised. Selection and prioritisation are a reality, but, as a discretionary process, not openly visible in the practice of the OTP. A step change in this practice provides opportunities to trigger debate

[1] *Situation in the Republic of Kenya*, Request for authorisation of an investigation pursuant to Article 15, OTP, ICC-01/09-3, 26 November 2009, paras 20–21; the same position is reflected in the ICC/OTP, Policy Paper on Preliminary Examinations, November 2013, para 2.

about alternatives to ICC investigation at the level of State Parties and raise the alarm in public about the need for investigation.

When the possibility of management through the length of preliminary examinations comes to a halt, because the duty to ensure effective investigations limits the conduct of preliminary examinations, as proposed in the previous chapter, the exercise of discretion is more visible and the discretionary element in the *proprio motu* powers gains new importance. Obviously, ideally the Prosecutor should aim at investigating all situations that meet the criteria in article 53(1) of the Statute. Whenever the OTP is confronted with more situations than it can pursue, it is suggested that one way forward could be to maximise ICC impact through targeted smaller-scale investigations into broader situations. This would allow for more diversity in the investigations. Such a step change in approach might not be feasible in all situations of conflict but could, in concert with other measures by the international community, allow for greater flexibility in ensuring that a range of different investigations can be conducted addressing a variety of situations.

Addressing mechanisms of accountability, I argue against the Pre-Trial Chamber's interference with prosecutorial discretion regarding the scope of potential investigations. Some Pre-Trial Chamber (PTC) decisions have contributed to creating expectations of the Court's constituents that the Prosecutor cannot fulfil. Having said that, the chapter ends with proposals to increase the pragmatic accountability of the Prosecutor through transparency in the criteria guiding prioritisation decisions, a call for inclusion of the reasons for prioritisation and selection decisions in reporting mechanisms, and a suggestion for a diverse advisory panel to the OTP for the process of the selection of situations for investigation. Such measures will greatly increase transparency in the process and aim at safeguarding the Court's legitimacy in one of the most contentious areas of the Prosecutor's work.

II. THE LEGAL FRAMEWORK FOR THE DECISION TO INITIATE AN INVESTIGATION

The main provision for the decision to initiate an investigation is article 53(1) of the Statute, providing the general parameters for any such decision that ends a preliminary examination.[2] Article 53(1) seems to suggest the duty to open an

[2] Art 53(1) ICCSt: 'The Prosecutor shall, having evaluated the information made available to him or her, initiate an investigation unless he or she determines that there is no reasonable basis to proceed under this Statute. In deciding whether to initiate an investigation, the Prosecutor shall consider whether:

(a) The information available to the Prosecutor provides a reasonable basis to believe that a crime within the jurisdiction of the Court has been or is being committed;
(b) The case is or would be admissible under article 17; and

investigation with the phrase 'the Prosecutor *shall* … initiate an investigation'. Based on article 53(1)(c) of the Statute, the Prosecutor can decide not to proceed with an investigation based on the interests of justice. The Prosecutor sees this provision as a potentially countervailing consideration that may provide a reason not to proceed under specific and highly exceptional circumstances.[3] In the practice of the OTP, it has not been used yet. The general parameters contained in article 53(1) of the Statute are applied regardless of the jurisdictional trigger mechanism.[4] They are the main factors for the decision whether to initiate an investigation.

A. The Low Threshold for the Initiation of an Investigation

The PTCs have interpreted article 53(1) of the Statute as only containing a very low threshold that is required for the start of an investigation.[5] The reasonable basis is the 'sensible or reasonable justification for a belief' that a crime in the jurisdiction of the Court has been committed.[6] Sensibly, the lowest evidentiary standard in the Rome Statute is required, because no investigation has taken place yet and any decision can only be based on the information available at the end of a preliminary examination. The application of this standard requires some subjective judgement on the part of the Prosecutor when she evaluates the available information, as such subjectivity is inherent in the task 'to believe'. Potential cases presented by the OTP at this early stage only serve to ascertain the threshold of a 'reasonable basis' to proceed, rather than predetermining or narrowing the scope of investigation at this point, as long as the investigation stays within the parameters of the authorisation.[7] The PTC decision in the

(c) Taking into account the gravity of the crime and the interests of victims, there are nonetheless substantial reasons to believe that an investigation would not serve the interests of justice.

If the Prosecutor determines that there is no reasonable basis to proceed and his or her determination is based solely on subparagraph (c) above, he or she shall inform the Pre-Trial Chamber'.

[3] Policy Paper Preliminary Examinations 2013 (n 1) paras 67–71.

[4] *Situation in the Republic of Kenya*, Decision pursuant to Article 15 of the Rome Statute on the Authorisation of an Investigation into the Situation in the Republic of Kenya, PTC II, ICC-01/09-19, 31 March 2010, para 20.

[5] For a critical account see M Ventura, 'The "Reasonable Basis to Proceed" Threshold in the Kenya and Côte d'Ivoire *Propio Motu* Investigation Decisions: The International Criminal Court's Lowest Evidentiary Standard?' (2013) 12 *The Law & Practice of International Courts and Tribunals* 49.

[6] *Kenya* Decision (n 4) para 35; *Situation in the Republic of Côte d'Ivoire*, Decision pursuant to Article 15 of the Rome Statute on the Authorisation of an Investigation into the Situation in the Republic of Côte d'Ivoire, PTC III, ICC-02/11-14, 3 October 2011, para 24; *Situation in Georgia*, Decision on the Prosecutor's Request for Authorization of an Investigation, ICC-01/15-12, 27 January 2016, para 25.

[7] *Georgia* Decision (n 6) para 64; *Situation in the Republic of Burundi*, Public Redacted Version of Decision pursuant to Article 15 of the Rome Statute on the Authorization of an Investigation into the Situation in the Republic of Burundi, ICC-01/17-X-9-US-Exp, 25 October 2017, para 193; *Situation in the People's Republic of Bangladesh/Republic of the Union of Myanmar*, Request for Authorisation of an Investigation pursuant to Article 15, ICC-01/19-7, 4 July 2019, para 22.

situation in Georgia suggested that the material presented by the Prosecutor need neither be conclusive, nor should any available information that points to the commission of a crime be disregarded unless it is manifestly false.[8] This basically allows the Prosecutor to draw on an extensive pool of information as long as this supports the claims that crimes in the jurisdiction of the ICC have been committed. Such material does not require corroboration by third parties, because it is the purpose of an investigation to substantiate the allegations.[9] Despite the inevitable scope for some subjective judgement in the application of such a standard, the 'reasonable basis' element does not contain any scope of discretion to impact on the Prosecutor's workload. This is because a reasonable basis to believe merely depends on the factual circumstances in the case; either they support the conclusion or they do not. In sum, the reasonable basis to believe is a very low bar.

Deviating from the above outlined approach, as the practice of the Court has developed over the last few years, it has become the PTC II's stance, regarding the scope of an authorisation in the decision, not to authorise an investigation in the situation in Afghanistan. The PTC suggests that the Prosecutor can only investigate incidents specifically mentioned in the request:

> The precise width and breadth of the Prosecutor's power to investigate are to be determined on the basis of the scope of the Chamber's authorisation: the Prosecutor can only investigate the incidents that are specifically mentioned in the Request and are authorised by the Chamber.[10]

Whether this approach will persist in the Court's future practice remains to be seen. The PTC bases its approach on the rationale of article 15 as providing an effective filtering function.[11] As will be discussed further below, this proactive stance overly curtails prosecutorial discretion. It would undermine the OTP's ability to effectively investigate crimes allegedly committed and ultimately demand the OTP to develop the ability to identify all specific cases and incidents before the start of an investigation. As such, it also demonstrates the need for a robust discussion about the PTC's role vis-a-vis the OTP.

The threshold with regard to the admissibility requirement is similarly low to that applied by the majority of PTCs with regard to facts that suggest crimes have been committed within the jurisdiction of the Court. The admissibility assessment has to be made with regard to potential cases arising from a situation.[12]

[8] *Georgia* Decision (n 6) para 25, with reference to *Situation on the Registered Vessels of the Union of Comoros, the Hellenic Republic and the Kingdom of Cambodia*, Decision on the request of the Union of the Comoros to review the Prosecutor's decision not to initiate an investigation, PTC I, ICC-01/13/34, 16 July 2015, para 35 purporting that no information should be disregarded.

[9] *Georgia* Decision (n 6) para 35.

[10] *Situation in the Islamic Republic of Afghanistan*, Decision pursuant to Article 15 of the Rome Statute on the Authorisation of an Investigation into the Situation in the Islamic Republic of Afghanistan ICC-02/17-33, 12 April 2019, para 40.

[11] *Afghanistan* Decision (n 10) para 42.

[12] *Kenya* Decision (n 4) paras 49–52.

However, it is not required that all potential cases that could arise from that situation need to meet the admissibility assessment. The PTC in the situation in Georgia found that a potential case concerning an attack on Russian peacekeepers might be inadmissible because of ongoing national proceedings by the Russian authorities; the authorisation to investigate was granted regardless.[13] The PTC left the Prosecutor to assess the admissibility of the case throughout the proceedings.[14] This finding is supported by a teleological interpretation given that any other understanding of articles 53(1)(b) and 17 of the Statute would allow domestic authorities to considerably delay the start of an entire ICC investigation through half-hearted domestic proceedings regarding some or even only one of the potential cases. In consequence, the Prosecutor does not need to await the result of ongoing domestic proceedings as long as the overall picture in the situation suggests that some potential cases would be admissible. Applying these findings to other preliminary examinations like Afghanistan would have allowed the Prosecutor to move forward much more quickly with a request for the authorisation of an investigation. In sum, the requirements to establish a reasonable basis to proceed with an investigation are low and would permit the Prosecutor to act faster.

B. The Ambiguity of Article 15 of the Statute

Article 15 of the Rome Statute governs the *proprio motu* powers of the Prosecutor that permit her to start an investigation in the absence of a referral. This widens the possibility for the Prosecutor to investigate situations in which crimes within the jurisdiction of the Court might have been committed. It therefore potentially increases the number of investigations that may be selected for investigation. Article 15(1) of the Statute provides that the 'Prosecutor *may* initiate investigations *proprio motu*'.[15] Article 15(3) of the Statute requires that 'if the Prosecutor concludes that there is a reasonable basis to proceed, he or she *shall* submit to the Pre-Trial Chamber a request for authorization of an investigation'.[16] The authorisation is the precondition for the Prosecutor to initiate an investigation.

[13] ibid, para 50.

[14] ibid.

[15] (Emphasis added). M Bergsmo, J Pejic and D Zhu 'Article 15' in O Triffterer and K Ambos (eds), *Commentary on the Rome Statute of the International Criminal Court*, 3rd edn (Munich, Beck, 2016) para 9: 'The terms "may" and "initiate" would indicate that article 15 provides the Prosecutor with an "unconditional and discretionary right" to initiate an investigation'. However, they do not resolve the tension between paras 1 and 3 pointing to the duty to request authorisation.

[16] (Emphasis added). Bergsmo, Pejic and Zhu, ibid, para 24, comment that 'he or she is not at liberty to exercise discretion in applying to the Chamber to proceed when he or she considers that there is a sufficient basis'. S Rohrer, *Legalitäts- oder Opportunitätsprinzip beim Internationalen Strafgerichtshof* (München, Carl Heymanns Verlag, 2010) 160 proposes that the wording of art 15(1) ICCSt would only indicate the permission to initiate investigations *propio motu* rather than any discretionary scope.

For determining whether a reasonable basis to proceed exists, the Prosecutor has to consider the factors set out in article 53(1)(a)–(c) of the Statute.[17] Once the reasonable basis has been established, a literal interpretation of article 15(3) ('shall … submit') would suggest that the Prosecutor must open an investigation and has no scope for any discretion at this point. But the Prosecutor would only be able to initiate such a *proprio motu* investigation if a reasonable basis to proceed is given. The question therefore is whether the Prosecutor may or must exercise the Court's jurisdiction through the initiation of an investigation in all those situations in which a reasonable basis to proceed has been established.

It appears that the Prosecutor – at least in the early practice of the OTP – seemed to use gravity as one of the statutory requirements in article 53(1)(b) of the Statute in a flexible manner to allow management of the Office's workload. In the first preliminary examination in Iraq, the Prosecutor decided not to initiate an investigation based on the lack of sufficient gravity and explained to that end that 'the Court is faced with multiple situations involving hundreds or thousands of crimes and must select situations'.[18] However, the admissibility criterion of gravity requires consistency in its application. A practice of increasing or decreasing the admissibility threshold, depending on the workload, would endanger the consistent enforcement of the law.[19] Admissibility criteria are not a viable tool for prioritising or selecting among situations. When the situations that would merit investigation exceed the OTP capacities, the Prosecutor faces the task of prioritising and selecting between situations, but she should do so openly, recognising that more situations would warrant investigation than the OTP is able to address. All this requires that the appropriate space for such considerations needs to be reassessed.

III. THE LEGAL BOUNDARIES OF THE DISCRETIONARY SCOPE FOR THE DECISION TO INITIATE AN INVESTIGATION

While the Prosecutor sees a broad scope for discretion throughout the preliminary examination, this discretionary scope appears not to exist in the Prosecutor's view, and change into a duty to act, once the OTP has determined a reasonable basis to proceed. The Prosecutor states in the Policy Paper on Preliminary Examinations:

> The Office will conduct, on the basis of its *proprio motu* powers under article 15 of the Statute, a preliminary examination of all situations that are not manifestly

[17] Rule 48 RPE (Rules of Procedure and Evidence).

[18] ICC/OTP, 'Letter to Senders of Iraq Communication', 9 February 2006, 8–9. This decision was revisited when the Prosecutor decided to reopen the preliminary examination.

[19] G-JA Knoops, 'The Legitimacy of Initiating Contemporary International Criminal Proceedings: Rethinking Prosecutorial Discretionary Powers from a Legal, Ethical and Political Perspective' (2004) 1 *International Studies Journal* 365, 377 points out that the lack of well-defined criteria for the selection of investigations 'may be perceived as political'.

> outside the jurisdiction of the Court. The goal is to collect all relevant information necessary to reach a fully informed determination of whether there is a reasonable basis to proceed with an investigation. If the Office is satisfied that all the criteria established by the Statute for this purpose are fulfilled, it has *a legal duty to open an investigation* into the situation.[20]

Other OTP statements confirm this position and express a duty to open an investigation.[21] This understanding of the Court's framework would leave no scope for the prioritisation or selection of situations according to the available capacities of the Court at the end of a preliminary examination.[22] Leading figures in the OTP, however, admit that selectivity exists and is not only limited to the discretionary selection of cases but extends to the selection of entire situations for investigation.[23] It is an absurd position to suggest that a preliminary examination can continue without time limits, but once the reasonable basis to proceed has been established, no choice would any longer exist. Why was the Prosecutor obliged to move to an investigation in the situation in Kenya, recalling the claim that it was the OTP's duty to investigate this situation, but not in Nigeria or Colombia? How can the different treatment of these situations be justified? Why would the OTP be more duty-bound to investigate the crimes committed in Kenya than those in Afghanistan?

The Prosecutor clearly exercised discretion when she prioritised one situation over the other. But such practice is incompatible with any claim of a *duty* to investigate. Deconstructing that claim is important to allow a reassessment of the overall approach taken to the selection of potential investigations. The Prosecutor is equipped with discretion regarding the exercise of her *proprio motu* powers. Acknowledging this discretion and introducing structured forms of prioritising between situations at the end of a preliminary examination will contribute to reducing the danger of arbitrary decisions.

Currently, the OTP over-extends the scope of discretion throughout a preliminary examination whereas, in contrast, the Prosecutor adopts an overly restrictive view at the end of such an examination. Not to acknowledge the existence of discretion is erroneous because it entails the danger of arbitrary results.

[20] Policy Paper Preliminary Examinations (n 1) para 2 (emphasis added).

[21] Deputy Prosecutor James Stewart, Public Lecture, 'Transitional Justice in Colombia and the Role of the International Criminal Court' (Bogota, 13 May 2015) 2, 5, available at: www.icc-cpi.int stated: 'Where a State Party fails to discharge its duties under the Rome Statute, then the ICC, as the "court of last resort", must intervene … Only where the State is unable or unwilling to act can the Prosecutor exercise her jurisdiction – and then she is under a duty to do so, a duty imposed by the Rome Statute'.

[22] W Schabas, 'Selecting Situations and Cases' in C Stahn (ed), *The Law and Practice of the International Criminal Court* (Oxford, Oxford University Press, 2015) 372 interprets the disapperance of any reference to the selection of situations in the 2013 policy paper as a desire to downplay the role of discretion.

[23] F Guariglia and E Rogier, 'The Selection of Situations and Cases by the OTP of the ICC' in C Stahn (ed), *The Law and Practice of the International Criminal Court* (Oxford, Oxford University Press, 2015) 352.

Where choices can be made, they need to be made consciously and according to consistent methods and criteria; otherwise justice cannot be delivered even-handedly. Therefore, it is time to reassess the appropriate place for discretionary choices that have to be made between a number of situations that would all merit investigation and provide no reason to apply the interests of justice. The interests of justice are not a concept that should be used to manage resources, as I will explain in more detail in chapter six. Justice never comes cheaply. To turn down an investigation simply because no resources are available might be a necessary choice, but it would not serve the interests of justice.

A. A Duty to Initiate *proprio motu* Investigations?

Articles 15(1), (3) and 53(1) of the Statute viewed together are ambiguous as regards the precise scope of discretion for the Prosecutor. The Prosecutor *may* initiate investigations *proprio motu*, which suggests discretion about whether to initiate an investigation. Such initiation of an investigation is only possible once the OTP has established a reasonable basis to proceed – at any earlier point in the proceedings the initiation of an investigation is not an option. When a reasonable basis has been established, however, the Prosecutor *shall* request authorisation for the initiation of an investigation according to article 15(3) of the Statute. In the French text, article 15(3) of the Statute reads 'S'il conclut … le Procureur présente à la Chambre préliminaire une demande d'autorisation'. As Schabas points out, any indicator for a truly mandatory provision such as 'doit présente' or 'est requis de présente' is missing.[24] The French text allows the interpretation of article 15(3) of the Statute as establishing the procedural requirement of requesting PTC authorisation rather than an all-encompassing duty. This would clarify that the discretion indicated in article 15(1) of the Statute does not cease to exist once a reasonable basis to proceed has been established.

The object and purpose of the Rome Statute allows the interpretation of the Statute in such a way that the ambiguity between article 15(1) and (3) can be resolved without the need for a strict legal obligation to initiate an investigation in any situation that would meet the statutory criteria of article 53(1) of the Statute. Neither the fight against impunity, nor the prevention of further crimes as object and purpose of the Rome Statute necessarily require a duty to investigate. Of course, the task of the Court to close the gap of impunity for international crimes can in theory best be achieved through investigations in all situations. The decision to investigate crimes is a vital first step for their prosecution and therefore also a step towards closing the gap of impunity. However, judging by the practice of the first 15 years of operations, investigations at the

[24] W Schabas, *The International Criminal Court: A Commentary on the Rome Statute* (Oxford, Oxford University Press, 2010) 321–22.

ICC result in only a handful of cases maximum per situation with one or two defendants per case. While it is the OTP's purpose to investigate international crimes, the aim of closing the impunity gap might equally well be served if the resources were concentrated on fewer investigations with more prosecutions following suit. Spreading the available resources too thinly might even be counterproductive to high-quality and effective prosecutions. Another point against the idea of a strict legal obligation to initiate investigations *proprio motu* – in every situation that would meet the statutory criteria – is that such a duty is not backed up by a duty to prosecute. It is ultimately in the discretionary power of the Prosecutor to decide whether she wants to start a prosecution.[25] It makes no sense to impose or read into the Rome Statute that the Prosecutor is obliged to investigate in every situation, but prosecution would not have to follow suit.[26] Ultimately, it does not further the purpose of the Rome Statute to have multiple investigations, requiring considerable resources, but which are not then followed by a duty to prosecute the cases resulting from it.

The design, size and resources of the ICC are another indicator of what kind of institution the drafters of the Rome Statute wanted to create. It would not be convincing to create an institution with a duty to investigate every theoretically admissible situation if the Prosecutor is not equipped for multiple large-scale investigations. Ultimately, it is up to the Assembly of State Parties to clarify whether a Prosecutor should investigate every situation arising. It is difficult to see how the Assembly of State Parties as the voice of those states that made up a vital part of those states that drafted the Rome Statute would have expected this from a Prosecutor when they now effectively force the Prosecutor to postpone needed investigations through their budgetary decisions.

Turning to the drafting history as a supplementary means of interpretation is helpful to get a better understanding of the difficult negotiation process. The proposal to introduce *ex officio* powers for the Prosecutor was highly controversial during the drafting of the Rome Statute and a consensus was only reached at the Rome Conference.[27] Article 54 of the draft statute reflects the different options discussed and provides for ex officio powers:

> On receiving a complaint [or upon notification of a decision of the Security Council referred to in article 10, paragraph 1,] [or ex officio upon any other substantiated

[25] *Situation in Darfur/Sudan*, Decision on Application under Rule 103, PTC I, ICC-02/05-185, 5 February 2009, para 14: 'The Chamber observes, nevertheless, that neither article 58(1) nor article 58(7) of the Statute require the Prosecution to request the issuance of an arrest warrant or a summons to appear whenever there is reasonable grounds to believe that a person is criminally liable under the Statute'.

[26] Schabas, 'Selecting Situations and Cases' (n 22) 380.

[27] F Guariglia, 'Investigation and Prosecution' in RS Lee (ed), *The International Criminal Court: The Making of the Rome Statute* (The Hague, Kluwer Law International, 1999) 230; P Kirsch and D Robinson, 'Initiation of Proceedings by the Prosecutor' in A Cassese, P Gaeta and J Jones (eds), *The Rome Statute of the International Criminal Court: A Commentary, Vol I* (Oxford, Oxford University Press, 2002) 657.

> information], the Prosecutor *shall* [subject to paragraphs 2 and 3] initiate an investigation unless the Prosecutor concludes that there is no reasonable basis for a prosecution under this Statute and decides not to initiate an investigation, in which case the Prosecutor shall so inform the [Presidency] [Pre-Trial Chamber].[28]

While the chosen wording 'shall' seems to support the idea that the drafters did not envisage any discretion to choose whether to proceed or not, article 54 of the draft statute was later split into articles 15 and 53 of the Statute with their differing wording. Also, the question of *ex officio* or *proprio motu* powers, basically the question regarding whether the Prosecutor could act at all, was highly controversial until the last day of the Rome Conference. Some delegations raised very serious concerns about the prospect of frivolous or politically motivated prosecutions.[29] An early judicial oversight mechanism was suggested to counterbalance any such dangers.[30] Despite these concerns, the proposal in favour of *proprio motu* powers gained the support of the great majority of delegations during the Rome Conference, a position summarised well by a remark of the German delegate in Rome who emphasised that '[v]iable and effective safeguards already existed against frivolous investigations by a mala fide Prosecutor' through the envisaged PTCs.[31] There is no indication in the materials that the idea of *proprio motu* powers was aimed at introducing a duty to investigate every possible crime within the jurisdiction of the Court. Instead, the main arguments in favour of these powers were concerned with the strengthened independence of the Prosecutor and efficacy of the Court. Those opposing *proprio motu* powers feared a politicised Prosecutor, but also addressed concerns stemming from the scale of the crimes and number of potential perpetrators that 'unless the prosecution were given certain discretionary authority to carry out its duties, it would be extremely difficult for it to fulfil its function effectively'.[32] While it is always difficult to determine a unified will of the drafters in multilateral treaty negotiations, in summary two strands of argument seemed to dominate the discussion: (1) the efficacy argument in order to broaden the potential scope of intervention by the Court; and (2) counterbalancing these broadened powers through judicial supervision to avoid politicisation. Based on these arguments, the proposition of *proprio motu* powers, coupled with early judicial oversight and equipped with explicit discretion through the 'interests of justice' found its way into the Rome Statute.[33] While the specific function of the interests of

[28] United Nations, 'United Nations Diplomatic Conference of Plenipotentiaries on the Establishment of an International Criminal Court, Report of the Preparatory Committee on the Establishment of an International Criminal Court', Vol III (1998) A/CONF.183/2, 41 (emphasis added).

[29] United Nations, *Official Records of the United Nations Diplomatic Conference of Plenipotentiaries on the Establishment of an International Criminal Court (Volume II)* (2002) A/CON.183/13, 322, para 28 exemplary with the US statement.

[30] Proposal by Argentina and Germany in A/Ac.249/1998/WG.4/DP.35, 25 March 1998.

[31] Mr Westdickenberg's remark, *Official Records Volume II* (n 29) 325, para 71.

[32] Guariglia (n 27) 230.

[33] ibid.

justice is a matter that is addressed in detail in chapter six of this book, the main point here is that the State Parties had no intention to introduce a Prosecutor with the comprehensive duty to investigate every crime potentially within the jurisdictional reach of the ICC.

In short, it is not convincing to interpret article 15(3) of the Statute as eliminating the discretionary power to choose whether or not to use the *proprio motu* powers. It is therefore recommended that the Prosecutor revises the position in the Policy Paper on Preliminary Examinations, pronouncing the OTP's legal obligation to investigate because anything else can create false expectations of the Court. The OTP is required to acknowledge that scope for discretion exists even at the point when a reasonable basis to proceed is given, no matter whether it is positively determined or not. The Prosecutor should commit herself to the aim of investigating all situations that warrant it, but she must acknowledge that this might, for capacity reasons, not always be feasible. One might at this point wonder why it should make any difference whether discretion that leads to selection is exercised throughout the preliminary examination process or at the end of it. The argument is that for discretion to be exercised in a structured and transparent way, avoiding the danger of arbitrariness, it is important to make these decisions visible. Additionally, openly acknowledging that specific situations would warrant investigations that the ICC is not able to cover at a specific point in time could ring alarm bells with State Parties and the broader international community that other mechanisms need to be put in place.

B. A Duty to Investigate State Party and Security Council Referrals?

The legal framework is far less ambiguous regarding referrals, because article 53(1) of the Statute clearly states that '[t]he Prosecutor shall … initiate an investigation unless he or she determines that there is no reasonable basis to proceed'.[34] The wording indeed suggests a duty to investigate every situation in which the low threshold of a reasonable basis to proceed is met. Any scope for procedural discretion beyond the interests of justice would have to be based on

[34] J Goldston, 'More Candour about Criteria: The Exercise of Discretion by the Prosecutor of the International Criminal Court' (2010) 8 *Journal of International Criminal Justice* 383, 391 suggests that the Prosecutor 'must initiate an investigation unless he determines that there is no reasonable basis to proceed'. JD Ohlin, 'Peace, Security, and Prosecutorial Discretion' in C Stahn and G Sluiter (eds), *The Emerging Practice of the International Criminal Court* (Leiden, Martinus Nijhoff, 2009) 185 even submits that the Prosecutor is obliged to initiate an investigation in case of an SC referral regardless of the factual circumstances. Based on the functions and powers of the Security Council (SC), he argues, that it would disregard the basic principles of international law if it grants the Prosecutor discretion to refuse a SC referral. However, the SC can only utilise the ICC on the basis of the Rome Statute which contains a judicial review mechanism in article 53(3)(a) of the Statute in case the Prosecutor decides not to initiate an investigation following an SC referral.

article 13 of the Statute providing that the 'Court may exercise its jurisdiction'.[35] But the Court is only in the position to exercise its jurisdiction through the decision of the Prosecutor to initiate an investigation, which brings the discussion back to article 53(1) of the Statute. Does article 53(1) contain a strict legal obligation or only a general principle that requires the Prosecutor to investigate all situations that meet the threshold of article 53(1) of the Statute?

The system must be fit for a scenario, in which multiple situations – and more than perhaps initially envisaged by the State Parties – warrant investigation by the Court. If the Prosecutor has no discretion in the case of a state or SC referral, beyond the narrow scope of the interests of justice, this would ultimately mean that referred situations have priority over *proprio motu* investigations, because only in the latter category is the Prosecutor equipped with some scope for discretion through article 15(1) of the Statute. Any scope for discretion would have to derive from the jurisdictional provision of article 13 ('The Court may exercise its jurisdiction'). A systematic look at articles 13 and 53 of the Statute suggests that the latter is *lex specialis* for the initiation of investigations. It is positioned in part V of the Statute titled 'Investigations and Prosecutions'. In contrast, the former is a provision in part II of the Statute concerning 'jurisdiction, admissibility and applicable law', designed to clarify the circumstances in which the Court is enabled to exercise its jurisdiction. Having said that, the main argument contradicting a duty to investigate is that the drafters of the Statute did not build a Court that is fit to investigate multiple complex situations but necessarily has to select among situations and cases. Therefore some scholars argue that the Prosecutor is equipped with discretion in the decision whether or not to proceed when considering a referral.[36] The drafting history would evidence a clear move towards discretionary powers for the Prosecutor: from what was initially envisaged as a Prosecutor without any discretion whatsoever to discretion for the Prosecutor at two levels: (1) through the insertion of *proprio motu* powers; and (2) because of the option implied in article 53(3) of the Statute that the Prosecutor decides not to investigate on referral.[37] And, indeed, at these two points discretion does exist, but the *proprio motu* powers are not applicable in the case of a referred situation. It is only the interests of justice that provide some leverage for the Prosecutor. Any discretion in case of referrals beyond the interests of justice, however, could hardly be reconciled with the wording of article 53(1) of the Statute.

Such an interpretation acknowledging a difference in the scope of discretion between *proprio motu* decisions and referrals finds support in different

[35] M Brubacher, 'Prosecutorial Discretion within the International Criminal Court' (2004) 2 *Journal of International Criminal Justice* 71, 75 argues that the word 'may' in article 13 ICCSt would indicate discretion even in referred situations.

[36] Schabas, 'Selecting Situations and Cases' (n 22) 370; A Marston Danner, 'Enhancing the Legitimacy and Accountability of Prosecutorial Discretion at the International Criminal Court' (2003) 97 *American Journal of International Law* 510, 519.

[37] Schabas, 'Selecting Situations and Cases' (n 22).

mechanisms of judicial review contained in article 53(3) of the Statute. Based on article 53(3)(a) of the Statute,[38] referring State Parties have the possibility to request judicial review of all three components (jurisdiction, admissibility, interests of justice) of a prosecutorial decision. In contrast, only article 53(3)(b)[39] provides the limited option for the PTC to review a negative decision in a non-referred situation if this decision is based on the interests of justice. This structure illustrates the dominance of the will of State Parties. They can take a very proactive role in shaping the Court's activities through the tool of state referrals based on article 14 of the Statute.[40] So far, the Court has predominantly received 'self-referrals' in which a country refers a situation of crisis with alleged crimes committed within its own jurisdiction.[41] The referral of the situation in Venezuela is the first referral by a group of states – Argentina, Canada, Colombia, Chile, Paraguay and Peru – that deals with a situation of crisis in another country. Self-referrals have a problematic side in that they contain a danger of focusing the Court on the conduct of non-state actors, rather than addressing the potential criminal conduct on all sides of the conflict to the extent necessary.[42] This is a challenge that the Prosecutor will have to tackle throughout the case selection stage. With the reduced scope of discretion regarding state referrals, the Statute reflects the traditional, state-centred structure of the international legal order, despite the introduction of the *proprio motu* powers of the Prosecutor. The structure of prosecutorial discretion can therefore be summarised in the formula that the Prosecutor must initiate an investigation in the case of a referral, and can initiate an investigation *proprio motu*, if a 'reasonable basis to proceed' based on article 53(1) of the Statute has been established.

[38] Art 53(3)(a) ICCSt: 'At the request of the State making a referral under article 14 or the Security Council under article 13, paragraph (b), the Pre-Trial Chamber may review a decision of the Prosecutor under paragraph 1 or 2 not to proceed and may request the Prosecutor to reconsider that decision'.

[39] Art 53(3)(b) ICCSt: 'In addition, the Pre-Trial Chamber may, on its own initiative, review a decision of the Prosecutor not to proceed if it is based solely on paragraph 1(c) or 2(c). In such a case, the decision of the Prosecutor shall be effective only if confirmed by the Pre-Trial Chamber'.

[40] Art 14 ICCSt:

> '1. A State Party may refer to the Prosecutor a situation in which one or more crimes within the jurisdiction of the Court appear to have been committed requesting the Prosecutor to investigate the situation for the purpose of determining whether one or more specific persons should be charged with the commission of such crimes.
> 2. As far as possible, a referral shall specify the relevant circumstances and be accompanied by such supporting documentation as is available to the State referring the situation'.

See Schabas, *The International Criminal Court* (n 24) 305–06 for an overview of the drafting history stating that there was unanimous support in Rome for the authority of State Parties to trigger the Court's jurisdiction.

[41] This form of referral has invited criticism as it was not envisaged by the drafters; see H van der Wilt, 'Self-Referrals as an Indication of the Inability of States to Cope with Non-State Actors' in C Stahn (ed), *The Law and Practice of the International Criminal Court* (Oxford, Oxford University Press, 2015) 211.

[42] F Mégret, 'Is the ICC Focusing Too Much on Non State Actors ?' in M deGuzman and D Amann (eds), *Arcs of Global Justice: Essays in Honor of William A Schabas* (Oxford, Oxford University Press, 2017) 184.

IV. GUIDING AIMS AND PRINCIPLES

Wherever the Prosecutor exercises discretion, this must be guided by the main aims contained in the Rome Statute. As discussed in the previous chapter, the exercise of the Prosecutor's *proprio motu* powers must aim at crime prevention and be geared towards realising victims' interests. Also, the duty to act impartially[43] – strictly speaking a limitation on discretion – has repercussions at this point. It requires that the Prosecutor treats all comparable situations the same.

A. A General Principle in Favour of Investigation

The OTP 2013 Policy Paper on Preliminary Examinations is silent on the question regarding what the Prosecutor considers a viable guiding principle for the prioritisation of investigations. The policy paper works on the assumption of investigating all situations that merit it. Given that this is not a workable assumption, the Prosecutor should reframe this policy. She should be guided by the general principle that, when exercising her *proprio motu* powers, she should always decide in favour of an investigation unless she faces severe resource constraints. The drafters have expressed this will in article 53(1) of the Statute, which indicates that generally situations should be investigated. However, this general principle does not solve the selection dilemma. The question here is what should guide the Prosecutor's procedural choice between different investigations when she faces considerable resource constraints and is therefore forced to select between them?

B. Maximising Impact Through Targeted Smaller-Scale Investigations into Broader Situations

Socio-legal research into prosecutorial decision-making in other areas suggests that a high degree of selectivity can strengthen the effect of those cases in which prosecutors choose to act.[44] The expressive force of investigations and prosecutions might be stronger in systems where a prosecutor only rarely acts. Hawkins suggests that 'choosing the strongest cases and the symbolically most important "targets", [allows] prosecutors [to] maximize the impact and effectiveness' of their actions'.[45] He extensively researched the exercise of prosecutorial discretion in the area of health and safety regulatory agencies in the UK, where prosecutors

[43] Art 45 ICCSt: '[T]he Prosecutor, the Deputy Prosecutors ... shall each make a solemn undertaking in open court to exercise his or her respective functions impartially and conscientiously'.
[44] K Hawkins, *Law as Last Resort: Prosecution Decision-making in a Regulatory Agency* (Oxford, Oxford University Press, 2003) 393.
[45] ibid.

generally only prosecute a select few cases that raise the level of public shaming drastically for those subject to prosecution.[46] The constraint in using these findings, however, is that they have been derived from a domestic legal system with businesses as potential objects of prosecution. A local business might want to avoid a prosecution that could ruin its reputation and, therefore, be more easily compelled to comply with health and safety regulations. The armed actor in a conflict might be less wary about an indictment by the ICC.[47] Having said that, research regarding the ICC suggests that actors concerned with their legitimacy, notably state actors or some separatist movements, do seem more concerned about ICC prosecution.[48] With this caveat in mind, Hawkins' research entails some valuable aspects for the question of how to maximise the impact of scarce resources. Choosing the strongest and most symbolic cases would increase the expressive force of the Court.

When the Prosecutor needs to make a decision on whether to initiate an investigation into a situation at all, of course, no clear cases have usually been identified. But the OTP has to identify *potential* cases throughout the preliminary examination stage, because the necessary admissibility assessment can only be based on potential cases rather than a whole situation. A way forward in the selection dilemma could be a change in the scope of potential investigations. Currently, the OTP works with open-ended in-depth investigations.[49] Targeting only a select few and strong cases for investigation, from what would be a very complex situation, to maximise the impact of those few cases would allow the Prosecutor to distribute investigations across all those situations that warrant investigation. It would indicate to states, as well non-state actors, that the aspect of ICC prosecution following suit after preliminary examinations is not only a hypothetical scenario. Perhaps this might better facilitate a catalysing effect in domestic states and contribute better to the deterrence potential of the Court. Considering the very low numbers of prosecutions deriving from every investigation, opening in-depth investigations into very broad conflicts creates very high expectations that can only leave many disappointed. Scaling back on the size of an investigation might allow addressing all those broader situations that would warrant investigation. Smaller-scale targeted investigations might be a better way to exercise discretion and select between investigations when resources are scarce. Such a proposal, however, should not be understood as making a decision not to investigate other cases at all. This is why the alarm function of the ICC becomes relevant and should be used to appeal to states and the international community to contribute through additional investigative mechanisms.

[46] ibid, 333 ff.

[47] This resonates with observations made by H Jo and B Simmons, 'Can the International Criminal Court Deter Atrocity?' (2016) 70 *International Organization* 443, 460 ff.

[48] ibid, 454.

[49] ICC/OTP, Strategic Plan 2016–2018, 6 July 2015, para 35.

V. ACCOUNTABILITY MECHANISMS FOR THE DECISION TO INVESTIGATE

Mechanisms of accountability play an important role in ascertaining that the discretionary decisions adhere to legal boundaries and are taken in a principled and structured manner. The Rome Statute contains judicial supervision and review mechanisms as checks and balances on the exercise of prosecutorial discretion.[50] Article 15(3) and (4) of the Statute requires the authorisation of *proprio motu* investigations, hence implementing the strongest legal constraints on prosecutorial discretion through the need for authorisation. In case of state or SC referrals, the OTP can proceed with an investigation without such a check and only the negative decision is subject to judicial review based on article 53(3)(a) of the Statute. Thirdly, PTCs may review any negative decision solely based on the interests of justice according to article 53(3)(b).

Calibrating this structure of checks and balances on prosecutorial discretion is of key importance for a balanced relationship between the OTP and PTCs. They 'strike at the core of the balance between the supervisory role of the Pre-Trial Chamber and the discretionary power of the Prosecutor during the early stages of the proceedings'.[51] Some PTCs adopted a proactive stance that unduly interferes with the exercise of prosecutorial discretion. It creates expectations on the Court that cannot be fulfilled. The Court has only limited capacities to address injustices from around the world. Equally damaging are decisions in which the PTC exercises discretion through non-authorisation based on the interests of justice decision as the PTC did regarding an investigation in Afghanistan. The PTC must refrain from interfering with a task explicitly assigned to the Prosecutor, that of strategic decision-making, deciding the feasibility and the scope of investigations as long as the legal prerequisites of jurisdiction and admissibility are met.

A. Judicial Authorisation of *proprio motu* Investigations

Article 15(1) and (4) of the Statute require that any investigation based on the *propio motu* powers of the Prosecutor are subject to PTC authorisation. The Chamber has to consider whether the requirements set out in article 53(l)(a)–(c) of the Statute are satisfied.[52] The authorisation requirement is a safeguard against an abuse of these powers.[53] The short formula most often used is that the authorisation by another organ of the Court, the PTC, would prevent

[50] Personal misconduct of the Prosecutor or failure to comply with Court orders can also be subject to sanctions based on art 71(1) ICCSt.

[51] *Comoros* Decision (n 8) para 43.

[52] *Kenya* Decision (n 4) para 24.

[53] ibid, para 18; *Georgia* Decision (n 6) para 3.

'unwarranted, frivolous or politically motivated investigations'[54] that 'could have a negative effect on its credibility'.[55] After the first years of the Court were dominated by self-referrals, this has changed since the 2010s and the OTP has started investigations in Kenya, Côte d'Ivoire, Georgia and Burundi based on the *propio motu* powers. PTC II refused authorisation for an investigation in Afghanistan as not being in the interests of justice despite finding that the potential cases identified by the OTP would be within the jurisdiction of the Court and meet the admissibility criteria.[56] Whether this decision will be reversed subject to an appeal is, at the time of writing, yet to be determined.[57] This decision goes right to the core question of delineating the competencies of PTCs and OTPs.

i. What is the Standard of Review?

A key issue in this context is what is the appropriate test for the PTC for the decision whether to authorise an investigation. Article 15(4) of the Statute demands a 'reasonable basis to proceed with an investigation, and that the case appears to fall within the jurisdiction', which is determined along the criteria set out in article 53(1). A key point of contention, however, is whether the interests of justice are included in the scope of review. Article 53(1)(c) of the Statute frames the interests of justice as a negative consideration ('nonetheless substantial reasons to believe') with an increased threshold, in contrast to the other statutory criteria that only demand a reasonable basis to believe.

The first PTC decisions suggest that the authorisation decision only requires the review of jurisdiction and admissibility of potential cases when the Prosecutor decides not to use the interests of justice.[58] The PTC III decision regarding Burundi in general accepted this standard of review, albeit hinting tentatively towards a middle ground when it deliberated that in particular the victims in the situation overwhelmingly support an investigation. Hence, 'the Chamber considers that there are indeed no substantial reasons to believe that an investigation would not serve the interests of justice'.[59] This seems to suggest that some consideration of the interests of justice did take place.

PTC II in the Afghanistan situation, however, adopted a very proactive and controversial position in fully reviewing the interests of justice and replacing the Prosecutor's judgement that there are no substantial reasons to believe

[54] *Côte d'Ivoire* Decision (n 6) para 21.

[55] *Kenya* Decision (n 4) para 32; *Afghanistan* Decision (n 10) para 29.

[56] *Afghanistan* Decision (n 10).

[57] *Situation in the Islamic Republic of Afghanistan*, Request for Leave to Appeal the Decision pursuant to Article 15 of the Rome Statute on the Authorisation of an Investigation into the Situation in the Islamic Republic of Afghanistan, ICC-02/17-34, 7 June 2019.

[58] *Kenya* Decision (n 4) para 24, fn 35: 'As for the assessment of "interests of justice" under article 53(l)(c), the Chamber considers that its review is only triggered when the Prosecutor decides not to proceed on the basis of this clause'.

[59] *Burundi* Decision (n 7) para 190.

that an investigation would not serve the interests of its justice with its own – discretionary – decision:

> [T]he scrutiny mandated to the Pre-Trial Chamber in the proceedings under article 15 is not limited to determining whether there is a reasonable basis to believe that crimes under the Court's jurisdiction have been committed, but must include a positive determination to the effect that investigations would be in the interests of justice.[60]

The wording of articles 53(1) and 15(4) of the Rome Statute has to be the starting point of any discussion regarding what the standard of review in authorisation proceedings should be. Article 15(4) refers to the PTC's conclusion that a reasonable basis to proceed with an investigation exists, whereas only article 53(1) addresses the different elements that would constitute such a reasonable basis to proceed. The 'reasonable basis' standard, however, is only required for jurisdiction and admissibility criteria in article 53(1) of the Statute, whereas a higher threshold with 'substantial reasons' is needed for the interests of justice. While this to some extent confirms the approach established in the Kenya situation and used since, it does not fully resolve the tension and ambiguity as the interests of justice are nevertheless part of the criteria in article 53(1).

In the vivid scholarly blogosphere surrounding the ICC Jacobs argues that the PTC acted ultra vires, suggesting that

> [i]t is only if the Prosecutor makes such a decision [that an investigation would not be in the interests of justice], that a Pre-Trial Chamber can review it (Article 53(3)(b)). The only job of the PTC when the Prosecutor requests the opening of an investigation is to determine jurisdiction and admissibility. And the 'interests of justice' fall under neither of these categories.[61]

Heller, in contrast, contends that the PTC can only effectively scrutinise the OTP request to fulfil its function if it addresses all three elements of article 53(1), jurisdiction, admissibility and the interests of justice.[62] Both scholars have a point; their contrasting views demonstrate how limited any interpretation based on the wording of the Statute alone is, given the tensions in the Statute that are the result of the complicated negotiations in Rome.[63]

So, what is necessary to achieve the object and purpose of the PTC authorisation, to filter out frivolous claims, avoiding a politicised[64] Court, and 'curb abuse'[65] of the Prosecutor's powers? PTC II in the Afghanistan decision described the purpose of the authorisation proceedings as providing scrutiny regarding

[60] *Afghanistan* Decision (n 10) para 35.

[61] D Jacobs, 'ICC Pre-Trial Chamber rejects OTP request to open an investigation in Afghanistan: some preliminary thoughts on an ultra vires decision', 12 April 2019, available at: dovjacobs.com.

[62] KJ Heller, 'Can the PTC Review the Interests of Justice?', 12 April 2019, available at: opiniojuris.org.

[63] See also *Kenya* Decision (n 4) para 67.

[64] W Schabas, *The International Criminal Court: A Commentary on the Rome Statute*, 2nd edn (Oxford, Oxford University Press, 2016) 406.

[65] *Burundi* Decision (n 7) para 28.

the 'legality and appropriateness of investigations'.[66] How the Chamber arrived at the conclusion though that it was tasked to test the appropriateness of a decision remains unknown. In my view, the appropriateness of proceedings is different from curbing abuse. Neither the text of the Rome Statute nor its drafting history supports the claim that the purpose of authorisation was to ensure appropriateness.

Vasiliev described the PTC decision as a 'thinly-guised surrender to power politics'[67] in the context of open and unprecedented US hostility towards the ICC with its threats of sanctions against ICC personnel and countries that would support an investigation aimed at US nationals. Besides, PTC II did not expose the Prosecutor's considerations, critically the expressed strong interest of victims in favour of an investigation, to judicial scrutiny. The Afghanistan decision illustrates well that the exercise of judicial discretion is just as susceptible to politicisation of the Court as the exercise of prosecutorial discretion. However, especially in highly contentious political situations, any Court decision will be perceived as politicised. Hence, the key focus should be on the requirements to curb the abuse of investigative prosecutorial powers.

A way to make sense of the provisions in the Rome Statute is to go back to the review structure in article 53(3) of the Statute in which drafters seem to have implemented the idea that a decision not to investigate based on the interests of justice requires two organs, the OTP and the PTC, acting to some degree in concert. The OTP is required to inform the PTC of decisions that are solely based on the interests of justice in order to provide the PTC with the chance of judicial review. This ensures that any discretionary decision to use the interests of justice can be exposed to judicial scrutiny to avoid errors in the use of the concept. The Rome Statute provides a safety net aimed at protecting against flawed discretionary decisions. At the same time, article 53 of the Rome Statute contains the assumption in favour of investigation and the discretionary decision not to do so ought to remain as the exception.

Allowing the PTC to trigger the exceptional discretionary use of the interests of justice on its own accord would disturb this structure. The Statute contains no safety net against a politicised or flawed judicial decision.[68] In my view, the PTC decision in Afghanistan is a clear example of an erroneous decision regarding the interpretation of the interests of justice, a matter I will return to in chapter six of this book. Together with the object and purpose of avoiding any abusive use of prosecutorial power, this militates against any possibility of the PTC replacing the Prosecutor's discretion with its own.

[66] ibid, para 36.

[67] S Vasiliev, 'Not just another "crisis": Could the blocking of the Afghanistan investigation spell the end of the ICC? (Part I)', 19 April 2019, available at: ejiltalk.org.

[68] Whether an appeal against such a decision, based on art 82 ICCSt, is possible is yet to be determined.

However, this should not close the door to judicial scrutiny entirely in order to ensure effective proceedings in which victims' voices are heard and understood. For example, in cases where victims' voices call for the interests of justice to be used not to investigate because of alternative justice mechanisms during fragile post-conflict scenarios but are disregarded by the OTP based on a flawed understanding of the interests of justice, judicial review might be warranted. Otherwise, victims' interests are without any protection despite being a core element of the interests of justice. As I argued earlier, the tension between articles 15 and 53(1) of the Statute cannot fully be resolved through a textual analysis. Yet, the object and purpose of filtering out 'frivolous' decisions could require a PTC to review whether any obvious circumstances have not been considered by the OTP such as an overwhelming expression by victims that an investigation would not be in the interests of justice. The Burundi PTC decision with its brief review of any substantial reasons that could suggest triggering the interests of justice could reconcile the ambiguous wording, the general review structure of article 53, and ensure effective judicial scrutiny without unduly interfering with prosecutorial discretion.

Such a proposed middle ground, however, must not amount to the exercise of judicial discretion replacing that of prosecutorial discretion as has happened in Afghanistan. Some insights into how to strike the balance between ensuring judicial scrutiny without interfering with prosecutorial discretion can be gained from an Appeal Court (AC) decision regarding the scope of review for gravity criteria.[69] For the gravity assessment, the AC has delineated the competences in such a way that the PTC may review the interpretation of the law whereas the Prosecutor has the final say over the factual assessment.[70] This finding addressed the use of the gravity concept, which is similar to the interests of justice concept that requires some interpretative discretion to make sense of it. As part of the judicial review process, the PTC might request the Prosecutor to reconsider its decision, as it did in the Gaza Flotilla incident which was at the core of the AC proceedings. The only scenario in the context of article 53 in which the PTC is explicitly equipped with the power to override a prosecutorial decision is when the OTP has decided not to investigate a situation based solely on the interests of justice.[71] The reverse position, when the PTC deems it warranted to use the interests of justice, poses the challenge as it is unclear whether the PTC has any leeway at all. The proposed reconsideration approach in this scenario is not unfamiliar to the Rome Statute.[72] Its analogous use could fill a gap that currently exists as the Rome Statute does not explicitly spell out how such scenarios could

[69] *Situation on the Registered Vessels of the Union of the Comoros, the Hellenic Republic and the Kingdom of Cambodia*, Judgment on the appeal of the Prosecutor against Pre-Trial Chamber I's Decision on the Application for Judicial Review by the Government of the Union of the Comoros, ICC-01/13-98, 2 September 2019.

[70] ibid, para 80.

[71] ibid, para 75.

[72] See art 53(3)(a) and (4) ICCSt.

be dealt with. Judicial review and scrutiny without the active use of discretion on the PTC's side would enable a more constructive dialogue between the two ICC organs, provide a chance for enhanced prosecutorial discretion through consideration and deliberation on the points raised in PTC proceedings, and avoid legally erroneous decisions.

ii. The PTC Tendency to Broaden the Scope of Investigation

Another example of an overly proactive stance is the PTC decision in the situation in Côte d'Ivoire with its tendency to broaden the scope of investigation.[73] In June 2011 the Prosecutor requested the authorisation to initiate an investigation into post-election violence from 28 November 2010 onwards because of the levels of violence thereafter and the wealth of supporting material for that time period.[74] However, after a review of further supporting material, the PTC authorised the investigation not only with the requested starting date but going back to 2002, an option that the Prosecutor had indicated in his initial request as an alternative to the preferred starting point of 28 November 2010.[75] Apart from expanding the requested starting date for the investigation, the Chamber also identified more possible criminal acts in the authorisation than initially presented by the Prosecutor.[76] This proactive stance of the PTC interfered with the initial exercise of prosecutorial discretion, in which the Prosecutor determined the scope of the potential investigation based on factors such as the evidence available and the level of violence. Despite the broad authorisation and years after commencing the investigation, the Prosecutor has not brought any cases that cover incidents from the period between 2002 and November 2010.[77] In retrospect, it seemed pointless for the PTC to have expanded the scope of the investigation, especially when, as here, the discretionary decision to limit the request was based on sound reasons like the wealth of evidence.

Avoiding such overly proactive PTC decisions that interfere with prosecutorial discretion is important for the following reasons. First, the OTP is best placed to review the potential for a successful investigation based on the possibilities of gathering evidence or drawing on existing pools of evidence. Second, the Prosecutor needs to oversee the resource management of the Office and might determine a narrow scope in order to ensure the feasibility of the investigation. For the closure of the gap of impunity, successful prosecutions are more important than extensive investigations that, ultimately, lead nowhere.

[73] *Côte d'Ivoire* Decision (n 6).

[74] *Situation in the Republic of Cote d'Ivoire*, Request for authorisation of an investigation pursuant to article 15, ICC-02/11-3, 23 June 2011, para 174.

[75] *Côte d'Ivoire* Decision (n 6).

[76] ibid, para 83 ff regarding the identification of torture and other inhumane acts as crimes against humanity.

[77] *Prosecutor v Blé Goudé and Laurent Gbagbo*, ICC-02/11-01/15; *Prosecutor v Simone Gbagbo*, ICC-02/11-01/12.

Third, expanding the scope of investigations creates (false) expectations of the affected communities, who hope to see justice done and who have suffered a decade of violence in their country. The PTC should therefore refrain from such interference with prosecutorial discretion and focus on their initially assigned task of preventing unwarranted investigations.

iii. End Dates to Investigations?

Another connected problem with a balance between prosecutorial discretion and judicial review is the question of determining the end point of an investigation. For the Côte d'Ivoire investigation, the PTC authorised the investigation of potential future crimes, as long as they were sufficiently linked to the referred situation[78] in accordance with the Prosecutor's request. The Chamber's approach contrasts to that taken in the situation in the Republic of Kenya. There, the PTC found that it would undermine its supervisory function if the investigation were extended beyond the date of the Prosecutor's request.[79] In the situation in Côte d'Ivoire, the Chamber wanted to ensure that ongoing or continuing crimes could be included in the investigation considering the volatile security situation.[80] Bearing in mind that the drafters of the Rome Statute aimed at the deterrence of future crimes, a limited authorisation into a situation of ongoing violence that only enables the Prosecutor to investigate crimes up to a specific date undermines the deterrence potential of the Court. In situations of continuing violence, future perpetrators would have little to fear from a Prosecutor whose hands are tied through the scope of authorisation. Another argument in favour of a more flexible approach is that the requirement of a nexus between past crimes, within the scope of the authorisation, and future crimes provides sufficient protection against politically motivated investigations by the Prosecutor. Having said all that, it is ultimately the Prosecutor who is and should be in the prime position to determine how broadly she wants to design investigations, given the management function over resources and capacities in the OTP. Any request should therefore precisely communicate how broad a mandate for investigation she seeks in order to allow effective investigations.

Given the discussed problems with either a too restrictive or too proactive stance on the part of the PTCs, the approach of PTC I in the situation in Georgia is a welcome development.[81] PTC I strictly limited its examination to assessing the merits of the prosecutorial request, because the authorisation 'serves no other purpose than to prevent the abuse of power on the part of the Prosecutor'.[82] The wording of article 15(4) of the Statute, which governs

[78] *Côte d'Ivoire* Decision (n 6) para 178.
[79] *Kenya* Decision (n 4) para 206.
[80] *Côte d'Ivoire* Decision (n 6) para 179.
[81] *Georgia* Decision (n 6).
[82] ibid, para 3.

the authorisation proceedings, requires the PTC to consider the prosecutorial request as well as the supporting material in order to determine the jurisdiction of the Court and the reasonable basis to proceed with an investigation. This is crucial to enable the PTC to assess the merits of any request independently and to filter out any abusive use of the Prosecutor's powers. However, this does not suggest that the Chamber may exceed the original request. The fact that rule 50(5) of the Rules of Procedure and Evidence provides that the PTC may authorise an investigation 'with respect to all or any part of the request by the Prosecutor', supports the limited approach taken by PTC I in the Georgia decision. While additional findings regarding further crimes by additional groups of perpetrators in the situation could strengthen the finding that an investigation would not be frivolous and could emphasise the scale of the conflict, this does not justify any interference with prosecutorial discretion.

PTC I chose a more cautious approach in that regard. The Chamber pointed out that the Prosecutor might have been too restrictive in the assessment of the available material with regard to the identification of potential crimes, given that the material also would have allowed a request based on crimes related to sexual and gender-based violence.[83] But, given that the request contained a basis broad enough to justify the authorisation of an investigation, the Chamber thought it sufficient to indicate that such crimes may be part of an investigation without exceeding the prosecutorial request.[84] This seems the preferable approach at such an early stage of the proceedings, which is only based on preliminary information gathering, while only a full investigation allows the Prosecutor to shed light on the full extent of crimes committed.

The procedural system of the ICC was still very much under construction at the time that the first two authorisation decisions were taken. A lesson to learn from those first decisions is that the PTCs should refrain from any interference with the scope of prosecutorial discretion by authorising wider investigations than requested. At the same time, the Prosecutor must ensure that she fully deliberates on her prosecutorial choice in order to clarify that the scope of investigation has not been determined arbitrarily. Given the possibility of increasing the deterrence potential for the Prosecutor, it seems important to keep the temporal scope flexible as long as this does not defeat the purpose of the authorisation. The decision regarding the situation in Georgia is a welcome development towards a balanced relationship between the OTP and the PTCs.

B. Judicial Review Based on Article 53(3)(a) of the Statute

Article 53(3)(a) of the Statute provides another avenue of judicial review for situations referred by the SC or a State Party, if the Prosecutor decides not to

[83] ibid, para 35.
[84] ibid.

proceed with an investigation. The Gaza Flotilla raid by Israeli forces, referred to the Court as *Comoros, Greece and Cambodia*, afforded the PTC[85] the first chance to use this review mechanism. It includes judicial scrutiny of the Prosecutor's assessment of the Court's jurisdiction, the admissibility of potential cases, and of any countervailing interests of justice issues.[86] The Prosecutor had based her decision regarding the Gaza Flotilla on the lack of gravity required for the admissibility of potential cases.[87] The PTC used the opportunity to assess in detail the use of the gravity notion. This is of key importance for the different dimensions of prosecutorial discretion as – within the Prosecutor's logic – the OTP decision was not a discretionary decision as such but based on the finding that the potential case would lack the gravity required to meet the admissibility threshold. Hence, no procedural choice presented itself in this context. The decision and the review process were nevertheless interesting from the perspective of prosecutorial discretion, as they entailed the review of the interpretative dimension of discretion that some of the open and indeterminate concepts in the Rome Statute contain.

i. Review of the Gravity Assessment

PTC I reviewed the Prosecutor's gravity assessment regarding the criteria used for the determination of gravity, more specifically the question of whether circumstances beyond the jurisdiction of the Court could be taken into account.[88] The PTC clarified that the 'Court has the authority to consider all necessary information, including as concerns extra-jurisdictional facts for the purpose of establishing crimes within its competence as well as their gravity'.[89] This finding allows us to grasp the gravity of crimes within its real life context rather than only in regard to the artificial boundaries set by the jurisdiction of the Court. It is an example for an important part of the review process, whenever interpretative discretionary elements are at stake. A parallel can be drawn here to how the PTCs should approach judicial scrutiny of an interests of justice assessment in which it might review what criteria are used to determine the interests of justice. A key element for the PTC review process must be to ascertain that the criteria used to determine the content of open notions, such as the interests of justice or gravity, are consistent and without legal errors.

However, coming back to the *Gaza Flotilla* decision and on a more critical note, the Chamber also confirmed the requirement of a perpetrator-based element ('those who bear the greatest responsibility') in the gravity assessment.[90]

[85] *Comoros* Decision (n 8).

[86] Art 53(1), (3)(a) ICCSt.

[87] *Situation on Registered Vessels of Comoros, Greece and Cambodia* 'Art 53(1) Report', OTP, 6 November 2014, para 150.

[88] ibid, para 15.

[89] ibid, para 17.

[90] ibid, para 22.

This criterion is inconsistent with an earlier AC decision[91] that refused to reduce the ICC focus to those who bear the greatest responsibility, thereby resulting in the different Chambers of the Court taking contrasting approaches. Achieving consistency and unity within the system, however, should be one crucial function of judicial supervision.

Another dimension in the use of indeterminate notions such as gravity, as in any legal process, is the application of the facts to the elements in the case. Exactly how far the PTC can claim competences to review the application of the facts to the criteria, and whether it can replace its own findings with that of the OTP, remains in dispute between the majority of PTC I, with Judge Kovacs dissenting, and the Prosecutor. The Chamber stated that the number of victims was a 'compelling' indicator for the gravity of the situation[92] whereas the OTP had considered these figures as 'relatively limited proportions'.[93] De facto, the PTC delivered a judgment on the merits as such a finding leaves no room for the OTP to genuinely reconsider its decision without appearing in public as defying a judicial decision.[94] At this point, it is important to remember that according to article 53(3)(a) the PTC 'may [merely] request the Prosecutor to reconsider' a decision. Again, the review presents parallels to the previously discussed 'interests of justice' review. Judicial scrutiny must ensure consistency in the interpretation and application of the legal framework but must also acknowledge that the Prosecutor is equipped with a margin of interpretative discretion.

> [T]he assessment of gravity involves ... the evaluation of numerous factors and information ..., which the Prosecutor has to balance in reaching her decision. In this regard, the Appeals Chamber, by majority, ... considers that the Prosecutor enjoys a *margin of appreciation*, which the pre-trial chamber has to respect when reviewing the Prosecutor's decision. Accordingly, the Appeals Chamber, by majority, finds that it is not the role of the pre-trial chamber to direct the Prosecutor as to what result she should reach in the gravity assessment or what weight she should assign to the individual factors.[95]

ii. Delineating the Boundary between OTP Discretion and PTC Supervision

So, where is the right boundary between the PTC and the OTP in this matter? The wording of article 53(3)(a) of the Statute only equips the PTC with the

[91] *Situation in the Democratic Republic of the Congo*, Judgment on the Prosecutor's appeal against the decision of Pre-Trial Chamber I entitled 'Decision on the Prosecutor's Application for Warrants of Arrest, Article 58', ICC-01/04-169, 23 September 2008, para 68 ff.

[92] *Comoros* Decision (n 8) para 26.

[93] Comoros, 'Art 53 Report', para 138 (n 87). See also A Pues, 'Discretion and the Gravity of Situations at the International Criminal Court' (2017) 17 *International Criminal Law Review* 960, 968.

[94] See for a scathing critique, KJ Heller, 'The Pre-Trial Chamber's Dangerous Comoros Review Decision' (*Opinio Juris*, 2015), available at: opiniojuris.org/2015/07/17/the-pre-trial-chambers-problematic-comoros-review-decision opiniojuris.org: 'Had the majority adopted an "abuse of discretion" standard of review, it would not have been able to engage in the kind of second-guessing that characterizes the Comoros decision'.

[95] AC Decision *Comoros* (n 69) para 81 (emphasis added).

competence to request that the Prosecutor reconsiders a decision rather than replaces that decision. This provision only makes sense if the PTC does not replace its subjective judgement with that of the Prosecutor. Otherwise this would duplicate the work of the different organs of the Court and would diminish the scope for 'reconsideration' for the Prosecutor. At this early stage, the Prosecutor is the only organ of the Court with a deeper insight into the circumstances of the situation and is therefore best placed to make the initial gravity assessment. This changes once proceedings are under way and the facts become clearer. Also, the possibility of a full review is difficult to reconcile with the fact that article 53(3)(a) of the Statute gives the PTC a discretionary choice: it 'may' conduct a review. It would lead to an unbalanced system if it were within the discretionary choice of the PTC to decide whether it wanted to review a decision at all or could exercise the freedom to basically replace the decision on its merits. For these reasons, the potential scope for review is more limited than a decision that basically offers a full gravity assessment.

The question that follows from this finding is whether Judge Kovacs was right in his dissenting opinion that the PTC as a supervisory organ is limited to filtering out any cases of abuse of power.[96] Preventing the abuse of discretion – as Judge Kovacs suggests – is an obvious function of judicial review. Others have suggested that the PTC should employ a test of 'patently unreasonable';[97] a proposal which resembles that of abuse of discretion and is strongly influenced by administrative law. Under this test, the PTC would only filter out a decision that 'plainly and unambiguously flies in the face of fundamental reason and common sense'.[98] However, it is suggested here that this alone would reduce the scope of review too much and render the work of the different organs of the Court ineffective. 'Abuse of discretion' contains a notion of arriving at a specific decision for unjustified purposes.[99] Both suggested tests would set a very high threshold before the PTC could ask the Prosecutor to reconsider a decision and would be able to address inconsistent developments in the ICC system. Rule 108 of the Rules of Procedure and Evidence requires that the Prosecutor reconsiders a decision as soon as possible to reach a final decision. To make the procedural system as effective as possible while strictly observing the different roles of the organs, the most coherent interpretation of the Rome Statute would be if the PTC was not only tasked with identifying abuse but also the erroneous interpretation of the law. This would allow clarification regarding whether gravity should be assessed just based on facts from within the jurisdictional reach of the Court, or whether it should include circumstances beyond that. This power, though, must strictly be distinguished from the competence to evaluate the facts

[96] Dissenting Opinion of Judge Péter Kovács, ICC-01/13-34-Anx, 16 July 2015, para 7.

[97] G-JA Knoops and T Zwart, 'The Flotilla Case before the ICC: The Need to Do Justice While Keeping Heaven Intact' (2015) 15 *International Criminal Law Review* 1069, 1081.

[98] ibid.

[99] Definition of abuse: 'Use (something) to bad effect or for a bad purpose'. In: Lexico.com.

at the preliminary stage of the proceedings. For that reason, it is proposed that PTC I acted within its competence when reviewing the abstract question of whether the concept of gravity permits factual analysis beyond the territorial parameters of a potential case.[100]

Having said all that, it is only a small but important difference that the PTC would need to make in its tone and findings to remain within its remit. The PTC is free to unpick the legal elements used to constitute the gravity notion, and it might also point to any apparent inconsistencies with other Court decisions. All this is part of the supervisory function to ensure that the Prosecutor remains within the limited scope of the interpretative discretionary dimension entailed in the gravity assessment[101] and the decision to investigate. However, the PTC should not make any judgement on the merits of the case. Limiting the decision to making the point that the decision appears inconsistent, when compared with other cases chosen for prosecution, providing guidelines as to which legal elements should apply, but refraining from statements on the merits ('a compelling indicator for … sufficient gravity') would allow the Prosecutor the genuine possibility to reconsider. Striking the right balance between holding the Prosecutor to account and respecting the scope of prosecutorial discretion is a fine line that has yet to be achieved.

C. Judicial Review Based on Article 53(3)(b) of the Statute

Article 53(3)(b) of the Statute extends the possibility of judicial review to prosecutorial decisions solely based on the interests of justice. To date, the Prosecutor has not used the interests of justice as the justification for a decision not to investigate a specific situation and views this possibility as a highly exceptional measure.[102] The judicial review is based on the discretion of the PTC and cannot be triggered by any non-state actors such as victim communities, who have no formal path to hold the Prosecutor to account for such decisions.

In parallel to the model developed here for the exercise of prosecutorial discretion, judicial discretion in the decision-making process regarding whether to commence a review of a decision not to investigate, that is solely based on the interests of justice, requires principle and structure. A key guide for the PTC ought to be victims' interests as these are at the heart of the interests of justice provision in article 53(1)(c). If victims indicate that it is in their interests to review such a decision, the PTC should weigh this as a key consideration in its decision. Only through such a commitment can the interests of victims – at the heart of the concept of the interests of justice – be fully realised.

[100] PTC Decision *Comoros* (n 8) para 16.

[101] See for a detailed discussion Pues (n 93).

[102] ICC/OTP, Policy Paper on the Interests of Justice, September 2007, para 3; Policy Paper Preliminary Examinations 2013 (n 1) para 71.

D. Pragmatic Accountability

The system of formal accountability contains gaps in the system. It does not include any review that would allow scrutiny of the prioritisation of investigations despite the impact that such decisions can have on the perceptions of legitimacy. The Rome Statute leaves victims of non-referred situations with no judicial remedies, when the Prosecutor decides not to proceed with an investigation. This increases the need for openness in the exercise of discretion to allow pragmatic forms of accountability. As part of the broader project to place prosecutorial discretion in the context of legitimacy at key points in the system, I argue for more avenues of pragmatic accountability to fill the gaps in the system. In the light of this, it is more coherent to actively decide to postpone investigations because of managerial requirements than to keep the potential situation on the back burner of the preliminary examination stage. Managing expectations, rather than nurturing false hope, is not only more honest but also the more sustainable approach. It would raise the alarm, and, not least, allow civil society to lobby for other solutions to achieve justice.

The wide jurisdictional reach, and a relatively low threshold regarding the evidence and facts, increase the need for prioritisation and selection of situations through the exercise of prosecutorial discretion. Developing guidelines or abstract criteria for this process seems hardly possible, given that they would need to be abstract enough to be generally applicable and specific enough to allow predictability and consistency in their application.[103] In the process, a multitude of factors will play a decisive role, like the security situation in a country, the support of the international community, state cooperation, the availability of evidence, resource availabilities, to name but a few. The current situation, with the occasional vague reference towards the gravity of a situation, is unsustainable for the future practice of the Prosecutor. But given that these decisions are critical for the legitimacy of the Court, it is important that the Prosecutor opens up and makes transparent those cornerstone choices that influence and guide her decisions. It is deliberately referred to cornerstones here given that these factors will neither reach the level of abstract criteria nor the detail of guidelines. A move to more transparency at this general level, publicising the factors that guide the prioritisation and selection process, would be an important step forward.

Equally important is the gap of supervision in the area of *proprio motu* decisions. Neither the initial prosecutorial request for authorisation, nor the PTC authorisation decision, deliberate on why that specific situation was chosen among various contenders for the active investigation stage at that point. To give an example: at no point was there ever discussion or deliberation as to why the situation in Georgia was moved to the stage of active investigation but not the much longer pending situation in Afghanistan. The work of the OTP is factually

[103] A Greenawalt, 'Justice without Politics? Prosecutorial Discretion and the International Criminal Court' (2007) 39 *New York University Journal of International Law and Politics* 584, 655.

constrained by multiple factors that can impact such decisions. This, however, remains largely unclear and unchecked. The OTP and the PTC only communicate in an isolated manner the legal merits of individual situations.[104] They do not explain how the – ultimately discretionary – choice between the pending situations has been taken. Filling these gaps is crucial to moving, in the exercise of prosecutorial discretion, towards genuine transparency and accountability.

The drafters expressed their will for the supervision of prosecutorial discretion in the process of selecting situations for investigation through the implementation of an authorisation procedure in article 15 of the Statute. At the same time, the drafters of the Statute have made the deliberate choice of creating a court with an independent Prosecutor.[105] However, only now that the ICC is in full working mode, is it possible to fully appreciate where the procedures are not satisfactory and should be enhanced. Apart from a lack of criteria, the current structure provides no supervision of the selection process whatsoever. It provides no access to formal accountability mechanisms, whenever the Prosecutor decides not to act *proprio motu*, unless this is based on the interests of justice. It affords no possibility to demand review by non-state actors or contested state actors.

As a way to enhance accountability, it has been proposed to create a group of advisers, reflecting the diversity of the international community, to hold open consultations with the Prosecutor on the selection of situations.[106] Such a group would only have an advisory status and therefore not interfere with prosecutorial independence.[107] Diverse international voices can contribute to a more holistic understanding of the complex situations of conflict and facilitate a better decision-making process. This might be particularly warranted for the identification of smaller-scale investigations into the most symbolic cases, whenever selection pressure is high. Such a panel would provide an informal mechanism to hold the Prosecutor to account for all those actors that are excluded from the formal mechanisms such as victims or contested state actors. It would allow these groups to lobby for their voices to be heard. At the same time, such a proposal would give the Prosecutor an additional forum to address issues such as the non-cooperation of states or resource constraints. Acknowledging the political in the process, rather than denying it, in a transparent way, might be the better way to preserve the Court's legitimacy.

Such a consultation alone, however, would not necessarily facilitate sufficient transparency for a broader debate. Only the transparent exercise of discretion

[104] See as an example in the *Situation in Georgia*, 'Request for Authorisation of an Investigation pursuant to Article 15', ICC-01/15-4, 13 October 2015.

[105] Art 42(1) ICCSt.

[106] This proposal was made by Schabas, 'Selecting Situations and Cases' (n 22) 375; it resonates to some extend with Greenawalt's suggestion, 671 f (n 103) that the Prosecutor might have a chance to moderate a legitimacy crisis by externalising some of the politically contentious choices to political actors with greater political legitimacy. However, Greenawalt's proposal is difficult to reconcile with the Prosecutor's independence.

[107] Schabas, 'Selecting Situations and Cases' (n 22) 375.

at the level of the individual decisions allows the Prosecutor to benefit from the forces of increased effectiveness through transparency. It forces the decision-maker to deliberate on the reasons for the decision, and it enhances the reflection of those aims and principles guiding the decision. It is therefore additionally proposed that the Prosecutor includes a section in the annual report that deliberates on the prioritisation and selection for that year. This might also raise the alarm if resource constraints are holding the Prosecutor back from moving forward. Such reports would be ideal to document and report on the consultation process. Combining the publication of those cornerstones that the Prosecutor uses in the exercise of discretion, with a consultation process with independent advisers that is documented annually, can be a way forward in striving for more transparency and accountability. An honest approach might be controversial but possibly the more sustainable for the credibility of the Court in the long run.

VI. CONCLUDING REMARKS

The Prosecutor needs to rethink the current policy on the initiation of investigations. So far, she has not acknowledged that prioritisation and selection of investigations takes place. The flawed claim to a duty to investigate all situations should rather be seen as a general principle that it is desirable to investigate all situations that warrant it. Nevertheless, the Prosecutor is equipped with discretion through the *proprio motu* powers even if a reasonable basis to proceed were given in a situation. This scope for discretion, however, only exists to manage scarce resources in an overcrowded system because of the clear preference in the Rome Statute in favour of investigation. But if resources are limited, choices are inevitable. In order to allow these choices to be made through the structured exercise of prosecutorial discretion as opposed to arbitrary choices, it is crucial to acknowledge that this discretion exists. To allow more flexibility and diversity in the investigations that the OTP focuses on, the Prosecutor should concentrate the resource management on smaller-scale investigations into the most symbolic cases rather than large-scale complex situations. Such management questions are entirely within the scope of the Prosecutor. The PTC must not attempt to broaden the scope of an investigation nor to manage resources instead of the OTP in its supervisory position. Judicial activism that interferes with inherently prosecutorial tasks will not help to increase legitimacy. Instead, any accountability gaps should be filled with more pragmatic accountability mechanisms. To that end, this book endorses a proposal that the appointment of an internationally diverse advisory panel be established to provide informal accountability for the prioritisation and selection of decisions. Combining this with a move to a genuine transparency of prioritisation decisions, added to the annual preliminary examination reports, could facilitate public scrutiny and debate. The Prosecutor has to be highly selective and should embrace this reality rather than deny it.

4

Case Selection

I. INTRODUCTION

FOLLOWING THE START of an investigation, the selection of cases for prosecution is the next big challenge for the Prosecutor. The Prosecutor is effectively the gatekeeper to the Court. If the selection of situations is the outer gate of the Court, case selection is the inner passageway into the centre of the Court. Case selection is a complex 'process of choosing the incidents, persons and conduct to be investigated and prosecuted within a given situation and across situations'.[1] The legal scope for discretion is very wide with barely any limitations on the choice of defendants and different options regarding the charging process, provided, of course, that a sufficient factual and evidentiary basis exists. Having said that, the choice of defendants is legally limited through the principle of equality before the law, and the choice of charges must adhere to fair trial provisions, providing clarity and information for the defendant and factually clearly limiting the scope of trial proceedings. The caveat with any of these selection choices, however, is that decisions made in this process are strongly influenced and constrained by a multitude of pragmatic circumstances. The availability of evidence, the focus of previous investigations, and not least the cooperation of state- and non-state actors in specific incidents have a strongly limiting effect beyond the law. Within this web of political and factual constraints and discretionary decisions, this chapter zooms in on the selection of defendants and the selection of the charges as two vital aspects in this process.

As has been shown for the exercise of procedural discretion at the preliminary stage of the proceedings, prevention and deterrence as well as victims' interests are paramount in providing guidance for the Prosecutor. Having said that, how these broad aims more specifically guide the exercise of discretion at the stage of case selection is entirely different. A key aim for the Prosecutor should be to maximise the deterrence potential through the expressive power

[1] ICC/OTP, Policy Paper on Case Selection and Prioritisation, 15 September 2016, para 1.

that a prosecution before the International Criminal Court (ICC) entails.[2] Furthermore, all main areas of victimisation either across a situation or within one case ought to be covered across the case selection choices. It is argued that the Prosecutor must ensure that she communicates the highly selective choices of cases in a transparent way. Changing perspective, the chapter also addresses how those defendants that have been selected can challenge their prosecution. Whenever the selection of a defendant appears as discriminatory, a stay of the proceedings should be the answer to the question 'why me?' Eichmann posed this question in the trial against him, asking: 'Why not the local policemen, thousands of them … Why me? Everybody killed the Jews?'[3] Providing coherent answers to the question 'why me' is a core challenge in the case selection process in situations of mass atrocity.

II. THE LEGAL FRAMEWORK AND THE CURRENT PRACTICE OF CASE SELECTION

Within the Rome Statute, a trio of provisions, articles 53(2), 58 and 61, forms the main procedural framework in the process of case selection. Article 53(2) of the Statute provides that the Prosecutor can decline a prosecution if a case would lack a sufficient legal or factual basis, be inadmissible, or not in the interests of justice.[4] Accordingly, the Office of the Prosecutor (OTP) uses these criteria for the selection of cases for investigation and prosecution in its ongoing practice.[5] Article 58 outlines the conditions for an arrest warrant or a summons to appear, which, in practice, is the formal starting point for a case against a specific defendant. Lastly, article 61 of the Statute sets the procedural requirements for the confirmation of charges before the Pre-Trial Chamber (PTC). Any case that the Prosecutor selects obviously needs to meet the conditions to pass the procedural hurdles, but beyond that, the Prosecutor has broad discretion to choose from within a pool of potential cases.

[2] M deGuzman, 'Choosing to Prosecute: Expressive Selection at the International Criminal Court' (2012) 33 *Michigan Journal of International Law* 265, 313 explains with further references to Kahan, Anderson and Pildes, and Sunstein how expressive theories of law include the idea of 'crafting law to express valued social messages and employing law as a mechanism for altering social norms'.

[3] Cited after L Horwitz and C Catherwood, *Encyclopedia of War Crimes & Genocide* (Facts on File, 2006) 140.

[4] Art 53(2) ICCSt: 'If, upon investigation, the Prosecutor concludes that there is not a sufficient basis for a prosecution because: (a) There is not a sufficient legal or factual basis to seek a warrant or summons under article 58; (b) The case is inadmissible under article 17; or (c) A prosecution is not in the interests of justice, taking into account all the circumstances, including the gravity of the crime, the interests of victims and the age or infirmity of the alleged perpetrator, and his or her role in the alleged crime; the Prosecutor shall inform the Pre-Trial Chamber and the State making a referral under article 14 or the Security Council in a case under article 13, paragraph (b), of his or her conclusion and the reasons for the conclusion'.

[5] Policy Paper Case Selection and Prioritisation (n 1) para 9.

A. Selecting Defendants

A pivotal part of case selection is the selection of the defendants that the OTP aims to target. The Rome Statute only demands that the perpetrators of the most serious crimes of concern to the international community as a whole must be prosecuted.[6] Other than that, the Court's jurisdiction excludes possible perpetrators under the age of 18 at the time of the alleged commission of a crime.[7] But other substantive provisions in the Rome Statute indicate that the ICC was designed as a Court for a broad variety of perpetrators. The Rome Statute, for example, provides for various forms of criminal liability, which indicates the broad scope of discretion to select defendants, from the principal perpetrator to those merely assisting.[8]

Regarding the selection of defendants, the gravity criterion, as part of the admissibility assessment, was at the heart of a judicial dispute in the case against Ntaganda. The PTC refused to issue a warrant of arrest against the suspect, in part based on the lack of gravity of the case, arguing that Ntaganda was not among the most senior leaders in this situation.[9] On appeal, the Appeals Chamber (AC) dismissed this approach, arguing that the Statute did not require any such criterion of seniority for the selection of an alleged perpetrator.[10] The need to preserve the deterrence effect of the Court would require that no potential perpetrators were excluded from potential prosecution before the ICC.[11] Furthermore, a teleological reading of the Statute, and in particular the provisions regarding the irrelevance of superior orders, suggests that it applies to more than just the highest-ranking leaders.[12] This ruling not only keeps the door open for a variety of different perpetrators, it also implies that the choice, regarding whom to prosecute, is a matter of prosecutorial discretion because this choice is not subject to PTC scrutiny at the stage of issuing a warrant of arrest or a summons to appear.[13] In a decision in the situation in Sudan, PTC I explicitly confirmed the Prosecutor's discretionary power to select defendants for prosecution:

> [N]either article 58(1) nor article 58(7) of the Statute require the Prosecution to request the issuance of an arrest warrant or a summons to appear whenever there is reasonable grounds to believe that a person is criminally liable under the Statute.[14]

[6] Preamble ICCSt.

[7] Art 26 ICCSt.

[8] Art 25 ICCSt.

[9] *Situation in the Democratic Republic of the Congo*, Judgment on the Prosecutor's appeal against the decision of Pre-Trial Chamber I entitled 'Decision on the Prosecutor's Application for Warrants of Arrest, Article 58', ICC-01/04-169, 23 September 2008, paras 56–65 with a summary of the PTC's reasoning and the procedural history.

[10] ibid, para 75.

[11] ibid.

[12] ibid, para 78.

[13] ibid, para 41.

[14] *Situation in Darfur/Sudan*, Decision on Application under Rule 103 PTC I, ICC-02/05-185, 4 February 2009, para 14.

i. The OTP Policy Approach

As a matter of policy, the OTP focuses its investigative and prosecution efforts on those most responsible for crimes that fall under the Court's jurisdiction.[15] This approach, however, has been amended in more recent policy papers. The OTP might now also use a strategy of building cases up through the investigation and prosecution of limited numbers of mid-level perpetrators in order to create a reasonable prospect of conviction for those most responsible.[16] The OTP also aims at commanders or other superiors, whereby command responsibility, as provided for in article 28 of the Statute, is invoked wherever suitable in order to reinforce the duty of commanders to prevent and punish crimes committed by their subordinates.[17] Furthermore, the Office will also consider the prosecution of lower-level perpetrators in cases where their conduct was particularly grave or notorious.[18] The adoption of these more nuanced policies evidences that the initially very narrow policy focus has been broadened, opening up space in individual case selection decisions for a more flexible exercise of prosecutorial discretion.

ii. Selection in Practice

Moving from the general policy commitments to the evaluation of individual selection decisions, the OTP policy of focusing on 'those most responsible' is reflected in a number of selection decisions in which the Prosecutor targeted senior leaders within a situation.[19] Yet, the willingness to pursue state actors as alleged perpetrators seems very low in situations referred by a State Party.[20]

[15] ICC/OTP, Policy Paper on Preliminary Examinations, November 2013, para 103; ICC/OTP, Policy on Children, November 2016, para 83.

[16] ICC/OTP, Strategic Plan 2016–2018, 6 July 2015, paras 35–36.

[17] Policy Paper Case Selection and Prioritisation (n 1) para 44.

[18] Policy on Children (n 15) para 83; ICC/OTP, Policy Paper on Sexual and Gender-Based Crimes, June 2014, para 52.

[19] Kenya: the current (as of 2018) President Kenyatta and Vice-President Ruto (cases closed now, both represented opposing sides during the conflict under investigation); Sudan: (ex)President Al-Bashir (arrest warrant issued) and Minister of the Interior Ahmad Harun, Abdallah Banda and Saleh Jerbo as leaders of armed units of one of the opposition forces; Ivory Coast: former President Gbagbo, no cases yet regarding the other side of the conflict; Uganda: Kony (arrest warrant) and Ongwen (at trial) as members of the leadership circle of the Lord's Resistance Army (LRA) (other alleged leaders deceased), no cases regarding the government forces; DRC: Lubanga as former President and Ntaganda as Deputy Chief of Staff of the armed militia Union of Congolese Patriots/Patriotic Force for the Liberation of Congo (UPC/FPLC), Katanga was Brigadier General in the Armed Forces of the Democratic Republic of the Congo (FARDC); the Central African Republic: Bemba was Vice-President of Congo, but charged as Commander of the Movement for the Liberation of the Congo (MLC). This list is not exhaustive but illustrates the point made. The information for all cases and the positions of the defendants mentioned here can be found on the Court's website: www.icc-cpi.int.

[20] See F Mégret, 'Is the ICC Focusing Too Much on Non State Actors?' in M deGuzman and D Amann (eds), *Arcs of Global Justice: Essays in Honor of William A Schabas* (Oxford, Oxford University Press, 2017).

Case selection has triggered considerable critique.[21] The OTP is doing the bidding of state governments,[22] bringing cases 'against individuals who threaten the present ruling political and military elites, leaving the crimes of such ruling elites unaccounted for'.[23] Case selection has also been perceived as one sided, featuring massive time lags between prosecutions of different parties to a conflict or a lack of explanation for why other parties to a conflict are not being prosecuted at all.[24] These are critical points for the discussion of case selection processes, feeding into the identification of those aims and principles that should guide the Prosecutor in such processes.

B. Selecting Charges

Throughout the pre-trial stage of the proceedings in a case, the Prosecutor has to make the decision about which charges to bring. The charges are a combination of the material facts and circumstances that describe specific incidents and their legal characterisation as crimes within the subject-matter jurisdiction of the Court. The Prosecutor has to provide a document containing the charges (DCC) with a 'detailed description of the charges … [and] a list of the evidence, which he or she intends to present at the hearing'.[25] Before the confirmation hearing, the Rome Statute provides the Prosecutor with free discretion to amend or withdraw charges; the only limitation being that the Prosecutor is required to 'give reasonable notice' to the suspect.[26] The significance of the charging decision lies in the fact that the confirmed charges set the parameters for the trial and have a binding effect, because the trial judgment must not exceed the facts and circumstances described in the charges.[27] Returning to the metaphor of the Prosecutor as a gatekeeper of the ICC, the selection of charges as the last step in the case selection process represents the inner gate to the ICC. Once that gate, in the form of the confirmation of the charges, has been passed, the case reaches the centre of the ICC, the trial stage.

[21] See A Tiemessen, 'The International Criminal Court and the Politics of Prosecutions' (2014) 18 *International Journal of Human Rights* 444, 445.

[22] D Bosco, *Rough Justice: The International Criminal Court in a World of Power Politics* (New York, Oxford University Press USA, 2014) 142: ICC officials were aware of perceptions that they were 'doing the bidding' of Kabila's government and that of Western countries backing him.

[23] Tiemessen (n 21) 445.

[24] See Human Rights Watch, 'Human Rights Watch Comments on the ICC Office of the Prosecutor Draft Policy Paper on Case Selection and Prioritisation', 3 May 2016, available at: www.hrw.org.

[25] Rule 121(3) RPE (Rules of Procedure and Evidence of the International Criminal Court).

[26] Art 61(4) ICCSt.

[27] Art 72(2) ICCSt.

i. The Confirmation Process

The confirmation process before the PTC requires the Prosecutor to support each charge with sufficient evidence 'to establish substantial grounds to believe that the person committed each of the crimes charged'.[28] The purpose of the confirmation proceedings is to ensure that only persons are prosecuted against whom sufficiently compelling charges 'beyond mere theory or suspicion have been brought' and to protect rights of the accused 'against wrongful and wholly unfounded charges'.[29] Based on the hearing, the PTC shall confirm the charges, decline the confirmation for those charges lacking sufficient evidence, or adjourn the hearing and request the Prosecutor to either submit more evidence or amend a charge.[30] After the charges are confirmed, the Prosecutor is dependent on the permission of the PTC to amend any charges; any addition or substitution of charges against more serious charges would be dependent on a new hearing and confirmation procedure.[31] With the confirmation decision the pre-trial stage ends and the assigned Trial Chamber (TC) will be responsible for future proceedings in that case.[32] After the commencement of the trial, the Prosecutor may only withdraw charges if the TC permits.[33] The overview indicates how the scope for discretion is narrowed down throughout the procedural stages. Therefore, a key decision is which charges to include in the DCC.

ii. Charging Techniques

The selection of charges at the ICC is particularly challenging because of the extraordinary complex factual circumstances in situations of mass violence containing a multitude of different crimes. In order to tackle the difficult process of charging in such complex settings, the Prosecutor employs different strategies in her practice: limiting the charges, bringing alternative charges, or applying them cumulatively.

The approach of limiting charges was prevalent in the *Lubanga* case as the first case before the ICC. The OTP focused on the war crimes of enlisting and conscripting children under the age of 15 years and using them to actively participate in hostilities,[34] whereas no charges related to sexual violence were

[28] Art 61(7) ICCSt.

[29] *Prosecutor v Lubanga*, Decision on the Confirmation of Charges, PTC I, ICC-01/04-01/06-803-tEN, 14 May 2007, para 37; *Prosecutor v Katanga and Chui*, Decision on the Confirmation of Charges, ICC-01/04-01/07-717, 30 September 2008, para 63 adding that the confirmation hearing is 'not a mini trial'.

[30] Art 61(7) ICCSt.

[31] Art 61(9) ICCSt.

[32] Art 61(11) ICCSt.

[33] Art 61(9) ICCSt.

[34] *Prosecutor v Lubanga*, Decision on the Confirmation of Charges (n 29).

brought, despite a considerable amount of evidence suggesting that such crimes had been committed.[35] With regard to sexual and gender-based crimes, the OTP has now changed its policy and will not exclude these charges through a limited approach but will strive to bring charges related to these crimes whenever sufficient evidence is available.[36]

The OTP uses cumulative charges 'in order to reflect the severity and multifaceted character of … crimes fairly'.[37] When cumulatively charged, the suspect is charged with more than one offence for the same conduct. In the initial DCC in the *Bemba* case, the Prosecutor chose this technique and used the factual circumstances of one incident of rape to present a number of different charges of war crimes and crimes against humanity.[38] Another option for the Prosecutor is to charge crimes or modes of liability in the alternative. In this case, a prevailing approach among pre-trial judges is that alternative charges (including alternative modes of liability) will be confirmed when the evidence is sufficient to sustain each alternative.[39] The OTP uses alternative charging in particular for different war crimes when it is not entirely settled as to whether a conflict is of an international or non-international character, or for the possible modes of liability.[40] The Rome Statute, however, is silent on the question of under what circumstances the Prosecutor may utilise these different techniques. When does the defendant's right to a fair trial limit the possibility to bring cumulative and alternative charges? Under what circumstances is a limited charging approach justified?

III. LEGAL LIMITATIONS

The broad scope of discretion with regard to the choice of defendants, as well as the choice of charges, is limited through the Prosecutor's obligation to act

[35] See S Sácouto and K Cleary, 'Importance of Effective Investigation of Sexual Violence and Gender-Based Crimes at the International Criminal Court' (2009) 17 *American University Journal of Gender, Social Policy & the Law* 337, 345.

[36] Policy Paper on Sexual and Gender-Based Crimes (n 18) para 71.

[37] ibid, para 72.

[38] *Prosecutor v Bemba*, Document Containing the Charges, ICC-01/05-01/08-136-AnxA, 3 October 2008, 26–28.

[39] ICC, 'Pre-Trial Practice Manual', September 2015, 18. This Manual is not part of the legal framework of the Court and has no authoritative character. However, it does set out the consensus among most judges and, as a living document, aims at contributing to the overall effectiveness and efficiceny of the proceedings.

[40] See as examples, *Prosecutor v Katanga and Chui*, Amended Document Containing the Charges pursuant to Article 61(3)(a) of the Statute, ICC-01/04-01/07-649-Anx1A, 26 June 2008, paras 93–95; *Prosecutor v Laurent Gbagbo*, Prosecution's Submission of Document Amendé de Notification Des Charges, l'Inventaire Amendé Des Éléments de Preuve À Charge, and Le Tableau Amendé Des Éléments Constitutifs Des Crimes, and Response to Issues Raised by Pre-Trial Chamber I, ICC-02/11/-1/11-592, 13 January 2014, para 11.

impartially. The OTP demonstrated its awareness of this constraint in the 2016 Policy Paper on Case Selection and Prioritisation in identifying impartiality, objectivity and independence as general principles applicable in the case selection process.[41] Intertwined with the principle of impartiality is the principle of equality before the law, a vital principle for case selection in which defendants might feel arbitrarily chosen or victims equally arbitrarily denied a pathway to justice. The Prosecutor has to square the circle of being highly selective because of the resource constraints that the Office faces but also appearing to be objective and impartial in often highly politicised environments. The criticisms of the selection decisions so far have demonstrated that.

A. Equality Before the Law

The OTP policy on case selection aims to provide some transparency on what considerations guide the exercise of the wide scope of discretion in the selection process.[42] However, the OTP cautiously explains that '[t]his is an internal document of the Office and as such, it does not give rise to legal rights, and is subject to revision based on experience and in light of evolving jurisprudence'.[43] For that reason, the developed policies of the Office do not amount to any legal constraint on the scope of discretion available to the Prosecutor. Neither does the Rome Statute limit the selection of defendants as long as the case against them meets all jurisdictional and admissibility criteria.

The Prosecutor's selective choices are nevertheless not entirely unconstrained. Adherence to the principle of equality is an essential ingredient of the Prosecutor's obligation to perform her duties impartially[44] and poses a legal constraint on prosecutorial discretion regarding the selection of defendants. At the International Criminal Tribunal for the former Yugoslavia (ICTY), the defendant Landžo had claimed that the enforcement against him had been unfairly selective. In response to this challenge, the ICTY AC developed the following test:

> [A] firmly established principle of international law … [is] equality before the law, which encompasses the requirement that there should be no discrimination in the enforcement or application of the law. Thus Article 21, and the principle it embodies, prohibits discrimination in the application of the law based on impermissible motives such as, inter alia, race, colour, religion, opinion, national or ethnic origin. The Prosecutor, in exercising her discretion under the Statute in the investigation

[41] Policy Paper Case Selection and Prioritisation (n 1) paras 16–23.
[42] Policy Paper Case Selection and Prioritisation (n 1) paras 1, 3.
[43] ibid, para 2.
[44] R Cryer, *Prosecuting International Crimes* (Cambridge, Cambridge University Press, 2005) 193.

> and indictment of accused before the Tribunal, is subject to the principle of equality before the law and to this requirement of non-discrimination.[45]

Given that the ICTY and ICC Prosecutors are equally obliged to act impartially, this test sets out the bottom line, or, put differently, the outer limit regarding the choice of defendants. The Prosecutor is required to enforce the law against the specific person chosen for prosecution based on objective criteria rather than any discriminatory grounds. Equally, incidents must not be chosen depending on the group of people targeted, as equality before the law requires law enforcement free from discrimination for all involved in the process. The 2016 policy paper attempts to achieve this by developing the same methods and criteria for all cases,[46] no matter which group the potential defendants might belong to. The OTP will not aim to prosecute perpetrators from all sides at any cost: 'Accordingly, the Office will not seek to create the appearance of parity within a situation between rival parties by selecting cases that would not otherwise meet the criteria set out herein'.[47] This was precisely the claim made by Landžo before the ICTY, who argued that he had only been chosen because the OTP wanted parity of the different warring groups. However, substantiating such a claim of discrimination will in practice be the problem. This is where the existence of clearly outlined policies is important. While the policy paper itself creates no rights or legal limitations, it makes it easier to detect any discrimination when clearly none of the selection or prioritisation criteria have been met.

B. Fairness in the Charging Process

As outlined above, in practice the Prosecutor uses cumulative and alternative charging techniques. Recalling the significance of the charging decisions as the parameters for the trial, this practice has implications for the right of the defendant to a fair trial. Article 67(1) of the Statute as the key provision in the Rome Statute for the fair trial rights of a defendant sets out that in 'the determination of any charge, the accused … [has] to be informed … in detail of the nature, cause and content of the charge'. These functions, of informing the defendant and of limiting the parameters of the trial, are essential, as both are key factors for an accused to be able to effectively defend himself against the accusations on which the trial is based. It is therefore vital to clarify under what circumstances the right to a fair trial limits the exercise of prosecutorial discretion regarding different charging techniques.

[45] *Prosecutor v Delalić, Mucić, Delić and Landžo*, Appeals Judgment, IT-96-21-A, 20 February 2001, para 605; see also Cryer (n 44) 193 pointing out that this test for a plea of selective enforcement with its high threshold can similarly be found in common law systems.

[46] Policy Paper Case Selection and Prioritisation (n 1) para 20.

[47] ibid.

i. Alternative Charging and the Right to be Informed

Bringing alternative charges has become a common tool for the Prosecutor in particular regarding modes of liability.[48] The Pre-Trial Practice Manual confirms this practice stating:

> [T]he Pre-Trial Chamber will confirm alternative charges (including alternative modes of liability) when the evidence is sufficient to sustain each alternative. It would then be the Trial Chamber, on the basis of a full trial, to determine which one, if any, of the confirmed alternatives is applicable to each case. This course of action should limit recourse to regulation 55 of the Regulations, an exceptional instrument which, as such, should be used only sparingly if absolutely warranted.[49]

The manual refers to regulation 55, a nod to a controversial practice exemplified in the *Katanga and Chui* case. The Prosecutor had charged Katanga as a co-perpetrator or alternatively with accessorial liability.[50] PTC I regarded the question of accessorial liability as moot, given that the judges confirmed the charges based on the defendants acting as principals – partly as co-perpetrators and partly having committed the underlying crimes jointly through another person.[51] During the trial stage, the TC took a controversial turn by utilising regulation 55 of the Regulations of the Court recharacterising the mode of liability and finding Katanga guilty, based on accessorial liability rather than the initially charged modes.[52] This in turn brings up a whole series of queries around the fair trial for the accused,[53] given that it was used only at a very late stage of the proceedings after the accused had chosen a defence strategy reliant on the charges as confirmed. From a fair trial perspective, the lesson learnt from

[48] *Prosecutor v Al Mahdi*, Decision on the Confirmation of Charges against Ahmad Al Faqi Al Mahdi, PTC I, ICC-01/12-01/15-84, 24 March 2016, para 22; see also *Prosecutor v Ntaganda*, Decision pursuant to Article 61(7)(a) and (b) of the Rome Statute on the Charges of the Prosecutor Against Bosco Ntaganda, PTC II, ICC-01/04-02/06-309, 09 June 2014; *Prosecutor v Gbagbo*, Decision on the Confirmation of Charges against Laurent Gbagbo, PTC I, ICC-02/11-01/11-656-Red, 12 June 2014; *Prosecutor v Blé Goudé*, Decision on the Confirmation of Charges against Charles Blé Goudé, PTC I, ICC-02/11-02/11-186, 11 December 2014; *Prosecutor v Bemba et al*, Decision pursuant to Article 61(7)(a) and (b) of the Rome Statute, PTC II, ICC-01/05-01/13-749, 11 November 2014.

[49] Pre-Trial Practice Manual (n 39) 18.

[50] *Prosecutor v Katanga and Chui*, Amended Document Containing the Charges pursuant to Article 61(3)(a) of the Statute (n 40) paras 93–95.

[51] *Prosecutor v Katanga and Chui*, Decision on the Confirmation of Charges, ICC-01/04-01/07-717, 1 October 2008, paras 471, 489.

[52] *Prosecutor v Katanga*, Decision on the implementation of regulation 55 of the Regulations of the Court and severing the charges against the accused persons, TC II, ICC-01/04-01/07-3319-tENG, 21 November 2012. See similarly *Prosecutor v Laurent Gbagbo and Blé Goudé*, Decision Giving Notice pursuant to Regulation 55(2) of the Regulations of the Court, TC I, ICC-02/11-01/15-185, 20 August 2015.

[53] See Minority Opinion of Judge C Van den Wyngaert, ICC-01/04-01/07-3436-AnxI, 7 March 2014, para 60 ff. Also M Dastugue, 'The Faults in "Fair" Trials : An Evaluation of Regulation 55 at the International Criminal' (2015) 48 *Vanderbilt Journal of Transnational Law* 273; H Friman, 'Trial Procedures – With a Particular Focus on the Relationship between the Proceedings of the Pre-Trial and the Trial Chambers' in C Stahn (ed), *The Law and Practice of the International Criminal Court* (Oxford, Oxford University Press, 2015) 917–18.

the *Katanga and Chui* case for the pre-trial stage is that it is preferable if the accused is fully alerted to different charges and modes of liability that he might face. It is proposed that the OTP's discretion should not be curtailed regarding the choice of charging techniques, as long as the charges are supported by sufficient evidence and attempt to precisely identify how specific facts link to the charged crimes and modes of liability.[54]

Fair trial requirements nevertheless provide limits to the Prosecutor's discretion. In *Mbarushimana*,[55] the Prosecutor included charges featuring patterns of behaviour without specifying all relevant factual circumstances. The DCC included phrases such as 'these locations included but not limited to' or 'and neighbouring villages' and 'surrounding villages'.[56] The PTC rightly dismissed this approach 'to keep the parameters of the case as broad and general as possible' finding that, at the time of the confirmation hearing, the Prosecutor ought to know the scope of the case and should be in a position to plead on more specific grounds. There are three arguments in support of the PTC's position, linked to the fairness of the proceedings. First, the suspect must be informed in detail of the facts underlying the charges brought against him 30 days before the commencement of the confirmation hearing.[57] Providing only an overview with some specific examples does not meet the requirement of providing detailed information for the suspect. Second, according to article 74(2) of the Statute, the TC's decision establishing criminal liability of the defendant has to be based on the facts and circumstances as described in the charges. Charging patterns of behaviour would undermine the limiting effect of the charges on the scope of the trial. And third, looking at the Statute systematically, it would undermine the procedure in article 61(9) of the Statute, which provides that any amendment of the charges after the confirmation procedure is subject to PTC permission and notice to the accused. Moreover, the addition of any more serious charges requires a formal new hearing. This provision would lose its important protective function with regard to the fair trial guarantees set out in article 67(1) of the Statute. Article 54(1)(c) of the Statute requires the Prosecutor to respect the fair trial rights of the accused. Charges that do not precisely specify the factual circumstances would breach the fairness of proceedings.

ii. Cumulative Charges and Fairness

At the ICC, PTC and TC practice has endorsed an approach to cumulative charges that limits the permissibility of cumulative charges to those that contain materially distinct legal elements from one another.[58] The *Bemba* case triggered

[54] Reg 52(c) Regulations of the Court.

[55] *Prosecutor v Mbarushimana*, Decision on the Confirmation of Charges, PTC I, ICC-01/04-01/10-465-Red, 16 December 2011.

[56] ibid, paras 79–80.

[57] Arts 61(3)(a), 67(1)(a) ICCSt; rule 121(3) RPE; Regulation 52 Regulations of the Court.

[58] Pre-Trial Practice Manual (n 39) 18.

the development of this approach. The Prosecutor initially charged Bemba with one incident of rape as a war crime, a crime against humanity, torture as a crime against humanity, and outrages upon personal dignity as a war crime. The PTC criticised this approach as an undue burden on the Defence that would lead to delays in the proceedings.[59] Based on these considerations, the OTP is currently limited to use cumulative charges only when 'each [charge] is sufficiently supported by the available evidence and each crime cumulatively charged contains a materially distinct legal element'.[60]

However, nothing in the Rome Statute seems to prescribe the requirements as spelled out by the PTC. A look at other international courts and tribunals, however, shows that cumulative charging has been widely practised.[61] To support the application of the 'different elements' test, the PTC references the ICTY AC decision in the case against Delalić. However, the PTC overlooks the important point that the AC found that cumulative *charging* is permissible while cumulative *convictions* should be subject to a test of distinct elements to ensure fairness for the accused.[62] The ICTY AC found:

> Cumulative charging is to be allowed in light of the fact that, prior to the presentation of all of the evidence, it is not possible to determine to a certainty which of the charges brought against an accused will be proven. The Trial Chamber is better poised, after the parties' presentation of the evidence, to evaluate which of the charges may be retained, based upon the sufficiency of the evidence.[63]

The jurisprudence of the *ad hoc* tribunals is not prescriptive for the ICC. However, the findings illustrate the important point that it is the TC that is best placed to determine the charges on which a conviction should be based. Considering the fairness of the proceedings, the pivotal point from a fair trial perspective for the accused is to be protected against being punished more than once for the same criminal conduct.[64] This, however, can be addressed by the

[59] *Prosecutor v Bemba*, Decision pursuant to Article 61(7)(a) and (b) of the Rome Statute on the Charges of the Prosecutor Against Jean-Pierre Bemba Gombo, ICC-01/05-01/08-424, 15 June 2009, paras 201–02; also *Prosecutor v Ruto, Kosgey and Sang*, Decision on the Confirmation of Charges pursuant to Article 61(7)(a) and (b) of the Rome Statute, ICC-01/09-01/11-373, 23 January 2012, para 277.

[60] Pre-Trial Practice Manual (n 39) 18.

[61] See S Sácouto and K Cleary, 'The Practice of Cumulative Charging at the International Criminal Court' (Washington, War Crimes Research Office, 2010), available at: www.wcl.american.edu/warcrimes/icc/documents/WCRO_Report_May2010.pdf, 6 ff; also J Locke, 'Indictments' in L Reydams, J Wouters and C Ryngaert (eds), *International Prosecutors* (Oxford, Oxford University Press, 2012) 635.

[62] *Prosecutor v Delalić et al* (n 45) paras 400–12 (emphasis added).

[63] ibid, para 400.

[64] *Prosecutor v Katanga*, Judgment pursuant to Article 74 of the Statute, ICC-01/04-01/07-3436-tENG, 20 April 2015, para 1695 outlining that cumulative convictions are permissible 'where the conduct in question clearly violates two distinct provisions of the Statute, each demanding proof of a "materially distinct" element not required by the other'. See also Sácouto and Cleary, 'The Practice of Cumulative Charging at the International Criminal Court' (n 61) 9.

TC at the conviction or sentencing stage and does not require a limitation of the Prosecutor's discretion at the pre-trial stage.

The PTC in *Bemba* based its arguments on fairness considerations attempting to avoid an undue burden for the defence and delays. A key burden in any (pre-)trial proceedings, however, is the amount of evidence and factual considerations. Curtailing cumulative charging does not reduce the level of evidence. Indeed, fairness considerations can weigh in favour of an extensive cumulative charging approach to ensure that the defendant is fully informed. According to regulation 55 of the Regulations of the Court,[65] the TC has the power to recharacterise charges against the accused during the trial stage.[66] The TC is only limited by the 'facts and circumstances' described in the charges.[67] It is the existence of this possibility that makes it important for the defendant to be prepared for, and informed of, any possible charges. It might be less prejudicial if the defendant was informed of, or alerted to, the possible range of charges he would have to face, given that the limited confirmation of charges would not rule out other charges at the trial stage.[68] The existence of regulation 55 greatly increases the need for the accused to be fully informed of all possibilities. Ultimately, fair trial considerations do not pose a limitation on the Prosecutor's discretion to bring cumulative charges, as long as this is sufficiently supported by evidence. The PTCs should create space for the Prosecutor to exercise the discretion placed with her by the Rome Statute.

C. The Rule of Speciality

The choice of charges is also limited through the rule of speciality. Article 101(1) of the Rome Statute provides for the application of the rule of speciality, which means that proceedings are limited to the conduct that formed the basis for the

[65] Reg 55 Regulations of the Court:

1. In its decision under article 74, the Chamber may change the legal characterisation of facts to accord with the crimes under articles 6, 7 or 8, or to accord with the form of participation of the accused under articles 25 and 28, without exceeding the facts and circumstances described in the charges and any amendments to the charges.
2. If, at any time during the trial, it appears to the Chamber that the legal characterisation of facts may be subject to change, the Chamber shall give notice to the participants of such a possibility and having heard the evidence, shall, at an appropriate stage of the proceedings, give the participants the opportunity to make oral or written submissions.

[66] See for a critical discussion, D Jacobs, 'Shifting Scale of Power: Who is in Charge of the Charges at the International Criminal Court and the Uses of Regulation 55' (2013) Grotius Centre Working Paper 2013/004-ICL, available at: papers.ssrn.com.

[67] Art 74(2) ICCSt.

[68] Similarly Locke (n 61) 637.

surrender of a person.[69] This provision has repeatedly been the reason for the defence to challenge the charges in cases before the ICC, arguing that some of the charges contained in the DCC had not been included in the warrants of arrest that formed the basis of the suspect's surrender. To date, however, the PTCs have interpreted the scope of article 101 of the Statute rather narrowly.[70] It seems to suffice that those charges not explicitly mentioned in the warrant of arrest but included in the DCC, have implicitly been part of the factual conduct included in the arrest warrant.[71] This finding was based on the 'more generic wording' of article 101 of the Statute ('conduct or course of conduct which forms the basis of the crimes').[72] The rule of speciality is linked to the underlying facts included in an arrest warrant rather than the legal qualification,[73] a convincing argument given the difference between the charges and the crimes. This illustrates how the rule of speciality constrains the choice of charges only in that any charges have to be linked to the factual conduct included in the arrest warrant on which the surrender of a suspect was based.

While the rule of speciality is a well-known principle in matters of international cooperation and judicial assistance in criminal proceedings, it will be of only limited relevance in proceedings before the ICC.[74] The Rome Statute explicitly provides for the possibility to request a waiver of the rule of speciality.[75] Hence, whenever the OTP assumes that they might not have covered the full range of alleged material conduct, requesting a waiver will enable the OTP to avoid legal constraints. State Parties are expected to provide such a waiver and are under a general obligation to cooperate with the Court.[76] Therefore, only when a non-State Party surrenders a suspect to the ICC might the rule of speciality pose a relevant constraint on prosecutorial discretion. In summary, the rule of speciality only provides a limited legal constraint for prosecutorial discretion.

[69] Art 101 ICCSt:

> '1. A person surrendered to the Court under this Statute shall not be proceeded against, punished or detained for any conduct committed prior to surrender, other than the conduct or course of conduct which forms the basis of the crimes for which that person has been surrendered.
> 2. The Court may request a waiver of the requirements of paragraph 1 from the State which surrendered the person to the Court'.

[70] *Prosecutor v Bemba et al*, Decision on Narcisse Arido's Request for an Order Rejecting the Prosecution's Document Containing the Charges and for an Order to the Prosecution to File an Amended and Corrected Document Containing the Charges, ICC-01/05-01/13-567, 15 July 2014; *Prosecutor v Mbarushimana*, Decision on the Confirmation of Charges (n 55) paras 90–92.

[71] *Prosecutor v Mbarushimana*, Decision on the Confirmation of Charges (n 55) para 91.

[72] *Prosecutor v Bemba et al* (n 70) 5.

[73] ibid.

[74] The rule of speciality is, for example, contained in article 14 of the 1957 European Convention on Extradition (with 50 Member States the biggest multilateral extradition regime).

[75] Art 101(2) ICCSt.

[76] Arts 101(2) and 86 ICCSt.

IV. GUIDING FACTORS IN THE CASE SELECTION PROCESS

Case selection and prioritisation is one of the essential areas where the Prosecutor exercises discretion. The selection of cases ultimately determines which crimes – often a matter of choosing between different incidents in situations of mass atrocity – and which defendants reach the trial stage of the ICC. This is a pivotal point at which the aims of international criminal law matter. Realising those aims strongly depends on the choice of cases. For the preliminary examination stage, I have demonstrated how prevention and deterrence as well as victims' interests ought to guide the exercise of discretion. The same principles apply throughout the process of case selection but, obviously, impacting differently on the question of how the Prosecutor should exercise discretion. But how can prevention and deterrence best be achieved? And how should other general aims of international criminal law feed into the decision-making process? Lastly, what precisely are these aims?

Retribution ('the most serious crimes ... must not go unpunished ... Determined to put an end to impunity') and the resolve 'to contribute to the prevention of such crimes'[77] are the justifications for the creation of the ICC and continue as justifications for its work. The reference in the Preamble to the need for punishment strongly connects to retributive theories that often refer back to Kant's philosophy.[78] A reading of Kant suggests that 'all and only those both morally and legally guilty should be punished'.[79] But this provides few answers to the questions 'who should be punished' and 'why'. It has implications for the question 'who should be put on trial' and 'why' in a highly selective environment in which not all, but only very few, will face trial before the ICC and might receive punishment subsequently. Yet, if retribution and deterrence are the key objectives of the ICC's work in general, they also represent the justifications for its trials.

Hence, retribution and crime prevention directly feed into case selection and the Prosecutor needs to work towards those objectives for a legitimate exercise of her power. Making sense of retribution and deterrence understood as crime prevention in a highly selective environment is therefore a key task.

In this vein, ICC sentencing decisions[80] are informative as they provide an insight into how the ICC judges interpret these objectives:

> With regard to retribution, the Chamber clarifies that it is not to be understood as fulfilling a desire for revenge, but as an expression of the international community's

[77] Preamble ICCSt.

[78] See A Duff and D Garland, 'Thinking about Punishment' in A Duff and D Garland (eds), *A Reader on Punishment* (Oxford, Oxford University Press, 1994) 2–3.

[79] T Hill, 'Kant on Punishment: A Coherent Mix of Deterrence and Retribution?' (1997) 5 *Jahrbuch fuer Ethik und Recht* 291, 298.

[80] *Prosecutor v Al Mahdi*, Judgment and Sentence, ICC-01/12-01/15-171, 27 September 2016, para 66; *The Prosecutor v Katanga*, Decision on Sentence pursuant to article 76 of the Statute, ICC-0 1/04-01/07-3484-tENG-Corr, 23 May 2014, paras 37–38; *Prosecutor v Bemba Gombo*, Decision on Sentence pursuant to Article 76 of the Statute, ICC-01/05-01/08-3399, 21 June 2016, para 10.

> condemnation of the crimes, which, by way of imposition of a proportionate sentence, also acknowledges the harm to the victims and promotes the restoration of peace and reconciliation. In respect of deterrence, the Chamber considers that a sentence should be adequate to discourage a convicted person from recidivism (specific deterrence), as well as to ensure that those who would consider committing similar crimes will be dissuaded from doing so (general deterrence).[81]

This interpretation connects retributive with restorative elements through the need to promote peace and reconciliation. The initial drafting history does not necessarily point to the ICC as a tool to promote peace. Nonetheless, more recent Assembly of States Parties (ASP) statements[82] do confirm that states want the ICC to work as a tool of peace and security and has an important role in delivering 'reparative' justice.[83] The concept of reparative justice places great emphasis on the reparations process, on the attempts to repair the harm done, as an essential step in delivering justice. The concept of restorative justice differs slightly in that it places greater emphasis on reconciliation processes. However, both concepts strongly overlap in that the attempt to repair the harm done is one piece in the jigsaw of achieving the restoration of relationships within a society torn apart by conflict. For the ICC to contribute to peace and security will only be possible if the restorative and reparative elements of justice play a key role.

Breaking this down for the case selection processes means that the OTP needs to ask itself which cases best express condemnation, how best to acknowledge victims, promote peace and reconciliation, and attempt to dissuade actors from similar criminal conduct. In short, how can the OTP make the most of the communicative and expressive functions of the trial?

A. Maximising the Impact of Selected Cases

Criminal trials in general have communicative functions.[84] One of those functions most prominent in domestic criminal law is the function to communicate to the offender that the criminal behaviour is unwanted and not to be repeated (special deterrence) as well as the material wrong of the act prosecuted. The ICC's communicative reach, however, is much broader. Case selection has further dimensions in that it emphasises the normative importance of specific values and rules but also affirms the state's failure through its unwillingness or inability to prosecute domestically. Beyond a specific state, it signals to states more generally that the Court is ready to step in where other jurisdictions fail to prosecute

[81] *Al Mahdi* Judgment (n 80) para 67.

[82] See ICC-ASP/17/Res.5 'Strengthening the International Criminal Court and the Assembly of States Parties', 12 December 2018, Preamble

[83] ibid, para 107.

[84] A Duff, L Farmer, S Marshall and V Tadros, *The Trial on Trial, Volume 3: Towards a Normative Theory of the Criminal Trial* (Oxford, Hart Publishing, 2007) 93.

international crimes. The Court addresses victim audiences, publicly acknowledging their suffering and affirming their status as victims. Where states failed to take action and no public forum exists to acknowledge wrongs done, the ICC is the alternative public forum to do so. It signals to non-state actors that specific conduct is wrong[85] and that harm has been done to particular groups of people. It also signals to the most abstract of all audiences, the international community, that specific values are protected and highlights their importance. In short, case selection expresses the point that specific sufferings matter. The dynamic of communicative effects can vary considerably, depending on the context-specific situation. As such, they need to be unpacked further to fully understand how the Prosecutor ought to use the communicative dimensions and expressive effects of case selection for the aims of deterrence and prevention.

i. Unpacking Deterrence Dynamics

Deterrence is a complex phenomenon that is tied in with the communicative functions of the trial. Deterrence includes elements of 'prosecutorial deterrence' and 'social deterrence' which both reinforce each other through the presence of legal authority and the threat of prosecution (prosecutorial deterrence), combined with extra-legal costs or effects for non-compliance with the legal authority (social deterrence).[86] If deterrence strategies are successful, they are difficult to measure because the non-commission of crimes and the reasons for peaceful conflict resolution are often influenced by a number of factors. Regarding prosecutorial deterrence, or deterrence through punishment, theorists have raised doubts about whether the ICC can effectively create a prosecutorial deterrence effect through the threat of punishment.[87] Prosecutions at the ICC are rare and slow and, therefore, far from certain.[88] Additionally, the most responsible perpetrators of mass atrocities are perhaps the least likely to 'contemplate the wrongfulness of their doings nor take seriously the threat of subsequent trials' in times when norms seem perverted.[89] Communication with the individual through ICC prosecution as a means of serving the aim of special deterrence seems ineffectual.

[85] See B Wringe, *An Expressive Theory of Punishment* (Basingstoke, Palgrave Macmillan, 2016) 130 for the signalling function that the arbitrary use of force would be prevented.

[86] H Jo and B Simmons, 'Can the International Criminal Court Deter Atrocity?' (2016) 70 *International Organization* 443, 444.

[87] M Mennecke, 'Punishing Genocidaires: A Deterrent Effect or Not?' (2007) 8 *Human Rights Review* 319; VE Collins and DL Rothe, 'The International Criminal Court: A Pipe Dream to End Impunity?' in D Rothe, J Meernik and T Ingadóttir (eds), *The Realities of International Criminal Justice* (Leiden, Brill Nijhoff, 2013); C Mullins and D Rothe, 'The Ability of the International Criminal Court to Deter Violations of International Criminal Law: A Theoretical Assessment' (2010) 10 *International Criminal Law Review* 771; K Cronin-Furman, 'Managing Expectations: International Criminal Trials and the Prospects for Deterrence of Mass Atrocity' (2013) 7 *International Journal of Transitional Justice* 434.

[88] Cronin-Furman (n 87) 454.

[89] Mennecke (n 87) 326.

Nevertheless, some empirical research does indicate that the ICC can indeed achieve deterrence effect.[90] The existence of the ICC increases the pressure for domestic prosecutions through the principle of complementarity.[91] Linking it back to the communication with states, the ICC should convey the message that if the state does not prosecute, it will. Internationally, pressure from the international community can follow, or be coupled with, the pressure of ICC investigations or prosecutions that highlight any norm violations by this state actor.[92] Case selection must therefore be utilised to trigger state activities. How best to achieve this will require further experiences and analysis of specific country dynamics.

General deterrence requires the Court to dissuade others from violating international norms. More generally, this entails an element of branding specific behaviour as unacceptable and of increasing specific norm awareness. This dynamic needs to be viewed together with the domestic responsibilities of State Parties to the Rome Statute. State Party territory should be no option for exile or as a safe haven for perpetrators of international crimes any longer, because these states have a duty to prosecute international crimes. Such domestic activity is very slowly emerging. One such example is the prosecution of crimes committed in the Democratic Republic of the Congo before a German court.[93] Although charges of sexual violence (rape as a crime against humanity) were dropped in the course of the trial, the responsible Federal Prosecutor expressed awareness of the importance of such charges for the historical record.[94] The ICC has an important part to play in further impressing and demonstrating the need to fully deliver justice for victims of sexual and gender-based crimes. Scholarly voices have identified a particularly important role of international criminal law for the expression of specific normative values in this context.[95] The German proceedings are an important starting point in this process without delivering in full. A pivotal point for case selection decisions is to increase norm awareness and reinforce the importance and the value of specific norms in order to build pressure for compliance.

Regarding deterrence dynamics aimed at specific actors engaged in conflicts, the ICC has to date not developed the ability to deliver successful prosecutions of state actors. Structurally, this is not surprising as state actors holding power can curtail an ICC investigation through non-cooperation and withdrawal as

[90] Jo and Simmons (n 86) 460 ff.

[91] ibid, 448 f.

[92] ibid, 463–65.

[93] OLG Stuttgart, 5-3 StE 6/10, Judgment of 28 September 2015.

[94] See S Studzinsky, 'Sexualstraftaten im ersten Völkerstrafrechtsprozess – ein Kommentar' (2017) 2 *Streit – Feministische Rechtszeitschrift* 51.

[95] See G Bass, *Stay the Hand of Vengeance: The Politics of War Crimes Tribunals* (Princeton, NJ, Princeton University Press, 2002); R Sloane, 'The Expressive Capacity of International Punishment: The Limits of the National Law Analogy and the Potential of International Criminal Law (2007) 43 *Stanford Journal of International Law* 39; deGuzman (n 2).

political instruments.[96] However, selecting cases, as such, against state actors might nevertheless signal to others that even state power does not go unchecked. An analysis of developments in Kenya, where leading politicians and office bearers were prosecuted, suggests that the ICC investigations did have the effect of deterring further election-related violence.[97] For rebel groups, it seems more difficult to achieve similar social pressure dynamics, because these groups largely operate outside the social realm of civil society or the international community. Having said that, rebel actors who strive for succession seem more responsive to social pressure.[98] Additionally, rebel actors do also seem to respond to prosecutorial action and 'are likely to alter their tactics in light of new evidence that the prosecutor's office intends to hold actors accountable for their atrocities'.[99] To achieve a maximum impact in terms of successful deterrence therefore requires addressing both components of deterrence: social deterrence through norm awareness and increased pressure, as well as prosecutorial action. What seems to matter most is not so much the attempt to communicate with the individual through individual prosecution, but the communication with broader publics about norms, their values and the need to enforce those values through cases selected for prosecution.

ii. *Maximising Impact*

Themed cases can be one vehicle to brand a specific behaviour as socially unacceptable.[100] Such cases highlight one specific incident or crime as the theme of the case. The ICTY was the first international court featuring themed cases. In the so-called *Foča* cases three middle-ranking Bosnian police officers were prosecuted and convicted for their individual responsibility for the rape and sexual enslavement of Muslim women in the municipality of Foča.[101] This case drew more media attention than most other cases at the ICTY.[102] Such cases may bear the danger of show trials,[103] but as long as cases are built on solid evidence and meet the admissibility criteria, choosing such a case is a good example of how a prosecution can create social pressure and public awareness. It can be

[96] Withdrawal does not hinder the exercise of ICC jurisdiction for the time while a state was still party to the Rome Statute but for future conduct. See the examples of Burundi and The Philippines.

[97] Y Dutton and T Alleblas, 'Unpacking the Deterrent Effect of the International Criminal Court: Lessons From Kenya' (2017) 91 *St John's Law Review* 105, 157–60.

[98] Jo and Simmons (n 86) 468.

[99] ibid.

[100] M deGuzman, 'An Expressive Rationale for the Thematic Prosecution of Sex Crimes' in M Bergsmo (ed), *Thematic Prosecution of International Sex Crimes* (FICHL Publication Series No 13) (Brussels, Torkel Opsahl Academic EPublisher, 2012).

[101] *Prosecutor v Kunarac, Kovac and Vuković*, Trial Judgment, IT-96-23-T and IT-96-23/1-T, 22 February 2001.

[102] M Schrag, 'Lessons Learned from the ICTY Experience' (2004) 2 *Journal of International Criminal Justice* 427.

[103] ibid, 431.

one pathway towards optimising sparse resources by focusing on a particular thematic area in suitable cases. At the ICC, the *Lubanga* case could serve as an example of a thematic case around the enlistment of child soldiers,[104] although it is unclear from the published prosecutorial strategies whether this was the intention. Retrospectively, Bensouda explicitly sought to connect the criticised discretionary choice that omitted charges related to sexual- and gender-based violence in the *Lubanga* case with values and principles underlying the Rome Statute. Bensouda explained how the OTP attempted to uphold children's rights with their charges against Lubanga connecting the OTP's exercise of discretion with a positive principle: the protection of children's rights.[105]

The *Lubanga* case is a good example that shows that a fine calibration between different aims and principles is required, because a limited, thematic charging strategy can undermine the aim of representing all areas of victimisation.[106] Choosing a limited charging approach and – even if it was meant to serve as a themed case – not to communicate this function appropriately was counterproductive. Beyond this particular case, however, the vehicle of a themed case can be reconciled with the aim of representing all areas of victimisation if other cases in the situation under investigation cover other areas. As long as those cases together address different types of crime and different groups of victims and perpetrators, a themed case can be a useful tool to maximise the ICC's impact.

Themed cases are just one example of how the Prosecutor can be guided by the aim of maximising the impact of every selected case. The 2016 Policy Paper acknowledges the need to strengthen the expressive force of cases selected for prosecution through its commitment to 'pay particular attention to crimes that have been traditionally under-prosecuted, such as crimes against or affecting children as well as rape and other sexual and gender-based crimes'.[107] According to the OTP, a similar effort will be made with regard to 'attacks against cultural, religious, historical and other protected objects as well as against humanitarian and peacekeeping personnel', aiming 'to highlight the gravity of these crimes'.[108]

[104] deGuzman (n 2) 314 suggests that the controversial *Lubanga* charging decision 'may have been animated by expressive goals'.

[105] F Bensouda, 'Children and International Criminal Justice' (2015) 43 *Georgia Journal of International and Comparative Law* 591, 594: 'This is a clear demonstration of the importance we attached to crimes against children from the inception of our work and we continue to do so. The guilty verdict against Mr Lubanga in 2012 was a landmark decision for the Court and I believe for the whole Rome Statute system'.

[106] See M Drumbl, 'The Effects of the Lubanga Case on Understanding and Preventing Child Soldiering' (2012) 15 *Yearbook of International Humanitarian Law* 87, 89 for the 'important didactic' function of international trials but critiquing that the *Lubanga* proceedings reinforced a stylised 'portrayal of the child soldier as a faultless victim' which bears the danger of hampering a full understanding of child-soldiering and development of a 'robust culture of juvenile rights'.

[107] Policy Paper Case Selection and Prioritisation (n 1) para 46.

[108] ibid.

The OTP notes that developing jurisprudence in such under-represented areas will contribute positively to the social deterrence potential of the ICC.[109] This is a clear shift towards more expressively condemning specific crimes.

The other component of maximising impact is the choice of potential defendants. Obviously, this choice will in the first instance be evidence led because of the presumption of innocence and the requirement of reasonable grounds to believe that the person has committed a crime in the jurisdiction of the Court.[110] But wherever the Prosecutor has selective choices to make, these should be made on the basis of maximising impact on the deterrence and expressive force of what is wrong.

One such choice can, for example, be to activate command responsibility through increased prosecution activities to reinforce the responsibility to prevent the commission of crimes and punish subordinates accordingly.[111] The policy paper states:

> In order to encourage military commanders and non-military superiors to deal effectively with the commission of [sexual and gender-based] crimes by their forces or subordinates, the Office will, as appropriate, increasingly explore the potential of bringing charges on the basis of article 28 as well as article 25. Under article 28, military commanders or non-military superiors may be held accountable ... also where they knew, or should have known about, or consciously disregarded information regarding, the commission of such crimes, and failed to take all necessary and reasonable measures within their power to prevent or repress such commission, or to submit the matter to the competent authorities for investigation and prosecution.[112]

This policy attempts to achieve deterrence effects by stimulating compliance at the level of military commanders or other superiors with their responsibility to punish and prevent the commission of crimes by their subordinates. When war crimes are not committed for tactical reasons, commanders who fail to prevent and punish violations do not have strong incentives to allow mass atrocity and 'therefore are more likely to be deterred by prosecutions of similarly situated individuals'.[113] The prosecutorial policy seems a step in the right direction. Ultimately, the challenge of maximising the impact of cases chosen for prosecution will require a careful case-by-case assessment of what message a specific case conveys will be sent to different audiences.

[109] The Policy on Children (n 15) paras 84–88 sets out that the aim of its policies is to achieve a greater deterrence effect in a two-fold way: (i) by strengthening accountability through prosecution; and (ii) through developing jurisprudence in this area.

[110] Arts 58 and 66 ICCSt.

[111] Art 28 ICCSt.

[112] Policy Paper on Sexual and Gender-Based Crimes (n 18) para 78.

[113] Cronin-Furman (n 87) 453.

B. Representing All Main Areas of Victimisation

Another key guiding principle for case selection is the need to represent all main areas of victimisation within a case and across a situation. The legal foundation for this principle is provided in article 54(1)(a) of the Statute obliging the Prosecutor 'to establish the truth' and 'to investigate incriminating and exonerating circumstances equally'. Any investigation therefore has to be conducted impartially and be aimed at the establishment of the 'objective' truth.[114] Literally, this provision only seems to extend to the investigation stage, because the provision refers solely to the investigation. Having said that, it only makes sense to provide for a duty to establish the truth for the investigation phase, when the result translates into a prosecution based on the evidence collected. Article 54(1)(b) of the Statute obliges the Prosecutor to 'take appropriate measures to ensure the effective investigation and prosecution … and in doing so, respect the interests … of victims'. Victims' interests can be multifaceted and are therefore not easy to determine. Nonetheless, one of the victims' rights that overlaps with the overwhelming account of what victims of atrocities formulate, is the right to truth,[115] and the interest in understanding what happened.

To gain a better understanding about the dimension of the right to truth, insights can be gained from the normative dimensions of a trial.[116] Taking a purely instrumentalist view, establishing the truth would only matter in as far as it could establish the guilt of the accused. This, however, would not explain why trials should be public and why they matter. If the underlying aim is to resolve a dispute – a dispute about the defendant's guilt – a trial is required to establish the truth because it matters what happened.[117] This matters to more than only the defendant and the prosecutor, as the key actors in the dispute about legal responsibility, it is important to a broader public.[118] In international criminal law in particular the underlying dispute is often a situation of mass violence and atrocity. The function of a trial and of the need to establish the truth can only be explained if the trial attempts to capture what has happened and establishes the responsibility of the defendant. Because the selection of cases and the choice of charges determines the extent to which the subsequent trial will be able to fulfil the function of holding the accused to account, the Prosecutor needs to attempt to adequately ensure accountability by aiming to represent all areas of

[114] G Turone, 'Powers and Duties of the Prosecutor' in A Cassesse, P Gaeta and J Jones (eds), *The Rome Statute of the International Criminal Court: A Commentary, Vol II* (Oxford, Oxford University Press, 2002).

[115] *Prosecutor v Katanga and Chui*, Decision on the Set of Procedural Rights Attached to Procedural Status of Victim at the Pre-Trial Stage of the Case, PTC I, ICC-01/04-01/07-474, 13 May 2008, paras 31–34 with further references to decisions of international human rights bodies.

[116] See Duff et al, *The Trial on Trial, Volume 3* (n 84) 57. This work is based on considerations mainly of the English system but speaks directly to the issues discussed here.

[117] ibid, 69.

[118] ibid.

victimisation. This way, the duty to establish the truth, victims' interests, and their right to truth can best be given effect.[119]

In the absence of any domestic efforts, prosecution before the ICC may be the only avenue for victims to have their suffering acknowledged. Yet, the nature of the criminal process, designed to assign individual responsibility, individualises collective injury.[120] The case selection process is inherently a process of exclusion for victims; it is a process of sub-division into collectives of injury, and for those whose suffering is not included in the selected incidents, a separation from the collective whose injury is acknowledged. The highly selective nature of ICC proceedings makes this an even more contentious point, because other jurisdictions such as domestic or hybrid courts, with a greater focus on one specific conflict, might have the chance to successively work towards prosecution of a multitude of offenders acknowledging the wrong done to victims. Selective processes and dynamics of exclusion are unavoidable but can be alleviated by gearing case selection towards representing the dimensions of victimhood through the cases chosen for prosecution.

i. Balancing the Scope of a Trial

The current prosecutorial policy contains a commitment to represent the main types of victimisation.[121] Coupled with the development of the policy on sexual- and gender-based crimes, it is a very good example of how the OTP can contribute to turning the ICC into a responsive institution, understood in the sense that social pressures are perceived as 'sources of knowledge and opportunities for self-correction'.[122] Policy commitments, of course, can change over time. It is therefore pivotal to understand that this is a task embedded in the Rome Statute and the exercise of discretion needs to be geared towards fulfilling it.

Yet, we need to acknowledge the limitations of what cases can deliver. A (single) trial will most likely not be able to provide an account of what happened

[119] C Aptel, 'Prosecutorial Discretion at the ICC and Victims' Right to Remedy' (2012) 10 *Journal of International Criminal Justice* 1357, 1374 calls in this context for mindfulness of the Prosecutor towards victim constituencies and their rights to justice.

[120] R Kesselring, *Bodies of Truth* (Stanford, CA, Stanford University Press, 2017) 6 with reference to W Brown. Kesselring demonstrates in her work on law, memory and emancipation in South Africa though that victims' participation in legal processes entails a chance to emancipate themselves from a discourse rather than subjection to it.

[121] Policy Paper Case Selection and Prioritisation (n 1) para 45: 'The Office will aim to represent as much as possible the true extent of the criminality which has occurred within a given situation, in an effort to ensure, jointly with the relevant national jurisdictions, that the most serious crimes committed in each situation do not go unpunished. Consistent with regulation 34(2) of the Regulations of the Office of the Prosecutor, the charges chosen will constitute, whenever possible, a representative sample of the main types of victimisation and of the communities which have been affected by the crimes in that situation'.

[122] P Nonet and P Selznick, *Law & Society in Transition: Towards Responsive Law* (New Brunswick, Transaction Publishers 2001) 77.

in a larger conflict. The practice to date provides some important lessons in that regard. Judge Henderson's opinion in the collapsed case against Laurent Gbagbo and Charles Blé Goudé provides important insights:

> [T]his case has suffered from being exceedingly complex. The Prosecutor, in a Herculean effort, has attempted to bring within the scope of this single litigation several years of Ivorian history. This has proved to be overly ambitious … although the available evidence is voluminous, a lot of essential information is still missing. Whether this is due to the information being unavailable to the Prosecutor or to the fact that the Prosecutor did not look (hard enough) for it is not for me to say. However, in framing the factual scope of the charges so broadly, the Prosecutor may have bitten off more than she could possibly chew with the resources that were available to her.[123]

The TC halted the trial against both accused and found that they had 'no case to answer' because of insufficient evidence, or evidence of insufficient quality, to support the charges against the accused. Judge Henderson offers the following lessons to be learned:

> [T]he Prosecutor cannot be expected to bring cases of this level of complexity and scope within a reasonable time frame with the limited resources that are currently available to her. While it is important for the Prosecutor to be ambitious in the way that she approaches her mandate, she ought also to be realistic about what is feasible.[124]

The example shows the limitation of trial proceedings and of establishing the truth. A case cannot be a vehicle to tell the full story, or, perhaps to put it more accurately, the multitude of different stories, of mass violence and be representative of it. In the first instance, case selection must solidly be grounded on the availability of evidence and feasibility. It is within those constraints that the Prosecutor needs to capture the variety of different forms of victimisation. The exercise of discretion must be guided by a fine balancing act that aims to represent all areas of victimisation but does not attempt to overload cases.

As part of the lessons learnt from the case against Gbagbo and Blé Goudé, Guilfoyle argues for fewer and deeper investigations, a point I agree with.[125] Yet, Guilfoyle further contends that Lubanga-style prosecutions, narrow cases, 'run against a rebel leader on relatively few (or at least closely related) charges'[126] would be a way forward. Themed cases can be one vehicle for the Court to highlight a specific wrong.[127] Such choices, however, require that further

[123] *Prosecutor v Gbagbo and Blé Goudé*, Reasons of Judge Geoffrey Henderson, ICC-02/11-01/15-1263-AnxB-Red, 16 July 2019, para 5.

[124] ibid, para 10.

[125] D Guilfoyle, 'A Tale of Two Cases: Lessons for the Prosecutor of the International Criminal Court (Part III)', 30 August 2019, available at: ejiltalk.org.

[126] ibid.

[127] See ICC/OTP, Strategic Plan 2019–2021, 17 July 2019, para 24 for the OTP's new future strategy to pursue narrower cases where appropriate.

prosecutions within the same situation address other wrongs and aim overall at providing a representative picture of victimisation. Guilfoyle's suggestion entails an instrumentalist approach to trial proceedings, solely geared at pinning some responsibility on some perpetrators. This runs counter to the principle of representing all areas of victimisation and will not strengthen the ICC's legitimacy in the long run.

The *Lubanga* case does offer some lessons though. As the first case before the ICC, it received strong criticism[128] because the charges did not appropriately represent the victims' plight with no charges brought relating to sexual violence despite a considerable amount of evidence suggesting that such crimes had been committed.[129] Narrowly designed cases require communication with victims groups about the reasons. For the OTP, it will be pivotal to work with victims participating in the proceedings towards developing a case within the practical constraints of prosecution that aims at responding to their expectations. Also, earlier in the process, the OTP needs to carefully plan its investigations to lay the foundations for the prosecution of all areas of victimisation.[130]

ii. Representing Diverse Victim Communities

Regarding the failure to represent different victim communities, the situation in Uganda provides a good example. The Ugandan security forces had been reported as having perpetrated numerous atrocities; the failure to bring any cases against these forces was widely seen as neglecting one side of the conflict.[131] Because of the seriousness of crimes committed not just by the LRA but also by government forces, and the lack of appropriate remedies for victims of those crimes within Uganda, Moffet suggested that the ICC's reputation for impartiality would suffer.[132]

[128] C Ferstman, 'Limited Charges and Limited Judgments by the International Criminal Court – Who Bears the Greatest Responsibility?' (2012) 16 *International Journal of Human Rights* 796, 799 and 808 accuses the Prosecutor of having been indifferent to any charges related to sexual violence.

[129] *Situation in the Democratic Republic of the Congo*, Request Submitted pursuant to Rule 103(1) of the Rules of Procedure and Evidence for leave to participate as amicus curiae in the article 61 confirmation proceedings with confidential annex 2, ICC-01/04-313, 13 November 2006, para 13 ff, in which the Women's Initiative for Gender Justice suggests that prosecutorial discretion is not unfettered in the area of case selection, in particular when the Prosecutor decided not to bring specific charges and that was contrary to victims' interests.

[130] Sácouto and Cleary, 'Importance of Effective Investigation of Sexual Violence and Gender-Based Crimes at the International Criminal Court' (n 35) 345.

[131] See L Moffet, *Justice for Victims before the International Criminal Court* (Abingdon, Routledge, 2014) 197 ff; M Kersten, *Justice in Conflict: The Effects of the International Criminal Court's Interventions on Ending War and Building Peace* (Oxford, Oxford University Press, 2016) 5, 15 (with further references) who argues that the ICC case selection impacted on the peace talks in Uganda because of the 'good' and 'evil' narrative that was being produced through the sole prosecution of LRA commanders despite mass atrocities having being committed on both sides.

[132] Moffet (n 131) 232.

Yet, the current prosecutorial policy suggests that impartiality requires that the membership of a perpetrator to a group should be irrelevant for the case selection process.[133] Yet, in highly politicised contexts and societies divided by conflict, no neutral ground exists. While it is agreed that there should be no 'equivalence of blame'[134] where the conduct of conflicting groups is remarkably different, not to bring any cases against one side of the conflict, despite this group being heavily implicated in crimes as well, sends a counterproductive message. It implies a message that accepts that some behaviour, namely that crimes committed by state actors, go unpunished if those state actors cooperate with the ICC. It further bears the danger of polarising discourse and creating obstacles to reconciliation by not publicly acknowledging the wrong done to 'the other side' and denouncing justice as one-sided and biased. The OTP seeks to assert its neutrality, but heavily politicised and loaded conflicts do not provide for any such neutrality. Expressive force therefore needs to be used equally to send messages to all sides in a conflict. Only a linkage between both guiding aims, being representative of all areas of victimisation, and being expressive through case selection, can together contribute to an enhanced process of case selection. Because of its highly symbolic power, a principled and responsive case selection process is crucial for the legitimacy of the Court.

Speaking to different audiences and avoiding a hierarchy of wrongs militates in favour of case selection that aims at representing the different dimensions of suffering in a conflict. Solely prosecuting one side of the conflict can create an obstacle to peace and reconciliation and ultimately undermine a key objective of the ICC, to prevent further crimes.

A holistic view throughout the series of individual selection decisions is important to adjust decisions to practical concerns and preserve the focus on the overarching aims. Investigative efforts, the selection of specific incidents for prosecution, the selection of charges within an identified case, as well as the selection of cases based on different perpetrators, all contain procedural decisions that together have to cover the main areas of victimisation. Having said that, it should be acknowledged that the OTP might choose between different possible strategies: (1) a comprehensive approach to charging that includes bringing charges reflecting all areas of victimisation in one case; or (2) a limited approach to charging that highlights one specific area of victimisation in a themed case. In the case of the latter, the Office should commit to ensuring that other cases within the same situation will be representative of other areas of victimisation. Equally, if the Prosecutor intends to use a bottom-up strategy in which she prosecutes a number of mid-level perpetrators, with the aim of bringing a case against those most responsible, the OTP might want

[133] Policy Paper Case Selection and Prioritisation (n 1) para 20.

[134] The OTP suggests that 'impartiality does not mean "equivalence of blame" [between different sides of the conflict] within a situation'. See Policy Paper Case Selection and Prioritisation (n 1) para 20.

to limit these cases to avoid clogging up the system. This is one of the lessons learned from the ICTY, where Prosecutors maintained a multilevel approach up until 2007, although it was criticised that the 'small fish' were indeed clogging up the system.[135] The ICTY experience provides an important argument to limit the remit of some cases instead of intending to use every individual case to be fully representative. The importance is that the Prosecutor aims at decisions that – across the board of potential cases – address the task of being representative. Ensuring a process of case selection that facilitates this representative function would show that the OTP as an institution is responsive to the critique voiced by a variety of different actors over the years.

C. The Role of Gravity in the Case Selection Process

In the current practice of the OTP, gravity is the predominant case selection criterion. The gravity of cases is assessed in relation to the degree of responsibility of alleged perpetrators and the potential charges.[136] Gravity features in the Rome Statute as an admissibility criterion in article 17(1)(d) and in the Preamble with its reference to the 'most serious crimes'. The lack of a definition provides scope for interpretive discretion because it cannot be determined to exacting legal requirements.[137] The exercise of discretion linked to the use of the gravity notion operates at different dimensions. On the one hand it contains an element of interpretative discretion regarding which criteria to use and how to weigh them in a specific context. Additionally, it serves procedural purposes as a criterion that should aid the case selection process:

> Gravity of crime(s) as a case selection criterion is assessed similarly to gravity as a factor for admissibility under article 17(1)(d). However, given that many cases might potentially be admissible under article 17, the Office may apply a stricter test when assessing gravity for the purposes of case selection than that which is legally required for the admissibility test under article 17.[138]

The use of the gravity notion in the practice of the ICC is strongly contested and has been subject to extensive scholarly debate as to how to develop a coherent understanding of the admissibility criterion and its additional function as a selection mechanism.[139] The admissibility criterion in article 17(1)(d) of the

[135] F de Vleming, 'Selection of Defendants' in L Reydams, J Wouters and C Ryngaert (eds), *International Prosecutors* (Oxford, Oxford University Press, 2012) 559.

[136] Policy Paper Case Selection and Prioritisation (n 1) para 6.

[137] See A Pues, 'Discretion and the Gravity of Situations at the International Criminal Court' (2017) 17 *International Criminal Law Review* 960, 964.

[138] Policy Paper Case Selection and Prioritisation (n 1) para 36.

[139] See, eg, S Sácouto and K Cleary, 'The Gravity Threshold of the International Criminal Court' (2008) 5 *American Journal of International Law* 807; M deGuzman, 'The International Criminal Court's Gravity Jurisprudence at Ten' (2013) 12 *Washington University's Global Studies Law Review* 475; I Stegmiller, *The Pre-Investigation Stage of the ICC* (Berlin, Duncker & Humblot, 2011).

Statute requires a consistent application across the board of different situations and cases given that all cases require equal assessment. Only a consistently applied admissibility threshold can fully give effect to the principle of equality before the law, which again is interconnected with the principle of impartiality and hence essential for the prosecutorial decision-making process. Hence admissibility considerations need to be made regardless of the caseload of the Court and solely on the merits of the individual case. Managerial considerations, such as a prioritisation of cases, therefore, have no place in the assessment of gravity as an admissibility criterion.

With this in mind, the seemingly solid legal foundation for the central place of gravity in case selection becomes rather shaky. Only the Preamble provides another legal anchor for gravity as a selection and prioritisation criterion. Yet, the affirmation in the Preamble of the Rome Statute that 'the most serious crimes of concern to the international community as a whole must not go unpunished' formed the justification for the creation of the Court as such. Can it also give guidance as to what is most serious among all those crimes in the jurisdiction of the Court? After all, can the commission of genocide be compared with the destruction of cultural heritage? And whose contribution to the commission of crimes is graver, that of the person shooting, that of the person giving the orders, or those who have produced the arms and that benefit materially from crimes? We should recall at this point that the AC has clarified that no lower-level perpetrators should be excluded from potential prosecution at the ICC.[140] Hence, gravity has been labelled as a 'fig leaf for what is really a form of unaccountable discretion'.[141] The quantitative element in the gravity notion – the number of victims of a specific crime – is combined with some qualitative components, but Mégret argues pointedly that this 'will only convince certain Western audiences horrified by the number of casualties in peripheral African armed conflicts. Worse, it risks being part of a very concrete politics that minimizes the collateral casualties of, for example, technologically sophisticated Western wars'.[142] Discretionary and highly selective decisions need to be made at the ICC but gravity as a selection criterion provides little guidance for the exercise of discretion in such a way that it could proffer the legitimacy of the Court.

V. MECHANISMS OF ACCOUNTABILITY

The Prosecutor has a wide scope for discretion in the case selection process, and, as has been shown throughout this chapter, has made extensive use of this discretion. The OTP practice falls short of the aim of representing all areas of victimisation. Whether in Uganda or in Côte d'Ivoire, the Prosecutor has,

[140] *DRC* Judgment (n 9) paras 73–79.

[141] F Mégret, 'Beyond "Gravity": For a Politics of International Criminal Prosecutions' (2013) 107 *Proceedings of the Annual Meeting (American Society of International Law)* 428, 430.

[142] ibid.

after years of investigations, only brought cases against one side of the conflict despite evidence of atrocities by the other side. These shortcomings show the necessity of mechanisms to hold the Prosecutor to account for case selection decisions. The PTC has a limited role through the necessity to issue warrants of arrest or summons to appear as well as the confirmation of charges proceedings. However, for victims of those cases that are not selected for prosecution, there are no direct avenues to hold the Prosecutor formally to account. For these victim communities, it is therefore crucial that the system provides pragmatic possibilities of accountability for the procedural choices that the Prosecutor makes.

Within the frameworks of articles 53(2) and (3), 58(1) and 61 of the Statute, the PTC is confined to reviewing only some specific choices made by the OTP. Regarding the issuance of a warrant of arrest or a summons to appear, based on article 58 of the Statute, the PTC reviews the material presented by the Prosecutor applying the test of whether a reasonable observer would be satisfied that the person may have committed the offence without the need for there to be certainty about this.[143] The confirmation of charges proceedings in article 61 of the Statute tests the strength of evidence in a case, designed to protect the accused 'against wrongful and wholly unfounded charges'.[144] However, the decision on what to charge, as well as on how the charges shall be formulated, is fully within the responsibility of the Prosecutor and not the PTC's responsibility.[145] Equally, the manner in which investigations are carried out – a crucial preliminary phase before any case can reach the prosecution stage – is entirely within the Prosecutor's authority and not subject to judicial review by the PTC.[146] None of these PTC proceedings leaves room to challenge shortcomings in how the exercise of prosecutorial discretion might address the identified principles that should guide the Prosecutor.

A. Article 53(2) of the Statute: A Redundant Mechanism?

Article 53(2) and (3) of the Statute is the only mechanism allowing the PTC to review decisions not to prosecute a case.[147] No judicial decisions on its scope

[143] This test was formulated in *Prosecutor v Al Bashir*, Judgment on the Appeal of the Prosecutor against the "Decision on the Prosecution's Application for a Warrant of Arrest against Omar Hassan Ahmand Al Bashir"', ICC-02/05-01/09-73, 3 February 2010, para 31, with reference to European Court of Human Rights, *Fox, Campbell and Hartley v United Kingdom*, Judgment, Application Nos 12244/86, 12245/86, 12383/86, 30 August 1990, para 32.

[144] *Prosecutor v Katanga and Chui*, Decision on the Confirmation of Charges (n 29) para 63.

[145] See Pre-Trial Practice Manual (n 39) 12.

[146] *Prosecutor v Muthaura, Kenyatta and Ali*, Decision on the Cofirmation of Charges pursuant to Article 61(7)(a) and (b) of the Rome Statute, PTC II, ICC-01/09-02/11-382-Red, 23 January 2012, para 63; *Prosecutor v Abu Garda*, Decision on the Confirmation of Charges, PTC I, ICC-02/05-02/09-243-Red, 8 February 2010, para 48.

[147] *Situation in the Republic of Kenya*, Decision on the Victims' Request for Review of Prosecution's Decision to Cease Active investigation, PTC II, ICC-01/09-159, 5 November 2015, para 18.

and interpretation exist yet, despite the ambiguous wording of paragraph two: 'If … the Prosecutor concludes that there is not a sufficient basis for a prosecution … the Prosecutor shall inform the Pre-Trial Chamber'. Theoretically, 'a decision not to prosecute' can mean different things in this context:

> (i) [A] decision not to prosecute a specific individual; (ii) a decision not to prosecute a certain group of persons in a given situation; (iii) a decision not to prosecute certain crimes; or (iv) a decision not to prosecute at all, ie the absence of any cases in the situation under investigation.[148]

The provision also contains an obligation to notify the PTC and a referring state or the Security Council (SC) of a decision not to prosecute. No such notification has yet been made. The OTP works on the basis that as long as it does not take a negative decision and is prosecuting *a case* in a situation under investigation, the review mechanism in article 53(3) of the Statute is not triggered.[149] This begs the question of how to make sense of article 53(2) of the Statute. Under what circumstances does it effectively provide a possibility to hold the Prosecutor to account?

Article 53(2) and (3) of the Statute provides the possibility of judicial review of decisions not to prosecute. Given the current practice of dividing between situations and cases, it is highly unlikely that there will be any practical relevance of article 53(2) of the Statute any time soon. The situations chosen for investigation are all large-scale with numerous potential cases; as long as the Prosecutor prosecutes one case within a given situation, article 53(2) seems redundant. This is even more pronounced given that the Prosecutor currently works with a strategy of open-ended investigations in which the OTP gradually develops case hypotheses and adjusts case selection decisions accordingly.[150]

The case selection process is flexible and complex. Such decisions not only require the evaluation of the evidence regarding specific incidents and persons but also the resources available to determine whether there is enough capacity to move to the prosecution stage. The Prosecutor uses a case selection document that lists potential cases across all situations that aims to facilitate a prioritisation and selection process across the board.[151] Disturbing that process, as long as an investigation has not been brought to an end, would infringe on the Prosecutor's authority to manage the Office and the resources available to it.[152] This leaves the question, under what circumstances could the mechanism in article 53(2) of

[148] C Stahn, 'Judicial Review of Prosecutorial Discretion: Five Years on' in C Stahn and G Sluiter (eds), *The Emerging Practice of the International Criminal Court* (Leiden, Martinus Nijhoff, 2009) 270.

[149] F Guariglia and E Rogier, 'The Selection of Situations and Cases by the OTP of the ICC' in C Stahn (ed), *The Law and Practice of the International Criminal Court* (Oxford, Oxford University Press, 2015) 363 (emphasis added).

[150] Policy Paper Case Selection and Prioritisation (n 1) para 5.

[151] ibid, para 11.

[152] Art 42(2) ICCSt.

the Statute be effective in terms of accountability for case selection decisions? And following on from that, how could a State Party contest inaction, when the OTP brings one case in a situation, where there might be hundreds of potential cases within one investigation of a situation? It is an uncomfortable thought to allow the broad area of case selection to go mainly unchallenged, because, as long as the Prosecutor does investigate the broader situation and prosecutes a case, the review possibility in article 53(2) cannot be triggered.

Part of the apparent redundancy of article 53(2) of the Statute is based on the situation/case divide. While this is a reality at the Court, this divide might require fresh thinking and not be as practical as it appears at first sight. The Court might have to investigate smaller incidents such as that of the Gaza Flotilla, a case in which Israeli forces raided a flotilla of ships bound for Gaza and allegedly committed a number of war crimes.[153] Also, should the OTP make a step-change towards more focused and limited investigations, article 53(2) of the Statute will have a role to play once an investigation has been concluded. The smaller the scale of an investigation, the more likely that the OTP concludes not to proceed with a prosecution, perhaps because – across the board of potentially admissible cases in all situations – any case deriving from that investigation does not meet the prioritisation criteria. At this point, the Prosecutor is under the obligation to inform the PTC, and, if applicable, the referring State Parties or the SC.[154] It will be in such a situation that the review process provided through article 53(2), (3) of the Statute becomes relevant.

B. Why Me: Scope for the Defendant to Challenge Case Selection?

Highly selective decisions can often appear arbitrary. The prosecutorial scope of discretion regarding the choice of defendants is very broad and only explicitly limited when the selection is based on discriminatory motifs. Given this low bar, it is probably not surprising that no challenge related to the choice of defendants has been successful before the ICC. The two pathways chosen by defence teams were a challenge of the admissibility of the case at the pre-trial stage of the proceedings and an application to decline the confirmation of charges on the basis of unlawful selection. Despite being unsuccessful in the specific cases, both are interesting pathways that deserve a closer look regarding whether they are generally feasible ways to pose the 'why me' challenge.

In the situation in Kenya, former police chief Ali challenged his selection on the grounds of the insufficient gravity of the case against him and, hence, a lack of admissibility at the pre-trial stage.[155] The defence argued that Ali's

[153] *Situation on the Registered Vessels of Comoros, Greece and Cambodia* ICC-01/13.

[154] Rule 106(1) RPE.

[155] *Prosecutor v Muthaura, Kenyatta and Ali*, Decision on the Cofirmation of Charges (n 146) paras 41, 45.

specific role did not meet the gravity threshold as a criterion of admissibility in article 17(1)(d) of the Statute, because he was not 'one of the most senior leaders', was neither accused as a principal nor direct perpetrator of the crimes, and his case only concerned an omission in his alleged failure to act as head of the Kenyan police.[156] The PTC refused these arguments based on the following considerations: the Statute could not be interpreted as excluding acts of omission, as this would contravene the object and purpose of the treaty.[157] Reduction to principals and direct perpetrators would leave article 25(3)(d) of the Statute redundant. The PTC also assessed the gravity of the case against Ali but focused entirely on the crimes that he was charged with, rather than the role that he might have had.[158] However, the confirmation of charges against Ali was declined on the basis of insufficient evidence.[159]

The PTC decision not to discuss any perpetrator-based element seems coherent with the AC judgment, attempting to safeguard the Court's deterrence potential by preventing too narrow a focus on those most responsible.[160] In contrast, the PTC, at the earlier stage of authorising the investigation into the situation in Kenya, required that 'persons that bear the greatest responsibility for the alleged crimes would be the potential objects of an investigation'.[161] The PTC based this requirement on the gravity of potential cases as part of the admissibility evaluation. Using such a filter before the start of an investigation, but then confirming prosecution decisions regardless of the standing of the perpetrator in question, is contradictory. The PTC stance for the stage of authorising investigations is difficult to reconcile with the AC's judgment that emphasises the openness of the Statute for perpetrators at different levels. The AC has made it clear that it is the crime that matters, and not the role of the perpetrator, because the Preamble demands that the perpetrators of the most serious crimes – and not only the most serious perpetrators – are brought to justice. Having said all that, it remains to be seen whether the Chambers will uphold this crime-focused stance in the (admittedly theoretical and rather unlikely) event that the OTP selects an ordinary soldier without any specific role or responsibility, whose conduct did not stand out, as a defendant in a case of war crimes charges. This question has yet to be answered. Any challenge that attempts to exclude a specific defendant from proceedings before the ICC would therefore have to focus on the criminal conduct being charged, rather than the position of the person. But successfully challenging the selection of a defendant

[156] ibid.
[157] ibid, para 46.
[158] ibid, para 49.
[159] ibid, paras 426–27.
[160] *DRC* Judgment (n 9) paras 75–78.
[161] *Situation in Kenya*, Decision pursuant to Article 15 of the Rome Statute on the Authorisation of an Investigation into the Situation in the Republic of Kenya, PTC II, ICC-01/09-19, 31 March 2010, paras 60–62; see similarly *Situation in Georgia*, Decision on the Prosecutor's Request for Authorization of an Investigation, ICC-01/15-12, 27 January 2016, para 51.

through an admissibility challenge, based on the lack of gravity of the role of the defendant, is not a promising path to pursue.

The other challenge was brought by the defence in the case against Arido in the context of offences against the administration of justice under article 70 of the Statute in the case against Bemba et al. The defence motion suggested that the PTC decline the charges against Arido claiming his unlawful selection, because the OTP had not justified the selection of this suspect over others or considered the gravity or interests of justice in the case.[162] This claim was rejected on two grounds: (1) gravity and interests of justice are not applicable for offences against justice, the underlying charges in this case; and (2) the powers of the PTC are confined to 'analysing the strength of the Prosecutor's evidence, while the selection of cases lies first within the powers of the Prosecutor'.[163] This argument resonates with the function of the confirmation of charges proceedings, the protection of the accused against wholly unfounded charges. Again, it is the criminal conduct that matters and not the person themselves.

The remedy of last resort to protect the accused against a selection decision, based on discriminatory motifs, can be the stay of proceedings. Article 21(3) of the Statute obliges the Court to ensure the non-discriminatory application of the Statute.[164] The Statute is silent on any remedies in that case. However, in the jurisprudence of the Court,[165] the stay of proceedings has been confirmed as the appropriate remedy for the abuse of process.[166] The AC set a high bar in the proceedings against Lubanga, which concerned disclosure issues, for a stay of proceedings:

> Where a fair trial becomes impossible because of breaches of the fundamental rights of the suspect or the accused by his/her accusers, it would be a contradiction in terms to put the person on trial. Justice could not be done. A fair trial is the only means to do justice. If no fair trial can be held, the object of the judicial process is frustrated and must be stopped.[167]

If indeed a defendant were singled out for prosecution based on discriminatory motifs, this would be a breach of the suspect's fundamental right to treatment

[162] *Bemba et al* (n 48) para 22.

[163] ibid.

[164] Art 21(3) ICCSt: 'The application and interpretation of law pursuant to this article must be consistent with internationally recognized human rights, and be without any adverse distinction founded on grounds such as gender as defined in article 7, paragraph 3, age, race, colour, language, religion or belief, political or other opinion, national, ethnic or social origin, wealth, birth or other status'.

[165] *Prosecutor v Lubanga*, Judgment on the appeal of the Prosecutor against the decision of Trial Chamber I of 8 July 2010 entitled 'Decision on the Prosecution's Urgent Request for Variation of the Time-Limit to Disclose the Identity of Intermediary 143 or Alternatively to Stay Proceedings Pending Further Consultations with the VWU', ICC-01/04-01/06-2582, 8 October 2010, para 55.

[166] Guariglia and Rogier (n 149) 363 for the abuse of process if the prosecution is based on impermissible criteria.

[167] *Prosecutor v Lubanga*, Judgment on the appeal (n 165) para 55.

free from discrimination. Such a breach would be unfair and could not be remedied other than through the permanent stay of proceedings, because no other, less drastic, measure would be able to appropriately address such a selection decision. That being said, the real challenge for the pathway to accountability would be to demonstrate that the selection was based on discriminatory grounds. A first step to provide any safeguards against discriminatory, and indeed arbitrary, selection, is transparency in the selection criteria.

C. Pragmatic Accountability

The discussion of formal accountability mechanisms regarding the case selection process shows how important forms of transparency and pragmatic accountability at the ICC are. Transparency is crucial in order to facilitate accountability and ultimately enhance the legitimacy of the Court. Transparency fosters integrity because it forces the Prosecutor to reveal the underlying rationale for decisions. Such deliberation on discretionary decisions also has a quality-enhancing effect in that it ensures a systematic reflection on the legal limits to discretion, the guiding principles, and reasons for a decision as a form of self-justification. The dynamic of transparency as a tool of pragmatic accountability works at two levels: at the general policy level, which determines case selection mechanisms and criteria in the abstract; and at the level of individual case selection decisions, which requires the use of these abstract criteria in the specific situation. The increase in policy papers that document the OTP's practice and thinking are important instruments in providing such transparency at the general level. They are crucial for an enhanced understanding of prosecutorial decisions.

Of specific importance is the 2016 Policy Paper on Case Selection and Prioritisation. The public consultation process is worth highlighting as a novel step of engagement with stakeholders and the public, as it invited comments on the draft policy paper from anyone interested.[168] This consultation provided the possibility of scrutinising the existing and the intended practice at the Court and of providing suggestions to further improve the process. The change between the draft and the final policy paper was notable. Beyond improving the quality of the policy, it further provided an informal avenue for preserving the Court's legitimacy. If selective processes are openly discussed and input is possible from diverse groups of Court constituents, it allows a more consensual process and is an important stepping-stone towards a more open and responsive Court.

As a pragmatic mechanism of accountability, the Prosecutor's commitment to provide the reasons for individual case selection decisions is highly relevant, because a policy paper alone does not ensure transparency of the exercise of

[168] ICC Press Release, 'ICC Prosecutor, Fatou Bensouda, issues Draft and Prioritisation, for comment', ICC-CPI-20160229-PR1192, 29 February 2016, available at: www.icc-cpi.int/Pages/item.aspx?name=pr1192&ln=en.

discretion in the specific case selection process. In the 2016 Policy Paper, the Prosecutor pledges that 'once a person has been arrested or appeared voluntarily before the Court, the Office will include, as part of its public information activities, its rationale for bringing forward the case for prosecution'.[169] Yet, the information available for cases made public since publication of the policy does not explain any reasons for the selective choices beyond outlining the alleged roles of defendants and the alleged criminal conduct the defendants will be charged with.[170]

Explaining the reasons for the selection of a specific case gives the Prosecutor a chance to fully use the expressive power that a case before the ICC can have. It allows the Prosecutor to demonstrate how the case selection choice is geared towards representing different areas of victimisation. And, if the chosen case cannot address all areas of victimisation, either because the choice of charges is limited in order to highlight a specific topic, or because it only addresses one side of the conflict, it gives her a chance to explain how she intends to balance this in further case selection choices. Such deliberation on the reasons of individual decisions also forces the Prosecutor to adhere to her policy commitments. Deviating from those criteria would be open to the public and therefore open to public scrutiny. It might not provide a formal remedy, but as an institution that has to rely on external support for the enforcement of its decisions, and whose budget is annually newly decided by the ASP, any inconsistencies here could very quickly have repercussions for the Prosecutor. This form of transparency is therefore pivotal as an accountability mechanism.

Because transparency regarding the reasons for a case selection decision is so important, the policy commitment to providing a rationale for individual decisions is a first step in the right direction. The current commitment seems to be rather informal though and, given that it has not been used yet, the envisaged form is unclear. Because of its crucial function, it is proposed that the OTP should commit to introducing specific public 'case reports', deliberating on discretionary decisions at a suitable point in the process after the case has been selected for prosecution. Such a proposed case report – resembling the 'Article 5 Reports' of the Office – could in a more formalised and systematic way explain the choices of charges in a specific case and highlight generally 'under-prosecuted' areas. Another reason for a more formalised form of information is that such official announcements allow better public scrutiny. The more formalised the deliberation process is, the better it can serve its function as an accountability mechanism.

The situation in Côte d'Ivoire serves as a good example for the importance of formalised mechanisms. Since the commencement of the investigation

[169] Policy Paper Case Selection and Prioritisation (n 1) para 15.

[170] See, eg, *Situation in the Central African Republic II: Prosecutor v Yekatom and Ngaïssona* ICC-01/14-01/18.

in 2011, there was a reasonable basis to believe that both sides of the conflict, pro-Gbagbo forces as well as pro-Ouatarra forces, committed crimes within the jurisdiction of the Court. Despite the Prosecutor's commitment to represent all areas of victimisation, up to now only cases against the Gbagbo side have filled the dock at the ICC. The Prosecutor faces widespread criticism for the one-sided prosecution efforts.[171] In interviews, the Prosecutor keeps communicating that she will prosecute both sides, but that she was constrained by the lack of funding.[172] Eight years into the investigation, the one-sided prosecution efforts with a collapsed case against Gbagbo and Blé Goudé represent a disastrous result which requires a radical revision of the investigation strategies. Perhaps better and formalised reasoning would have served as an internal quality control mechanism, as well as improved transparency in the situation.

VI. CONCLUDING REMARKS

The Prosecutor at the ICC needs to be highly selective when choosing cases for prosecution. Among the pool of potentially admissible cases resulting from the investigation into one situation alone, the Prosecutor is always only able to choose a very limited number of cases. Accordingly, the scope for prosecutorial discretion is wide. Regarding the choice of defendants, the Statute only imposes a bottom line that does not allow the Prosecutor to choose a defendant based on discriminatory motifs. Equally, the Prosecutor can use a variety of charging techniques: she can bring cumulative or alternative charges, where the legal criteria have been met, or she can choose to limit the charges she brings. Only a few legal constraints, such as the rule of speciality or the prohibition to select a defendant on discriminatory motifs, apply to the broad procedural choices. For that reason, it is crucial that the Prosecutor directs her efforts towards some key aims.

Bearing this in mind, it is particularly critical that all areas of victimisation are represented, not only in relation to the choice of charges but also to address different groups of perpetrators and groups of victims. Such decisions are of the utmost importance for the legitimacy of the Court. If the Prosecutor is perceived as only addressing one side of the conflict, as not administering justice in an even-handed manner, it is only a small step to perceptions of arbitrariness. Equally, the Prosecutor needs to ensure the maximum impact of prosecution decisions on the deterrence potential for the Court and use the expressive force inherent

[171] See Human Rights Watch, 'Making Justice Count, Lessons from the ICC's Work in Côte D'Ivoire', 4 August 2015, available at: www.hrw.org.

[172] See T Miles, 'ICC Prosecutor vows to investigate both sides in Ivory Coast' (*Reuters*, 3 June 2016), available at: af.reuters.com/article/topNews/idAFKCN0YP251. The reason given for the slow progress was the lack of funding.

in prosecutions at the ICC. Achieving these aims requires that the Prosecutor communicates the reasons for the choices that she has made. Communication means transparency, and transparency will in turn further accountability. Where the Rome Statute provides some accountability mechanisms that protect the defendant in the cases that have been chosen for prosecution, the Statute offers little accountability for those cases that have not. Communication and transparency are therefore key signals of the openness of the Court and allow responses for those whose hopes for justice seem unfulfilled.

5

Plea Agreements

I. INTRODUCTION

> [W]e always have to keep in mind that this Tribunal is not a municipal criminal court but one that is charged with the task of trying persons accused of the gravest possible of all crimes. The persons appearing before us will be charged with genocide, torture, murder, sexual assault, wanton destruction, persecution and other inhumane acts. After due reflection, we have decided that no one should be immune from prosecution for crimes such as these, no matter how useful their testimony may otherwise be.[1]

Judge Antonio Cassese made this statement in his capacity as President of the International Criminal Tribunal for the former Yugoslavia (ICTY) during the early years of the Tribunal. It sums up well some of the tensions around plea bargaining[2] in the context of international criminal courts. In many domestic jurisdictions, plea bargaining has become an important tool of prosecutorial discretion to deal with the pressures arising from overloaded dockets.[3] At the international level, plea bargaining has gradually found its way into the courts. The developments at the ICTY showcase this well, with the initial principled stance expressed by Cassese to the introduction of rules 62*bis* and 62*ter* in the Rules of Procedure and Evidence (RPE) making way for a regulated use of plea bargains[4] and seen as a 'triumph of pragmatism'.[5]

The Rome Statute allows the Prosecutor to enter into discussions with the defendant but not into binding plea agreements. Article 65 of the Rome Statute sets out '[a]ny discussions between the Prosecutor and defence regarding modification of the charges, the admission of guilt or the penalty to be imposed shall

[1] Statement by the President of the ICTY, Judge Antonio Cassese, made at a briefing to Members of Diplomatic Missions, IT/29, 11 February 1994, cited after M Scharf, 'Trading Justice for Efficiency' (2004) 2 *Journal of International Criminal Justice* 1070, 1073.

[2] Plea bargains or plea agreements are used synonymously in this chapter.

[3] S Thaman (ed), *World Plea Bargaining: Consensual Procedures and the Avoidance of the Full Criminal Trial* (Durham, NC, Carolina Academic Press, 2010) with an account of plea bargaining procedures across different domestic systems.

[4] JN Clark, 'Plea Bargaining at the ICTY: Guilty Pleas and Reconciliation' (2009) 20 *European Journal of International Law* 415, 416.

[5] N Jørgensen, 'The Genocide Acquittal in the Sikirica Case Before the International Criminal Tribunal for the Former Yugoslavia and the Coming of Age of the Guilty Plea' (2002) 15 *Leiden Journal of International Law* 389, 407.

not be binding on the Court'.[6] This was the compromise that emerged during the Rome negotiations; negotiators were influenced by the chequered experiences from the *ad hoc* tribunals as well as the attitudes in their own legal traditions.[7] The compromise contained in the Rome Statute is a blend of 'Anglo-American and Continental European forms of criminal justice, [f]ollowing the former, international courts tolerate inter-party negotiations and, following the latter, they insist that deals arising from these negotiations have no binding effect on the court'.[8] Against this backdrop, this chapter discusses the scope of prosecutorial discretion for plea bargaining at the International Criminal Court (ICC), framing its arguments around the case against Ahmed Al Mahdi. It is one of the few convictions at the ICC to date, and, the only one based on a plea agreement.

The arguments pro and contra plea bargaining have been made many times. Arguments in favour of plea bargaining procedures are expedited cases, reduced costs and the potential to induce cooperation from defendants. Arguments against include the danger of generating arbitrary sentencing disparities, obscuring the true facts and distorting the historic record, leading innocent defendants to plead guilty, and to undermine the educative function of the trial.[9] Negotiated justice, however, is particularly contentious in the context of mass atrocities and has been subject to extensive debate.[10] The Trial Chamber (TC) remarked on the advantages:

> An admission of guilt can lead to a swifter resolution of a case, giving much needed finality in an otherwise unmatchable timeframe. While there may be victims who prefer to testify, others may wish to be spared the stress of having to testify to their personal tragedies and being exposed to cross-examination. Accused admitting guilt pursuant to an agreement to testify in subsequent trials can contribute to the search for the truth as insider witnesses in cases against others. Perhaps most importantly, the speed at which cases can be resolved following admissions of guilt saves the Court both time and resources, which can be otherwise spent advancing the course of international justice on other fronts.[11]

As a court often criticised for the low level of convictions, these benefits are most welcome for the ICC. Hence, the *Al Mahdi* case might be a first stepping-stone in an emerging practice.

But when should the Prosecutor seek discussions and where are the limits to such agreements? What is required to render a plea agreement and the subsequent trial a fair procedure? These are some of the questions at the core of this chapter.

[6] Art 65(5) ICCSt.

[7] M Damaška, 'Negotiated Justice in International Criminal Courts' (2004) 2 *Journal of International Criminal Justice* 1018, 1022–27.

[8] ibid, 1038.

[9] See J Turner, 'Plea Bargaining and International Criminal Justice' (2017) 48 *The University of the Pacific Law Review* 219, 239–42.

[10] See, eg, Scharf (n 1); Damaška (n 7); R Henham, 'The Ethics of Plea Bargaining in International Criminal Trials' (2005) 26 *Liverpool Law Review* 209; N Combs, *Guilty Pleas in International Criminal Law* (Stanford, CA, Stanford University Press, 2007).

[11] *Prosecutor v Al Madhi*, Judgment and Sentence, ICC-01/12-01/15-171, 27 September 2016, para 28.

In addressing them, I argue that plea agreements have considerable potential for the ICC despite the tensions created in relation to some of the broader aims of the Court and international criminal law more generally. However, it will be demonstrated that any plea agreement requires efforts on the part of the Office of the Prosecutor (OTP) to address informational asymmetry and ensure that due process requirements are met. De facto, the scope for the Prosecutor to secure an agreement and maintain some control over the outcome is greatest at the pre-trial stage regarding the choice of charges; yet, this is the most contentious area of bargaining. Throughout the previous chapters of this book, I have extensively discussed the need to ensure that cases are representative of areas of victimisation, the need to safeguard victims' interests, and have referred to the expressive force of international trials. In this regard, how can a negotiated result, relating to either the charges brought or to the sentence, contribute to establishing the truth? Yet, plea agreements are a reality. Thus, I argue that the Prosecutor is limited through the need to ensure a representative account of what happened and is not driven by efficiency gains that aim at securing a quick conviction. Any legitimate practice of plea bargaining must aim to construct a restorative justice approach.[12] Efficiency should always only be the by-product of any agreements.

II. THE LEGAL FRAMEWORK AND THE ADMISSION OF GUILT

The legal framework for the admission of guilt is provided in articles 64(8)[13] and 65[14] of the Rome Statute allowing for an abbreviated procedure before the TC on the admission of guilt and providing safeguards for the protection of the accused. These safeguards have emerged as a minimum standard across

[12] Combs (n 10).

[13] Art 64(8)(a) ICCSt: 'At the commencement of the trial, the Trial Chamber shall have read to the accused the charges previously confirmed by the Pre-Trial Chamber. The Trial Chamber shall satisfy itself that the accused understands the nature of the charges. It shall afford him or her the opportunity to make an admission of guilt in accordance with article 65 or to plead not guilty'.

[14] Art 65 ICCSt:

> '1. Where the accused makes an admission of guilt pursuant to article 64, paragraph 8 (a), the Trial Chamber shall determine whether:
>
> (a) The accused understands the nature and consequences of the admission of guilt;
> (b) The admission is voluntarily made by the accused after sufficient consultation with defence counsel;
>
> and (c) The admission of guilt is supported by the facts of the case … presented by the Prosecutor or the accused.
>
> 2. Where the Trial Chamber is satisfied that the matters referred to in paragraph 1 are established, it shall consider the admission of guilt, together with any additional evidence presented, as establishing all the essential facts that are required to prove the crime to which the admission of guilt relates, and may convict the accused of that crime.
>
> 3. Where the Trial Chamber is not satisfied that the matters referred to in paragraph 1 are established, it shall consider the admission of guilt as not having been made, in which case it shall order that the trial be continued under the ordinary trial procedures provided by this Statute and may remit the case to another Trial Chamber.

different systems[15] and include that the defendant is able to fully understand the nature and consequence of his plea, acts voluntarily and has had the chance to sufficiently consult with defence counsel; additionally, the TC is required to ensure that the plea reflects the facts of the case. Such an admission does not necessarily need to be connected to a plea agreement between defence and prosecution, although in practice it most likely will. A pivotal point is that no such agreement is binding on the TC.[16] Rule 139 of the RPE additionally sets out that the TC may invite the OTP and Defence to submit their views on the admission of guilt before reaching a decision and placing the reasons for it on the record. The provisions confirm the strong role of the TC throughout the trial proceedings, being more than the independent arbiter between two parties but charged with the protection of the interests of justice, and victims' interests in particular, as well as the fairness of the proceedings.

A. The First Plea Agreement before the ICC

The conviction of Ahmed Al Faqi Al Mahdi for the war crime of intentionally directing attacks against historic monuments and buildings dedicated to religion was based on a plea agreement. The case derived from the investigation into the situation in Mali and addressed the destruction of cultural heritage (nine mausoleums and one mosque) in Timbuktu. Very soon after his surrender from Niger to the ICC, Ahmed Al Mahdi and his defence entered into discussions with the OTP. The OTP successfully seized the chance to reach a plea agreement during the pre-trial phase of the proceedings.[17] The document containing

4. Where the Trial Chamber is of the opinion that a more complete presentation of the facts of the case is required in the interests of justice, in particular the interests of the victims, the Trial Chamber may:

   (a) Request the Prosecutor to present additional evidence, including the testimony of witnesses;

   or (b) Order that the trial be continued under the ordinary trial procedures provided by this Statute, in which case it shall consider the admission of guilt as not having been made and may remit the case to another Trial Chamber'.

[15] *Prosecutor v Erdemović*, Appeals Chamber Judgment, IT-96-22-A, 7 October 1997, para 20 for the requirement that a guilty plea must be entered on a fully informed basis. *Natsvlishvili and Togonidze v Georgia*, ECtHR Judgment, 9043/05, 29 April 2014, para 92: '[T]he bargain had to be accepted by the first applicant in full awareness of the facts of the case and the legal consequences and in a genuinely voluntary manner; and (b) the content of the bargain and the fairness of the manner in which it had been reached between the parties had to be subjected to sufficient judicial review'. See also IACH, Report on Measures Aimed at Reducing the Use of Pre-Trial Detention in the Americas OEA/Ser.L/V/II.163, 3 July 2017, para 60 requiring that 'the acceptance of the accused is voluntary and based on full knowledge of the facts of the case and of the legal consequences of such acceptance'.

[16] See similarly, ICTY Rule 62 *ter* Rules of Procedure and Evidence (13 December 2001); ICTR Rule 62 *bis* Rules of Procedure and Evidence (27 May 2003).

[17] See for positive reactions, M Aksenova, 'The Al Mahdi Judgment and Sentence at the ICC: A Source of Cautious Optimism for International Criminal Justice', 13 October 2016, available at: EJILTalk.org; M Karnavas, 'Al Mahdi Culturecide Judgment: A watershed moment for plea agreements', 30 September 2016, available at: michaelgkarnavas.net.

the charges (DCC) was filed on 17 December 2015, the plea agreement signed on 18 February 2016, and the charges confirmed on 24 March 2016.[18] The Prosecutor had limited the charges to one war crime charge linked to the destruction of cultural heritage[19] and the Defence neither objected to the charges nor challenged any of the evidence.[20] All these aspects allowed the confirmation proceedings to progress at unprecedented speed.[21]

Previously during the first status conference before the TC, all parties and participants had worked on the assumption of a guilty plea[22] before OTP and Defence publicly disclosed the plea agreement in a joint submission in August 2016.[23] The trial was held between 22 and 24 August 2016 in an abbreviated procedure in which the accused admitted his guilt and publicly apologised, oral submissions relating to the judgment and sentencing were received, and the prosecution presented the testimony of three witnesses.[24] As agreed, the Prosecutor recommended a sentence of nine to 11 years, and the TC ultimately sentenced him within this range to nine years. As part of the mitigating circumstances the TC found:

> The Chamber further observes that Mr Al Mahdi took responsibility for his actions as early as the first day of his interviews with the Prosecution. Subsequently, the parties reached an agreement sufficiently early in the proceedings, namely before the confirmation of charges, to help substantially speed up the proceedings.[25]

These considerations are in line with jurisprudence in other international criminal tribunals on the mitigating effect of guilty pleas[26] and showcase the importance of the right timing. The earlier in the proceedings that the accused takes responsibility, the more effective in making mitigation work for the accused. According to the TC in *Al Mahdi*, article 65(5) of the Statute provides a 'third avenue'[27] between common and civil law approaches that would 'implicitly authorise discussions corresponding to plea agreements in common law legal systems'.[28]

[18] *Prosecutor v Al Madhi*, Decision on the Confirmation of Charges against Ahmad Al Faqi Al Mahdi, ICC-01/12-01/15-84-Red, 24 March 2016, paras 5–12.

[19] *Prosecutor v Al Madhi*, Chef d'accusation retenu par l'Accusation contre Ahmad Al Faqi Al Mahdi, ICC-01/12-01/15-62, 17 December 2015.

[20] *Al Mahdi* Decision on the Confirmation of Charges (n 18) para 28.

[21] In a separate opinion, Judge Péter Kovács, ICC-01/12-01/15-84-Anx, 09 May 2016, para 7 heavily criticised the Majority approach to the review of evidence: 'Being at the pre-trial phase does not justify a light assessment of facts or disregarding the proper presentation of evidence submitted'.

[22] Transcript of Hearing, ICC-01/12-01/15-T-3-CONF-ENG.

[23] *Prosecutor v Al Madhi*, Version publique expurgée du 'Dépôt del'Accord sur l'aveu deculpabilité de M Ahmad Al Faqi Al Mahdi', 25 février 2016, ICC-01/12-01/15-78-Conf-Exp, ICC-01/12-01/15-78-Red2, 19 August 2016.

[24] *Al Mahdi* Judgment (n 11) para 7.

[25] ibid, para 98.

[26] Jørgensen (n 5) 401.

[27] *Al Mahdi* Judgment (n 11) para 46.

[28] ibid, para 47.

> Pursuant to Articles 64(8)(a) and 65 of the Statute, an accused is afforded an opportunity to make an admission of guilt at the commencement of the trial, a procedure which looks not dissimilar to the traditional common law 'guilty plea'. Article 65(5) of the Statute also implicitly authorises discussions corresponding to plea agreements in common law legal systems. However, Article 65 also requires the Chamber to conclude that the admission is 'supported by the facts of the case', specifically requiring it to consider both the admission of guilt 'together with any additional evidence presented'. This is more analogous to a summary or abbreviated procedure traditionally associated with civil law systems.[29]

While this judgment sets no precedent, it will be an important point of reference for the future practice of the Court.[30] Hence, delineating the scope of prosecutorial discretion within this 'third avenue' is critical.

B. Scope for Discretion During the Different Stages of the Proceedings

The key space for the exercise of discretion is the possibility of 'discussions' between the OTP and the defence, which may be aimed at identifying common ground regarding the charges, the evidence or other factual circumstances related to the case.[31] A central point that made the *Al Mahdi* case a success is the early agreement between the parties. The defendant fully secured the mitigating circumstances derived from a plea agreement, and the OTP secured a successful conviction and a widely noted landmark case addressing the destruction of cultural heritage in a very timely fashion. While article 65 does not specify when the discussion should be had, the *Al Mahdi* case evidences that timing is important.

The scope for discretion is greater at the pre-trial stage, because it is within the Prosecutor's discretion to determine the charges and to provide the factual narrative for the Court. Although no agreement is binding on the TC at the later stage of the proceedings, the parties can seize some control by narrowing the scope of the charges and facts.[32] Also, from the defence perspective, it seems advisable to enter into discussions early – of course, only if the defence contemplates plea bargaining – in order to secure the chance of mitigating circumstances through accelerated proceedings. Once trial proceedings have started, article 64(8) of the Statute affords the accused the chance to enter a plea. Hence, ideally the parties should be ready to go with any agreement before this, making it more likely to convince a TC that an abbreviated procedure, based on

[29] ibid.

[30] Art 21 (2) ICCSt: 'The Court may apply rules and principles as interpreted in its previous decisions'.

[31] Art 65(5) ICCSt.

[32] Art 74(2) ICCSt: 'The decision shall not exceed the facts and circumstances described in the charges and any amendments to the charges. The Court may base its decision only on evidence submitted and discussed before it at the trial'.

the plea agreement and possibly within the sentencing range of the agreement, is appropriate.

Throughout the trial stage, or, put differently, once inside the courtroom, any scope to reach a plea agreement is drastically reduced. Article 65 is clear in this respect that the TC has the final say. Should, for example, the Defence and the OTP reach an agreement throughout ongoing trial proceedings – a dynamic which might very well unfold during the course of years of trial proceedings in which both sides might have realised that some of their case is not going to plan[33] – it will strongly depend on the judges' approach within the Chambers regarding their openness to any such agreement.

In any case, the judges need to take into consideration that the negotiating countries were divided on the issue of plea agreements during the drafting process. Concerns had been raised that plea bargaining would not be appropriate for cases likely to come before the Court.[34] 'The Court is not just a criminal court but must additionally fulfil the historical role of clarifying the events in the situations brought before it'.[35] To use Cassese's words, the ICC is not any municipal court, but a court designed to deal with the gravest of all crimes. The compromise formula in article 65 IV of the Statute allowing 'discussions … regarding modification of the charges, the admission of guilt or the penalty to be imposed' implies that it is within the Prosecutor's discretion to discuss a potential modification of the charges or aspects of sentencing. Despite these concerns, it seems unavoidable and even 'desirable in the interest of a speedy and focused trial'[36] that parties might come to agreements. The drafters' considerations reflect the experiences from the *ad hoc* tribunals, which saw a considerable practice of plea agreements[37] with about 12 per cent of all cases resolved by plea agreements.[38] Equally, other international or hybrid courts feature the possibility of plea agreements.[39] All these courts have to negotiate the tension between the broad aims of truth finding, of setting a historical record, delivering on the task of contributing to reconciliation of conflicted societies, and pressures to perform efficiently. Hence, the compromise formula reflects developments in international criminal law more broadly. To make the formula of a third avenue at the ICC a practical reality, prosecutorial, as well as judicial,

[33] Jørgensen (n 5) 397 discussing a similar scenario before the ICTY in the *Sikirica* case.

[34] H-J Behrens 'The Trial Proceedings' in R Lee, *The Making of the Rome Statute* (The Hague, Kluwer Law International, 1999) 242.

[35] ibid, 242.

[36] ibid.

[37] See Combs (n 10) 57 ff for the ICTY; and 91 ff for the International Criminal Tribunal for Rwanda (ICTR).

[38] J Dieckmann and M O'Leary, 'The Role of Defense Counsel in Pre-Trial' in C Rohan and G Zyberi (eds), *Defense Perspectives on International Criminal Justice* (Cambridge, Cambridge University Press, 2017) 273.

[39] See Combs (n 10) 114 for the practice at the Special Panels in East Timor. Also Rule 94 of the Rules of Procedure and Evidence before the Specialist Kosovo Chambers, KSC-BD-03/Rev1/2017/59 of 127, 25 August 2017.

discretion contained in article 65 must carefully negotiate the legal limitations on plea bargaining and be strongly guided by the broader aims of international criminal law.

III. LIMITATIONS ON PLEA AGREEMENTS

The non-binding nature of any agreement between the OTP and the Defence at the ICC will act as a factual barrier to widespread plea bargaining because of the uncertainty attached to it. Yet, similar rules at the ICTY did not stop the establishment of a practice of plea bargaining. Additionally, the Prosecutor is legally limited in the scope that is available for any plea agreement. At the macro level, international treaty obligations, combined with the specific task of creating a historical record, create a limiting effect on the scope of prosecutorial discretion, when plea bargaining, specifically through charge bargaining, amounts to a distortion of the historical record. At a micro level within a specific case, due process requirements place some additional legal limits on the Prosecutor. This uncertainty requires counterbalancing through the provision of the highest standards of fairness in the proceedings. The Prosecutor has to approach any plea agreement in a fair and balanced way appropriate for an international criminal court, which also has to deliver the highest standards of justice to instil 'lasting respect for and the enforcement of international justice'.[40]

A. Due Process Requirements

The need for fairness in the proceedings and safeguards for the rights of the accused are key limitations on the exercise of prosecutorial discretion. The principle of a fair trial is tightly woven into the Rome Statute. Article 54(1)(c) of the Statute requires the OTP to 'fully respect the rights of persons arising under this Statute'; article 55 spells out the fair trial provisions during investigations; article 66 provides for the presumption of innocence; and article 67 contains procedural rights of the accused to secure fairness in the trial proceedings. It is therefore crucial that the Prosecutor ensures that fair trial standards are applied to any negotiating process between the defendant and the OTP. If the OTP cannot or does not address all fairness issues within its competence and ensures that the suspect is fully aware of those, the OTP would be barred from seeking to secure a plea agreement. The 'procedural "short-cut" [of plea-bargaining] must not … be allowed to curtail the rights of the accused or, more generally, prove detrimental to the general principle of fair trial'.[41] Article 65(1)

[40] Preamble ICCSt.

[41] *Prosecutor v Erdemović*, Separate and Dissenting Opinion of Judge Cassese, IT-96-22, 7 October 1997, para 9.

of the Statute reflects this idea when placing the obligation on the TC to ensure that any guilty plea is entered on a well-informed, voluntary basis, is free from coercion and backed up by legal advice. Accordingly, in *Al Mahdi*, the TC tested whether the guilty plea was entered on a voluntary basis, fully informed, with adequate translation at hand and supported by legal counsel.[42]

These criteria have important repercussions for the OTP. It is not only defence counsel's duty to advise the accused with due diligence,[43] but it requires the OTP to ensure that the Defence is fully informed and supported. Eliminating informational asymmetry is one key problem in this context.[44] US case law, as the system with an extremely strong plea bargaining culture,[45] is informative in this respect. The US Supreme Court found that any guilty plea as part of a bargain must be 'voluntary' and 'intelligent'.[46] These components did not initially include full information on the strength of the Prosecution's case.[47] However, exonerating material must be disclosed to the defendant.[48] In its subsequent case law, the US Supreme Court developed the concept that a defendant is entitled to effective assistance from counsel at the plea bargaining stage.[49] Effective assistance, however, requires that counsel ensures that any advice given is based on the knowledge and analysis of relevant facts and the applicable law, including a review of any exonerating circumstances that would be available for counsel through a disclosure request. For the OTP at the ICC, it is therefore critical to diligently fulfil its disclosure obligations and assist defence counsel in effectively accessing the materials, as these will often amount to thousands of pages of information.

Disclosure of critical parts of the evidence is the only way to ensure that counsel is enabled to give informed and full advice to the suspect as a key component for the fairness of any plea agreement. Additionally, the OTP must in any case seek to move a case towards trial stage as swiftly as possible. Extremely long detention periods can negatively impact the free choice of a defendant to strike a plea agreement. Considering the length of pre-trial and trial proceedings,[50] a rational accused might well come to the conclusion that a favourable plea

[42] Transcript of Proceedings, ICC-01/12-01/15-T-4-Red-ENG WT 22-08-2016, 10–11.

[43] Dieckmann and O'Leary (n 38) 274 argue that it is counsel's duty to provide a defendant with sufficient information to make an informed decision about a guilty plea.

[44] E Hashimoto, 'Towards Ethical Plea Bargaining' (2008) 30 *Cardozo Law Review* 949 argues that some level of informational symmetry is critical to the plea process.

[45] About 95% of all convictions are based on plea bargains. See R Covey, 'Plea-Bargaining Law after Lafler and Frye' (2013) 51 *Duquesne University Law Review* 595, 600.

[46] *Brady v United States* 397 US 742, 748 (1970).

[47] ibid.

[48] According to a majority of US Circuit Courts, the obligation to disclose exonerating evidence applies at the plea-bargaining stage; see with further references to the case law Covey (n 45) 601–02.

[49] *Lafler v Cooper* 566 US (2012).

[50] *Prosecutor v Bemba*, ICC-01/05-01/08: It took 10 years from arrest to acquittal which the accused spend in detention (although it should be noted that the accused was convicted of offences against the administration of justice in a distinct trial before the ICC with a sentence of one year).

bargain might be a quicker avenue to regain freedom than a lengthy trial. In such a case, the system would have failed as it 'would conceal rather than establish the relevant truth, and a wrongdoer is not being brought to answer for her [or his] wrong'.[51] This shows that the due process guarantees that limit the exercise of discretion, and place specific burdens on the OTP to secure an environment in which plea agreements might be possible, serve not only the protection of the accused but safeguard broader justice aims.

The OTP, and the Court more generally, must stay very alert to the fact that a variety of circumstances can negatively impact on the permissibility of a plea agreement, even if the OTP is not acting in bad faith. A key point is that utmost consideration must be given to full disclosure, swift proceedings, and support for the Defence in such a way that due process guarantees are fully met, and any direct or indirect coercion is avoided. Should the OTP not be willing to do so, and, more generally, should the OTP engage in any conduct that would negatively impact on the fairness of the proceedings and unduly pressurise the accused, plea bargaining would be beyond limits.

B. Charge Bargaining?

Returning from this micro-perspective to the macro level, respect for international criminal justice also requires respect for the particular functions of international criminal trials. Concerns have been raised that charge bargaining may obscure the true facts of the case and the full extent of a defendant's culpability.[52] Yet, the scope for discretion seems greatest at the pre-trial stage, when the OTP determines the potential charges and the factual narrative to be presented to the Pre-Trial Chamber for confirmation and ultimately to the TC. At the ICTY, cases of charge bargaining caused some dissent on the judges' benches, which are valuable to understand the limits of prosecutorial discretion:

> If the Prosecutor makes a plea agreement such that the totality of an individual's criminal conduct is not reflected or the remaining charges do not sufficiently reflect the gravity of offenses committed by the accused, questions will inevitably arise as to whether justice is in fact being done. The public may be left to wonder about the motives for guilty pleas, whether the conviction in fact reflects the full criminal conduct of the accused and whether it establishes a credible and complete historical record.[53]

[51] A Duff, L Farmer, S Marshall and V Tadros, *The Trial on Trial, Volume 3: Towards a Normative Theory of the Criminal Trial* (Oxford, Hart Publishing, 2007) 170.

[52] Turner (n 9) 229.

[53] *Prosecutor v Momir Nikolić*, Sentencing Judgment, IT-02-60/1-S, 2 December 2003, para 66.

Judge Schomburg made similar points:

> [I] it is for the Prosecutor alone to decide whom, and under which charges, to indict ... However, it is also for the Prosecutor to safeguard that justice is seen to be done and to convince, in particular, those people on whose behalf this Tribunal is working that there is no arbitrary selection of persons to be indicted and no arbitrary selection of charges or facts in case of an indictment.
>
> ... [and] promises ... [as part of a plea bargain] can not result in *de facto* granting partial amnesty/impunity by the Prosecutor, particularly not in an institution established to avoid impunity.[54]

Both pinpoint the dangers of the exercise of prosecutorial discretion in which the charges are extremely limited. Judge Schomburg described the indictment against Deronjić at the ICTY as involving 'clinically clean' selected facts that omit the presentation of broader criminal conduct beyond some specific killings in one village only.[55] Such charging can impact on, or even distort, the historical record and allow impunity if considerable additional criminal conduct is omitted. These voices highlight the critical point that justice is more than just delivering a conviction.

At first sight, the Rome Statute seems to offer a safety mechanism against such extensive bargaining through the option to demand a more complete presentation of the facts. This, however, can only be linked to the charges brought rather than to entirely different conduct that has been omitted from the DCC. Earlier in this book, I have argued that the case selection process must attempt to capture the full extent of victimisation where the factual basis allows. This principle provides guidance for the Prosecutor in the case selection process, and, as its flipside, also a limitation to any discussions with the accused.

The European Court of Human Rights (ECtHR)[56] suggests that plea bargaining is impermissible when it runs counter to any important public interest. Uncovering a substantive truth, or setting the historical record straight, would seem to serve the public interest in this regard, as these are often cited aims of international criminal trials. However, as mentioned previously, these are meta-aims often difficult to achieve; criminal lawyers are rarely historians[57] and plea bargaining has a 'complicated relationship to the goal of establishing an accurate record of international crimes'.[58] Yet, plea bargaining should not distort the perception of what happened in a conflict. This could be the case when, for example, selected charges would not adequately reflect the role and responsibility of key individuals – specifically important for persons with leadership

[54] *Prosecutor v Deronjić*, Sentencing Judgment, Dissenting Opinion of Judge Schomburg, IT-02-61-S, 30 March 2004, paras 10–11.

[55] ibid, para 9.

[56] *Natsvlishvili* Judgment (n 15) para 91.

[57] R Rauxloh, 'Negotiated History: The Historical Record in International Criminal Law and Plea Bargaining' (2010) 10 *International Criminal Law Review* 739, 742

[58] Turner (n 9) 244.

roles – even though a factually and evidentiary sufficient basis existed to charge the accused with particular crimes. Understanding the role that a particular individual has played would be of considerable public interest. Additionally, a conviction that is seen as unjust could disturb societal processes in a transitional or post-conflict setting. For those reasons, the third avenue approach at the ICC ought to exclude excessive charge bargaining that omits large parts of criminal conduct for which a sufficient evidentiary basis exists. Providing genuine accountability through a trial for wrong done is an important interest, ensuring an accurate historical record. Any discretion aiming at a plea agreement at the ICC must work towards safeguarding those aims.

The last and strongest argument that militates in favour of conceptualising the scope of discretion regarding charge bargaining as limited through public interest is that the crimes within the jurisdiction of the Court are mostly deemed to be serious breaches of (customary) international law protecting fundamental values of the international community as a whole.[59] Cassese expressed this forcefully in his statement at the beginning of this chapter. The prohibition of genocide or torture are *ius cogens* norms and the enforcement of those prohibitions are obligations *erga omnes*.[60] Additionally, some of the crimes within the jurisdiction of the ICC are derived from multilateral treaties. The four Geneva Conventions of 1949 require the prosecution of specific grave breaches of international humanitarian law, the Genocide Convention implements the obligation to prosecute genocide, and the Convention against Torture places an obligation on states to prosecute torture.[61] Yet, the addressees of these treaties are states and in international legal terms not directly binding on the ICC.[62] In the same vein, the obligation to prohibit and prevent crimes such as genocide does not extend to the ICC. Nonetheless, we need to remember that the ICC has been created to close the gap of impunity, when states abandon or are unable to fulfil their international obligation to prosecute and punish perpetrators of international crimes.

It would undermine a core purpose of the ICC if the Court did not ensure the prosecution and punishment of such crimes. Scharf comes to the conclusion that plea bargaining related to specific charges at international tribunals 'might violate the spirit, though not the letter, of the international duty to prosecute'.[63] Although there is no direct obligation for the ICC, the duty to prosecute has a binding effect in that it must not amount to de facto impunity by entering into excessive charge bargains that would, for example, omit a charge of genocide in favour of a very limited war crimes charge. 'Plea-bargaining that results in

[59] E Cimiotta, 'The Relevance of *Erga Omnes* Obligations in Prosecuting International Crimes' (2016) 76 *Zeitschrift für ausländisches öffentliches Recht und Völkerrecht* 687, 629.

[60] ibid. For the crime of genocide see also *Jorgic v Germany*, Judgment, Application No 74613/01, 12 July 2007, para 20.

[61] Scharf (n 1) 1075.

[62] ibid.

[63] ibid, 1070.

the dropping of charges has the effect of editing out the full factual basis upon which a conviction rests and thus has the potential to distort the historic record generated by the Tribunal'.[64] The scope for any charge bargains is therefore limited and delineating these depends on the specific charges in question.

IV. GUIDING AIMS FOR PLEA AGREEMENTS

The limitations outlined above lead directly towards those aims that should guide the Prosecutor in the decision-making process regarding whether to pursue a plea agreement. Whether this will be a practical challenge for the ICC remains to be seen. Although beyond the scope of prosecutorial discretion, which is the focal point of this book, such a principled exercise of discretion should also extend to the judicial level. Judges will have to exercise discretion when deciding on the acceptance of a plea agreement. Accused and the Defence are left with little guidance as to the criteria by which judges apply their exercise of discretion when deciding whether to follow any recommendations made.[65] I will return to this point later in this chapter.

The *Al Mahdi* case was clearly perceived as a success and served a variety of different interests: abbreviated procedures served the interests of the Court; Al Mahdi's cooperation and information for further investigations served the interests of the Prosecutor, communities in Mali and the broader public who have an interest in clarity on what happened in the conflict in Mali; a very moderate sentence was in the interests of the defendant; and lastly, the apology and a relatively quick reparations decision served the interests of victims. Additionally, the *Al Mahdi* conviction was critical in bringing the protection of cultural heritage firmly onto the public agenda. In conjunction with scholarly contributions that construct a principled approach to plea bargaining in international criminal justice,[66] this can provide some guidance as to how to approach the exercise of discretion.

Critical here though is that any plea agreement involves some form of trade-off.[67] Even within the legal limitations that ensure an environment able to produce fair procedures and freedom from coercion, and that refrains from significant charge bargaining, plea bargaining always operates within the tension of the prosecution making some form of compromise. Limited charges, or frankly the agreement on a story the OTP and the defence can live with, bears

[64] ibid, 1081.

[65] R Henham and M Drumbl, 'Plea Bargaining at the International Criminal Tribunal for the Former Yugoslavia' (2005) 16 *Criminal Law Forum* 49, 66 critiquing the lack of framework at the ICTY for when to disregard a Prosecutor's recommendations and equally, what circumstances should impact sentencing at the ICC in cases of guilty pleas (at 73).

[66] See Combs (n 10).

[67] I thank Lindsey Farmer for very insightful comments on this chapter and the point here in particular.

the danger of negatively impacting on uncovering the truth. But what is this truth? As I have explained at other points in this book, the trial truth can never fully provide an account of what happened. But it is important to bear in mind that truth finding must be a key aim for the Court. The Prosecutor is directly tasked to 'establish the truth'[68] in her investigations, a provision that binds the Prosecutor not only during investigations but also at the prosecution stage. The purpose of any investigation is ultimately to understand what happened, and, following on from that, through prosecution to provide an accurate account of events[69] and ensure equally accurate accountability.

The aim for accuracy in the account serves the establishment of a historical record and of assigning adequate responsibility to the defendant, hence, any plea agreement must aim to ensure that the task of uncovering the truth can still be achieved. International trials have communicative functions beyond those of domestic trials. As discussed in the previous chapter, international trial proceedings fulfil communicative functions aimed at a variety of different audiences. This brings me back to the importance of establishing that the truth accurately captures what has happened within the situation that is at the heart of trial proceedings.

A. Efficiency Gains?

From the institutional perspective, efficiency gains are one of the key aspects of plea bargaining. This is the key reason why plea bargaining, a legal transplant from common law systems,[70] has become a reality in civil law systems. It appears to be a convenient tool to ensure that a justice system under pressure is able to function. However, as shown before, the ICC as a system *sui generis* aims at ensuring that justice is done in cases in which gaps of impunity exist and that contribute to deterrence and prevention of mass atrocity crimes. It also has considerable symbolic and educational power. Efficiency gains should only be of importance for the ICC Prosecutor[71] if the same case (or plea agreement) in addition substantially contributes to the broader aims of the Court.

Securing cooperation and information are important considerations in this context. If an agreement can secure pathways for a strategy of building up further cases, this can be of utmost importance as it allows better insights into what happened and to hold those most responsible to account. However, any

[68] Art 54(1)(a) ICCSt.

[69] Duff et al (n 51) 178.

[70] M Langer, 'From Legal Transplants to Legal Translations: The Globalization of Plea Bargaining and the Americanization Thesis in Criminal Procedure' (2004) 45 *Harvard International Law Journal* 1.

[71] Henham and Drumbl (n 65) 56 remark in this context that the 'pragmatic goals of plea bargaining are at odds with the goals of punishment'.

agreement that rewards cooperative behaviour must not lose sight of the fact that punishment in the first instance must reflect the gravity of the crime and the individual level of responsibility.[72] Equally, pragmatic considerations, such as saving Court resources through abbreviated procedures, should only be of very limited guidance to the ICC.

Judge Schomburg ended his dissenting opinion with the words of a victim; these words might help to understand that pragmatic considerations cannot be the priority but rather the by-products of plea agreements that serve further purposes:

> I saw Miroslav Deronjić plead guilty on the television. The Bosnian Muslims in the community that I have spoken to, felt relieved because he admitted his guilt. This is a positive thing and can heal the wounds of the community provided that he is punished adequately. A mild punishment however would not serve any purpose; he does not deserve any compassion as he did not show any not only to people of Glogova but also to the other Muslim Bosnians of Bratunac and Srebrenica.[73]

The exercise of prosecutorial discretion in cases of plea bargains must deliver an exercise of anticipated sentencing considerations, based both on the full extent of the criminal conduct known and a sound evidentiary base. The victim's voice cited above demonstrates the danger of plea bargains. Henham and Drumbl's analysis fits aptly here in that the exercise of discretion in such processes must aim to avoid the charge that 'positive aspects of plea bargains – namely, the dissemination of some truth and accountability' are not 'overshadowed by corrosive contempt among victim communities'.[74] 'This should ensure that a realistic bargain is struck and, most importantly, that the result of the case is perceived as just. Otherwise plea bargains might impede, rather than foster, transitional justice in conflicted and post-conflict societies'.[75]

B. Towards Restorative Justice

Implementing restorative justice elements will be of key importance for plea agreement procedures at the ICC to contribute to respect for international justice. Combs even suggests that 'guilty pleas often possess greater potential to restore and reconcile than full-scale trials'.[76] Her work is based on the analysis of domestic and international plea bargaining procedures as well as existing restorative justice approaches. She identifies a number of key elements for plea bargaining procedures that entail and strengthen restorative justice that are informative here.

[72] ibid.
[73] Cited after Schomburg Dissenting Opinion (n 54) para 20.
[74] Henham and Drumbl (n 65) 85.
[75] ibid.
[76] Combs (n 10) 191.

A plea agreement with restorative components must entail an element of truth telling. However, as Combs puts it, it would be an account that seeks to 'obtain more and different kinds of information'[77] as it seeks not only to answer the Prosecutor's questions but also those of victims. Pressing questions might concern the whereabouts of the disappeared, finding their remains, or learning about their fate. Answers to such questions are often more important than the number of years the accused has to serve behind bars. The ICC does provide mechanisms to allow victims to raise their views and concerns, although with the numbers of participating victims at the ICC this might pose a challenge. Understanding which questions are important, thinking beyond the ordinary procedures of a criminal trial to allow such truth telling to take place would require some creativity. Accommodating a flow of information that allows communication and truth telling to take place would be an innovative feature, and prosecutorial discretion plays a critical role in making this happen.

Intertwined with and yet distinct from the function of truth telling is a clear and unequivocal show of remorse and apology.[78] 'Conventional' plea bargaining often contains an apology issued as part of the guilty plea. However, research into restorative justice mechanisms suggests that this 'may leave victims and community members uncertain about its "authenticity."'[79] Acknowledging distinctions between legal and moral responsibility[80] can aid an approach aimed at a guilty plea procedure that, at the same time, removes this uncertainty and provides an opportunity for the accused to show the genuineness of the apology. Providing answers to the best of the accused's knowledge can be a testament of moral responsibility.

A genuine apology is also a step towards reparations and restoration. The nature of the crimes before the ICC makes it impossible to literally repair the harm. Nevertheless, apologies can be an important form of symbolic reparations.[81] Recalling the Bosnian victim cited earlier, feelings of relief might allow (at least some) victims to move on and feel a process of healing. A plea agreement at the ICC additionally paves the way for the Court to issue a reparations decision, as a restorative justice element implemented in the Rome Statute, in a timely fashion. In the *Al Mahdi* case, the Court issued a reparations order 11 months after the conviction, again, at unprecedented speed. The TC had granted 139 applicants victim status for reparations purposes, awarding individual, symbolic and collective reparations, holding Al Mahdi liable for reparations

[77] ibid, 141.

[78] ibid, 199 highlights that studies in the domestic contexts have shown that an apology is a key element in efforts to advance reconciliation.

[79] RL Cohen, 'Restorative Justice' in C Sabbagh and M Schmitt (eds), *Handbook of Social Justice Theory and Research* (New York, Springer, 2016) 258.

[80] ibid.

[81] Combs (n 10) 144.

at US$2,700,000.[82] Additionally, the Trust Fund for Victims was asked to complement the reparations award and provide assistance for victims.[83] The *Al Mahdi* case therefore features considerable elements of a restorative approach to justice, perhaps a key ingredient in why the judgment was generally well received.

For the Prosecutor at the ICC, plea agreements can be an important tool to advance the interests of justice and fulfil the ICC's mission. Any such plea bargain, however, ought to be driven by the aim of implementing restorative justice elements, with institutional efficiency gains being a by-product but nothing more. This task demands creativity, openness to thinking beyond the traditional criminal trial procedures, and critical assessment on a case-by-case basis of what might best contribute to justice and peace in situations of (post-) conflict, and, last but not least, the ICC's legitimacy.

V. ACCOUNTABILITY

Any form of plea bargain requires judicial supervision to safeguard the rights of the accused, the interests of justice and those of victims. The most direct form to ensure that the Prosecutor cannot engage in any plea agreement running counter to the legal limitations or aims of international justice is the non-binding nature of the plea agreements. Hence, the TC has a critical role. Having said that, these judicial decisions, whether to accept a guilty plea, how much factual presentation to request, and what the appropriate sentence is, are acts of judicial discretion that are not always free from legal or factual mistakes. Additionally, judicial control through the trial is limited to the charges and facts presented before the Chamber. Because of these limitations, providing accountability for plea agreements is pivotal.

A. Waiving the Right to Appeal?

The Rome Statute provides that any trial judgment convicting and sentencing an accused may be subject to an appeal according to the conditions set out in article 81 of the Rome Statute. This affords an important layer of protection against procedural errors, errors of law or facts. Yet, the *Al Mahdi* plea agreement contained a notable feature – the mutual waiver of the right of appeal. The plea agreement sets out that Al Mahdi 'agrees that he will not appeal his conviction, and further agrees that he will not appeal any sentence imposed by the Trial Chamber within the range set forth at paragraph 19(a) below'.[84]

[82] *Prosecutor v Al Mahdi*, Reparations Order, ICC-01/12-01/15-236, 17August 2017.
[83] ibid.
[84] *Prosecutor v Al Mahdi*, Agreement regarding admission of guilt, ICC-01/12-01/15-78-Anx1-tENG-Red, 9 September 2016, para 13.

Equally, the Prosecutor committed not to appeal any sentence within the recommended range.[85] At the ICTY, the prosecution introduced the use of appeal waivers after the first defendants, who had pleaded guilty,[86] albeit not based on a plea agreement, had launched appeals.[87] At a later stage defendants at the ICTY became more reluctant to enter into plea agreements that included such a waiver. The prosecution subsequently dropped such clauses leading to the Appeals Chamber (AC) in consequence being 'well-occupied with appeals to sentences in guilty-plea cases'.[88] Is such a waiver of the right to appeal permissible, or even desirable just because it preserves efficiency gains? Or is the possibility of appeals one of those crucial checks and balances on the trial practices to safeguard the interests of justice?

An important function of the TC is assessing whether a more complete presentation of the case is required in the interests of justice and particularly the interests of victims. What the interests of justice might require, though, and how to address the interests of victims appropriately, are both aspects that allow broad scope for judicial discretion. And, as I have demonstrated repeatedly in this book, wherever discretionary decisions are made, whether by the Prosecutor or ICC judges, the danger of erroneous decision-making is real. In a worst case scenario, a culture of plea agreements at the ICC could evolve without providing any chance for the AC to assess if, and to what extent, this practice, the third avenue can be reconciled with the Rome Statute. Against the background of the drafting history, in which the drafters were divided on the possibility of plea agreements, this seems a worrying prospect. This could portend the introduction of an appeal waiver element as is often used in common law systems such as in the US. But exposing international criminal justice to bargaining procedures without the additional layer of protection through the AC seems at odds with the idea of a 'third avenue' that aims to bridge the gap between the pragmatic common law approach and the unease expressed by representatives from civil law countries during the drafting process.

Although the ICC is a system *sui generis*, a brief look at domestic systems might be informative at this point. Germany, with its continental civil law system, introduced the Plea Bargaining Act[89] to regulate an often criticised but widespread informal plea-bargaining practice. The informal practice included the expectation that prosecution and defence would waive their right to appeal. The Plea Bargaining Act clarified that a waiver of the right to appeal is not possible whenever a judgment includes a plea bargain.[90] The German Federal Constitutional Court, tasked with assessing whether the plea bargaining

[85] ibid, para 19b.
[86] See, eg, *Erdemović* Judgment (n 15).
[87] Combs (n 10) 86.
[88] ibid, 87.
[89] §257c Strafprozessordung.
[90] §302(1), second sentence Strafprozessordung.

mechanisms would appropriately safeguard the basic rights of the accused and the rule of law, found:

> [The aim of the Plea Bargaining Act was] not to introduce a new 'consensual class' of proceedings. Instead, the Plea Bargaining Act integrates the forms of plea bargaining it allows into the existing system of criminal procedure with the aim of ensuring that criminal proceedings continue to be committed to ascertaining the substantive truth and to arriving at a just punishment that is commensurate with the crime. The legislature expressly stated that plea bargains as such may never constitute the sole basis of a judgment, but that instead the courts continue to be bound by their duty to investigate *ex officio* … [the] legislature added specific safeguard mechanisms to its statutory framework, which guarantee that the steps leading to a plea bargain are completely transparent and that they are documented, thus enabling the exhaustive monitoring of the plea bargaining process by the public, the prosecution and the appellate courts.[91]

The features of the German system are similar to the ICC's approach. The trial procedure is not open to a contractual agreement of two parties; the non-binding nature of any such decision before the TC makes this abundantly clear. The two systems also share the aim of ascertaining the 'substantive truth', although a criminal trial will never fully reach this aim. The idea of international criminal trials contributing to the historical record of conflict and atrocity mirrors the search for substantive truth. Because of the need to safeguard such public interests, the judicial process cannot be subdued to a private contractual logic. This is a core argument that explains the need for judicial control and the non-binding nature of any 'discussions' between the OTP and defence before the ICC. Against this background, the emphasis on accountability, or, in the words of the Federal Constitutional Court, for 'exhaustive monitoring', inter alia through the appellate courts, gains importance. Effective accountability through appeals procedures, as envisaged by the drafters, should not be subject to the parties' discretion.

But why should it be possible for an accused to appeal a judgment and sentence that he or she had agreed to in the first instance? Would it not be a waste of important Court resources? At the core of this argument is, again, the rather contractual view of plea agreements. Beyond the argument made above about the need to safeguard public procedures, an additional point against this logic is that the two parties, the Prosecutor and the accused, are not parties on an equal footing. The fact that an accused has entered a plea agreement voluntarily, free from coercion and well informed, does not fully address the vulnerability and pressure that can arise through pre-trial detention and the prospect of years of trial proceedings. Another issue is the exceptional nature of any case before the ICC with the extraordinary public interest and potential political pressures from all sides. Additionally, it must be borne in mind that the ICC provides a role for victims as participants in the proceedings. Although

[91] German Federal Constitutional Court (BVerfG), Judgment of the Second Senate, 19 March 2013, 2 BvR 2628/10, para 65.

article 81 does not afford victim participants a separate right to launch an appeal, they would potentially have a chance to voice their views and concerns during any appeals proceedings. For all those reasons, the contractual or private law logic of the argument against the right to appeal seems unfit to serve the purposes of international criminal trials. In the emerging procedural system at the ICC, such a waiver should have no place.

B. Towards a Court-Wide Policy

Throughout this book, I have advocated an approach of radical transparency to the exercise of prosecutorial discretion. The OTP has taken the laudable path of developing detailed policies in key areas of its activities. Equally, a protocol or policy ought to be in place to structure the approach to plea bargaining.[92] It would provide a further element of transparency to the Court's approach and contribute to more structure in the exercise of discretion. A policy paper opens the space for debate and forces the OTP to reflect and deliberate on the general approach to plea agreements. A clear commitment to strengthening restorative justice functions, and transparency to allow monitoring through the public, should be essential parts of that. Having said that, and considering the unease during the drafting process, a policy determined by the OTP alone might not be sufficient in this context and might be open to considerable critique, opening up a divide between common and civil law countries.

To date, the OTP policy papers, touching on a number of different areas of prosecutorial discretion, have been drafted by the OTP alone, albeit with varying but considerable input from consultations with experts. Given how important an agreed approach between the judiciary and the OTP is, to ensure a consistent approach to the acceptance of plea agreements, I propose here to aim for a court-wide policy. A joint policy paper, agreed by all organs of the Court, might considerably strengthen the legitimacy of a policy. Because of the concerns regarding plea agreements in Rome, it would furthermore seem pertinent to strive for endorsement by the Assembly of States Parties. This could pave the way for a modern approach to plea agreements that demonstrates respect for the gravity of the crimes, the fairness of the proceedings, the credibility and not least legitimacy of the Court's proceedings.

VI. CONCLUDING REMARKS

The *Al Mahdi* case was a starting point in what could be an emerging practice of plea bargaining before the ICC. Constructing a third avenue to plea bargaining

[92] See with a call for such a policy and some policy ideas, A Whiting, 'Encouraging the Acceptance of Guilty Pleas at the ICC' (Blog post, 11 February 2015), available at: postconflictjustice.com.

requires a joint approach between the Prosecutor and the judiciary. This approach must clearly recognise the need to secure due process requirements, not only for the sake of safeguarding the rights of the accused but to ensure that a trial delivers accurate accountability. The Rome Statute does leave scope for discretion at the pre-trial stage before the charges are confirmed as to entering an agreement with the defendant on specific, limited charges. However, the public interest of the international community and of those communities affected by the crimes in question require that the Prosecutor refrains from excessive plea bargaining that would distort the account of events. Despite these limitations, plea agreements can create space for strengthened restorative justice elements in the Court's procedures. Elements that ensure information for victims, even if not in all circumstances reflected in the charges, can satisfy the need for truth although not fully secured through formalised trial proceedings. The OTP should refrain from simply adopting an approach directly transferred from other systems. Institutional efficiency gains can be a by-product of plea agreements but should not dominate prosecutorial considerations. Any future practice should therefore refrain from curtailing the right to appeal. Plea bargaining done well has considerable potential for the Prosecutor and the ICC.

6

The Interests of Justice

I. INTRODUCTION

THE ROME STATUTE provides scope for prosecutorial discretion in article 53(1) and (2) of the Statute in that the Prosecutor is authorised to choose not to initiate an investigation or prosecution based on the interests of justice.[1] In the early academic contributions on prosecutorial discretion at the International Criminal Court (ICC), the 'interests of justice' concept in article 53 of the Rome Statute was much discussed.[2] Indeed, the introduction of the concept into the Rome Statute was perceived as 'introducing prosecutorial discretion'[3] into the ICC system, although, as demonstrated throughout this book, the proceedings provide ample scope for discretion beyond the interests of justice. The concept has been largely irrelevant in the practice of the Court,

[1] Art 53 ICCSt:

'1. The Prosecutor shall ... initiate an investigation unless he or she determines that there is no reasonable basis ... the Prosecutor shall consider whether: ...

(c) Taking into account the gravity of the crime and the interests of victims, there are nonetheless substantial reasons to believe that an investigation would not serve the interests of justice.

If the Prosecutor determines that there is no reasonable basis to proceed and his or her determination is based solely on subparagraph (c) above, he or she shall inform the Pre-Trial Chamber.

2. If, upon investigation, the Prosecutor concludes that there is not a sufficient basis for a prosecution because: ...

(c) A prosecution is not in the interests of justice, taking into account all the circumstances, including the gravity of the crime, the interests of victims and the age or infirmity of the alleged perpetrator, and his or her role in the alleged crime; the Prosecutor shall inform the Pre-Trial Chamber and the State making a referral under article 14 or the Security Council in a case under article 13, paragraph (b), of his or her conclusion and the reasons for the conclusion'.

[2] See P Kirsch and D Robinson, 'Initiation of Proceedings by the Prosecutor' in A Cassese, P Gaeta and J Jones (eds), *The Rome Statute of the International Criminal Court: A Commentary, Vol I* (Oxford, Oxford University Press, 2002); D Robinson, 'Serving the Interests of Justice: Amnesties, Truth Commissions and the International Criminal Court' (2003) 14 *European Journal of International Law* 481; M Brubacher, 'Prosecutorial Discretion within the International Criminal Court' (2004) 2 *Journal of International Criminal Justice* 71.

[3] G Bitti, 'The Interests of Justice – where does that come from? Part II', 14 August 2019, available at: ejiltalk.org.

because the Prosecutor has not based any of her decisions on this provision. The prosecutorial strategies and policies are built on the assumption that a decision not to proceed in the interests of justice is exceptional; for the Office of the Prosecutor (OTP), there is a 'presumption in favour of investigation or prosecution wherever the criteria established in article 53(1)(a) and (b) or article 53(2)(a) and (b) have been met'.[4] The debate on the interests of justice was reignited when Pre-Trial Chamber (PTC) II refused the authorisation of an investigation into the situation in Afghanistan.[5] The commencement of an investigation had been long awaited, and to many the PTC refusal to provide the authorisation, based on the interests of justice, was a bombshell.

Against this background, the following chapter will reassess the role that the interests of justice can have for the scope of prosecutorial discretion. It provides a novel interpretation of the concept, in the context of the Statute, potentially providing the Prosecutor with greater flexibility in taking temporary procedural measures to react and adjust to still evolving situations. The use of the interests of justice triggers two dimensions of discretion: (1) the indeterminacy of the concept requires the use of interpretative discretion to determine the constituting elements of the interests of justice in the cases and situations; and (2) the procedural discretionary dimension provides flexibility for the Prosecutor in the decision-making process regarding whether to investigate a situation or prosecute specific cases. A key argument advanced in this chapter is that the interpretative discretionary dimension does not provide any space for managerial issues, such as the prospect of a difficult investigation, political considerations or budget pressure. The Prosecutor should be guided by peace and human rights considerations in the use of the interests of justice. Furthermore, I suggest that the concept allows flexibility to adjust the notion to the justice conceptions of local communities affected by conflict. Such flexibility provides space for legal pluralism in international criminal law and allows the use of prosecutorial discretion to turn the ICC into a more responsive institution.

The chapter proceeds as follows. It outlines the legal framework and current OTP policy position. It will address developments in Sudan and Uganda to illustrate how the Prosecutor could have used the interests of justice in the specific scenarios and analyse the Afghanistan decision. Examining the limitations of the concept, I will show that the interests of justice were not made for the purpose of providing a viable selection or management tool for the Prosecutor. Resource constraints, political pressures or other managerial considerations are beyond the concept's limits. Yet, I will demonstrate how the interests of justice can actually provide more flexible decision-making processes through measures such as a withdrawal of charges based on the concept. In the subsequent section, the

[4] ICC/OTP, Policy Paper on the Interests of Justice, September 2007, 1.

[5] *Situation in the Islamic Republic of Afghanistan*, Decision pursuant to Article 15 of the Rome Statute on the Authorisation of an Investigation into the Situation in the Islamic Republic of Afghanistan, ICC-02/17, 12 April 2019.

chapter argues for a principled understanding and use of the interests of justice in such a way that it dissolves the dichotomic relationship between peace and justice. The interests of justice should be guided by a sense of local ownership over justice processes, the need to acknowledge that human rights and peace are part of a balancing exercise in the understanding of justice, without giving up on the idea of holding those to account that have committed crimes. Addressing accountability, I argue that the flexible use of the interests of justice with measures short of the full deferral of an investigation should be based on formal decisions that allow judicial review. Additionally, I suggest in this chapter that the Prosecutor provide reasons for all those decisions in which the OTP does not use the concept despite relevant stakeholders arguing for it. Lastly, this chapter opposes the suggestion made in the literature to introduce a higher degree of accountability through specific guidelines. Instead, this chapter opts for a middle ground and advocates a revised policy that sets out some key principles, committing to a transparent use of the interests of justice responsive to the local communities affected by international crimes.

II. THE LEGAL FRAMEWORK, POLICY AND PRACTICE

Article 53 of the Rome Statute is at the heart of the OTP's work and provides the legal framework for the interests of justice. It is a provision that no other international court has featured before and provides ample challenges in its use. In what follows, I will outline the structure of article 53 before discussing the current prosecutorial policy as well as the practice of using the interests of justice to date.

A. The Structure of Article 53

At the stage of deciding whether to initiate an investigation based on the results of the preliminary examination, the Prosecutor determines whether there is a 'reasonable basis' to proceed and, for that, considers the jurisdiction of the Court and admissibility issues. If those criteria are met, article 53(1)(c) of the Statute implements an additional threshold not to initiate an investigation as this requires 'nonetheless substantial reasons to believe that an investigation would not serve the interests of justice'. However, the provision does not offer any definition of the interests of justice. It only identifies two potential factors for consideration: the gravity of the crime and the interests of victims. If the Prosecutor determines not to proceed based on the interests of justice, article 53(1) of the Statute obliges her to inform the PTC.

Article 53(2) of the Statute refers to the prosecution of specific cases on investigation. To a large extent, it mirrors the requirements of article 53(1) of the Statute. Again, the Prosecutor ought to evaluate jurisdictional issues, the admissibility of the case, and can decide not to prosecute based on the interests of justice. In addition to the gravity of the crime and the interests of victims, at this point the Prosecutor has to consider all the circumstances of the case including the personal circumstances of the alleged perpetrator, such as age and infirmity, and his or her role in the alleged crime. Also, in paragraph 2, the Prosecutor is not only obliged to inform the PTC about the determination but also to provide reasons for the conclusion and – if the jurisdiction of the Court has been triggered by a referral – to inform the State Party or the Security Council (SC) respectively. This obligation on the part of the Prosecutor is more complex than at the start of an investigation, when no specific deliberation is required. However, whether it is a decision not to investigate or not to prosecute, the extent of judicial review is in any case based on article 53(3) of the Statute.

Article 53(3)(b) of the Statute provides the PTC with the discretionary power to review any decision of the Prosecutor not to investigate a situation or prosecute a case, based on article 53(1) and (2) of the Statute that is solely based on the interests of justice. If the PTC does so, this has a direct effect on the competence of the Prosecutor: the decision of the Prosecutor is only effective if confirmed by the PTC. Beyond article 53, PTC II has found in its Afghanistan decision that the authorisation proceedings in article 15(4) of the Statute would entail a review and use of the interests of justice, even if the Prosecutor did not make any submission on the interests of justice.[6] As discussed extensively in chapter three of this book, this interpretation of article 15(4) in its interplay with article 53(1) of the Statute is disputed. The higher degree of accountability provided through the possibility of full judicial supervision on the PTC's own motion indicates the exceptional status of the 'interests of justice' in article 53 of the Statute.

B. The Policy and Practice

The OTP has never decided not to investigate or prosecute based on the interests of justice. The Office has a policy in place that rests on the presumption in favour of investigation and prosecution.[7] Accordingly, the majority of PTC decisions considered the interests of justice to be a countervailing circumstance that required no further consideration whenever jurisdictional and admissibility criteria were met and the Prosecutor sought to proceed with an investigation.[8]

[6] ibid, para 35.

[7] Policy Paper Interests of Justice (n 4) 1, 5.

[8] *Situation in the Republic of Kenya*, Decision pursuant to Article 15 of the Rome Statute on the Authorisation of an Investigation into the Situation in the Republic of Kenya, ICC-01/09-19, 31 March 2010, para 63. Similar, albeit with a brief reference to victims' interests as an indicator: *Situation in Côte d'Ivoire*, Decision pursuant to Article 15 of the Rome Statute on the Authorisation of an Investigation into the Situation in the Republic of Côte d'Ivoire, ICC-02/11-14, 3 October 2011, paras 207–08; *Situation in Georgia*, Decision on the Prosecutor's Request for Authorization of an Investigation, ICC-01/15-12, 27 January 2016, para 58.

Thus, the aforementioned PTC decision not to authorise an investigation in Afghanistan,[9] based on the interests of justice, marks a drastic change in the Court's practice.

The PTC decision came after an 11-year-long preliminary examination into the conflict. The Prosecutor sought authorisation for an investigation into war crimes and crimes against humanity allegedly committed by a variety of actors, among them the Taliban, the Afghan Forces and most critically US (CIA) personnel. The PTC refused the necessary authorisation for *propio motu* investigations reasoning that although jurisdiction and admissibility criteria were met, an investigation would not be in the 'interests of justice'. Key considerations included problems in securing evidence, the volatility of the political landscape and an expected lack of meaningful state cooperation, the risk of frustrating victims and creating the potential for hostility towards the Court.[10] This is a contentious and, as will be demonstrated in the subsequent discussion, indeed flawed interpretation of the interests of justice.

Apart from the Afghanistan decision, the 2007 Policy Paper on the Interests of Justice is the key point of reference for the OTP policy approach. The exceptional nature of a decision not to investigate or prosecute based on the interests of justice is one key characteristic. The policy further suggests rather vaguely that the OTP will be guided in the determination of the interests of justice by the prevention of crimes through ending impunity, and that the interests of justice are a distinct concept to the interests of peace, with the latter being within the competence of other international institutions.[11] Additionally, the Prosecutor acknowledges that the role of transitional or other justice mechanisms are elements to consider within the interests of justice.[12] This would include truth seeking and reparations programmes, institutional reform and traditional justice mechanisms in the pursuit of a broader justice.[13] These points provide some guidance as to the elements that the OTP considers as part of the concept. Yet, these policy features contain some contradictions to other practices of the OTP.

i. The Presumption in Favour of Investigation and Prosecution

The presumption in favour of investigation,[14] whenever the jurisdictional and admissibility criteria have been met, corresponds with the OTP's practice in as far as all decisions not to investigate specific situations have so far been made

[9] *Afghanistan* Decision (n 5).
[10] ibid.
[11] ibid, 1.
[12] ibid, 7.
[13] ibid, 8.
[14] ibid, 1, 5.

based on the lack of jurisdiction or non-admissibility.[15] Some of the preliminary examinations leading up to the potential start of an investigation have been or are extremely long. The Afghanistan situation is a good example; the preliminary examination in Colombia is another such example having been started in June 2004. Such a delayed decision about the start of an investigation resembles a negative decision, because, in those years in which the situation was potentially within the jurisdictional reach of the ICC and would have met the admissibility criteria, the necessary investigation was warranted but not conducted. I have argued elsewhere for a policy change towards more confined time frames for preliminary examinations.[16] A practice of delay is not consistent with the announced presumption in favour of investigation. If the interests of justice only provide a possibility not to investigate in exceptional circumstances, what are the legal foundations for the factual non-investigation of situations that have undergone preliminary examination for a prolonged time period? This incoherence and the lack of open debate about the necessary prioritisation and selection is a critical point that requires resolution.

Equally incoherent is the theoretical presumption in favour of prosecution, in contrast to the practice of selecting and prioritising cases. Only a handful of cases are selected for prosecution from within large-scale situations of violence. The 2016 Policy Paper on Case Selection confirmed that such a selection process takes places and that not all potentially admissible cases would always be prosecuted.[17] Similarly, the OTP announced in the context of the Colombian preliminary examination that, as a matter of policy and prosecutorial discretion, the ICC would normally only prosecute 'persons at the highest echelons of authority, who are alleged to have directed, financed, or otherwise organized Rome Statute crimes'.[18] These policies were designed to allow the Office to manage its resources and provide transparency in this process.[19] In light of this selection process, which is undoubtedly necessary given the limited resources of the Office, the policy presumption in favour of prosecution rings hollow. Therefore, the 2007 Policy Paper on the Interests of Justice requires adjustment to achieve greater coherence with the more recent policy statements.

[15] *Situation in the Republic of Korea*, Article 5 Report, June 2014; *Situation in Honduras*, Article 5 Report, October 2015; Letter to Senders of Communcations Related to Venezuela, 9 February 2006.

[16] See A Pues, 'Towards the "Golden Hour"? A Critical Exploration of the Length of Preliminary Examinations' (2017) 15 *Journal of International Criminal Justice* 435.

[17] ICC/OTP, Policy Paper on Case Selection and Prioritisation, 15 September 2016, para 35 stating that this policy facilitates 'how to prioritise amongst those cases if the demands placed upon the Office exceeds the Office's resources'.

[18] J Stewart, Public Lecture, 'Transitional Justice in Colombia and the Role of the International Criminal Court', Bogota, 13 May 2015, 14, available at: www.icc-cpi.int.

[19] ICC/OTP, Strategic Plan 2016–2018, 6 July 2015, para 38.

ii. Justice Versus Peace Considerations

The interests of justice seem redundant in the prosecutorial practice to date. The reason lies in the exercise of prosecutorial discretion beyond the interests of justice. But the redundancy is not only caused through the way the OTP prioritises and selects investigations and cases. A further contributing factor is the Prosecutor's refusal to include peace within the interests of justice.[20] The OTP policy is very narrow in its view: while justice considerations were a matter for the OTP, the Rome Statute recognises the role for the SC to maintain peace and security issues through the possibility of deferring investigation or prosecution based on article 16 of the Statute.[21] The Office recognises that there might be some overlap through issues such as crime prevention, security and the OTP's duty to protect victims and witnesses. Although, it notes that 'the broader matter of international peace and security is not the responsibility of the Prosecutor; it falls within the mandate of other institutions'.[22]

Sudan is one example where the Prosecutor has not used the concept of the interests of justice. Sudanese 'Citizens Organisations' requested the ICC not to issue arrest warrants for the sake of furthering peacebuilding efforts.[23] These organisations argued that issuing arrest warrants would have considerable implications for the peacebuilding process, contributing to negative perceptions of the Court, and could thus lead to a deterioration in the security situation in Sudan. Alternative means of transitional justice were being pursued and so there was no need for the ICC to become involved at this stage.[24] While the Prosecutor did not substantively respond to the request, the PTC dismissed the application arguing that it lacked any review power in circumstances where the Prosecutor opted not to use the interests of justice.[25] At this point, it is interesting to note that the Prosecutor initially indicated that he would monitor efforts that were being made to achieve peace. The Prosecutor reported to the SC:

> In addition to the issue of admissibility, I am also required by the Rome Statute to consider whether a prosecution is not in the interest of justice. In considering that factor, I will follow the various national and international efforts to achieve peace and security, as well as the views of witnesses and victims of the crimes.[26]

This 2005 report indicates that the Prosecutor at that point considered efforts to achieve peace in Sudan as relevant for the possible application of the interests

[20] Policy Paper Interests of Justice (n 4) 8–9.
[21] ibid.
[22] ibid, 9.
[23] *Situation in Darfur/Sudan*, Decision on the Application for Leave to Appeal the Decision on Application under Rule 103, PTC I, ICC-02/05-192, 19 February 2009.
[24] ibid, 3.
[25] *Situation in Darfur/Sudan*, Decision on Application under Rule 103, PTC I, ICC-02/05-185, 4 February 2009.
[26] Second report of the Prosecutor to the Security Council pursuant to UN SC Res 1593(2005), 13 December 2005, S/PV.5321, 3.

of justice. The later policy paper, however, contradicts this approach with its stated position that peace and security were not within the responsibility of the Prosecutor.

The interests of justice and its application in potential peacebuilding efforts also became relevant in the early years of ICC activities in Uganda. The Prosecutor had to consider his activities in the light of the possibility that the Lord's Resistance Army (LRA) might join peace negotiations,[27] if the threat of ICC prosecutions was removed.[28] At this early time of ICC activities in 2004 and 2005, Luis Moreno-Ocampo refused to end investigations in the interests of justice but responded to the possibilities of a peace process by only conducting 'low-key' investigations in order not to interfere with any political developments towards a peace process.[29] According to Moreno-Ocampo, he based his exercise of discretion on the interests of victims because it is a key consideration in article 53(1)(c) of the Statute.[30] While some elements of the interests of justice therefore influenced the Prosecutor's exercise of discretion through the delay of decisions, he did not use the full extent of his power under article 53(1)(c) of the Statute. The long-term impact of ICC intervention in Uganda, and the question of how the interests of justice could best be served, are yet to be determined.[31]

The first trial against a member of the LRA did not commence until December 2016.[32] Earlier that year, ICC Prosecutor Bensouda publicly conveyed a message to LRA fighters suggesting that they would not face any proceedings at the ICC for crimes they might have been involved in.[33]

> [M]any within the ranks of the LRA are still being misled by Joseph Kony and other senior LRA commanders that you will … be imprisoned like Dominic Ongwen, … if you surrender and try to return home. As it concerns judicial proceedings, only the cases of Joseph Kony or Dominic Ongwen are before the ICC. No other LRA member is subject to ICC proceedings. We have seen encouraging trends: many LRA fighters are returning home and reintegrating into their communities. I urge those still

[27] L Moreno-Ocampo, 'Keynote Address: Integrating the Work of the ICC into Local Justice Initiatives' (2005) 21 *American University International Law Review* 497.

[28] See K Hanlon, 'Peace or Justice: Now That Peace is Being Negotiated in Uganda, Will the ICC Still Pursue Justice?' (2007) 14 *Tulsa Journal of Comparative & International Law* 295.

[29] Moreno-Ocampo (n 27) 497.

[30] ibid.

[31] LM Keller, 'Achieving Peace with Justice: The International Criminal Court and Alternative Ugandan Mechanisms' (2008) 23 *Conneticut Journal of International Law* 209, 251 tentatively suggests that the Prosecutor might have been right not to decline prosecution in the interests of justice. She argues that a determination that the prosecution would be prohibitively harmful would require speculation, especially considering the shortcomings of the Ugandan judicial system, and would probably even undermine deterrence.

[32] *Prosecutor v Dominic Ongwen*, ICC-02/04-01/15.

[33] ICC/OTP Press Release, 'Message from the Prosecutor of the International Criminal Court, Fatou Bensouda, calling for defection by LRA fighters', 1 April 2016, available at: www.icc-cpi.int/Pages/item.aspx?name=160401-otp-stat.

> in the bush to also seize any opportunity to stop fighting and return home, where you have a chance to rebuild your lives ... Dominic Ongwen was arrested and is now being tried at the ICC because he was one of the five top commanders.[34]

This declaration implies that no LRA cases other than that of Ongwen and Kony will be selected for prosecution. Clearly, Bensouda's message was designed to encourage soldiers to defect from the LRA. It can only be explained through a motivation to further the return of soldiers to their communities and hence strengthen the peace process, rather than achieving justice in the form of providing accountability for international crimes at the ICC level. How the Prosecutor can convey such a message, which would entail a discretionary decision that no other cases will be brought, in the light of the policy that peace is distinct to the interests of justice, and in the light of the extent of the atrocities underlying the situation in Uganda, remains a riddle.

According to the OTP, '[t]he best guidance on [its] approach to [the interests of justice] can be gathered from the way it has dealt with real situations'.[35] But, as the examples above illustrate, the current practice lacks coherence. The same applies to the role of transitional justice mechanisms. As outlined above, the Prosecutor has endorsed the role for different justice and truth-finding mechanisms in the interests of justice as policy.[36] Yet, in Colombia, the OTP[37] insisted on judicial accountability for all perpetrators of international crimes and only granted leeway for domestic governments with regard to the sanctions system.[38] This stance was perceived as rather uncompromising, considering the lengthy struggle within the country to end a 50-year-old war in Colombia.[39] Later in the process, the OTP explained that it was crucial that 'national laws ... produce investigations, prosecutions and sanctions that support the overarching goal of the Rome Statute system of international criminal justice – to end impunity for mass atrocity crimes'.[40] None of this, though, was reflected in the message to

[34] ibid.

[35] Policy Paper Interests of Justice (n 4) 9.

[36] ibid, 8.

[37] See Stewart (n 18).

[38] NC Sanchez Leon, 'Could the Colombian Peace Accord Trigger an ICC Investigaton on Colombia?' [2016] *AJIL Unbound* 172, 175.

[39] See R Uprimny and NC Sanchez, 'The ICC and Negotiated Peace: Reflections from Columbia', available at: www.opendemocracy.net, 11 February 2015, who wrote shortly before Stewart's lecture: 'The ICC should have more flexibility and prudence when it evaluates whether to open a case in a country that is negotiating a peace agreement. It must take into consideration the various forms of transitional justice adopted during peace processes, often after incredibly difficult and complex negotiations. Thus, in principle, peace processes that rule out general and unconditional amnesties should be respected, even if the provision for justice does not meet a strict interpretation of the duty to prosecute ... For this reason, we consider that in such cases it is unlawful for the ICC Prosecutor to open investigations and threaten the stability of the peace process. Such an intervention would violate article 53 of the Rome Statute, which indicates that the Prosecutor should not open investigations when there are "substantial reasons to believe that an investigation would not serve the interests of justice"'.

[40] Stewart (n 18) 10.

Ugandan LRA fighters. Instead, Bensouda's words appear to send a message that accepts a degree of impunity for the crimes allegedly committed by LRA fighters in exchange for them abandoning the organisation. These examples evidence the dilemma for when and to what extent 'criminal justice may be compromised for the sake of peace'.[41]

III. THE LIMITS OF DISCRETION IN THE INTERESTS OF JUSTICE

The lack of coherence in ICC practice is perhaps not surprising given that the interests of justice are not defined in the Rome Statute. The OTP was left with no guidance when it commenced its task of making a court work on the basis of a legal framework riddled with ambiguities. Similar to the gravity notion, the interests of justice represent an indeterminate, or, as I prefer to think of it, an open legal concept lacking definition in the Rome Statute. Thus, the exercise of discretion in the use of the interests of justice entails two intertwined dimensions. First, the interests of justice require the Prosecutor to exercise a degree of interpretative discretion to identify and weigh the elements that should be taken into consideration when filling the interests of justice. Second, it has a procedural dimension in that it produces a procedural consequence. Dissecting these processes can better aid us in understanding what the interests of justice are and how to make them work effectively and consistently.

Article 53 of the Statute provides some cornerstones for the interpretation of the concept: the interests of victims, the gravity of the crimes, and, at the prosecution level, also the age or infirmity of the alleged perpetrator or his role in the crime. But this list of factors is not exhaustive. The drafters opted for 'intentional ambiguity' of the concept to allow for broad interpretation.[42] This ambiguity facilitated agreement on what became the Rome Statute after the negotiating parties had encountered massive difficulties in finding a common denominator on issues such as the acceptability of transitional justice mechanisms.[43] For the understanding of interpretative spaces provided through such open concepts, the relevant point is that the drafters gave the Prosecutor, and the Court more generally, a flexible concept that allows a case-by-case approach adjustable to every specific situation.[44]

[41] A Greenawalt, 'Complementarity in Crisis: Uganda, Alternative Justice, and the International Criminal Court' (2009) 50 *Virginia Journal of International Law* 108.

[42] M Scharf, 'The Amnesty Exception to the Jurisdiction of the International Criminal Court' (1999) 32 *Cornell International Law Journal* 507, 522.

[43] Robinson (n 2) 483.

[44] See Greenawalt, 'Complementarity in Crisis' (n 41) 139; M Bergsmo and P Kruger, 'Article 53' in O Triffterer (ed), *Commentary on the Rome Statute of the International Criminal Court*, 2nd edn (Munich, Beck, 2008) 1073, para 29.

A. Understanding the Interpretative Dimension of Discretion

The components mentioned in article 53(1)(c) and (2)(c) of the Statute are only examples of an open-ended[45] list of factors to be considered for the determination of the interests of justice.[46] This is indicated in the wording of article 53 with phrases such as 'nonetheless ... reasons to believe' in paragraph 1 and 'taking into account all the circumstances, including' in paragraph 2. But, even the explicitly mentioned factors pose difficulties in that neither the interests of victims nor the gravity of the crime are clear-cut. This allows the Prosecutor to exercise interpretative discretion. In the first instance, it is down to her judgement to decide how to understand these criteria, which other criteria to take into account, and what weight to attach to them.

A parallel can be drawn to the process of interpreting the gravity notion in article 17(1)(d) of the Statute when deciding whether to initiate or authorise an investigation. The Appeals Chamber (AC) describes the process of using the gravity notion, albeit in the context of delineating the OTP and PTC competences, as follows:

> [T]he assessment of gravity involves ... the evaluation of numerous factors and information ..., which the Prosecutor has to balance in reaching her decision. In this regard, the Appeals Chamber, by majority, ... considers that the Prosecutor enjoys a *margin of appreciation*, which the pre-trial chamber has to respect when reviewing the Prosecutor's decision. Accordingly, the Appeals Chamber, by majority, finds that it is not the role of the pre-trial chamber to direct the Prosecutor as to what result she should reach in the gravity assessment or what weight she should assign to the individual factors.[47]

The considerations regarding the review powers are similarly instructive for the discussion of review mechanisms subsequently in this chapter; although, the scope of judicial review differs regarding gravity and the interests of justice. Critical here is the outline of the discretionary process at work.

Open concepts such as the interests of justice or gravity cannot be determined to 'exacting legal requirements'.[48] Hence, the traditional means of treaty

[45] LM Keller, 'Comparing the "Interests of Justice": What the International Criminal Court Can Learn from New York Law' (2013) 12 *Washington University Global Studies Law Review* 1, 5; Greenawalt, 'Complementarity in Crisis' (n 41) 133.

[46] *Sudan* Decision (n 25) para 17. See also J Goldston, 'More Candour about Criteria: The Exercise of Discretion by the Prosecutor of the International Criminal Court' (2010) 8 *Journal of International Criminal Justice* 383 observes that article 53 is 'even more open-ended' than the complementarity provisons.

[47] *Situation on the Registered Vessels of the Union of Comoros, the Hellenic Republic and the Kingdom of Cambodia*, Judgment on the appeal of the Prosecutor against Pre-Trial Chamber I's Decision on the Application for Judicial Review by the Government of the Union of the Comoros, ICC-01/13-98, 2 September 2019, para 81 (emphasis added).

[48] *Situation on the Registered Vessels of the Union of Comoros, the Hellenic Republic and the Kingdom of Cambodia*, Decision on the request of the Union of the Comoros to review the Prosecutor's decision not to initiate an investigation, PTC I, ICC-01/13-34, 16 July 2015, para 14.

interpretation do not effectively aid in the interpretation and determination of the elements of the interests of justice.[49] The wording of the provision does not facilitate a better understanding of what type of justice the drafters envisaged. Indeed, the wording was deliberately chosen to be ambiguous. Regarding the purpose and objectives of the Rome Statute as another means of treaty interpretation, ending impunity and crime prevention are the two explicit aims spelled out in its Preamble. These broad objectives, however, do not aid a better understanding of when investigation or prosecution are not in the interests of justice. Additionally, the drafting history only informs the discussion to the extent that the interests of justice were deliberately ambiguous. References to early discussion papers, such as that proposed by the United Kingdom,[50] merely confirm that some states intended the notion to contain wide discretion on the part of the Prosecutor, whereas other states were completely opposed to the concept of interests of justice.[51] All this confirms that no one unique interpretation will allow a successful application of the concept, but that each situation and case provides scope for interpretative discretion.

B. Beyond Bounds: Management and Political Considerations

When interpretative discretion is at work, the consistency of the law becomes a key concern. As I have argued in some of my previous work regarding gravity it matters that the Prosecutor aims to provide a consistent application of the gravity concept in order to ensure that the admissibility threshold is set consistently.[52] Only if all situations have the same chance of getting over that threshold, can the principle of equality before the law be secured. But how can equality before the law be ensured when a concept as open as the interests of justice is at play? For the gravity notion, I have argued that resource or management concerns must not influence the Prosecutor when exercising interpretative discretion.[53] Management considerations are all those pragmatic considerations that influence procedural decision-making and concern questions such as the availability of evidence, the resources available overall and for a specific

[49] N Jain, 'Interpretive Divergence' (2017) 57 *Virginia Journal of International Law* 45, 89–92 uses the difficutlies in the interpretation of the interests of justice as one example to underline her call for a 'revolution' in the interpretation of modern, multilateral treaties.

[50] 'UK Discussion Paper International Criminal Court Complementarity' (1996) para 30, available at: www.iccnow.org: 'The reference to "in the interests of justice" is intended to reflect a wide discretion on the part of the prosecutor to decide not to investigate comparable to that in (some) domestic systems, eg if the suspected offender was very old or very ill or if, otherwise, there were good reasons to conclude that a prosecution would be counterproductive'.

[51] See Bitti 'The Interests of Justice – where does that come from? Part II' (n 3).

[52] A Pues, 'Discretion and the Gravity of Situations at the International Criminal Court' (2017) 17 *International Criminal Law Review* 960.

[53] ibid, 984.

investigation, or also political pressures that could have an impact on compliance and cooperation. But is this also applicable for the process of filling the interests of justice with meaning in a given case or situation?

In the PTC decision regarding Afghanistan, managerial considerations are very much to the fore. The PTC bases its reasoning on 'predictably inconclusive investigations' that 'would necessarily infringe on fundamental individual rights without serving either the interests of justice or any of the universal values underlying the Statute'.[54] The latter part of this finding is wholly based on the assumption that investigations would, in any of the cases, be inconclusive and evidence less readily available. If so, no reasonable basis would exist to allow a prosecution to proceed and not infringe on the rights of any accused as fundamental individual rights. If an investigation, however, will necessarily be inconclusive is based on a purely theoretical exercise that attempts to anticipate the course of events. Feasibility is a criterion unfit for the interests of justice because it is difficult to predict as political circumstances can change, or evidence might appear unexpectedly. Additionally, evidential difficulties are inherent in criminal investigations, particularly so in international criminal law, which deals with large-scale violence and perpetrators far removed from the scene. But going back to criminal legal considerations: is the 'perfect murder' not worth investigating only because the perpetrator has left no trace? Is an inquiry into historical wrongs such as child abuse not in the interests of justice because most evidence has vanished? Scarce evidence underscores the need to investigate and find evidence to ensure that victims' rights to truth and justice can be served and to understand what happened.

Another consideration for the PTC was that the political landscape in Afghanistan and key states 'coupled with the complexity and volatility of the political climate still surrounding the Afghan scenario, make it extremely difficult to gauge the prospects of securing meaningful cooperation from relevant authorities'.[55] Such political assessments are ultimately part of managerial considerations; they aim to manage the institution's, or, court's performance, steering it through the rough waters of international politics. Bosco has outlined in his work how the Prosecutor has done so during the first decade of its operations.[56] This is part of the Prosecutor's task; yet, it is part of the role as a manager not as a law interpreter. Exercising interpretative discretion to fill the ambiguities in the Rome Statute has to be free from political power play.

The drafting history provides some important insights into delineating the boundaries of the concept of the interests of justice. Bitti recalls that 'the developments in the negotiations regarding the interests of justice were spurred on

[54] *Afghanistan* Decision (n 5) para 34.

[55] ibid, para 94.

[56] D Bosco, *Rough Justice: The International Criminal Court in a World of Power Politics* (New York, Oxford University Press USA, 2014).

by a fear of unequal treatment of States before the Court'.[57] He summarises the fear of some of the delegations in Rome as follows:

> ([P]owerful) States may push the Prosecutor, by threatening for example not to cooperate with the Court, to use the 'interests of justice' criterion in order not to start an investigation or a prosecution for the purposes of protecting their own nationals. Other (less powerful) States may not be in a position to push the Prosecutor to use the 'interests of justice' to their advantage in a similar way.[58]

The PTC position would allow precisely such political dynamics in through the back door. This understanding fundamentally undermines the compromise found in Rome that entailed an understanding of the interests of justice facilitating some discretion in exceptional circumstances. The drafters of the Rome Statute have made it clear that they wanted to create a court that could strike at the heart of states and hold the powerful to account. Article 27, with the exclusion of head of state immunity before the ICC and the inclusion of the crime of aggression, which is a state leadership crime, in the jurisdiction of the Court evidence this. It is only with a robust court system, without mechanisms that could encourage pressure on the Court and non-cooperation, that the Court will be able to deliver on its mission.

A pragmatic scholarly view is that the Court's viability is in the interests of justice.[59] Some circumstances, such as too many investigations or losing a major donor to the Court, might have the capacity to damage its ability to fulfil its mission to close the impunity gap.[60] These are ultimately managerial considerations similar to those that the PTC made. Such a position would risk damaging the ICC's impartiality, allowing exceptions in the pursuit of justice influenced by pecuniary considerations and would do longer-lasting damage. If the Prosecutor were to decide not to open the preliminary examination into Palestine, because any cases against Israeli forces would risk the financial support of the Court by some influential Western states, this would most certainly further delegitimise the Court in the perception of many in the developing world. It has also been argued that considering the likely length and financial expense of a trial and given the limited resources of the ICC, declining to pursue charges in particularly complex cases might allow the Court to consider more cases.[61] At the international level particularly, the complexity of the trial is often increased by the seniority of the position of the accused and the gravity of the crime.

[57] G Bitti, 'The Interests of Justice – where does that come from? Part I', 13 August 2019, available at: ejiltalk.org.

[58] ibid.

[59] C Davis, 'Political Considerations in Prosecutorial Discretion at the International Criminal Court' (2015) 15 *International Criminal Law Review* 170, 178; P Webb, 'The ICC Prosecutor's Discretion Not to Proceed in the "Interests of Justice"' (2005) 50 *Criminal Law Quarterly* 305, 346.

[60] C Davis (n 59) 180.

[61] A Marston Danner, 'Enhancing the Legitimacy and Accountability of Prosecutorial Discretion at the International Criminal Court' (2003) 97 *American Journal of International Law* 510, 545.

Therefore, such a consideration would potentially contradict the express will of the drafters that the gravity of the crime potentially weighs within the interests of justice as a consideration in favour of investigation and prosecution.

Having said all that, I have acknowledged throughout the book that prioritisation and selection of investigations and prosecutions is inevitable and a constant feature in the work of the OTP. So, why not interpret the interests of justice broadly and allow managerial concerns to be part of the concept? This would provide greater control through the PTCs as the interests of justice are counterbalanced by the review structure in article 53(3)(b) of the Statute. Yet, my contextual analysis throughout this book has shown that the Rome Statute provides ample scope for prosecutorial discretion. If one were to locate the only selection mechanism in the interests of justice, this would require that all selection and prioritisation – as the latter always contain an element of selection – processes were subject to judicial review. This is not a feasible proposal and, as a contextual argument, would undermine the independent status of the Prosecutor.[62] The other reason is a more principled argument: because ICC decisions have a very pronounced expressive power, it would damage the respect for international justice, if the ICC decided on a regular basis that the investigation of crimes against humanity, of war crimes, of genocide, and perhaps even of aggression would not be in the interests of justice. This would send a signal of acceptance of impunity and would ultimately undermine the respect for international justice.

The finding that a specific investigation would not be in the interests of justice, when no other local or regional mechanisms are in place to provide diverse forms of accountability and no form of justice is being done, does not raise the alarm in the international community. It also does not have any specific potential to activate other actors to step in and help address the gap of impunity, for example, through a domestic mechanism or a hybrid tribunal. Using the interests of justice for managerial concerns ultimately sends the signal that this investigation or prosecution, that the suffering of the victims in the incidents in question, is not worth it. A signal of acceptance of gaps of impunity as not within the interests of justice, would not ensure respect for international justice but erode its legitimacy even further.

C. Procedural Discretion: Towards a More Flexible Approach

Article 53 applies before the start of an investigation or prosecution respectively and allows the Prosecutor to decline the start of an investigation or a prosecution. So, while the determination of the elements of the interests of justice contains interpretative discretion, the application of the concept also entails a

[62] Art 42 ICCSt.

direct procedural dimension. But is this procedural dimension limited only to the starting point of proceedings? Or can the Prosecutor decide to discontinue an investigation or prosecution in the interests of justice?

Looking at the wording of the provision, no other option than not to commence proceedings is provided. Having said that, the Prosecutor is provided with other options to (dis-)continue proceedings. Article 61(4) of the Statute allows the Prosecutor to withdraw the charges throughout the confirmation hearing before the PTC without requiring any specific conditions that would have to be met for this. Also, article 61(9) of the Statute gives the Prosecutor the chance to withdraw charges against an accused, once the trial stage has been reached, as long as the TC (Trial Chamber) has given its permission for withdrawal.[63] In the case against Kenyatta, the Prosecutor withdrew the charges against the accused after the evidentiary basis had eroded throughout the case.[64] It is pivotal to note the TC's opinion that the withdrawal at that stage of the proceedings would not trigger the principle of *ne bis in idem* and therefore not bar the Prosecutor from bringing new charges against the accused at a later point, should the OTP obtain sufficient evidence to do so.[65] The withdrawal of charges does not necessarily signify a final decision that would cut off any avenues to accountability under changed circumstances. Indeed, it might provide an interesting opportunity for the Prosecutor to react flexibly to changing circumstances.

A contextual analysis of the Statute allows a broader variety of procedural consequences of the interests of justice than the wording would initially suggest. The approach proposed here to utilise the withdrawal of charges based on interests of justice considerations rests on two grounds. First, the withdrawal of charges is not linked to any preconditions in the Rome Statute and does not therefore exclude the withdrawal of charges based on the interests of justice. Second, such a decision is not necessarily the final one in the attempt to hold an alleged perpetrator of international crimes to account. There might be scenarios, when the halting of a prosecution at the international level could positively impact on a transitional peace process and contribute to crime prevention as one of the aims of the ICC. Such a scenario would not necessarily allow for impunity in the long run. Accountability may be provided through the continuation of the trial at the ICC, or through domestic proceedings, depending on developments in the transitional situation. Furthermore, if the Prosecutor is equipped with discretion not to investigate, or not to start a prosecution at

[63] Art 61 ICCSt: (4) 'In case of withdrawal of the charges, the Prosecutor shall notify the Pre-Trial Chamber of the reasons for the withdrawal.
(9) After commencement of the trial, the Prosecutor may, with the permission of the Trial Chamber, withdraw the charges'.

[64] *Prosecutor v Kenyatta*, Decision on the Withdrawal of Charges, ICC-01/09-02/11-1005, 13 March 2015. The TC had requested the Prosecutor to either file a withdrawal request or show that the evidentiary basis had considerably improved (para 3).

[65] ibid, para 9.

all, it follows as an *argumentum a maiore ad minus* that the interests of justice should also allow flexibility for the Prosecutor to exercise discretionary choice to delay proceedings. This is, de facto, what the Prosecutor did with regard to the delay of arrest warrants in the Uganda situation, although he did not base his decision on this legal consideration. Perhaps, it would have been more helpful in the dialogue with all stakeholders if the Prosecutor had used the interests of justice to formally delay proceedings and give the peace process a chance. A more flexible approach might better facilitate changing circumstances in a country – an avenue that specifically State Parties involved in transitional justice scenarios might positively respond to. The possibility of such flexibility in its use would enable the OTP to be more responsive, and nuanced in its reaction, to the complex realities in transitional (post-conflict) scenarios.

IV. A PRINCIPLED EXERCISE OF DISCRETION: PEACE, FAIRNESS AND HUMAN RIGHTS

When asked about what the interests of justice would mean, one victim of crimes in Afghanistan answered 'Fair Justice. It is that the powerful and weak are equal before the law'.[66] This very simple understanding of the interests of justice goes right to the core of the argument here. Any form of discretion ought to be exercised in a principled way that connects with and represents the joint values of the different constituents of the Court. Fairness, human rights and peace are key components in this context. A central argument in this chapter is that the Rome Statute provides the Prosecutor with more procedural flexibility in the interests of justice than appears at first sight. This flexibility allows a more nuanced approach that would break through the dichotomous understanding between peace and justice. A responsive approach to societies in conflict that allows local ownership of the justice process and creates space for legal pluralism[67] could greatly enhance a genuinely international understanding of justice.

A. Discarding the Peace versus Justice Dichotomy

The Prosecutor's policy suggests that peace is beyond the limits of the concept of interests of justice although leaving some ambiguity, because it also acknowledges the intertwined relationship between peace and justice.[68] The OTP derives

[66] Submission of a victim in the Situation in Afghanistan, see ICC-02/17-58-Anx, 12 July 2019, para 1.

[67] Greenawalt, 'Complementarity in Crisis' (n 41) emphasises that the interests of justice should create the space for the different forms of local and alternative justice mechanisms that a country in transition might employ but which fall short of triggering complementarity.

[68] Policy Paper Interests of Justice (n 4) 1, 8.

its distinction mainly from the divergent competences ascribed to the different international institutions. It specifically refers to the role of the SC as the institution mandated to safeguard international peace and security through its competences in chapter VII of the UN Charter. This acknowledgement alone already reveals that the OTP's argument that peace is a distinct concept to justice is a flawed one. It references the UN Secretary General stating that '[j]ustice, peace and democracy are not mutually exclusive objectives, but rather mutually reinforcing imperatives'.[69]

The mutually reinforcing relationship between justice, peace and democracy is reflected in the Rome Statute. The SC, acting on the basis of chapter VII of the UN Charter, can trigger the jurisdiction of the Court based on peace considerations.[70] This evidences that the competences of different international institutions are not exclusive but overlap. Furthermore, if justice is an essential part of peace, as the OTP argues in its policy paper, then, as an *argumentum e contrario*, peace has to be an essential part of the concept of justice.[71] The interrelationship between peace and justice is also acknowledged in the UN sustainable development goals. Goal 16 on peace, justice and strong institutions promotes peaceful and inclusive societies for sustainable development with access to justice for all.[72] Peace and sustainable development are intertwined, and sustainable development can only be achieved through justice and the rule of law.[73] Ultimately, this brings us back to the mutually reinforcing relationship between peace and justice. The UN explains in the 2030 Agenda for Sustainable Development:

> The new Agenda recognizes the need to build peaceful, just and inclusive societies that provide equal access to justice and that are based on respect for human rights (including the right to development), on effective rule of law and good governance at all levels and on transparent, effective and accountable institutions.[74]

The intertwined relationship demonstrates that the policy to treat peace and justice as distinct concepts, to the extent that peace issues are not to be considered as part of the interests of justice, is inherently flawed.[75]

[69] ibid, 8.

[70] The SC acted under Chapter VII in the situations in Libya and Darfur/Sudan, UNSC Res 1593 (2005), 31 March 2005, S/RES/1593(2005) and UNSC Res 1970 (2011), 26 February 2011, S/RES/1970/(2011).

[71] Policy Paper Interests of Justice (n 4) 8: 'The ICC was created on the premise that justice is an essential component of a stable peace'.

[72] UNGA Res 70/1 (2015) Transforming our world: the 2030 Agenda for Sustainable Development, 21 October 2015, A/RES/70/1, Goal 16.

[73] Preamble and target 16.3 UNGA Res 70/1 (2015).

[74] UNGA Res 70/1 (2015) para 35.

[75] See also K Rodman, 'Is Peace in the Interests of Justice? The Case for Broad Prosecutorial Discretion at the International Criminal Court' (2009) 22 *Leiden Journal of International Law* 99 arguing that peace can be a part of the interests of justice because international law cannot be decontextualised from the political context it operates in.

The different competences of the SC and the ICC Prosecutor in the areas of peace, security and justice can be reconciled through the conceptualisation of article 16 of the Rome Statute as a tool to manage regime collision.[76] This provision allows the SC acting under chapter VII of the UN Charter to defer investigations or prosecutions and bring them to a halt for up to 12 months. Article 16 of the Statute facilitates the management of clashes in the competences through the introduction of a deference rule; if there is a collision, the SC prevails.[77] This conception derives from scholarship in the area of regime theory that addresses regime overlaps and interplays in the growing but fragmented landscape of international institutions.[78] In this fragmented setting, different logics or rationalities apply in different institutions and therefore the collision potential between the regimes is high.

The SC is first and foremost a political organ that addresses conflict with political or even military measures, while the ICC is responsible for legal interventions based on the Rome Statute. Both institutions, however, address the intertwined areas of peace and justice. In this setting, the SC as a political institution may fail to react to threats of peace and security,[79] and has done so in the past.[80] The understanding of article 16 of the Statute as a collision rule implies that the Prosecutor does have an overlapping competence to the SC. This competence may become important in situations where the SC is paralysed but in which addressing peace issues would be vital. Peace is an element within the interests of justice that the Prosecutor could take into account as a guiding consideration. The dichotomous OTP position does not aid a principled use of the interests of justice.

B. Legal Pluralism and Local Ownership of the Process

The situation in Uganda was one of the focal points for the peace versus justice debate[81] and provides some lessons for the use of the interests of justice. Developing a pluralistic understanding of justice and allowing local ownership

[76] K Blome and N Markad, '"Contested Collisions": Conditions for a Successful Collision Management – The Example of Article 16 of the Rome Statute' (2016) 29 *Leiden Journal of International Law* 551.

[77] ibid, 562.

[78] See also K Blome et al, *Contested Regime Collisions: Norm Fragmentation in World Society* (Cambridge, Cambridge University Press, 2016).

[79] Blome and Markad (n 76) 24.

[80] As an example of the SC's inability to act see UN GA Resolution 'Uniting for peace' 377, 3 November 1950: 'Conscious that failure of the Security Council to discharge its responsibilities … does not relieve Member States of their obligations or the United Nations of its responsibilities … to maintain international peace and security'.

[81] See M Kersten, *Justice in Conflict: The Effects of the International Criminal Court's Interventions on Ending War and Building Peace* (Oxford, Oxford University Press, 2016) 92 ff for an in-depth analysis of the developments towards peace talks between the Ugandan government and the LRA and the effect of ICC intervention on it.

over the process to achieve a development towards peace can and should guide the exercise of prosecutorial discretion.

Although an analysis of the complex situation in Uganda is beyond the scope of this book, a short recap of developments is necessary for illustrative purposes. In 2003, Uganda referred the conflict with the LRA to the ICC, followed in 2005 by the Prosecutor issuing arrest warrants against the senior leadership of the LRA. Between 2006 and 2008 the government in Uganda and the LRA negotiated a possible peace agreement; and, in 2008, negotiations came to a halt and neither side signed the negotiated agreement.[82] In his detailed analysis of the effects of ICC intervention in Uganda, Kersten concludes that it 'would be impossible to know whether Kony [as the main LRA leader but absent from the peace talks] would have attended the peace talks had the ICC warrants not been issued or had they been revoked'.[83]

In the 2006–08 peace talks in Juba, justice, accountability and reconciliation were at the forefront of the negotiations; a crucial point was therefore how to resolve the existence of the ICC arrest warrants.[84] The draft peace agreement envisaged a special war crimes chamber in Uganda to prosecute those bearing the greatest responsibility for international crimes in order to facilitate trials against the indicted LRA leaders in Uganda rather than at the ICC.[85] Uganda would have needed clear guidance on how to approach transition towards a peace process through alternative justice mechanisms if it wanted to stop ICC investigation by either triggering the complementarity principle or the interests of justice. Such guidance, however, was lacking.[86] Moreno-Ocampo insisted in the situation in Uganda that the group of wanted senior LRA leaders ought to be tried by the ICC.[87] Greenawalt pointedly challenged this position, asking:

> Can it really be that the Rome Statute requires Uganda to put an entire peace process on hold to force the prosecution of just four – and now possibly three – perpetrators, while at the same time expressing juridical indifference as to countless other perpetrators who have also committed serious atrocities? This indifference would seem to concede so much to the proponents of alternative justice that it undermines the insistence on prosecuting the few.[88]

Ultimately, such situations can contribute to the erosion of the Court's legitimacy. The outlined OTP position appears inadequate and creates obstacles for a State Party to take back ownership of the proceedings in a transitional situation from conflict to peace.

[82] ibid for the details of the situation in Uganda.
[83] Kersten (n 81) 98.
[84] ibid; also Greenawalt, 'Complementarity in Crisis' (n 41) 144.
[85] Kersten (n 81) 100–01.
[86] Greenawalt, 'Complementarity in Crisis' (n 41) 145.
[87] ibid, 143.
[88] ibid, 144.

As argued above, the interests of justice do not necessarily need to be the end point of any prosecution. Ending the cases against the LRA leadership at that point would have been possible, based on the interests of justice and on the assumption that a peace agreement would come into effect that could facilitate prosecution of those most responsible in Uganda. If the expectations of peace and prosecution of those most responsible within Uganda had been disappointed, the Prosecutor could have used this as new circumstances at a later point to return to the prosecution of these cases based on article 53(4) of the Statute. The interests of justice allow flexibility, and therefore should be exercised flexibly.

The theme of allowing more local ownership of justice processes by the conflicted societies affected by ICC intervention links to another point of critique that was raised with regard to the Uganda situation. Based on a cultural and historical analysis of justice perceptions in African cultures that influence the actors in the Ugandan situation, Hanlon observes that the 'local culture of Uganda, wanting peace above all else, is at odds with the Western world, wanting justice as it is known in Western jurisprudence'.[89] She argues that allowing reconciliation through traditional justice mechanisms as a valid method for conflict resolution would have given Uganda the autonomy it had been seeking in handling its own affairs ever since the end of colonialism.[90] This feeds back to the acknowledgement of legal pluralism and the understanding of international justice as a genuine international notion; any interpretation of the interests of justice in the Rome Statute needs to acknowledge and embrace such a genuine international understanding of justice.

Generally, the Prosecutor has endorsed traditional and transitional justice mechanisms as part of the interests of justice.[91] However, in Uganda he did not actively, or at least openly, explain why any of the proposed accountability procedures for those most responsible would have been insufficient for the OTP to satisfy the interests of justice. Committing to legal pluralism would also mean challenging an understanding of justice built around Western values and norms.[92] It is therefore proposed that the Prosecutor needs to apply and interpret the interests of justice informed by the local cultural context and conceptions of justice of the conflicted community.

This proposal, beyond its theoretical underpinning of an international understanding of justice, can also be linked back to the Rome Statute itself because victims' interests are a paramount consideration within the interests of justice. It is the victims' culture and understanding of justice that have to be taken into account as guiding aims in evaluating the elements constituting the

[89] Hanlon (n 28) 298.

[90] ibid, 336.

[91] Policy Paper Interests of Justice (n 4) 8.

[92] J-M Coicaud, 'Crime, Justice, and Legitimacy: A Brief Theoretical Inquiry' in J Tankebe and A Liebling (eds), *Legitimacy and Criminal Justice: An International Exploration* (Oxford, Oxford University Press, 2013), 41.

interests of justice. Having said that, the interests of victims must be understood here in a much broader way than merely those that would have participatory rights in ICC proceedings. Victimisation through war and conflict can take many different forms: children might lose their education, abusive and violent behaviour might become more relevant because of the brutalisation of the society, environmental damage through conflict might have direct or indirect effects on people's livelihoods. All these effects lead to victimisation through conflict without necessarily allowing these people to participate as victims in proceedings at the ICC, depending on the focus of investigations and charges that are being brought.[93] It is therefore crucial that victims' interests are understood in a broad, inclusive manner that can take into account all elements of society that have suffered from the conflict.

C. Fairness and Human Rights

At this point I want to recall the voice of one of the Afghan victims and the expressed hope for fairness. A broad and inclusive culture and context-specific determination of the interests of justice resonates with the idea of a fairness-based theory of prosecutorial discretion and the interests of justice.[94] Similar to the approach taken here, Varaki, as its proponent, argues for the exercise of prosecutorial discretion to be geared towards achieving legitimacy.[95] Specifically focusing on legitimacy from the perception of the stakeholders on the grounds, the affected communities, she argues that the interests of justice provision is an important tool for the Prosecutor to calibrate and adjust prosecutorial decisions to the 'particularities' of the affected societies.[96] The awareness and ability to adjust to different social and legal cultures and traditions is a quality of fairness as well as justice. Varaki describes fairness therefore as a virtue of the right balance that would liberate the Prosecutor from legalistic constraints and guide her towards fair and contextualised decisions.[97] Her argument is based on Franck's conception of fairness and legitimacy that requires the right process and the need to produce results that do not feel grossly offensive. This fairness component is not only a due process component towards the accused but has a second dimension 'reflected in the broader implications of the prosecutorial exercise'.[98]

[93] E Ludwin King, 'Does Justice Always Require Prosecution? The International Criminal Court and Transitional Justice Measures' (2013) 45 *George Washington International Law Review* 85, 111 argues for the inclusion of the 'popular will', which would be one way of including all forms of victimisation through war, if all sectors of society agree on a transitional justice mechanism.

[94] M Varaki, 'Introducing a Fairness-Based Theory of Prosecutorial Legitimacy before the International Criminal Court' (2016) 27 *European Journal of International Law* 769.

[95] ibid, 781.

[96] ibid, 787.

[97] ibid.

[98] ibid, 788.

The idea that the principled exercise of discretion in the interests of justice requires fairness in the form of a balancing act between all different interests is also supported by a contextual analysis of the interests of justice notion in the ICC system. A number of provisions in the Rome Statute and the Rules of Procedure and Evidence of the International Criminal Court (RPE) refer to the interests of justice and aim for fairness and balance between different interests beyond the need to provide due process for the accused. Article 64(4) of the Statute, for example, provides that the TC in a case of admission of guilt nevertheless may require a more complete presentation of the facts of the case if required by the 'interests of justice, in particular the interests of victims'.[99] Pursuant to Rule 100(1) RPE, a trial might be moved to a place other than the host state, if this is in the interests of justice. For such a decision, a balance between a number of different interests needs to be found including the potential host state's interests, the security situation, and the accused's interests.[100] While only the interests of justice in article 53 of the Statute are designed as an instrument of discretion for the Prosecutor, the provision must be interpreted in a coherent way throughout the procedural system. In general, the interests of justice focus on fairness and a balance between the interests of the different parties and participants; at the same time, they clearly aim at safeguarding the interests of victims.[101] Bringing this back to the principled exercise of discretion in article 53(1)(c) and (2)(c) of the Statute, it equally requires that the Prosecutor attempts to strike a balance between all the different interests at stake.

Ultimately, such broad balancing acts require the Prosecutor to think in much wider than purely legal terms. The exercise of discretion in general, and specifically within the interests of justice, needs to reach beyond the legalist – the frame provided by the law – and become an exercise at the intersection of law, morals and politics.[102] Shklar's critique of legalism feeds into this proposition; she challenges the divide between these fields as artificial, because law is not a discrete entity out there but 'part of a social continuum'.[103] The law cannot be considered 'on neutral grounds' beyond any politics especially in highly politicised contexts

[99] Similar provisions include Rule 68(2)(b)(i), (d)(i) RPE allowing the introduction of pre-recorded testimony in the interests of justice; Rule 69 RPE allows a more complete representation of the facts in a case in the interests of justice and in particular the interests of victims despite the parties' agreement on specific facts.

[100] *Prosecutor v Gbagbo and Ble Goude*, Decision on the Gbagbo Defence Request to Hold Opening Statements in Abidjan or Arusha, TC I, ICC-02/11-01/15-316, 26 October 2015, para 15.

[101] *Prosecutor v Ongwen*, Decision on Contested Victims' Applications for Participation, Legal Representation of Victims and Their Procedural Rights, PTC II, ICC-02/04-01/15-350, 27 November 2015, para 24: Implementation of 'the best possible legal representation for participating victims … is in the interests of justice'.

[102] JN Shklar, *Legalism, Law, Morals, and Political Trials*, Reprint (Cambridge, MA, Harvard University Press, 1986) 3.

[103] ibid.

like the ICC.[104] It would be artificial to reduce the Prosecutor to a legal actor only, who does not need to be concerned with peace issues. Kersten's analysis of the situation in Uganda evidences this. Despite crimes having been committed from both sides of the conflict, the Uganda government as well as the LRA, the Prosecutor only selected the senior commanders of the LRA for prosecution.[105] This cemented a 'good' versus 'evil' narrative that had considerable impact on the peace talks because any concerns for accountability focused on the LRA, whereas accountability for international crimes committed by government forces was marginalised and would ultimately have allowed a gap of impunity.[106]

The divide between law and politics is as artificial as the peace versus justice divide. Based on this premise, pragmatic propositions have been made for broad prosecutorial discretion extending into the political realm with regard to the application of the interests of justice in the Rome Statute. Part of this proposition is also the call for the Prosecutor to actively engage in a dialogue with other political actors.[107] As one of the pragmatic proponents, Rodman makes his argument based on examples like the experience in Darfur, where the ICC impact was rather limited due to the 'mismatch between legal and political strategies'.[108] Taking political considerations into account would not impair the Prosecutor's role as an independent judicial institution, he argues; she should therefore strive for cooperation rather than opposition to other international efforts to resolve situations of conflict.[109] While it is agreed here that political considerations must not be beyond the Prosecutor's horizon, such a proposition must be handled with care. The Prosecutor must preserve her independence and impartiality. Political strategies are often based on geopolitical interests in a specific region, or influenced by the desire to bring about regime change.[110] A strategy embedded in such political processes runs counter to the idea of genuinely offering a forum for the societies on the ground and their interests. The acknowledgement that law and politics are not two entirely distinct areas should not go as far as the Prosecutor turning into a political actor.

This discussion takes us back to the limits of interpretative discretion in the interests of justice. The reader will recall that I argued earlier in this chapter that managerial considerations are 'out of bounds' for the Prosecutor in the interests of justice. The proposition[111] to use the interests of justice when an

[104] See also K Rodman, 'Justice as a Dialogue Between Law and Politics: Embedding the International Criminal Court within Conflict Management and Peacebuilding' (2014) 12 *Journal of International Criminal Justice* 437, 463.

[105] Kersten (n 81) 100–01.

[106] ibid.

[107] Rodman, 'Justice as a Dialogue Between Law and Politics' (n 104) 437.

[108] Rodman, 'Is Peace in the Interests of Justice? (n 75) 118.

[109] ibid, 122.

[110] For details of the interests of various political actors in the situations in Libya and Sudan, see N Mcmillan and D Mickler, 'From Sudan to Syria: Locating "Regime Change" in R2P and the ICC' (2013) 5 *Global Responsibility to Protect* 283, 306.

[111] C Davis (n 59) 182.

investigation does not seem feasible because state cooperation is lacking is based on the acknowledgmeent of the overlap between law and politics. It is motivated by efficiency considerations, because the ICC is depending on state cooperation.[112] Grounded on soft power theory, Davis argues that the ICC lacks any power, if it is not supported by states: 'if the OTP can utilise its discretion in a way that gets states to want what it wants, the ICC is going to remain a viable institution'.[113] This argument, however, is flawed, because it ultimately incentivises non-compliance with the Court. Such pragmatic approaches to prosecutorial discretion are therefore contested here, because they ultimately turn the Prosecutor into a political actor.

Instead, mediation between law and politics, between justice and peace, is possible through a human rights centred approach. Changing the perspective, instead of either attempting to separate law and politics (artificial) or extending the political into the legal (pragmatic), the exercise of discretion from the perspective of ethical and legal principles for the protection of human dignity and the duty to respect human rights offers an alternative and more productive way.[114] If the Prosecutor considers the impact of a prosecution on reconciliation and peacebuilding in a country, this can affect the exercise of human rights.[115] For example, if a prosecution is likely to stall settlement efforts and thereby result in many more future civilian deaths, then 'justice' may not be served in this larger sense.

Pursuant to article 21(1) of the Statute, the application and interpretation of law must be consistent with internationally recognised human rights. Placing the most effective strategy of human rights protection at the centre of the interests of justice, combined with an openness for the legal and cultural diversity of the societies affected by the ICC's actions, and based on a balanced and fair approach to the interests of all stakeholders, will help to enhance the exercise of discretion through the interests of justice.

V. ACCOUNTABILITY

Compared with other areas of prosecutorial discretion, article 53 of the Statute provides an exceptionally dense structure of judicial review. The potential to hold the Prosecutor to account, whenever the Prosecutor decides to decline an investigation or prosecution based on the interests of justice, is extensive. In case of non-investigation, the Prosecutor has to inform the PTC; in case of non-prosecution, the obligation to inform the PTC includes the reasons for

[112] ibid.
[113] ibid, 185.
[114] See for the ethical perspective, B Lepard, 'How Should the ICC Prosecutor Exercise His or Her Discretion: The Role of Fundamental Ethical Principles' (2009) 43 *John Marshall Law Review* 553.
[115] ibid, 566.

the decision.[116] Disregarding these differences, in both settings, the PTC has the discretionary power to fully review the prosecutorial decision based on article 53(3)(b) of the Statute, if it is solely based on the interests of justice.[117] If the PTC does so, this has an important effect on prosecutorial decisions, because its legal effects depend on the confirmation by the PTC.[118] Another route to judicial review is the request by a referring State Party or the referring SC according to article 53(3)(a) of the Statute. This provision, however, has a less powerful effect on prosecutorial discretion, because the PTC may merely request the Prosecutor to reconsider a decision – leaving the latter with the final decision.

A. Determining the Interests of Justice in Article 15(4)

In contrast to these two options, review mechanisms are disputed when the Prosecutor decides not to use the interests of justice and seeks authorisation to commence an investigation. Readers will recall the discussion in chapter three of this book which extensively addresses the scope of review in PTC authorisation proceedings based on article 15(4) of the Rome Statute. As a brief recap, it suffices at this point to say that PTC practice is split on the question if and to what extent a decision not to use the interests of justice can be reviewed. As outlined above, the majority of PTCs do not require the Prosecutor to provide any reasons, if the Office does not base its decision on the interests of justice. The PTC for the situation in Burundi chose a slightly different emphasis when considering that the submissions of victims in the situation confirmed the non-use of the interests of justice.[119] Despite the broad consent among the Chambers, PTC II proactively chose to review the interests of justice and sought to override the Prosecutor's assessment that no substantial reasons existed that would warrant the use of the interests of justice with its own discretionary decision.[120] The question regarding whether the PTC is mandated to positively determine

[116] Art 53(1), (2) ICCSt.

[117] Art 53(3) ICCSt:

> '(a) At the request of the State making a referral under article 14 or the Security Council under article 13, paragraph (b), the Pre-Trial Chamber may review a decision of the Prosecutor under paragraph 1 or 2 not to proceed and may request the Prosecutor to reconsider that decision.
>
> (b) In addition, the Pre-Trial Chamber may, on its own initiative, review a decision of the Prosecutor not to proceed if it is based solely on paragraph 1(c) or 2(c). In such a case, the decision of the Prosecutor shall be effective only if confirmed by the Pre-Trial Chamber'.

[118] Art 53(3)(b) ICCSt.

[119] *Situation in the Republic of Burundi*, Public Redacted Version of Decision pursuant to Article 15 of the Rome Statute on the Authorization of an Investigation into the Situation in the Republic of Burundi, ICC-01/17-X-9-US-Exp, 25 October 2017, para 190. Similarly also *Côte d'Ivoire* Decision and *Georgia* Decision (n 8).

[120] *Afghanistan* Decision (n 5) para 35 (emphasis added).

the interests of justice is contested with leave to appeal the PTC *Afghanistan* Decision requested by the OTP.[121]

As argued before, the PTC decision appears flawed.[122] In the context here the interpretative discretionary dimension of the interests of justice helps provide a more coherent understanding as to the potential standard of review. The interests of justice and gravity both contain an interpretative discretionary dimension. For the gravity notion, the AC has now delineated the review competences, divided along the lines of law and facts. Whereas the judges have the last say on the interpretation of the law – or the determination *in abstracto* which legal elements might fill an open concept – the Prosecutor has a remaining margin of appreciation regarding how to apply the facts to these elements and how to weigh them.[123] For a balanced approach, one that safeguards the consistent application of the law and provides an effective and robust system of review, I argue in this book for a middle ground. If circumstances appear obvious that would militate in favour of using the interests of justice such as victims' groups submissions, PTCs ought to alert the Prosecutor to those substantial legal aspects that might require reconsideration. This can aid a correct understanding of the interests of justice without interfering with the Prosecutor's competence to make the final decision.

B. The Scope of Judicial Review in Article 53(3)(b) of the Statute

Given the absence of any prosecutorial decisions to utilise the interests of justice, no judicial decisions exist to date based on article 53(3)(b) of the Statute. Yet, participating victims in the proceedings in the situation in Kenya attempted to trigger a judicial review of the Prosecutor's decision to cease active investigation.[124] This was a first attempt by victims participating in the proceedings to formally hold the Prosecutor to account for her discretionary decision based on article 53(3) of the Statute.

In the situation in Kenya, the Prosecutor had initially brought two cases forward for prosecution. Both cases, however, basically collapsed after the evidential basis had eroded significantly. In the case against Kenyatta, the TC had requested the Prosecutor to either withdraw the charges or present new evidence.[125]

[121] *Situation in the Islamic Republic of Afghanistan*, Request for Leave to Appeal the Decision pursuant to Article 15 of the Rome Statute on the Authorisation of an Investigation into the Situation in the Islamic Republic of Afghanistan, ICC-02/17-34, 7 June 2019, para 16.

[122] See ch 3 V.A.i.

[123] AC Judgment *Comoros* (n 47) para 81.

[124] *Situation in the Republic of Kenya*, Decision on the Victims' Request for Review of Prosecution's Decision to Cease Active Investigation, PTC II, ICC-01/09-159, 5 November 2015.

[125] *Prosecutor v Kenyatta*, 'Decision on Prosecution's Application for a Further Adjournment', TC V(B), ICC-01/09-02/11-981, 3 December 2014. The TC identifies a number of reasons for the development, see paras 50–57: non-cooperation by the Kenyan government; failures in the investigative steps of the OTP; and allegedly third-party interference, although the Chamber emphasises that no evidence with regard to the latter had been presented.

> [I]t would be contrary to the interests of justice for the Prosecution to proceed to trial in circumstances where [the OTP] believes it will not be in a position to present evidence sufficient to prove the guilt of the accused beyond reasonable doubt.[126]

The Prosecutor accordingly withdrew the charges, although without any reference to the interests of justice. Instead, she relied on the possibility of bringing new charges based on the same or similar factual circumstances, should the OTP obtain new evidence.[127]

The participating victims sought judicial oversight over the prosecutorial decision to cease active investigation that had been linked to these developments. The request was in part based on the argument that such a decision would mean not proceeding either based on article 53(1)(c) or (2)(c) of the Statute.[128] De facto, the victims' representative argued that the decision was based on the interests of justice and would therefore be open to review according to article 53(3)(b) of the Statute.[129] While this request was unsuccessful, the PTC findings are nevertheless pivotal for the scope of formal accountability of the Prosecutor.

i. The Standing of Victims in Proceedings

Critically, the PTC found that the victims generally have the judicial standing to request a review in order to prompt it to exercise its *proprio motu* powers to judicial review based on article 53(3)(b) of the Statute.[130] Victims were 'not precluded from seeking participation in any judicial proceedings ... provided their personal interests are affected by the issues'.[131] The participation could take the form of attempting to trigger judicial proceedings.[132] The Prosecutor had opposed this with the argument that the ICC system would distinguish between referring State Parties and the SC with a formal right to request review, and victims, who did not have such a right. Only the referring entities were entitled to notification by the Prosecutor of a decision, which should be understood as a clear indication of victims' lacking the right to request review.[133] This distinction, however, is not persuasive because the different forms of notification only indicate the privileged position of the referring party to directly request judicial review. Victims, instead, are dependent on whether the PTC chooses to exercise its discretionary power based on article 53(3)(b) of the Statute.

[126] ibid, para 61.

[127] *Prosecutor v Kenyatta*, Notice of Withdrawal of the Charges against Uhuru Muigai Kenyatta, OTP, ICC-01/09-02/11-983, 5 December 2014, para 3.

[128] ibid, para 1.

[129] ibid.

[130] ibid, para 7.

[131] ibid.

[132] ibid.

[133] *Situation in the Republic of Kenya*, Prosecution's Application to Dismiss in Limine the Victims' Request for Review of Prosecution's Decision to Cease Active Investigation, ICC-01/09-156, 25 August 2015.

The Prosecutor feared that the acknowledgement of legal standing for victims would lead to an open-ended right for victims to make submissions in the absence of proceedings as long as they were 'couched as a request for a Chamber to intervene'.[134] In my view, these fears are unsubstantiated. The specific request relates to explicitly recognized *proprio motu* powers of the PTC. These powers are limited in the ICC system and can therefore not lead to open-ended possibilities for victims. On the contrary, with this decision the PTC recognises the importance of victims' interests in article 53 of the Statute. It opens up avenues to hold the Prosecutor to account in those circumstances where the OTP attempts to circumvent a formal decision based on article 53(3)(b) of the Statute. Despite granting the victims legal standing, the PTC did not open the door far for any formal accountability.

ii. The Requirement of a Specific Decision

In its findings on the merits of the victims' claim, the PTC found that article 53(1)(c) of the Statute was not applicable in this situation, because an investigation had been initiated. With regard to article 53(2) of the Statute, the PTC reiterates that the OTP has brought forward cases for prosecution and that these could be brought again, because the charges had been withdrawn and no judgment of acquittal had been issued.[135] Additionally, the Chamber refers to the absence of a declaration of the OTP according to Rule 106 RPE not to prosecute explicitly based on the interests of justice. It would only be this narrow area of decision-making, clearly using the interests of justice, that would allow judicial review based on article 53(3)(b) of the Statute.[136] Beyond this limited scope, article 53(3)(b) of the Statute does not allow for the review of broader discretionary decisions that are based on factual considerations such as the lack of prospects of any further effective investigations. The Chamber found:

> [T]he decision 'not to conduct any further investigations at present' is, … not a result of the Prosecutor's conclusion that a prosecution is not in the interests of justice, but it is due to an objective circumstance of temporary nature, namely the absence of genuine cooperation from Kenya with the resulting lack of an immediate prospect of strengthening the evidence already gathered. As this Court cannot operate without the cooperation of States in accordance with Part 9 of the Statute, in particular of the State on the territory of which the concerned crimes have allegedly been committed, this lack of genuine cooperation has crucial consequences for the Court and its ability to properly investigate.[137]

With this pragmatic decision the Court acknowledges the practical constraints of the Prosecutor, who, unlike prosecutors in domestic systems, has no other

[134] *Kenya* Decision on Victims' Request (n 124).
[135] ibid, para 27.
[136] ibid.
[137] ibid, para 25.

effective means of investigation because of the lack of effective enforcement power on the territory of the State Party. While the PTC has not made any attempt to procedurally qualify the grounds for such a decision, the Prosecutor must have discretionary scope to adjust her decisions, once the factual basis changes to such an extent that a reasonable basis to proceed no longer exists.

It is part of the Prosecutor's general competence in article 53(1) of the Statute to assess the factual basis for a reasonable basis to proceed. The PTC further confirmed the division of functions at the pre-trial stage of the proceedings, leaving it entirely to the discretion of the Prosecutor as to whether to initiate a case through a summons to appear, or the request of an arrest warrant based on article 58 of the Statute.[138] The broad discretion granted to the Prosecutor in the decision to start a case against a specific person also means that this exercise of discretion cannot be reviewed unless a specific decision is based on the interests of justice. Case selection is therefore in the sole competence of the Prosecutor.

But what happens when the Prosecutor does not formally close down an investigation but remains inactive without bringing any further prosecutions or taking any decision based on the interests of justice? In the decision in the Kenya situation, the PTC also remarked that 'there exists no reason or information available to the Chamber to conclude that an investigation into these alleged crimes has been closed preventing the bringing of any further prosecution'.[139] Reading between the lines, this remark suggests that, in such a case, the Chamber might change its formal stance and allow judicial review despite the lack of a formal decision. How this could be reconciled with the position outlined above, requiring the need for a decision not to proceed based on the interests of justice, remains unclear. This area reveals a gap in the system of accountability, whenever no further prosecutions are being pursued. In order to provide a robust selection system at the ICC it is important to re-evaluate the role of article 53(2) and (3) of the Statute. Also, because of the gaps in the accountability system, it is crucial that avenues of pragmatic accountability are being pursued.

C. Pragmatic Accountability: A Role for *ex ante* Criteria or Guidelines?

The lopsided structure of judicial review mechanisms, with a dense mechanism for supervision in the case of the use of the interests of justice, but absence of an equivalent in the case of a negative decision, begs the question of how pragmatic forms of accountability can enhance the system. Calls have been made for the introduction of specific guidelines and *ex ante* criteria for the Prosecutor

[138] *Sudan* Decision on the Application for Leave to Appeal (n 23); *Kenya* Decision on Victims' Request (n 124) para 27.

[139] *Kenya* Decision on Victims' Request (n 124).

regarding the use of the interests of justice.[140] Such guidelines containing *ex ante* criteria for the determination of the interests of justice can in theory have an effect at two levels. First, internally, it might lead to a more structured decision-making process[141] that systematically addresses the formulated criteria and therefore reduces the risk of arbitrary decisions.[142] Second, it increases the level of informal accountability, because it allows a wider public to scrutinise whether the decision adheres to the formulated criteria. Although the underlying aims of those calling for guidelines to find ways of enhancing the Prosecutor's discretionary decision-making processes and the Court's legitimacy are laudable, it is doubtful that *ex ante* criteria for the interests of justice would achieve that.[143]

Marston Danner has made one of the key contributions in this debate, building her argument for *ex ante* criteria combined with extensive guidelines in the form of commentary on practices at the domestic level, specifically that of Canadian and British prosecutors.[144] The British Crown Prosecution Service, for example, introduced specific *ex ante* criteria for the determination of 'public interests'. These criteria, some socio-legal research has found, made prosecutors think more precisely about whether particular discretionary decisions conformed to the public interest.[145] Based on these experiences, she argues that guidelines can enhance the discretionary decision-making process, because they can give content to the 'nebulous phrase' interests of justice.[146] Additional commentary could help to describe how the Prosecutor will assess the relevance of a domestic truth commission, and what types of truth commission proceedings might constitute an adequate alternative to international prosecution.[147]

Other domestic experiences with statutory criteria for the interests of justice, however, seem less positive. For example, an analysis of the use of the interests of justice in New York does not support the argument that guidelines and *ex ante* criteria would necessarily enhance the legitimacy of decisions made in the interests of justice.[148] Keller found that the statutory criteria guiding prosecutorial discretion in New York are often not effectively providing more transparency or consistency in the use of the law. Instead, legal reasoning in many

[140] A Mcdonald and R Haveman, 'Prosecutorial Discretion: Some Thoughts on "Objectifying" the Exercise of Prosecutorial Discretion by the Prosecutor of the ICC' [Expert Consultation Process on General Issues Relevant to the ICC Office of the Prosecutor] (2003), available at: www.issafrica.org/anicj/uploads/McDonald-Haveman_issues_relevant.pdf; Webb (n 59).

[141] KC Davis, *Discretionary Justice, A Preliminary Inquiry* (Baton Rouge, LA, Louisiana State University Press, 1969) 198.

[142] See also Webb (n 59) 324.

[143] Goldston (n 46) 383; A Greenawalt, 'Justice without Politics? Prosecutorial Discretion and the International Criminal Court' (2007) 39 *New York University Journal of International Law and Politics* 584; Keller, 'Comparing the "Interests of Justice"' (n 45) 1.

[144] Marston Danner (n 61).

[145] ibid, 543, fn 273.

[146] ibid, 543.

[147] ibid, 545.

[148] Keller, 'Comparing the "Interests of Justice"' (n 45).

cases is reduced to only one or two sentences and to 'boilerplate language'.[149] This is an important point: standardised decisions cannot genuinely contribute to an enhanced decision-making process if they appear to be reduced to tick-box exercises without genuinely deliberating on the key considerations in the specific case. This might be a danger inherent in domestic systems, where the concept of interests of justice is a central tool to manage overcrowded systems. The exceptional nature of a decision based on the interests of justice, and the densely woven structure of judicial review in the use of the concept at the ICC, would probably avert the danger of 'boilerplate' language. Obviously, this has to remain an assumption that cannot yet be backed up by empirical evidence because of the lack of practice.

The main critique of these arguments here is of a more general nature. Domestic systems operate in such different circumstances that there are only limited lessons to learn for the ICC. The relatively small number of cases before the ICC cannot be compared with that of often overcrowded domestic systems. Big numbers of investigations and cases in domestic systems will mean that the circumstances in cases repeat themselves. Guidelines can be based on these practices. *Ex ante* criteria can be more easily identified, because case patterns can be anticipated. This is different at the ICC, where it would be very different to anticipate transitional processes in one part of the world based on experiences gained in an entirely different culture. Also, the impact of any ICC investigation or prosecution is entirely different from the consequences of decisions at the domestic level. Hence, prosecutorial discretionary decisions at the ICC need to ensure, and be guided by, consideration of the specific cultural and societial context in the situation of conflict. As said before, this is usually not something that can be anticipated.[150]

The necessity of remaining flexible in order to provide a tailored assessment for every situation of conflict also contradicts the assumption that guidelines and *ex ante* criteria could avert the danger of politicisation.[151] The need for flexibility is high, specifically because local communities should take ownership of accountability processes as much as possible, and the Prosecutor must create space for legal pluralism and diversity on the ground. Also, the positive determination of an indeterminate concept – or, to call it more positively, an open legal concept – is impossible. Therefore, any attempt to create an exhaustive list of *ex ante* criteria will fail. Instead, it seems far more helpful to emphasise the broad principles that should guide the exercise of prosecutorial discretion in that area. In this context, some of Marston Danner's points about providing commentary on transitional justice mechanisms can be of help without

[149] ibid, 23.

[150] With a similar critique Greenawalt, 'Justice without Politics?' (n 143) 652.

[151] Webb (n 59) 324 sees potential to avoid politicisation through the dialogue that would be facilitated between the OTP and PTCs and because of the greater transparency of such decisions. Goldston (n 46) 403, however, points out that the importance of flexibility would require guidelines only to guide but not to prescribe.

exhausting possibilities. The Prosecutor should be guided by the idea of allowing legal pluralism through a broad and context-specific understanding of justice mechanisms that can provide justice in conflicted societies. The OTP should opt for a fair exercise of discretion that balances the interests of all stakeholders fairly and is geared towards the protection of human rights to the greatest extent possible. In that context, peace is one important consideration.

Over time, a more structured exercise of discretion is still possible without *ex ante* criteria for the Prosecutor. It is important to move beyond a middle ground position in providing more transparency in the use of the concept through a revised policy that comments on some features. Additionally, deliberation on the merits of a specific decision requires a more structured decision-making process. In order to provide transparency and dialogue with the stakeholders, the Prosecutor should provide reasoned decisions on her (non-)use of the interests of justice in all those situations and cases in which stakeholders raise concerns. This could also provide the basis for a more effective form of legal review on the part of the PTCs. The Rome Statute only requires such a deliberation when the Prosecutor intends to use the interests of justice. This, however, did not provide any explanation for the people in Uganda in 2008/09, who were hoping for a successful outcome from the Juba peace talks and perceived the ICC investigation as a hurdle to achieving this. In such a situation, the OTP must enter into an active and flexible dialogue that allows an open discussion about the use of the interests of justice. Similarly, the Prosecutor needs to engage in any situation where an investigation is still pending, but cases are no longer being prosecuted, as is the case in Kenya.

For those reasons, it is proposed that the Prosecutor revises the current, inflexible policy position on peace and justice as distinct concepts, replacing it with a commitment to a principled exercise of discretion aiming at human rights protection, peace and fairness through an active dialogue with the affected communities. The Rome Statute allows more flexibility than the Prosecutor currently seems to be aware of for such a dialogue. She should use the full variety of possibilities, from signalling that she would halt proceedings for a specific time, based on the interests of justice, to ending an investigation or prosecution if developments justify such an action. Working together with the specific stakeholders on the requirements that ought to be met for a country to take ownership of proceedings through the clear communication of expectations, would be a step towards a court that can connect better with and respond to its diverse audiences, thereby enhancing the legitimacy of its actions in the perception of these audiences.

VI. CONCLUDING REMARKS

The current policy on prosecutorial discretion renders an important concept in the Rome Statute redundant. This instrument provides the Prosecutor with two dimensions of flexibility: it allows her to determine the elements of the interests of justice through the exercise of interpretative discretion, while also providing for some procedural discretionary scope. The scope for interpretative discretion is great because the open concept cannot be determined exhaustively. This openness, coupled with the variety of procedural consequences, allows flexibility to reconcile the Rome Statute's quest to closing the gap of impunity with the need of societies in conflict to achieve justice and peace. The relationship between justice and peace, however, is not a mutually exclusive one. The ICC is certainly not the primary actor in the field of peace. But the distinction made in the Policy Paper on the Interests of Justice is artificial and, indeed, counterproductive with a view to effective human rights protection.

The Prosecutor should commit to a principled and structured exercise of discretion that is geared towards human rights protection through justice and peace. The interests of justice should be used to allow conflicted societies to take ownership of the justice and peace processes as far as possible. For that, the Prosecutor has to engage in proactive dialogue with affected communities. The OTP should guide communities and states by outlining in specific circumstances how the interests of justice would allow deference of international judicial proceedings at the ICC. Allowing space for legal pluralism will not only require the exercise of interpretative discretion to capture the context-specific cultural setting, but also challenge the Prosecutor to exhaust the full scope of procedural discretion provided in the Rome Statute. The Prosecutor should therefore not shy away from using the interests of justice even in those situations where only a temporary measure is taken. This, however, should explicitly be based on the interests of justice in order to ensure that the will of the drafters is taken into account and formal judicial review is accessible for the referring entities or victims. It would include the PTC in the dialogue and can shield the Prosecutor from accusations of politicisation. This will greatly benefit the respect for international justice in the long run.

7

Discretion and Completion

I. INTRODUCTION

THE COMPLETION OF activities has been a major challenge for international courts and tribunals. The pressure to close down entails major questions on how to clear the dock of cases, how to reach out to communities, and how to ensure that the work of these tribunals leaves a positive legacy. Although the International Criminal Court (ICC), as a permanent Court, is here to stay, it is under similar pressure to end some of its activities. At its Assembly in December 2018, the State Parties declared:

> [G]reater consideration should be given to how the Court will complete its activities in a situation country and that possible completion strategies could provide guidance on how a situation country can be assisted in carrying on national proceedings when the Court completes its activities in a given situation.[1]

But the pressure to develop completion strategies also stems from the fact that the Court, and specifically the Office of the Prosecutor (OTP), has only limited capacities. As long as these are bound by ongoing investigations, it cannot start other necessary investigations and prosecutions.

The OTP will be required to decide on when and where to wind down its activities in a situation. This is a new challenge for an international criminal court because of the unique jurisdictional scope of the ICC. With the lack of a designated framework, it is a major task to develop a coherent completion approach, and prosecutorial discretion is at the heart of this challenge.[2] The permanent nature of the Court alleviates some of the practical questions such as the need for any residual mechanism to deal with remaining cases or continued witness protection measures. Nevertheless, the completion of the Court's activities in a given situation is complex. Of course, cases will come to an end in the conventional way through the judicial proceedings. But when are investigations into the broader situation in conflict complete? How many cases does the ICC

[1] ICC-ASP/17/Res.5 'Strengthening the International Criminal Court and the Assembly of States Parties', 12 December 2018, Preamble.

[2] ICC/OTP, Strategic Plan 2019–2021, 17 July 2019, 5 acknowledges the need for increasing 'the speed, efficiency and effectiveness of preliminary examinations', of 'optimising preliminary examinations' and 'developing a clear completion strategy for situations under investigation'.

need to bring to legitimately be able to claim that it has contributed to closing the gap of impunity? When is it justified to end preliminary examinations in which the OTP seemingly pursues a strategy of positive complementarity? How far advanced do domestic developments have to be before the Court can convincingly close its preliminary examination? These questions are at the heart of this chapter.

Understanding the dynamics, how to address the challenge of completion, is the final element in the construction of the ICC system. This chapter will be based on an analysis on the existing provisions in the Rome Statute, which do provide some cornerstones for completion processes with the principle of complementarity and the interests of justice. It will focus predominantly on the role of prosecutorial discretion in this context; although, persuasive completion strategies will require the different organs of the Court, and the Trust Fund for Victims, to work hand in hand. They also need to work in close partnership with other international, national and local actors. To date, there is neither explicit Court practice nor any policy papers to guide the approach expected from the Court. Therefore, the discussion in this chapter will look at potential completion scenarios through the lens of two emerging completions: (1) the situation in Colombia which has been under preliminary examination since June 2004; and (2) the investigation of the situation in Uganda, opened in July 2004.

There will be no one-size-fits-all completion strategy, because the situations before the Court are highly diverse. Comparing the dynamics in Colombia and Uganda reveals some incoherence in the ICC's approach. Preliminary Examinations into large-scale conflicts such as in Colombia, despite their complexity, do not provide an open-ended transition-supervision mandate. The situation in Uganda, in contrast, demonstrates the importance of a principled exercise of discretion at all stages of the proceedings. One-sided case selection provides no basis in the long run to build a legacy of justice in the country. I demonstrate in this chapter that prosecutorial discretion is at the heart of devising completion strategies. The principle of complementarity limits this discretion; it requires the Prosecutor to defer to domestic proceedings wherever these are genuine efforts to provide accountability. Yet, no such deference is owed to proceedings that blatantly disregard minimum due process guarantees. Ultimately, completion processes should be guided by an interests-of-justice-based approach that allows for local ownership, pluralism in the understanding of justice, and a holistic assessment of the transition process in the country in question. Anti-impunity efforts must be seen in context. The need to address the often socio-economic root causes of crimes cannot be ignored in any assessment, when further investigation would be in the interests of justice. The chapter also addresses avenues for accountability and demonstrates that article 53(3) has an important role in completion settings. Lastly, it is important that the ICC develops a court-wide policy. The ICC needs to act with one voice.

II. THE LAW AND PRACTICE

The critical cornerstones for completion processes are the principle of complementarity as expressed in the Preamble, article 1 and article 17 of the Statute, as well as the interests of justice in article 53(1)(c) and (2)(c) of the Statute. Both concepts come into play at different stages of the proceedings. They form core components of a preliminary examination, determine the question regarding whether to commence an investigation, and within an investigation about whether to commence a specific prosecution. These rules also, in the reverse, provide guidance regarding the ending of proceedings.

Difficulties stem from the need for dynamic complementarity assessments because of potentially unexpected developments in a given situation.[3] Even if initial state failure triggered the Court's jurisdiction, Minow suggests that the ICC 'loses its authority to proceed'[4] if an affected state genuinely starts undertaking its own investigations and efforts to prosecute international crimes in its jurisdiction. She argues that alternative justice mechanisms such as truth commissions could potentially bar ICC jurisdiction.[5] Her argument is broadly based on the need to acknowledge forms of restorative justice that do not follow an adversarial trial model but seek to 'genuinely contribute to individual accountability, justice and prevention of future harms'.[6] Contrary to Minow's position, article 17 of the Statute seems to be clear when using the language of investigations and prosecutions, rather than accountability, that this would refer to criminal prosecutions. Yet, the admissibility criteria do not fully answer the question of what the ICC's complementary position should be in a setting of transitional justice. Where is the tipping point when the ICC mandate ceases? From the perspective of states, these questions are particularly pressing in situations of evolving peace negotiations in which questions of transitional justice mechanisms and amnesties loom large. Although legal institutions speak predominantly through Court decisions, a closer look at the developments in Colombia and Uganda challenges us to conceptualise completion not as a matter of prosecutorial or Court decisions but as processes that go beyond the investigation and prosecution of specific cases.

A. Preliminary Examinations, Transitional Justice and Colombia

Colombia faces a clear challenge to develop transitional justice mechanisms that are sufficient to fulfil the country's obligation to investigate and

[3] See Assembly of States Parties (ASP), Report of the Bureau on Complementarity, ICC-ASP/16/33, 22 November 2017, para 18 reporting on a conference, chaired by the ASP President on 'Capacity-building with regards to African judicial systems through effective and dynamic complementarity and cooperation with the International Criminal Court'.

[4] M Minow, 'Do Alternative Justice Mechanisms Deserve Recognition in International Criminal Law?: Truth Commissions, Amnesties, and Complementarity at the International Criminal Court' (2019) 60 *Harvard International Law Journal* 1, 4.

[5] ibid.

[6] ibid, 39.

prosecute international crime, while at the same time struggling to both reach and implement peace agreements to end over 50 years of armed conflict. This is at the heart of the preliminary examination into the situation in Colombia.[7] For years, the OTP has marked the examination as pending at the phase of assessing the admissibility of potential cases. Additionally, the OTP has engaged with the Colombian efforts, such as legislation and investigative activities from the perspective of what the OTP believes are the Colombian obligations deriving from the Rome Statute. The 2018 Preliminary Examination Report contained a level of detail on potential cases and numbers of ongoing investigations and prosecutions that has not hitherto featured in any other preliminary examination.[8] The recorded number of cases under investigation by Colombian authorities and legislative initiatives make it difficult to envisage how the OTP could credibly move towards an investigation based on the reasoning that Colombia could be unwilling or unable to investigate and prosecute.

Only reflecting on the last few years of developments in Colombia, it becomes evident that the state is seeking to find the right balance between justice and the need for peace agreements. One step in the process included the judicial review of the Justice and Peace Law in 2015 by the Colombian Constitutional Court, which included alternative, reduced sentences aimed at facilitating truth and peace mechanisms.[9] The Court noted that

> it is impossible to restore justice, peace and victims' rights at the same time … Peace does not justify everything. The value of peace cannot be absolute in scope, since it is also necessary to ensure fairness, and the victims' right to justice … the Constitutional right to justice may take a wide range of forms … [however, the] substantial reduction of punishment is constitutionally necessary in the pursuit of peace.[10]

The decision acknowledges Colombia's responsibility to investigate and prosecute. But it also expresses the need to balance these obligations and the victims' rights to truth and justice, with the need for peace, giving both obligations a constitutional footing. Moving on from this ruling, the government and the Revolutionary Armed Forces of Colombia (FARC) signed the Final Peace Agreement in 2016.[11] The agreement entails the 'creation of a Comprehensive System for Truth, Justice, Reparation and Non-Repetition, including the establishment of a Special Jurisdiction for Peace designed to investigate and punish serious conflict-related crimes'. This started operations in March 2018.[12] These legal developments have

[7] See H Alviar García and K Engle, 'The Distributive Politics of Impunity and Anti- Impunity: Lessons from Four Decades of Colombian Peace Negotiations' in K Engle, Z Miller and D Davis (eds), *Anti-Impunity and the Human Rights Agenda* (Cambridge, Cambridge University Press, 2016) 216–18.

[8] ICC/OTP, Report on Preliminary Examination Activities 2018, 5 December 2018, paras 133–59.

[9] ibid, 230.

[10] Cited after ibid.

[11] ibid, para 129.

[12] ibid.

to be contrasted with the fragility of the political process on the ground. Some of the FARC commanders have taken up arms again, frustrated by the lack of commitment to the peace process. Meanwhile, peace negotiations with another major armed group, attempting to reach a similar peace agreement, have come to a halt.

In May 2018, Deputy Prosecutor James Stewart delivered a critical public lecture on the role of the ICC in the transitional justice process in Colombia, giving some valuable insights into the OTP's understanding of its role in this transition process. The OTP focuses on monitoring criminal prosecutions within the broader framework of transitional justice, while acknowledging that this might also feature truth commissions or reparations.[13] The OTP only perceives a mandate for its work, 'if the authorities of the State concerned are not themselves conducting genuine proceedings for Rome Statute crimes'.[14] This understanding of the OTP's mandate, with its strong focus on criminal prosecution, appears somewhat flawed in a transitional justice situation where a holistic view of political and legal developments is the most critical element. Although Stewart acknowledges the need for a 'holistic evaluation', he does so only in the context of assessing the seriousness of national efforts but, 'in and of themselves, [such efforts] would not be capable of rendering a case inadmissible before the ICC'.[15] This view seems to overly reduce the preliminary examination process to the admissibility of cases rather than an active consideration of the interests of justice, a much broader concept than article 17 of the Statute. With a view to completing a preliminary examination, the OTP's approach does not take into consideration the whole range of discretionary powers available to it.

The Stewart speech also provides a guide, albeit based on flawed legal assumptions, of how the OTP envisages justice arrangements in transitional justice scenarios. It presents a pyramid of measures: amnesties, pardons or waivers of prosecution may not be granted to any perpetrator of international crimes, not even war crimes that are neither systematic nor particularly grave.[16] This position assumes that the OTP has a legal mandate to consider and comment on such a scenario. Recalling, however, that article 17(1)(d) of the Statute reduces the admissibility to those cases that are of sufficient gravity to justify further action by the Court, it is difficult to see how Stewart can claim a mandate to comment on the prosecution of all international crimes regardless of their gravity. The admissibility criteria delineate the Court's mandate. Accordingly, the OTP considers the gravity of potential cases as part of the initial assessment regarding whether the Court's jurisdiction ought to be triggered. As an OTP representative, the Deputy Prosecutor is bound to act within the OTP mandate.

[13] J Stewart, 'The Role of the ICC in the Transitional Justice Process in Colombia', 30 May 2018, Bogota, para 47.

[14] ibid, para 48.

[15] ibid, para 54.

[16] ibid, paras 126–30.

This does not extend to formulating expectations on how a country ought to exercise its criminal jurisdiction concerning issues that are beyond the Court's jurisdiction.

Yet, Stewart continues to suggest that criminal prosecution is required,[17] and sentencing needs to be proportionate to the offence. As such, reduced sentences might be permissible, he suggests, if they are part of broader measures such as acknowledgement of criminal responsibility, demobilisation and disarmament, guarantees of non-repetition, full participation in the process of establishing the truth about serious crimes, a possible temporary ban from taking part in public affairs, or non-custodial sentences involving restrictions on liberty or supervision.[18] These requirements, however, have no foundation in the Rome Statute. Beyond the argument made above – that the Court only has a limited mandate – the Statute only requires states to 'exercise their criminal jurisdiction'.[19] How states choose to do so is not regulated in the Rome Statute. For those bearing the greatest responsibility, the Deputy Prosecutor states that 'the suspension of sentences would be manifestly inadequate, as this would, in effect, allow individuals who bear the greatest responsibility for the commission of the most serious crimes to avoid any real punishment'.[20] Anything short of genuine criminal investigation, targeting those bearing the greatest responsibility with progressive steps to achieve prosecution[21] with proportionate sentences, would fall short of the required genuine proceedings. Then, 'and only then – would the OTP step in to deliver one component of "transitional justice", namely, criminal investigations and prosecutions'.[22] This, however, begs the question of what would happen if a country such as Colombia chose to prosecute those most responsible but opted to ignore the requirement to prosecute every perpetrator of war crimes.

With the interests of justice, article 53(1)(c) of the Statute provides an answer to those scenarios where the country seems to be on the path of transitional justice. Suggestions have been made that the OTP could have invoked the interests of justice for issues such as mitigated or suspended sentences.[23] Indeed, which scenarios, other than those of countries addressing situations of mass violence, does the Prosecutor have in mind, when the interests of justice would come into play? The OTP expectations formulated in the Stewart speech

[17] ibid, para 53.
[18] ibid, paras 145–49.
[19] Preamble ICCSt. See also, S Nouwen, Complementarity in the Line of Fire: The Catalysing Effect of the International Criminal Court in Uganda and Sudan (Cambridge, Cambridge University Press, 2013) 38.
[20] Stewart (n 13) para 145.
[21] ibid, para 80
[22] ibid, para 54.
[23] C Stahn, M Bergsmo and H Chan, 'On the Magic, Mystery and Mayhem of Preliminary Examinations' in M Bergsmo and C Stahn (eds), *Quality Control on Preliminary Examinations, Vol I* (Brussels, TOAEP, 2018) 16.

show no consideration for domestic needs or cultural variations in perceptions of justice. It neither draws on what victims' groups might have conveyed, as expectations in the context of Colombia, nor on specific needs within the peace process. Not to even consider using the full scope of discretion provided in the Statute would be legally flawed.

In Colombia, the OTP appears to signal that it will analyse the operation of the Special Jurisdiction for Peace and to verify the execution of sentences imposed,[24] before a final decision regarding the preliminary examination in Colombia can be expected. The OTP position towards transitional justice, although not formulated in a policy paper, but conveyed through the Deputy Prosecutor, seems rigid and inflexible. Important for any completion scenario is that the OTP develops a coherent approach within the scope of its mandate, based on the needs of the society in question. Indeed, whether the mandate of the ICC even covers the supervision of an entire legislative framework in a country in a transitional justice setting is a contentious question. As I argue below, the principle of complementarity limits the Prosecutor's scope for discretion. The Rome Statute does not provide an all-encompassing mandate to the Prosecutor at the preliminary stage.

B. Uganda and the Completion of Situation Investigations

Uganda represents a case study of a situation nearing completion. The fact that the ICC is on its way out in Uganda becomes visible when piecing together different aspects of the Court's work and reported activities. The Prosecutor has made it clear that the OTP will not request further arrest warrants against Lord's Resistance Army (LRA) fighters.[25] The announcement, perhaps inadvertently, contained a statement that the investigation is coming to an end. Accordingly, Uganda does not feature on the OTP's list of active investigations in the latest report to the ASP.[26] The ongoing trial against Ongwen and the need to preserve the investigation pending arrest of Joseph Kony, both LRA leadership cases, are the only prosecution activities.[27] Beyond those cases, the OTP is currently attempting to enhance domestic capacities. Although not labelled as part of any completion strategy, OTP representatives are engaging with domestic Ugandan actors. An example is a workshop on addressing international crimes where the

[24] Stewart (n 13) para 155.

[25] ICC/OTP, 'Message from the Prosecutor of the International Criminal Court, Fatou Bensouda, calling for defection by LRA fighters', 1 April 2016, available at: www.icc-cpi.int/Pages/item.aspx?name=160401-otp-stat.

[26] ICC, Report on activities and programme performance of the International Criminal Court for the year 2017, ICC-ASP/17/2, 60. The report lists six active investigations: six active investigations (CAR IIa, CAR IIb, CIV 2, Libya 3&4, Georgia and Darfur).

[27] ibid.

OTP 'shared their experiences, lessons learned and best practices with a wide range of stakeholders, namely law enforcement and justice sectors'.[28]

At the domestic level, the response to the brutal conflict in northern Uganda includes a variety of measures.[29] In terms of criminal proceedings, a key development is the establishment of the International Crimes Division (ICD) in the High Court of Uganda. The ICD is a response to 'the civil wars and a series of other internal conflicts, … to try the perpetrators of war crimes and crimes against humanity including commanders of the LRA and other rebel groups'.[30] After implementation of key provisions of the Rome Statute into Ugandan law, the ICD has subject-matter jurisdiction covering, inter alia, genocide, crimes against humanity and war crimes.

> While originally meant to be part of a comprehensive peace agreement with the LRA, the International Crimes Division has come to be viewed as a court of 'complementarity' with respect to the International Criminal Court, thus fulfilling the principle of complementarity stipulated in the preamble and Article 1 of the Rome Statute.[31]

From an institutional perspective, the ICD's complementarity is a clear signal that Uganda wants to reassert its sovereignty through the enactment of its own law provisions that would demonstrate its ability and willingness to address international crimes domestically.

The first case before the ICD is that of ex-LRA commander Thomas Kwoyelo. In 2009, he surrendered to government forces and benefited from an amnesty designed for former LRA fighters. Contesting prosecution before the ICD, the Supreme Court ruled in 2015 on the extent of the amnesty granted to him and provides critical insights into the limitations of the 2000 Amnesty Act.[32] The Court paved the way for the prosecution of Kwoyelo when it found that '[w]illful murder of civilians is a crime against humanity which, … cannot be granted amnesty under the Laws of Uganda particularly the Geneva Conventions Act, and the Amnesty Act does not purport to do so'.[33] The Court further found that even the peace agreement, although never signed, suggested that both parties distinguished between 'acts of rebellion [as covered by amnesty provisions] from acts of grave criminal conduct that amounted to commission of international

[28] ICC Press Release, 'ICC Office of the Prosecutor participates in training initiative in Uganda: Collaboration is key to closing the impunity gap', ICC-CPI-20180313-PRPR1368, 13 March 2018, available at: www.icc-cpi.int/Pages/item.aspx?name=pr1368.

[29] One of the alternatives to prosecution, traditional Acholi justice practices that had been promoted, have lost their traction as an alternative to the ICC. Yet, these practices remain relevant in the local context. See in detail for the debates, Nouwen (n 19) 158.

[30] See the Court's website: judiciary.go.ug.

[31] ibid.

[32] *Uganda v Thomas Kwoyelo*, Supreme Court Judgment, Constitutional Appeal No 01 of 2012, 8 April 2015.

[33] ibid, 43.

crime [as those that are not]'.[34] Following this judgment, Kwoyelo now stands trial as one of the LRA's commanders for crimes against humanity and war crimes charges.

Viewing these legal developments in isolation would seemingly be a clear-cut case for the completion of the ICC's investigation with legislation in place and domestic institutions addressing crimes within the jurisdiction of the Court. Yet, a more holistic view of developments paints a very different picture. Kwoyelo's defence argued that 'other LRA Commanders … and 26,000 other rebels who had been captured under similar circumstances were granted certificates of amnesty'.[35] For the vast majority of LRA defectors, Uganda's amnesty law has been the main reason for doing so.[36] Many of those fighters will at some point have been involved in some of the LRA's operations that constituted grave breaches of international humanitarian law such as wilfully targeting civilians. Applying the reasoning in Kwoyelo to those numbers of ex-LRA fighters would ultimately require revisiting large numbers of cases – a challenge for the Ugandan legal system, but more importantly, a societal challenge that could seriously negatively impact the country's development.[37] Not surprisingly, there is no indication at this point for any such plans from the Ugandan side, nor ICC expectations to that extent.

Another important aspect is the lack of accountability to date for crimes committed by government forces. During the war, northern Uganda civilians were subjected to brutality from both sides. Drawing on extensive field work in Uganda, MacDonald summarises the government strategy in the fight against the LRA as follows:

> [The Ugandan government's] response was to combine military offensives with forced crowding of civilians into camps. While they were ostensibly 'protected' by Uganda People's Defence Forces (UPDF) soldiers, abuses by both the UPDF and the LRA were a regular feature of camp life. Described as a form of 'social torture', the camps devastated Acholi livelihoods, and led to a far larger number of deaths than those caused by direct LRA violence.[38]

[34] ibid, 46.

[35] ibid, 3.

[36] J McKnight, 'Accountability in Northern Uganda: Understanding the Conflict, the Parties and the False Dichotomies in International Criminal Law and Transitional Justice' (2015) 59 *Journal of African Law* 193, 200.

[37] See Z Lomo and L Hovil, 'Whose Justice? Perceptions of Uganda's Amnesty Act 2000: The Potential for Conflict Resolution and Long-Term Reconciliation' (2005) Refugee Law Project Working Paper No 15, 15 February 2005, for the overwhelming support among the population for the amnesty and its importance to the peace process. While this study captures the attitudes up until 2005, it is still relevant for the meaning of the amnesty process in the Ugandan context.

[38] A MacDonald, 'Somehow this Whole Process Became so Artificial: Exploring the Transitional Justice Implementation Gap in Uganda' (2019) 13 *International Journal of Transitional Justice* 225, 231. See also M Kersten, *Justice in Conflict: The Effects of the International Criminal Court's Interventions on Ending War and Building Peace* (Oxford, Oxford University Press, 2016) 66.

The extent of brutality of government troops and its impact is even more powerfully summed up in the words of one Acholi:

> [U]nder the cover of the war against these outlaws [the LRA], an entire society, the Acholi people, has been moved to concentration camps and is being systematically destroyed – physically, culturally, and economically … 'Everything Acholi is dying'.[39]

Despite crimes committed on both sides of the conflict, the ICC's focus rests solely on the LRA, and in Uganda itself, no state actors have been investigated.[40] Many of the acts go back as far as the mid-1990s and are hence not covered by the temporal jurisdiction of the Court. However, government operations continued until 2006, and, from the temporal perspective, would allow the Court to exercise jurisdiction. The Court's sole focus on the LRA created 'a widespread feeling within affected communities that ICC engagement was partisan'.[41] According to Nouwen, whose insights are also based on extensive fieldwork in Uganda, the ICC had 'provided "partial" or "selective" justice, an injustice in itself'.[42] Divisions and inequalities between north and south Uganda have been deeply entrenched along ethnicities in the history of Uganda.[43] The distribution of efforts to hold perpetrators of crimes to account mirrors these divisions, and justice for crimes committed by government forces seems to be missing from the ICC's engagement.[44]

A core lesson from completion processes of other international courts and tribunals is the importance of legacy building.[45] Not least for this reason, it is critical to ensure that accountability for government crimes is not left unaddressed. Can the Court rightfully claim to have fulfilled its mission of closing the gap of impunity in Uganda? It will be critical for the development of coherent completion strategies to explore the perceptions and expectations of those affected by the conflict, as it is their right to justice that is at stake. Some insights do exist, although further research will be needed.

[39] Cited after Nouwen (n 19) 127.

[40] MacDonald, 'Somehow this Whole Process Became so Artificial' (n 38) 231.

[41] ibid. Kersten (n 38) 74 reports: '[I]n virtually every interview and conversation conducted with citizens of northern Uganda about the causes of the conflict, the atrocities committed by the government were highlighted. As noted above, evidence has been collected and presented about crimes committed by UPDF troops. The people of northern Uganda have suffered atrocities at the hands of *both* the [Government of Uganda] GoU and the LRA; *both* are responsible for the plight, suffering, and abuse of citizens'.

[42] Nouwen (n 19) 143.

[43] Kersten (n 38) 67–69.

[44] Only a small number of military court cases address the conduct of government forces. See McKnight (n 36) 206.

[45] E Evenson and A Smith, 'Completion, Legacy and Complementarity at the ICC' in C Stahn (ed), *The Law and Practice of the International Criminal Court* (Oxford, Oxford University Press, 2015) 1262.

A useful Avocat Sans Frontières study explored the expectations and needs of victim communities in Uganda, highlighting that victims' expectations and needs in Uganda are much more focused on the reparative aspects of justice than on the trial proceedings and their outcome.[46] It is reparative rather than retributive justice that seems to matter for victim communities:

> [A]spects such as truth-seeking and prosecution rank low on victims' lists of priorities. Such transitional justice processes may run their course, but to these victims, they only attain credibility following the establishment and implementation of a much more urgently needed reparations program that caters for their basic needs.[47]

The choice of cases and charges leads to direct differences in the potential for victims to realise reparations. Some findings of the study exemplify this:

> [V]ictims are expressing their disappointment for not having the opportunity to participate in the Ongwen case … [because] the people of areas such as Lukodi (which is covered by the Ongwen charges) are already receiving assistance from the ICC while they are not.[48]

Thinking about such inequalities at the start of investigations and prosecutions has at least the potential to alleviate some of the effects of selectivity and impact on the potential legacy of the ICC's involvement.

With regard to completion strategies, the point that comes out of the analysis here is that the OTP needs to give much greater thought to reparative justice working hand-in-hand with victims groups in its processes, especially with the Trust Fund for Victims. In partnership with other organisations, the Trust Fund is – as of 2019 – involved in four projects across northern Uganda that aim at psychological (and to a smaller extent also physical) rehabilitation programmes.[49] While the work of the Trust Fund has been perceived as positive, it did at times raise unfulfilled expectations, leaving victims frustrated.[50] These findings emphasise the need for carefully planned outreach activities from the outset and follow-up with victims,[51] a task for the Registry as the organ conducting outreach as much as the OTP.

C. Completion as a Court-Wide Process

A comparison of the OTP approaches in Colombia and Uganda suggests that a country receives much greater scrutiny from the ICC at the preliminary stage than the investigation stage. This risks inviting state actors to aim at having a

[46] Avocat Sans Frontières, A Beggar has no Choice, Victims' Perspectives on a Reparations Framework for Uganda (2017), available at: www.asf.be.

[47] ibid, 13.

[48] ibid.

[49] See for information on the specific projects: trustfundforvictims.org.

[50] ASF Study (n 46) 28.

[51] ibid, 31.

given situation in their jurisdiction move to the investigation stage, since this could in fact decrease the exposure to overall scrutiny. Inconsistency is also evident regarding the de facto acceptance of amnesties in Uganda but not in Colombia. Variations in the Court's position as such might be necessary, as the type of amnesty can vary considerably and serve different purposes.[52] Any of these considerations, however, would need to be openly addressed. Inconsistency also exists regarding the formulated need to address a variety of types of crime that have occurred in Colombia, whereas the need for accountability for government crimes in Uganda is at least not openly addressed by the OTP.

There will be no-size-fits-all approach. For the conduct of preliminary examinations, the end is much easier to determine for a smaller-scale situation such as that in Guinea, which centres around a more limited event in Conakry in 2009. The complementarity assessment in Guinea focuses on the domestic investigation of that attack and seems now in the end stages with the beginning of trial proceedings against 13 high-ranking officials imminent.[53] The end to such an examination will clearly be much easier to determine than that in Colombia.

Equally, considerations as to the potential if and how to end any investigation require careful planning and recalibrating at different stages of the investigation. The examples here have shown that the completion of the ICC's activities entails dimensions well beyond those of the OTP investigation. Based on article 79 of the Statute, the Trust Fund for Victims plays a critical role at this stage. It is mandated with the implementation of Court-ordered reparations and the provision of physical, psychological and material support to victims and their families. Hence, the ICC and the Trust Fund are required to work in institutional partnership. Equally, the ICC Registry plays a role for the 'non-judicial' aspects of the Court's work.[54] It conducts and coordinates public information and outreach activities in the communities affected by the investigated crimes.[55] Effective communication of investigation and prosecution results, and of any prosecutorial decisions to end its activities, will be critical for the legacy of the Court's involvement in a country.

III. LIMITS TO COMPLETION

Completion is not a distinct stage of the proceedings as such and no distinct set of legal provisions is applicable to this process. Only very limited scenarios

[52] Prosecutions have gained prominence since the 1990s and Latin America has led the way here where amnesties were tried but did not work. See K Sikkink, *The Justice Cascade: How Human Rights Prosecutions are Changing World Politics* (New York, Norton, 2011).

[53] Preliminary Examination Report 2018 (n 8) 184.

[54] Art 43 ICCSt.

[55] The Registry is also responsible for organising the protection of victims and witnesses, where needed. The permanence of the Court allows the continuation of this work after completion of a situation investigation. For the completion strategies of other courts and tribunals, this was one of the particular challenges. See KJ Heller 'Completion' in L Reydams, J Wouters and C Ryngaert (eds), *International Prosecutors* (Oxford, Oxford University Press, 2012) 914.

allow a clearly determined completed preliminary examination or investigation. Once the prosecution of these perpetrators has ended, the Court would have broadly achieved its aim. In the currently pending situations, however, the Court mostly deals with protracted armed conflicts entailing a variety of different actors, different areas of crime and, accordingly, large numbers of potential cases. The examples of Colombia and Uganda show that it is more difficult in these circumstances to clearly identify when the Court's mission is fulfilled. The completion process is influenced by different aspects, including the scope of a given examination or investigation, the cases chosen for prosecution and the Court's aims in a situation. Delineating the boundaries to a process based on a multitude of decisions at various junctures, however, means that these boundaries have to be more broadly construed.

A. The Principle of Complementarity Beyond Admissibility

The central limitation to the Court's mandate and the Prosecutor's discretion is the principle of complementarity. It is embodied in the Preamble and in article 1 of the Rome Statute stating that the Court 'shall be complementary to national criminal jurisdictions'. This prominent position in the Rome Statute emphasises its importance. Its purpose is the protection of sovereign interests in the pursuit of justice for crimes within the Court's jurisdiction.[56] Previously, the *ad hoc* tribunals had a primary role in relation to domestic courts. Instead, the ICC is portrayed as a court of last resort when states fail to provide accountability for international crimes.[57] Article 17 of the Rome Statute addresses the relationship between national and international proceedings further through the criteria for the admissibility of cases before the ICC. What matters is whether a case is or has been investigated or prosecuted by a state which has jurisdiction over it, and that those proceedings are not conducted for the purpose of shielding the person from criminal responsibility.[58] The Court perceives the principle of complementarity as 'relating to the admissibility of cases before the Court

[56] *Prosecutor v Muthaura, Kenyatta, and Ali*, Decision on the Application by the Government of Kenya Challenging the Admissibility of the Case pursuant to Art 19(2)(b) of the Statute, ICC-01/09-02/11, 30 May 2011, para 40: 'The Chamber is well aware that the concept of complementarity and the manner in which it operates goes to the heart of States' sovereign rights'. Also, Nouwen (n 19) 58; J Holmes, 'The Principle of Complementarity' in RS Lee (ed), *The International Criminal Court: The Making of the Rome Statute* (The Hague, Kluwer Law International, 1999) 74.

[57] See P Kirsch, 'The Role of the International Criminal Court in Enforcing International Criminal Law' (2007) 22 *American University International Law Review* 539, 543.

[58] Art 17(1) ICCSt:

> 'Having regard to paragraph 10 of the Preamble and article 1, the Court shall determine that a case is inadmissible where:
>
> (a) The case is being investigated or prosecuted by a State which has jurisdiction over it, unless the State is unwilling or unable genuinely to carry out the investigation or prosecution;

pursuant to article 17 of the Statute'.[59] Yet, it is safe to assume that the ICC will not be able to prosecute all crimes under its jurisdiction in a given situation.[60] For that reason, the reference to admissibility alone for determining when a preliminary examination or a situation investigation can come to an end is not helpful for developing a structured approach to completion. Complementarity contains multiple aspects that go beyond the scope of the enquiry here.[61] In what follows, therefore, I will focus on developing my core argument that the principle of complementarity is more than merely a rule to regulate the admissibility of cases before the ICC. It is a limitation on prosecutorial discretion through the need to respect state sovereignty and allow deference to the domestic exercise of jurisdiction.[62]

The admissibility rules in article 17 set the bar very high for proceedings that could render a case inadmissible. In a first step, an assessment is necessary whether any proceedings at the national level exist,[63] and, if so, whether these 'cover the same individual and substantially the same conduct as alleged in the proceedings before the Court'.[64] For ongoing investigations, concrete and specific steps at the national level are required.[65] Generally, the Prosecutor must defer to the national efforts, unless the state is genuinely 'unwilling' or 'unable' to carry out the proceedings. This requires proceedings not to be a mere sham to prevent ICC action.

A key point of criticism that has been developed around these requirements is that this interpretation leaves little room for national investigations. For the

(b) The case has been investigated by a State which has jurisdiction over it and the State has decided not to prosecute the person concerned, unless the decision resulted from the unwillingness or inability of the State genuinely to prosecute;
(c) The person concerned has already been tried for conduct which is the subject of the complaint, and a trial by the Court is not permitted under article 20, paragraph 3'.

[59] ASP Report (n 3) para 23.

[60] C Stahn, 'Bridge Over troubled Waters?' in C Stahn and M El Zeidy (eds), *The International Criminal Court and Complementarity: From Theory to Practice* (Cambridge, Cambridge University Press, 2011) 3.

[61] See C Stahn, M El Zeidy (eds), *The International Criminal Court and Complementarity: From Theory to Practice* (Cambridge, Cambridge University Press, 2011) for an excellent overview over the different aspects of the principle of complementarity.

[62] P Clarke, *Distant Justice: The Impact of the International Criminal Court on African Politics* (Cambridge, Cambridge University Press, 2018) 28 frames this aspect of complementarity politically as the need for deference to domestic institutions.

[63] *Prosecutor v Katanga and Ngudjolo Chui*, Judgment on the Appeal of Mr Germain Katanga against the Oral Decision of Trial Chamber II of 12 June 2009 on the Admissibility of the Case, ICC-01/04-01/07-1497, 25 September 2009, paras 75–79.

[64] *Prosecutor v Ruto, Kosgey and Sang*, Judgment on the appeal of the Republic of Kenya against the decision of Pre-Trial Chamber II of 30 May 2011 entitled 'Decision on the Application by the Government of Kenya Challenging the Admissibility of the Case pursuant to Article 19(2)(b) of the Statute', ICC-01/09-01/11-307, 30 August 2011, para 1.

[65] *Prosecutor v Muthaura, Kenyatta and Ali*, Judgment on the appeal of the Republic of Kenya against the decision of Pre-Trial Chamber II of 30 May 2011 entitled 'Decision on the Application by the Government of Kenya Challenging the Admissibility of the Case pursuant to Article 19(2)(b) of the Statute', ICC-01/09-02/11-274, 30 August 2011, paras 1, 2, 40.

end of ICC investigations, regarding cases that have already been chosen by the OTP for prosecution, this requires a state to select the same person and the same factual conduct, potentially even the same charges, for domestic proceedings in order to trigger inadmissibility.[66] This turns the relationship between the Court and domestic jurisdictions on its head as the domestic jurisdictions should take the lead in their primary role rather than the ICC determining the parameters of domestic investigation:

> Once the Court's jurisdiction has been triggered, the state that wishes to avoid or end ICC involvement thus loses all prosecutorial discretion. The ICC Prosecutor, by contrast, has in practice total discretion in his or her decision which person, conduct, incident and mode of liability to charge. This inequality in discretion is difficult to square with any idea of primacy of domestic justice systems.[67]

Heller calls in this context for radical complementarity that would shift the focus back to domestic action.[68] Based on the analysis of Appeals Chamber (AC) complementarity decisions, Heller argues for radical complementarity, departing from the current tests. He demonstrates that the current interpretation of article 17 of the Statute would force a domestic investigation to adjust to, or pre-empt the focus of an ICC investigation, even if a strategy of building up a case against a more senior leader through the prosecution of other cases might be more promising than the ICC approach.[69] Similarly to Nouwen's critique, a key point is the inconsistency with the principle of complementarity designed to protect sovereignty.[70] It should be the state's first point of call to determine the need for investigations rather than the ICC investigation determining the boundaries of what the national state ought to do. It is worth reiterating here that the ICC was designed as a court of last resort. Currently, the primary role for states exercising their criminal jurisdiction becomes merely theoretical once the ICC has started investigations.

An additional critical dimension in the admissibility assessment is the dynamic development of potential domestic proceedings. The case against Simone Gbagbo illustrates this well. This case has been pending at the ICC in parallel to the case against Laurent Gbagbo. While he was on trial at the ICC, she had been investigated and prosecuted domestically in Côte d'Ivoire. The country saw a period of post-election violence from 2010 to 2011, which forms the core of ICC investigations. To date, the OTP has focused its investigations on one side of the conflict, Ex-President Gbagbo's side, whereas the crimes of the pro-Ouattara forces, the current head of state, have been left unaddressed. According to the OTP, domestic proceedings against Simone Gbagbo appeared

[66] Nouwen (n 19) 51.
[67] ibid, 52–53.
[68] KJ Heller, 'Radical Complementarity' (2016) 14 *Journal of International Criminal Justice* 637.
[69] ibid, 643.
[70] Heller, 'Radical Complementarity' (n 68) 648.

'to bear broad similarity to the case before the Court'.[71] The admissibility challenge was rejected on the ground that the conduct was not substantially the same in the domestic case as in the ICC case.[72] Heller[73] highlights the timing in this case: the Pre-Trial Chamber (PTC) rejected the admissibility challenge two weeks before the trial against her opened in Abidjan, and the AC judgment was issued two months after conviction and sentencing to 20 years' imprisonment for her role in the post-election violence.[74] Admissibility proceedings only appear to provide a small amount of flexibility to reassess and adjust to dynamic developments in a specific situation. This point reinforces Heller's call for radical complementarity:

> [T]he idea that as long as a state is making a genuine effort to bring a suspect to justice, the ICC should find his or her case inadmissible regardless of the conduct the state investigates or the prosecutorial strategy the state pursues.[75]

This call is addressed to the OTP as much as the judiciary to revisit its interpretation of article 17 of the Rome Statute.

The argument advanced here, however, aims at developing an understanding of the principle of complementarity that, beyond the admissibility of specific cases, inserts respect for the primary role of domestic proceedings in the exercise of prosecutorial discretion. The prosecutorial task to devise strategies for the completion of investigations, and accordingly for preliminary examinations, requires the exercise of discretion in such a way that the domestic proceedings can take a primary role. The observations on the law in action regarding the interpretation of article 17 of the Statute have made it clear that the current ICC position undermines this relationship.

The principle of complementarity has a dimension beyond the admissibility of cases. The Rome Statute refers to the principle of complementarity in article 1 of the Statute independently of the admissibility criteria in article 17 of the Statute. The latter might be understood as a specific admissibility rule, whereas the former contains a broader and all-encompassing principle that addresses the general relationship between the Court and states ('shall be complementary to national jurisdictions'). The ordinary meaning of complementarity is that of a 'relationship or situation in which two or more different things improve or emphasize each other's qualities'.[76] The notion contains an element

[71] *Prosecutor v Simone Gbagbo*, Decision on Côte d'Ivoire's challenge to the admissibility of the case against Simone Gbagbo, ICC-02/11-01/12-47-Red, 11 December 2014, para 17.

[72] ibid, para 78.

[73] Heller, 'Radical Complementarity' (n 68) 639.

[74] An interesting twist for any future proceedings before the ICC against Gbagbo is the amnesty granted to Simone Gbagbo and hundreds of Gbagbo supporters in 2018 in a move by Ouattara to contribute to peace and reconciliation in the country.

[75] Heller, 'Radical Complementarity' (n 68) 637.

[76] Definition of 'complementarity': Lexico.com.

of enhancement rather than competition. Once ICC proceedings have been reduced to competition for the ownership of a case, rather than jointly focusing efforts on closing the gaps of impunity in a given situation, or respecting state sovereignty, the principle of complementarity is no longer being served.

Thus, the principle of complementarity limits the exercise of prosecutorial discretion in such a way that it must ensure a primary role for domestic proceedings in the strategic planning for the completion of its activities in a given situation. This requires a proactive approach from both sides, genuine state efforts as well as cooperation. OTP cooperation with domestic states can take a variety of forms, such as information sharing as well as sharing best practice. In this context, the efforts in Uganda on participation in training programmes exemplify such cooperation.[77] Additionally, the OTP is mandated to share information with countries on the basis of article 93(10) of the Statute linked to its investigations for the purpose of further proceedings at the domestic level.[78]

The preliminary examination in Colombia currently shows little sign of deference to national ownership over the process. The principle of complementarity provides no mandate to act as transitional justice supervisor. However, it has to be acknowledged that it is the OTP's duty to provide guidance to situation countries regarding the scope of the cases pending before the ICC, and how it understands its complementary role. The ASP's call for greater clarity in its guidance,[79] albeit with due respect for the sovereign exercise of criminal jurisdiction, shows the need for clearer, but in my view also more restrained, OTP messages. This would allow a state to initiate proceedings and could 'have the potential to shape complementarity's catalysing effect'.[80] States emerging from conflict that make genuine and substantial efforts to provide accountability for international crimes require some flexibility on the ICC's part to reassert their own sovereignty to exercise their jurisdiction over international crimes.

B. Minimum Due Process Guarantees in Domestic Proceedings

Article 17 of the Statute provides further boundaries for the completion of given situations. Although the principle of complementarity aims to delineate the relationship between the Court and states, it implements a further boundary regarding the types of efforts that are needed. The Libyan cases triggered a controversy in how far fair trial standards are required to ensure that domestic proceedings render a case inadmissible. The AC in *Al Senussi* found that

[77] Although this must not amount to capacity-building efforts, as this is not within the Court's mandate.

[78] S Shoamanesh, 'Institution Building: Perspective from within the Office of the Prosecutor of the International Criminal Court' (2018) 18 *International Criminal Law Review* 489, 507.

[79] 'Strengthening the International Criminal Court and the Assembly of States Parties' (n 1).

[80] Nouwen (n 19) 70.

extreme cases of due process violations would be 'inconsistent with the intent to bring the person to justice'.[81] The AC reasoned:

> [D]epending on the facts of the individual case, whereby violations of the rights of the suspect are so egregious that the proceedings can no longer be regarded as being capable of providing any genuine form of justice to the suspect so that they should be deemed, in those circumstances, to be 'inconsistent with an intent to bring the person to justice'.[82]

This finding has to be placed in context in that it is not potential human rights infringements, but only extreme due process violations that could be taken into consideration for the admissibility of cases before the Court.[83] For the exercise of prosecutorial discretion, this provides a further limitation in that the completion of an investigation with a view to national efforts would be barred in the case of gross due process violations in the national setting. A not entirely hypothetical scenario would be one in which alleged perpetrators of international crimes are exposed to gross human rights violations through prolonged detention, exposed to torture and inhumane conditions, are faced with a trial that might last for 10 minutes or an hour before being sentenced to death. Currently, this seems to be the 'justice' response to the crimes committed by Da'esh fighters.[84] A scenario, in which the Prosecutor should defer to such national proceedings – or sham justice?

The AC position reverberates with the jurisprudence of the International Criminal Tribunal for the former Yugoslavia (ICTR) on completion processes. The ICTR discussed the due process requirements that a national jurisdiction must meet when prosecuting international crimes in a situation of concurrent jurisdiction with an international court.[85] In contrast to the ICC, the ICTR had a primary role towards national jurisdictions. However, the constrained time frame for the closure of the *ad hoc* tribunals triggered referrals of cases from the international to the national level to clear the decks. The introduction of rule 11*bis* of the Rules of Procedure and Evidence in the ICTR basically shifted the relationship with national courts to a 'more or less' complementarity role of the ICTR.[86] The ICTR had refused referrals to national courts based on due

[81] *Prosecutor v Gaddafi and Al Senussi*, Judgment on the appeal of Mr Abdullah Al-Senussi against the decision of Pre-Trial Chamber I of 11 October 2013 entitled 'Decision on the admissibility of the case against Abdullah Al-Senussi', ICC-01/11-01/11-565, 24 July 2014, para 1.

[82] ibid, para 3.

[83] ibid, para 169.

[84] According to newspaper reports, these are conditions in which some captured Daesh fighters find themselves in. See A Rubin, 'France hands ISIS suspects to Iraq, which sentences them to hang' *New York Times* (29 May 2019), available at: nytimes.com.

[85] A Marong and C Jalloh, 'Transfer of Cases under the Jurisprudence of the ICTR and Lessons Learnt for the ICC' in C Jalloh and A Marong, *Promoting Accountability under International Law for Gross Human Rights Violations in Africa* (Leiden, Brill Njihoff, 2015) 411.

[86] See similarly United Nations, ICTR Office of the Prosecutor, Complementarity in Action: Lessons Learned from the ICTR's Prosecutor's Referral of International Criminal Cases to National Jurisdictions for Trial, February 2015, 6.

process considerations.[87] It considered that judicial capacities were only slowly developing in Rwanda's justice system.[88] However, in contrast to article 17 of the Rome Statute, rule 11*bis* in the *ad hoc* tribunals explicitly refers to the fairness of proceedings,[89] therefore providing a clear legal basis for such consideration, making a comparative argument slightly less compelling.

The findings in the Libyan situation have provoked the critique that these requirements would not fit complementarity and even amount to 'norm hijacking'.[90] The AC acknowledged that the ICC is not designed to address due process violations at a different jurisdictional level. Nevertheless, the AC position touches on the core of international criminal justice. The not too far-fetched scenario above does not even entail a minimum of due process guarantees, lacks proper evidence gathering and the potential exposure to conditions that amount to torture and inhumane treatment as *ius cogens* violations. Such proceedings do not 'close the gap of impunity' but create new gaps. Normatively, as I have argued in chapter four on case selection, trials can be justified as truth-seeking mechanisms and as practices of accountability. Yet, a trial in the scenario above does neither. It does not contribute to the aim of establishing the truth, nor does it provide accountability. Such proceedings provide mere vengeance against the (alleged) enemy. Due process considerations hinder the Prosecutor in such circumstances from deferring to national proceedings for the sake of completing a given situation.

IV. GUIDING FACTORS

The completion of ICC interventions, either through a preliminary examination or through a full investigation, is closely linked with the preceding OTP strategies. The initial scope of an investigation, as well as case selection, has an important impact on the question on when an investigation is complete. Consideration and communication of the precise aims of any investigation right from the outset, and adjusted to developing circumstances, is therefore important. The discussion in the previous chapters has attempted to translate these broad aims into guiding principles for the exercise of discretion at the specific stages of the proceedings. Principles of fairness, of human rights considerations,

[87] *Prosecutor v Munyakazi*, Decision on the Prosecutor's Request for Referral of Case to the Republic of Rwanda, Case No ICTR-97-36-R11bis, 28 May 2008.

[88] See ICTR, *Lessons Learned* (n 86) 16–18 for further case law. The OTP responded to the refusal of referrals with roadmaps for Rwanda on how to tackle legislative reform, which led to renewed cooperation and reform.

[89] Rule 11*bis* (C):

> 'In determining whether to refer the case in accordance with paragraph (A), the Trial Chamber shall satisfy itself that the accused will receive a fair trial in the courts of the State concerned and that the death penalty will not be imposed or carried out'.

[90] See Nouwen (n 19) 192.

of being representative of all sides of the conflict where all sides have committed crimes, of allowing diversity and local ownership, and of being guided by victims' interests, all also play critical roles for completion processes. These principles make up an important part of the fabric of the ICC.

Considering the expressive power of the ICC, the end of an investigation and completion of the ICC's work can send strong messages. It can signal approval for domestic developments and communicate acceptance of specific transitional justice mechanisms. Any completion strategy needs to take these communicative effects into account.[91] Any investigation ought not to be limited through specific deadlines or be driven by performance indicators. Justice does not come cheaply and can take a long time. An investigation might encounter a multitude of problems such as non-cooperation or security issues. Perhaps an investigation will lie dormant or hibernate[92] until fundamental political change in a country takes place and enables the ICC to access important evidence. In such instances, although it is important to minimise the cost of such investigations, given the available budget, closing the investigation would give the impression that justice has not been done. Having said that, resource constraints and pressures on the Court are a reality.

A. An Interests-of-Justice-Based Approach

Justice will only be done if it respects those who have suffered. The answer to the exercise of discretion, when having to develop a strategy for the completion of complex and large-scale situations such as in Uganda and Colombia, must ultimately lie with the interests of justice. Article 53(1)(c) for the decision not to investigate and (2)(c) for the decision not to prosecute any further cases are the statutory answer to the question of completing the Court activities in complex situations in which not all crimes will be sufficiently addressed. The text of the Statute makes clear that the victims' voices play a critical role in this regard. In the previous chapter, I have argued for an approach to the interests of justice that creates space for legal pluralism and allows local ownership of the process. Calls have been made to use article 17 of the Statute to bar ICC activities, when transitional justice mechanisms are the favoured approach in the domestic context, to avoid the imposition of Western expectations on other legal cultures.[93] However, article 17 does not provide the flexibility to adjust the approach in a given situation to a broad variety of possible scenarios. In some situations, alternative forms of justice might be required to provide justice for

[91] See Heller, 'Completion' (n 55) 909 on the impact of completion strategies on the legitimacy of other international tribunals.

[92] This was the language adopted in the situation in Kenya.

[93] Minow (n 4) 8.

victims beyond Western norms. This will depend strongly on the cultural and political context. My argument is that this is precisely where the interests of justice provide the flexibility to reconcile the need for alternatives with the need for accountability.

As the situations in Uganda and Colombia demonstrate, state actors are often implicated in scenarios facing the ICC. Reliance on domestic actors, and an overemphasis on the sovereign will of states linked to a situation, can even risk fundamentally undermining the aims of international criminal law. The task for the ICC is to close the gap of impunity where state actors have failed to prevent and/or are responsible for crimes such as genocide, crimes against humanity or war crimes – and, one day, the crime of aggression. The tension between state sovereignty and individual criminal responsibility is a major difficulty for the ICC and international criminal law more broadly.

I have argued above that genuine state efforts should limit the Prosecutor's discretionary power and require deference to state efforts. Nevertheless, often situations will feature a grey zone in which states might be compelled to take some action but lack the resolve to fully address all sides of the conflict and genuinely provide accountability for crimes by state actors. It is this grey zone that the Prosecutor needs to address, and which contains a core challenge for the completion of situations. Victims' voices and the voices of the affected communities more broadly ought to have a mediating function in ensuring that the Prosecutor can strike a balance between state sovereignty and the need for criminal accountability. Local communities, those directly affected by conflict, are those best able to judge whether state efforts are genuine and whether the transitional scenario provides justice for them. Legally, the vehicle to provide space for this mediating influence and provide a voice for affected communities are the interests of justice.

A parallel to the completion of judicial intervention can be drawn to the exit in the context of post-conflict state-building activities. In that context, exit is defined 'as the transition of political authority from international to legitimate local institutions'.[94] This definition contains a couple of important aspects for the challenge of a principled stance to the completion of ICC investigations. It is a transitional process in which slowly emerging justice processes might run in parallel at different levels. In Uganda, and similarly in the Central African Republic (CAR), states initially triggered the Court's jurisdiction through referrals. While cases at the ICC are still ongoing, domestic proceedings emerge. The legitimacy of these domestic proceedings matters in this context. Such legitimacy of the local justice mechanism is determined through a variety of components such as the fairness of proceedings at the local level and the acceptance among the local communities. Readers will recall that I have argued previously in the book that local ownership of the justice processes is important in the context

[94] D Zaum, 'The Norms and Politics of Exit: Ending Postconflict Transitional Administrations' (2009) 23 *Ethics & International Affairs* 189, 193.

of the interests of justice. This goes precisely to the heart of the matter here. Taking communities in their self-determination seriously requires acceptance of those local mechanisms that are deemed legitimate among the population as an answer to the crimes that happened, as long as those answers create no new injustices through human rights violations.

Although the interests of justice are one of the *sui generis* features of the Rome Statute, the central place for affected communities in completion processes connects directly to some of the lessons that can be learned from other tribunals, in which outreach is often identified as a critical aspect for successful processes. '[T]here is a need to be responsive to what local populations think on the matter, otherwise irrespective of the excellent work the ICC may do, its departure risks leaving a bitter taste in too many mouths'.[95] Outreach, in this context, is not to be understood as a one-way street of explaining Court activities, but also to listen to affected communities and provide avenues for their input.[96] Such consultation has to be a broad exercise – as consideration beyond the interests of justice as such – to develop a genuine understanding of how best to create dynamics that contribute to building a sustainable legacy of justice. Government officials will be one part in the picture, but also civil society, victim and witness groups, voices of minorities[97] and whoever else has a role to play for the transition of a conflicted society to one that achieves reconciliation and peace.

B. Building a Legacy of Justice

Based on the local context, discretion should furthermore be guided by the aim to contribute to a legacy of justice, one not only focused on criminal accountability but a broader notion of justice. Clearly, the Prosecutor is a legal actor and her remit is limited. However, where the law does provide flexibility, contributing to a more holistic form of justice is important. One of those obvious points to make, and which links back to case selection processes, is the need to work towards an outcome that communities perceive as fair. Fairness is not only linked to procedures but also to the outcome of an investigation. Is it fair if all sides in a conflict have committed war crimes and yet only one side is being held to account, because the crimes from one side appeared graver than that of the other? It will be difficult for the OTP to contribute to a legacy of justice without addressing crimes in northern Uganda committed by the Ugandan state. Recent research into the developments in Uganda, based on field work and interviews

[95] Evenson and Smith (n 45) 1272.
[96] Heller, 'Completion' (n 55) 917.
[97] ibid.

in Uganda, revisits the peace talks in Juba against the backdrop of the ICC investigation. One of its conclusions is sobering:

> A key, enduring ICC legacy in northern Uganda is not justice, nor peace. It is something more modest but no less significant: a set of domestic transitional justice accords designed to 'protect' both government and rebel leaders from ICC style accountability.[98]

Another dimension for the OTP to consider is that the need for the prosecution of international crimes has to compete with other urgent political, social and economic demands.[99] Resources in the justice system and the state more generally have to address other forms of crimes and violence, and overburdened courts are obvious challenges in these environments. The UN suggests that 'an overly ambitious approach to prosecutions may cause a backlash, including potential threats to stability … and renewed calls for legislative barriers, such as amnesty laws'.[100] But the need to consider the socio-economic context in a given situation goes well beyond avoidance of a backlash. A lasting justice legacy cannot ignore the root causes of conflict and violence. The recurring theme in Colombia and Uganda is that through ICC intervention the narrative has shifted to an 'anti-impunity' agenda,[101] pushing the broader problems in the background.[102] Yet, the 'armed conflict was not only about national security, crime, or violence, but also about economic, social, and political exclusion'.[103] The Prosecutor has to be sensitive to the dangers of an anti-impunity agenda that can open the door to hard-nosed law-and-order politics rather than transformational societal processes that address inequalities. Context-sensitivity can express itself in greater deference to a domestic agenda with a strong focus on reforms aimed at alleviating the root causes of conflict through measures such as land reforms.[104] In Uganda, reparative forms of justice were more important for communities than the aspect of retribution through specific forms of punishment. For a lasting legacy, the Prosecutor needs to exercise discretion in the completion process in a way that positively considers the embeddedness of transitional justice measures in broader (eg, social, environmental) justice initiatives.

[98] A Macdonald, '"In the Interests of Justice?" The International Criminal Court, Peace Talks and the Failed Quest for War Crimes Accountability in Northern Uganda' (2017) 11 *Journal of Eastern African Studies* 628, 642.

[99] Office of the United Nations High Commissioner for Human Rights, *Rule-of-Law Tools for Post-Conflict States*, HR/PUB/06/4, New York, Geneva 2006, 5.

[100] ibid.

[101] K Engle, 'Anti-Impunity and the Turn to Criminal Law in Human Rights' (2015) 100 *Cornell Law Review* 1069.

[102] Kersten (n 38) 73 remarks on the conflict in Uganda: 'The political causes and dynamics of the war are largely ignored in favour of a narrative that views the LRA's actions as being propelled by an irrational need to commit atrocities and as being responsible for a humanitarian rather than political crisis'.

[103] Alviar García and Engle (n 7) 225.

[104] ibid, 239 demonstrating the problem for Colombia, where by 2014 'only 0.005 percent of all the land that has "forcibly changed hands" during the conflict' has been restored.

V. ACCOUNTABILITY

Rooting discretion within the law requires scrutiny as to its rightful exercise. This is as critical for the end of an investigation as it is for the beginning of the Court's activities. In this context, the identification of avenues for accountability is one of the overarching themes throughout this book. In particular the absence of a clear legal framework makes it more difficult to identify the mechanisms through which completion strategies can be exposed to some form of scrutiny. Also, I have demonstrated earlier that completion processes will require the OTP to work in concert with other actors such as the Trust Fund for Victims and the Registry. Formal judicial review mechanisms in the Rome Statute are ill-fitting as accountability mechanisms over what hopefully will emerge as holistically designed completion processes. For prosecutorial decisions over the formal end of an investigation and the non-prosecution of cases, however, accountability and the mechanisms in Article 53(3) are critical.[105]

A. Preliminary Examinations, the Interests of Justice and Article 53(3)

For preliminary examination processes, the decision not to investigate based on the interests of justice after a period of positive complementarity might be one option for the OTP to end such examinations. Perhaps, the preliminary examination in Colombia will be the first to end on that note. Article 53(3) of the Statute would allow states or the Security Council (SC) to trigger judicial review, and, additionally, the PTC may review such a decision on its own motion. The discussion above and throughout the book, in particular in chapter six, has demonstrated that, to date, the OTP seems reluctant to use the interests of justice. However, ongoing 'supervision of domestic proceedings' appears increasingly difficult to justify in situations such as Colombia. But moving from the specific example to the more abstract considerations, a decision not to investigate in the interests of justice would not have a *res judicata* effect. The ICC could revisit the situation, should a positive transition process in a country stall or be abandoned.

[105] Art 53(3) ICCSt:

'(a) At the request of the State making a referral under article 14 or the Security Council under article 13, paragraph (b), the Pre-Trial Chamber may review a decision of the Prosecutor under paragraph 1 or 2 not to proceed and may request the Prosecutor to reconsider that decision.

(b) In addition, the Pre-Trial Chamber may, on its own initiative, review a decision of the Prosecutor not to proceed if it is based solely on paragraph 1(c) or 2(c). In such a case, the decision of the Prosecutor shall be effective only if confirmed by the Pre-Trial Chamber'.

Proactively using the interests of justice as a concept for a structured and principled completion process provides the advantage of a more persuasive decision that is not based on prosecutorial discretion alone but has been exposed to judicial scrutiny. This applies to all those preliminary examinations in which a 'grey zone' of potential criminal conduct exists that would be in the Court's remit and in which domestic proceedings or mechanisms are slow. Yet, the relationship between the OTP and PTCs regarding the proper scope of judicial review of prosecutorial discretionary decisions has at times been rather troublesome. With more case law emerging as the Court consolidates its work, these problems will hopefully peter out, and the positive effects of judicial review can strengthen the Court's work.

B. Ending Situation Investigations: A Role for Article 52(2)?

The OTP is entering entirely novel legal ground with the completion of situation investigations. Yet, the PTC decision in Kenya[106] might inadvertently provide one of the first building blocks for the task of the ICC in formulating a procedural structure for the completion of situations. I want to recall that victims sought judicial review of the Prosecutor's decision in Kenya to withdraw the charges against Kenyatta and cease active investigation, after the evidential basis had collapsed. The PTC found that article 53(1) of the Statute was not applicable since an investigation had started and the provision only referred to the initiation of an investigation.[107]

The Rome Statute, as such, provides no guidance although the structure of article 53 suggests that the drafters aimed to cover investigations in paragraph 1 as well as prosecutions in paragraph 2. There are varying scenarios for situations in which the OTP has initiated investigations that are coming to an end. In detail, this will depend on how the OTP structures its investigations. If an overarching 'situation investigation' is branched out into more specific investigations focusing on clearly identified cases, it becomes easier to identify at what point those investigations might come to an end. In such a scenario article 53(2)[108]

[106] *Situation in the Republic of Kenya*, Decision on the Victims' Request for Review of Prosecution's Decision to Cease Active investigation, ICC-01/09-159, 5 November 2015.

[107] ibid, para 21.

[108] Art 53(2) ICCSt:

> 'If, upon investigation, the Prosecutor concludes that there is not a sufficient basis for a prosecution because:
>
> (a) There is not a sufficient legal or factual basis to seek a warrant or summons under article 58;
> (b) The case is inadmissible under article 17; or
> (c) A prosecution is not in the interests of justice, taking into account all the circumstances, including the gravity of the crime, the interests of victims and the age or infirmity of the alleged perpetrator, and his or her role in the alleged crime; the Prosecutor shall inform the Pre-Trial Chamber and the State making a referral under article 14 or the Security Council in a case under article 13, paragraph (b), of his or her conclusion and the reasons for the conclusion'.

becomes relevant.[109] If the Prosecutor has reached the decision to complete an investigation into a situation, she will also have to take decisions not to prosecute specific cases that would have been within the pool of admissible cases but not prioritised. The decision not to prosecute any further cases that would provide a sufficient evidentiary basis for prosecution might be made on the basis of complementarity, or such a decision might be based on the interests of justice. In those situations, article 53(2) requires the Prosecutor to inform the PTC, and a State Party or the SC for referred situations, which might in turn lead to judicial review based on article 53(3) of the Statute.[110]

In the situation in Uganda, judges decided to convene a status conference after the Prosecutor had signalled (in 2005!) that the investigation was 'nearing completion'.[111] Other cases than those against LRA commanders would be presented if they reached the 'gravity standards of the Statute'.[112] At that point, five arrest warrants against the LRA leadership had been issued. This early decision seems to indicate that the PTC interprets article 53(2) and (3)(b) in such a way that it would grant them the authority to review the OTP's decision not to pursue further prosecutions.[113] The drafting history of article 53(2) of the Statute provides little insight into the aim of this provision.[114] Interpreting article 53(2) of the Statute contextually suggests that the drafters aimed at inserting judicial review at investigation as well as prosecution stage. The overall aim of installing PTCs in the ICC system was to prevent a politicised Prosecutor. To give full effect to this aim, article 52(2) of the Statute should be interpreted in such a way that it allows a PTC review of cases that are not being prosecuted even if other prosecutions are under way. Such an understanding could, for example, counter a danger that the focus remains on one side of a conflict only.

C. Pragmatic Accountability: Towards a Court-Wide Policy

The ICC needs a court-wide completion policy that links different main themes such as the complementary role of the Court, its understanding of the interests of justice and, most critically, spells out the vision of the Court and its broader aims.[115] Such a policy requires a much needed debate that should be as wide and

[109] See for a detailed discussion ch 4 V.A.

[110] The need for notification is backed up by Rule 106 of the Rules of Procedure and Evidence of the International Criminal Court.

[111] *Situation in Uganda*, Decision to Convene a Status Conference on the Investigation in the Situation in Uganda in Relation to the Application of Article 53, ICC-01/04-01/05-68, 2 December 2005, para 8.

[112] ibid, para 9.

[113] R Hamilton, 'Closing ICC Investigations: A Second Bite at the Cherry for Complementarity?' (2012) Harvard University Human Rights Program, Research Working Paper Series HRP 12-001, May 2012, 9.

[114] ibid, 10.

[115] ibid, 13.

inclusive as possible. The broad aims of closing the gap of impunity, of deterrence and prevention, do not aid the Court sufficiently in its work, as scholars have lamented repeatedly. The question of completion makes this problem even more painfully clear, because only when an aim has been clearly defined, is it feasible to determine whether the mission has been accomplished.

To construct a meaningful policy, the Court needs to develop a multi-actor approach. For a legal institution, this will be an extremely challenging task. Prosecutorial and judicial independence do not easily fit into joint debates about what the interests of justice might mean, and about the aims pursued in specific situations. Legal institutions usually communicate through litigation: a specific decision is contested, and through contestation, the law develops. In this way, the Court has, for example, developed its approach regarding how to make sense of article 68(3) of the Statute and developed victim participation processes. For a successful completion strategy, however, different organs of the Court need to work in concert – and perhaps more so than at any other international court or tribunal that has existed to date. The judiciary will have a key role in determining the interests of justice. The concept will in many transitional settings be of critical importance for the task of completing the work of the Court. Therefore, the Court needs to speak with one voice, if and how a diverse range of transitional mechanisms might allow the Court to defer to such mechanisms. The Registry and the Trust Fund for Victims play pivotal roles in contributing to perceptions of justice and delivering key tasks. The Registry facilitates outreach activities and it will be critical that the Court as such, rather than only the OTP, communicates with and responds to those communities in a situation. The Trust Fund for Victims is tasked with the development and realisation of reparation schemes, another critical point in building a legacy of the Court's involvement. All this requires joined-up thinking across the different organs of the Court.

Such a court-wide policy will provide some much needed guidance for domestic actors, in relation to what to expect of ICC intervention. There will be no one-size-fits-all approach, because of the diversity of situations before the Court and the changing dynamics in them. It will nevertheless provide clarity, which in turn will allow states to better reassert sovereignty, where justified, and hopefully provide local communities with a pathway to take ownership over justice processes at the international or national level.

VI. CONCLUDING REMARKS

The task of completing the Court's long-pending preliminary examinations in transitional scenarios, as well as situation investigations, demonstrates the need for a principled exercise of discretion right from the start of preliminary examinations. The reflections on the investigation in Uganda have shown that a flawed investigation strategy that only focuses on one side of the conflict cannot create a legacy of justice. Any investigation will have to be carefully thought through from the start and has to be extremely sensitive to the political, social and economic context. Emerging or existing justice processes – even if they do not model on to the ICC system of criminal justice – might be valuable pathways to accountability.

How the ICC can contribute to the emergence of a more holistic justice agenda is still an open question. The ICC has to be sensitive to domestic transition efforts that address the root causes of crime, violence and conflict. An 'anti-impunity' agenda alone will not achieve this. Sustainable crime prevention requires efforts that tackle the root causes and see international crimes not as isolated phenomena but as the expression of greater problems. The Court only has a limited mandate in contributing to such efforts through the investigation and prosecution of the most serious crimes. Context-sensitivity could be one way for the ICC to become a part of the jigsaw of sustainable development towards peaceful and inclusive societies.[116]

The need to develop a court-wide completion policy provides an invaluable opportunity to take stock, to learn from past experiences, and to debate in depth how the broad aims of closing the impunity gap and prevention can be translated into more tangible aims. There will be no one-size-fits-all approach to the task of completing the Court's interventions, whether it is a more low-key examination or a full investigation. Prosecutorial discretion has a key role to play, but the Court needs to speak with one voice. It is critical to leave autonomous legal thinking behind and work towards a court-wide understanding of the interests of justice and of the principle of complementarity. The Prosecutor will only be able to provide valuable and much-needed guidance to domestic actors if there can be a degree of certainty among State Parties that judges will broadly support formulated OTP positions. Prosecutorial and judicial independence should not stand in the way of a fruitful dialogue between the different organs of the Court to develop a unified voice and a joint understanding of the Court's role.

Negotiating the tension between state sovereignty and individual criminal responsibility is a core challenge in international criminal law. The question of completion makes this ever more visible. Beyond the admissibility of cases before the Court, the principle of complementarity limits the Prosecutor's scope for action and requires deference to state sovereignty wherever genuine efforts are visible. The vehicle to provide the necessary flexibility for the OTP to provide space for diverse domestic developments is the interests of justice. In the Rome Statute, victims' interests are the backbone of this concept. Their voices,

[116] UN Sustainable Development Goal 16 aims at the '[promotion of] peaceful and inclusive societies for sustainable development, provide access to justice for all and build effective, accountable and inclusive institutions at all levels'.

the voices of those communities affected most by conflict and crime, must be listened to carefully. Doing so will allow the Prosecutor and the Court to mediate between state sovereignty and the need for holding those most responsible to account. Victims know best whether state efforts will genuinely provide justice for them. It will be the victims' perceptions that will judge the ICC's legitimacy and decide its future in the long run.

Conclusion

More than 20 years after the Rome Conference in 1998, the international legal and political landscape has changed dramatically. Right-wing populism is on the rise and attacks against the international legal order and multilateralist regimes have become part of nationalist populist agendas. State actors implicated in gross human rights violations are in positions of power across the world. Children in cages, deadly border regimes, and reports of detention facilities for millions are only some of the realities that draw into question if and what impact the emergence of modern international criminal law can have on deterring crime and violence.

The International Criminal Court (ICC) has experienced a backlash not only from African states but also from a number of state actors for whom the delegitimisation of the Court is a strategy of defence against possible investigations of them. One of the most powerful features of the Rome Statute was the codified commitment by State Parties to submit their own state power to the scrutiny of the Court and to waive any immunity for those state actors responsible for the commission of international crimes. Yet, to date, the ICC has not developed the ability to hold state actors to account. Investigations have been started, arrest warrants have been issued, prosecutions have begun. But, at the same time, states have withdrawn from the Rome Statute, arrest warrants have been met with non-compliance and prosecutions have fallen apart.[1]

Despite all this, the Office of the Prosecutor (OTP) has gradually sought to address more diverse situations. It has tried to pursue investigations in situations that entail crimes allegedly committed by Russian and US actors, challenging some of the most powerful countries in the world. When waves of violence drove hundreds of thousands of Rohingya out of Myanmar, the Prosecutor used the very limited jurisdictional power she had to start a preliminary examination and subsequently requested the authorisation to investigate. The statistics on successful convictions, however, suggests a rather chequered account. Nevertheless, the Office has used its expressive power to raise awareness of crimes in other areas such as the use of child soldiers and the destruction of cultural heritage

[1] Burundi is one of the investigations in which state actors are heavily implicated in crimes. The government declared its withdrawal from the Rome Statute after the Prosecutor opened the preliminary examination. The arrest warrant against the (now ex-)President of Sudan, Omar Al Bashir, triggered waves of non-compliance by African states. Prosecutions in the situation in Kenya aimed at the Kenyan state leadership, but the prosecution cases fell apart after witnesses withdrew their statements. The investigation stalled, and arrest warrants have been issued alleging the corrupt influence of witnesses.

and to put them onto the international agenda. The Office has published a series of remarkable policy papers. The Policy on Children and on Sexual and Gender-Based Crimes are genuinely groundbreaking and will hopefully have a lasting impact on the prosecution of international crimes at the international but also at the regional and domestic level.

The ICC as a forum of prosecution might be contested. At the same time, the Rome Statute has gradually developed normative ripple effects into domestic and regional orders. States have started implementing the Rome Statute, and in some of the countries under investigation, capacities are building up to address genocide, crimes against humanity and war crimes.[2] These developments are very gradual and questions regarding the normative influence of the Rome Statute can only be answered by future research projects. What ties the issues of prosecution fora and normative effects together, though, is how the Prosecutor at the ICC seeks to use her or his mandate. What I have argued throughout the book is that the exercise of prosecutorial discretion goes to the heart of all these issues. Prosecutorial discretion influences the choice of the ICC as a forum for prosecution and, through the selection of cases and the formulation of policies, potentially inspires normative developments. Developing a solid understanding of the discretionary processes at work is therefore critical for the operations of the ICC and, more broadly, to shape international criminal justice.

To enhance our understanding of prosecutorial discretion at the ICC, the book makes critical contributions in three distinct areas that cut across all chapters. First, embedded in general studies of discretion, this book offers a conceptualisation of prosecutorial discretion that can lead to a more precise and principled exercise of discretion that is geared towards safeguarding the Court's legitimacy. Second, looking at discretion in action, the book makes a series of proposals on reshaping current practice with the aim of contributing to the development of a much more coherent overall system. Flowing from this analysis, the book also contains a plea for radical transparency. Third, looking forward, it argues that the Prosecutor should use her or his discretionary powers to turn the Court into a more responsive institution capable of shaping a much more holistic understanding of justice.

This book conceptualises prosecutorial discretion with the aim that its exercise can contribute to safeguarding and enhancing the legitimacy of the ICC. The argument here is that the exercise of discretion within the frame of legality is insufficient, or, as the first Prosecutor Luis Moreno Ocampo put it 'respect for the law', is not enough. International criminal law always operates in a highly politicised context. This book therefore offers a conceptual approach to discretion that engages with those elements that form the foundations for the legitimacy of the Court. Legitimacy is a complex notion with different layers. The legitimate exercise of discretion requires engagement with process as well

[2] One such example is the Special Criminal Court in the Central African Republic.

as outcomes of the law in action. Any exercise of discretion has to engage with the legal boundaries derived from the Rome Statute, as well as other international legal principles and the guiding principles and values that are important to the constituents of the Court. Crucially, the system needs to offer mechanisms of formal and pragmatic accountability. Rethinking prosecutorial discretion in the way that is suggested here will provide a less fragmented and more structured form of discourse targeted at enhancing the legitimacy of the Court.

The analysis of prosecutorial discretion has revealed that the ICC system requires different dimensions of discretion in its operations. The dominant form is procedural in nature. It is characterised as the freedom for the Prosecutor to choose between different procedural courses of action as the result of applying the facts to the legal framework. This procedural dimension is present in all areas of the proceedings, namely, how to conduct preliminary examinations, how to choose between situations for investigation, how best to engage in the process of case selection, whether to start discussions in the quest of striking a plea agreement, and how to complete an investigation into a broader situation of conflict. Even in the day-to-day work of the Court, procedural discretionary decisions are continually present, for example, in the decision-making processes on how to structure and recalibrate specific investigations or whether to launch an appeal against a specific judgment. All these procedural discretionary decisions address very different areas of law but follow the same structure. They are those decisions where the Prosecutor, after applying the law, is equipped with a choice between different legal consequences.

Procedural discretion is limited through the general duties of the Prosecutor, such as the duty to undertake effective investigation and prosecution, to ensure fairness towards the accused, to act impartially but also to appear as impartial to an outside observer. However, the Prosecutor also has to consider managerial considerations such as staffing constraints, the availability of evidence and state cooperation, or the security situation in a country. Procedural discretion is the right instrument for a balancing exercise that takes these factual constrains on the OTP into account. Negotiating such factual constraints, the decision-making process should be guided by the question of how to contribute best to those values and aims expressed in the Rome Statute in the factual and legal space that is available. Yet, prevention and deterrence, closing the gap of impunity, responding to victims' interests, and the respect for human rights are very broad aims and values. They can nevertheless provide guidance for discretion at the specific stages of the proceedings. Based on a growing body of research in different disciplines, these aims need to be translated into more clearly specified strategies. The Prosecutor must actively use this knowledge to continuously enhance her exercise of discretion.

Applying the Rome Statute, however, is not a straightforward task, because the Statute contains some indeterminate – or open – legal concepts such as the gravity notion in article 17(1)(d) of the Statute and the interests of justice. Chapter one introduces the different dimensions in operation and embeds them in the broader theoretical context. Open legal concepts provide the Prosecutor with some freedom to choose which circumstances to take into consideration and how to weigh them in relation to one another. This dimension of discretion, interpretative in nature, is not exclusively prescribed to the Prosecutor. Whether it is the Prosecutor or the judges who are charged with exercising this dimension of discretion depends on the stage of the proceedings. What ties the interpretative dimension for different open concepts together, is that it does not allow the Prosecutor to use the interpretative act as a tool to manage the Office's workload. Responding to resource constraints or other practical pressures is beyond the limits of interpretative discretion. Acknowledging the interpretative dimension of discretion increases the awareness that this form of discretion exists, so that it is used with caution and the limitations of the different dimensions of discretion are recognised. The open concepts provide the Prosecutor with flexibility to apply the law to very diverse factual circumstances. Acknowledging this dimension of discretion is critical: where choices are available, these need to be made consciously to avoid the erroneous use of the law. Raising the bar of admissibility to the Court higher or lower through a different understanding of gravity depending on the workload of the Court entails the danger of severely undermining perceptions of the Court. Yet, pretending exactitude where there is none, creates false expectations. Identifying the scope for interpretative discretion also allows a better delineation of the scope of judicial review, one of the ongoing issues between the OTP and the Pre-Trial Chambers. Bowing to outside political pressure and non-cooperation as part of the interests of justice invites political power play rather than striving to realise justice for those who have suffered.

These procedural and interpretative dimensions of discretion are very closely intertwined, and, at times, it is only a matter of degree in the distinction between both, as the discussion on the interests of justice in chapter six demonstrates Identifying the content of the interests of justice in a particular situation is an interpretative act, yet, direct procedural consequences flow from it. This fluidity of the system is partly inherent in the nature of discretion with its elements of freedom and flexibility. And partly it is caused by the nature of the Rome Statute, an intriguing new system that melds different legal cultures together. It is an international treaty full of compromises and creative ambiguities. For those reasons, it would be too much to expect a mature system that is always dogmatically fully consistent.

For the development of a consistent system, it is important to rethink the approaches to the exercise of discretion at the different stages of the proceedings, because the analysis of the law in action and ICC practice has revealed some critical incoherence. The discussion of completion processes in chapter seven demonstrates the need for joined-up thinking from the start of preliminary examinations onwards. Hence, chapter two to chapter seven contain multiple practical suggestions for the different stages of the proceedings.

At the preliminary examination stage, prosecutorial discretion is not unlimited. A clear distinction between the analysis of criteria for the start of an investigation and strategies of positive complementarity is necessary at the preliminary stage. Prioritisation and selection processes must not be hidden away but should openly be addressed, because prolonged preliminary examinations can, for example, negatively impact on the quality of subsequent investigations. This point links closely with the Prosecutor's assertion of a duty to investigate. Chapter three has deconstructed this position, it is legally flawed to assert a duty where the *propio motu* powers provide scope for discretion. It is proposed that the Prosecutor should openly acknowledge if investigation is warranted but not possible because of practical constraints. Using the expressive power of the ICC to ring the alarm bells internationally provides a chance to call other actors onto the agenda.

In those situations where investigations have been started, discretion in the case selection process should be exercised in a principled and structured way that always goes back to actively asking the question of how a specific decision can contribute best to the aims and values of the Rome Statute. Chapter four suggests that a critical aim must be to represent all areas of victimisation in a specific situation of conflict. This applies as much to the different sides of a conflict – wherever evidence provides a basis for prosecution – as to potential charges. Once prosecutions are under way, chapter five outlines how plea agreements can provide a chance for the ICC but should be based on a court-wide policy that seeks to implement restorative justice elements in the proceedings.

Taking a more overarching view, chapter six turns to the non-use of the interests of justice in the practice of the Prosecutor. The chapter demonstrates that the Statute allows a more flexible use of the interests of justice. The OTP can, for example, facilitate the delay of an investigation for a specific time for reasons such as peace negotiations through the interests of justice. But, more generally, the concept should also serve as a tool to provide space for local ownership of justice processes and to contribute to a more holistic understanding of justice. The discussion links up closely with reflections on completion processes in which prosecutorial discretion will play a major role. In transitional justice scenarios, an interests-of-justice-based approach can ensure that victims' voices allow mediation between deference to domestic jurisdictions and the need for accountability. Overall, there will be no 'one size fits all' approach. The Prosecutor's discretion will be critical to shape international criminal justice in such way that it can complement other dimensions of justice and further those efforts that address the root causes of crime, conflict and violence.

One of the recurrent themes in this book is the role of transparency. An important conclusion that can be drawn from the book is the need for genuine transparency. Transparency has gained increasing importance for the Prosecutor.[3]

[3] ICC/OTP, Policy Paper on Preliminary Examinations, November 2913, para 15; Policy Paper on Case Selection and Prioritisation, 15 September 2016, para 3; Strategic Plan 2012–2015, 11 October 2013, para 5; Strategic Plan 2016–2018, 6 July 2015, para 81.

A series of policy papers and annual reports on preliminary examination activities have been published. Despite these efforts, the exercise of prosecutorial discretion remains largely opaque. There is in particular a lack of explanation about how different interests and principles are balanced. It is crucial to change this practice. Because the exercise of discretion serves the function of selecting among many meritorious complaints only a few for investigation and prosecution at the ICC, disappointment and critique will be inevitable. For that reason, it is crucial to use the expressive power that goes with such selection decisions to the fullest extent. It is important to explain why a particular decision has been taken. It is pivotal to explain how a specific investigation or prosecution will contribute best to prevention and deterrence of future crimes and how victims' interests are being served through the decisions taken because this is seldom self-evident. Furthermore, open discretionary processes have an impact on the quality of a decision because the decision-maker has to rationalise and deliberate on the reasons. It alerts the decision-maker to the need to exercise discretion, it requires the identification of the reasons for the decision, and it requires a balancing act between the different reasons. In this respect, a key finding of this book is that the Prosecutor is not using her powers in such a way that she could make the fullest use of all these benefits.

The plea for genuine transparency is combined with the acknowledgement that the duties of the OTP do not always permit full transparency. The transparency of discretion needs to be balanced and weighed against disadvantages and obstacles. The Prosecutor, already on the weak end of the enforcement side, might not want to lose the element of surprise when planning enforcement action, such as the execution of an arrest warrant, or when conducting a specific investigation. The need for the safety of witnesses and victims is the other balancing factor that does not always allow full transparency at all stages of the proceedings. These scenarios, however, will remain the small minority. With the need for a balancing act in mind, a radical increase in the transparency of discretionary decisions will be of benefit to the Court. It will trigger dissent but also greater understanding and acceptance, one of the elements at the core of legitimacy.

The most powerful states openly violate human rights on a massive scale and, yet, these human rights violations are left unaccounted for. Climate change will exacerbate conflict and insecurity. For the ICC to contribute to peace, security and sustainable development, it will need to become a persuasive institution that can overcome perceptions of bias and selectivity. The Prosecutor plays a critical role in shaping the practice of the Court, and, more broadly, of shaping the role of international criminal justice in the global legal order. If the ICC is to contribute to peace and security in the long run, it must develop a more responsive approach to its key constituencies, State Parties, affected communities and the international community at large. A more responsive approach would be one that is context-sensitive, allows scope for diverse approaches to accountability and that focuses on the needs of societies in conflict. The ICC should show its flexibility through the multiple discretionary mechanisms at the disposal of its Prosecutor. Ultimately, the Court has to persuade the international community that it is an institution fit for purpose, with the right balance between integrity and openness, rule and discretion, one that can work for the sake of future generations.

Bibliography

BOOKS

Ambos, K, *The Colombian Peace Process and the Principle of Complementarity of the International Criminal Court* (Heidelberg, Springer, 2010).

Bass, GJ, *Stay the Hand of Vengeance: The Politics of War Crimes Tribunals* (Princeton, NJ, Princeton University Press 2002).

Bergsmo, M, *Criteria for Prioritizing and Selecting Core International Crime Cases*, 2nd edn (Brussels, Torkel Opsahl Academic Epublisher, 2010).

Blome, K, Fischer-Lescano, A, Franzki, H, Markad, N and Oeter, S, *Contested Regime Collisions: Norm Fragmentation in World Society* (Cambridge, Cambridge University Press, 2016).

Bosco, D, *Rough Justice: The International Criminal Court in a World of Power Politics* (New York, Oxford University Press USA, 2014).

Chayes, A and Handler Chayes, A, *The New Sovereignty: Compliance with International Regulatory Agreements* (Cambridge, Cambridge University Press, 1995).

Clarke, K, Knottnerus, A and de Volder, E, *Africa and the ICC, Perceptions of Justice* (Cambridge, Cambridge University Press, 2016).

Clarke, P, *Distant Justice: The Impact of the International Criminal Court on African Politics* (Cambridge, Cambridge University Press, 2018).

Combs, N, *Guilty Pleas in International Criminal Law* (Stanford, CA, Stanford University Press, 2007).

Cottrell, PM, *The Evolution and Legitimacy of International Security Institutions* (Cambridge, Cambridge University Press, 2016).

Crawford, J, *Brownlie's Principles of Public International Law*, 8th edn (Oxford, Oxford University Press, 2010).

Cryer, R, *Prosecuting International Crimes* (Cambridge, Cambridge University Press, 2005).

Cryer, R, Friman, H, Robinson, D and Wilmshurst, E, *An Introduction to International Criminal Law and Procedure*, 3rd edn (Cambridge, Cambridge University Press, 2014).

Davis, AJ, Arbitrary Justice: *The Power of the American Prosecutor*, new edn (Oxford, Oxford University Press, 2009).

Davis, KC, *Discretionary Justice, A Preliminary Inquiry* (Baton Rouge, LA, Louisiana State University Press, 1969).

Duff, A, Farmer, L, Marshall, S and Tadros, V, *The Trial on Trial, Volume 3: Towards a Normative Theory of the Criminal Trial* (Oxford, Hart Publishing, 2007).

Dworkin, R, *Taking Rights Seriously* (London, Duckworth, 1977).

Fionda, J, *Public Prosecutors and Discretion: A Comparative Study* (Oxford, Oxford University Press, 1995).

Franck, T, *Fairness in International Law and Institutions* (Oxford, Clarendon Press, 1995).

Galligan, DJ, *Discretionary Powers: A Legal Study of Official Discretion* (Oxford, Clarendon Press, 1986).

Hawkins, K (ed), *The Uses of Discretion* (Oxford, Clarendon Press, 1992).

Hawkins, K, *Law as Last Resort: Prosecution Decision-making in a Regulatory Agency* (Oxford, Oxford University Press, 2003).

Horwitz, L and Catherwood, C, *Encyclopedia of War Crimes & Genocide* (Facts on File, 2006).

Kelsen, H, *Pure Theory of Law*, translation from the second German edition (Union, NJ, The Lawbook Exchange, 2005).

—— *The Law of the United Nations: A Critical Analysis of its Fundamental Problems*, 7th printing (Union, NJ, The Lawbook Exchange, 2008).

Kersten, M, *Justice in Conflict: The Effects of the International Criminal Court's Interventions on Ending War and Building Peace* (Oxford, Oxford University Press, 2016).

Kesselring, R, *Bodies of Truth* (Stanford, CA, Stanford University Press, 2017).

Kloss, B, *The Exercise of Prosecutorial Discretion at the International Criminal Court* (München, Hermann Utz Verlag, 2017).

Koskenniemi, M, *The Gentle Civilizer of Nations: The Rise and Fall of International Law 1870–1960* (Cambridge, Cambridge University Press, 2001).

—— *From Apology to Utopia: The Structure of International Legal Argument* (Cambridge, Cambridge University Press, 2006).

Minow, M, True-Frost, C and Whiting A (eds), *The First Global Prosecutor: Promise and Constraints* (Ann Arbor, MI, University of Michigan Press, 2015).

Moffet, L, *Justice for Victims before the International Criminal Court* (Abingdon, Routledge, 2014).

Nichols, L, *The International Criminal Court and the End of Impunity in Kenya* (Heidelberg, Springer, 2015).

Nonet, P and Selznick, P, *Law & Society in Transition: Towards Responsive Law* (New Brunswick, Transaction Publishers 2001).

Nouwen, S, *Complementarity in the Line of Fire: The Catalysing Effect of the International Criminal Court in Uganda and Sudan* (Cambridge, Cambridge University Press, 2013).

O'Malley, T, *Principled Discretion: Developing a Coherent Sentencing Policy* (Newbridge, Irish Academic Press, 2010).

Onuf, NG, *World of Our Making: Rules and Rule in Social Theory and International Relations* (London, Routledge, 2013).

Reydams, L, Wouters, J and Ryngaert, C (eds), *International Prosecutors* (Oxford, Oxford University Press, 2012).

Rohrer, S, *Legalitaets- oder Opportunitaetsprinzip Beim Internationalen Strafgerichtshof* (München, Carl Heymanns Verlag, 2010).

Safferling, C, *International Criminal Procedure* (Oxford, Oxford University Press, 2012).

Schabas, W, *The International Criminal Court: A Commentary on the Rome Statute* (Oxford, Oxford University Press, 2010).

—— *The International Criminal Court: A Commentary on the Rome Statute*, 2nd edn (Oxford, Oxford University Press, 2016).

Shklar, JN, *Legalism, Law, Morals, and Political Trials*, Reprint (Cambridge, MA, Harvard University Press, 1986).

Sikkink, K, *The Justice Cascade: How Human Rights Prosecutions are Changing World Politics* (New York, Norton, 2011).

Simpson, G, *Great Powers and Outlaw States: Unequal Sovereigns in the International Order* (Cambridge, Cambridge University Press, 2004).

Stahn, C (ed), *The Law and Practice of the International Criminal Court* (Oxford, Oxford University Press, 2015).

Stahn, C and Sluiter, G (eds), *The Emerging Practice of the International Criminal Court* (Leiden, Martinus Nijhoff, 2009).

Stahn, C and El Zeidy, M (eds), *The International Criminal Court and Complementarity: From Theory to Practice* (Cambridge, Cambridge University Press, 2011).

Stegmiller, I, *The Pre-Investigation Stage of the ICC* (Berlin, Duncker & Humboldt, 2011).

Thaman, S, (ed), *World Plea Bargaining: Consensual Procedures and the Avoidance of the Full Criminal Trial* (Durham, NC, Carolina Academic Press, 2010).

Triffterer, O, *Commentary on the Rome Statute of the International Criminal Court*, 2nd edn (Munich, Beck, 2008).

Venzke, I, How *Interpretation Makes International Law: On Semantic Change and Normative Twists* (Oxford, Oxford University Press, 2012).

Wringe, B, *An Expressive Theory of Punishment* (Basingstoke, Macmillan, 2016).

CHAPTERS IN BOOKS

Alviar García, H and Engle, K, 'The Distributive Politics of Impunity and Anti-Impunity: Lessons from Four Decades of Colombian Peace Negotiations' in K Engle, Z Miller and D Davis (eds), *Anti-Impunity and the Human Rights Agenda* (Cambridge, Cambridge University Press, 2016).

Beale, SS, 'Prosecutorial Discretion in Three Systems: Balancing Conflicting Goals and Providing Mechanisms for Control' in M Caianiello and JS Hodgson (eds), *Discretionary Criminal Justice in a Comparative Context* (Durham, NC, Carolina Academic Press 2015).

Beetham, D, 'Revisiting Legitimacy, Twenty Years on' in J Tankebe and A Liebling (eds), *Legitimacy and Criminal Justice: An International Exploration* (Oxford, Oxford University Press, 2013).

Behrens, H-J, 'The Trial Proceedings' in RS Lee (ed), *The International Criminal Court: The Making of the Rome Statute* (The Hague, Kluwer Law International, 1999).

Bergsmo, M and Kruger, P, 'Article 53' in O Triffterer (ed), *Commentary on the Rome Statute of the International Criminal Court*, 2nd edn (Munich, Beck, 2008).

Bergsmo, M, Pejic, J and Zhu, D, 'Article 15' in O Triffterer and K Ambos (eds), *Commentary on the Rome Statute of the International Criminal Court*, 3rd edn (Munich, Beck, 2016).

Burke-White, W, 'Maximizing the ICC's Crime Prevention Impact Through Positive Complementarity and Hard-Nosed Diplomacy' in RH Steinberg (ed), *Contemporary Issues Facing the International Criminal Court* (Leiden, Brill Nijhoff, 2016).

Cohen, RL, 'Restorative Justice' in C Sabbagh and M Schmitt (eds), *Handbook of Social Justice Theory and Research* (New York, Springer, 2016).

Coicaud, J-M, 'The Evolution of International Order and Fault Lines of International Legitimacy' in H Charlesworth and J-M Coicaud (eds), *Fault Lines of International Legitimacy* (Cambridge, Cambridge University Press, 2010).

—— 'Crime, Justice, and Legitimacy: A Brief Theoretical Inquiry' in J Tankebe and A Liebling (eds), *Legitimacy and Criminal Justice: An International Exploration* (Oxford, Oxford University Press, 2013).

Collins, V and Rothe, D, 'The International Criminal Court: A Pipe Dream to End Impunity?' in D Rothe, J Meernik and T Ingadóttir (eds), *The Realities of International Criminal Justice* (Leiden, Brill Nijhoff, 2013).

Côté, L, 'Independence and Impartiality' in L Reydams, J Wouters and C Ryngaert (eds), *International Prosecutors* (Oxford, Oxford University Press, 2012).

Cryer, R, 'The ICC and its Relationship to Non-States Parties' in C Stahn (ed), *The Law and Practice of the International Criminal Court* (Oxford, Oxford University Press, 2015).

deGuzman, M, 'An Expressive Rationale for the Thematic Prosecution of Sex Crimes' in M Bergsmo (ed), *Thematic Prosecution of International Sex Crimes* (FICHL Publication Series No 13) (Brussels, Torkel Opsahl Academic EPublisher, 2012).

Dieckmann, J and O'Leary, M, 'The Role of Defense Counsel in Pre-Trial' in C Rohan and G Zyberi (eds), *Defense Perspectives on International Criminal Justice* (Cambridge, Cambridge University Press, 2017).

Duff, A and Garland, D, 'Thinking about Punishment' in A Duff and D Garland (eds), *A Reader on Punishment* (Oxford, Oxford University Press, 1994).

Evenson, E and Smith, A, 'Completion, Legacy, and Complementarity at the ICC' in C Stahn (ed), *The Law and Practice of the International Criminal Court* (Oxford, Oxford University Press, 2015).

Farrior, S, 'Equality and Non-Discrimination under International Law' in S Farrior (ed), *The Library of Essays on International Human Rights, Volume II: Equality and Non-Discrimination* (Farnham, Ashgate Publishing, 2015).

Feldman, M, 'Social Limits to Discretion: An Organizational Perspective' in K Hawkins (ed), *The Uses of Discretion* (Oxford, Clarendon Press, 1992).

Fernandez de Gurmendi, S, 'The Role of the International Prosecutor' in RS Lee (ed), *The International Criminal Court: The Making of the Rome Statute* (The Hague, Kluwer Law International, 1999).

Friman, H, 'Investigation and Prosecution' in RS Lee (ed), *The International Criminal Court: Elements of Crimes and Rules of Procedure and Evidence* (New York, Transnational Publishers, 2001).

—— 'Trial Procedures – With a Particular Focus on the Relationship between the Proceedings of the Pre-Trial and the Trial Chambers' in C Stahn (ed), *The Law and Practice of the International Criminal Court* (Oxford, Oxford University Press, 2015).

Fuijiwara, H and Parmentier, S, 'Investigations' in L Reydams, J Wouters and C Ryngaert, (eds), *International Prosecutors* (Oxford, Oxford University Press, 2012).

Gawronski, M, 'The Legalistic Function of Preliminary Examinations: Quality Control as a Two-Way Street' in M Bergsmo and C Stahn (eds), *Quality Control in Preliminary Examinations, Volume I* (Brussels, Torkel Opsahl, 2018).

Guariglia, F, 'Investigation and Prosecution' in RS Lee (ed), *The International Criminal Court: The Making of the Rome Statute* (The Hague, Kluwer Law International, 1999).

Guariglia, F and Hochmayr, G, 'Article 65' in O Triffterer (ed), *Commentary on the Rome Statute of the International Criminal Court*, 2nd edn (Munich, Beck, 2008).

Guariglia, F and Rogier, E, 'The Selection of Situations and Cases by the OTP of the ICC' in C Stahn (ed), *The Law and Practice of the International Criminal Court* (Oxford, Oxford University Press, 2015).

Hawkins, K, 'The Use of Legal Discretion: Perspectives from Law and Social Science' in K Hawkins (ed), *The Uses of Discretion* (Oxford, Clarendon Press, 1992).

Heller, KJ, 'Completion' in L Reydams, J Wouters and C Ryngaert (eds), *International Prosecutors* (Oxford, Oxford University Press, 2012).

Holmes, J, 'The Principle of Complementarity' in RS Lee (ed), *The International Criminal Court: The Making of the Rome Statute* (The Hague, Kluwer Law International, 1999).

Kendall, S and Nouwen, S, 'Representational Practices at the International Criminal Court: The Gap between Juridified and Abstract Victimhood' (2013) 76 *Law & Contemporary Problems* 235.

Khojasteh, A, 'The Preliminary Examination Stage: Theory and Practice of the OTP's Phase 1 Activities' in M Bergsmo and C Stahn (eds), *Quality Control in Preliminary Examinations, Volume I* (Brussels, Torkel Opsahl, 2018).

Kirsch, P and Robinson, D, 'Initiation of Proceedings by the Prosecutor' in A Cassese, P Gaeta and J Jones (eds), *The Rome Statute of the International Criminal Court: A Commentary, Vol I* (Oxford, Oxford University Press, 2002).

—— 'Reaching Agreement at the Rome Conference' in A Cassese, P Gaeta and J Jones (eds), *The Rome Statute of the International Criminal Court: A Commentary, Vol I* (Oxford, Oxford University Press, 2002).

Lacey, N, 'The Jurisprudence of Discretion: Escaping the Legal Paradigm' in K Hawkins (ed), *The Uses of Discretion* (Oxford, Clarendon Press, 1992).

Leonard, E, 'From Realism to Legalization: A Rationalist Assessment of the International Criminal Court in the Democratic Republic of Congo' in SC Roach (ed), *Governance, Order, and the International Criminal Court: Between Realpolitik and a Cosmpolitan Court* (Oxford, Oxford University Press, 2009).

Locke, J, 'Indictments' in L Reydams, J Wouters and C Ryngaert (eds), *International Prosecutors* (Oxford, Oxford University Press, 2012).

Marong, A and Jalloh, C, 'Transfer of Cases under the Jurisprudence of the ICTR and Lessons Learnt for the ICC' in C Jalloh and A Marong, *Promoting Accountability under International Law for Gross Human Rights Violations in Africa* (Leiden, Brill Nijhoff, 2015).

Mégret, F, 'Accountability and Ethics' in L Reydams, J Wouters and C Ryngaert (eds), *International Prosecutors* (Oxford, Oxford University Press, 2012).

—— 'Is the ICC Focusing Too Much on Non State Actors ?' in M deGuzman and D Amann (eds), *Arcs of Global Justice: Essays in Honor of William A Schabas* (Oxford, Oxford University Press, 2017).

Moreno Ocampo, L, 'Prologue: The Prosecutor's Use of Legal Policies' in M Minow, C True-Frost and A Whiting (eds), *The First Global Prosecutor: Promise and Constraints* (Ann Arbor, MI, University of Michigan Press, 2015).

Nouwen, S, 'The International Criminal Court and Conflict Prevention in Africa' in T Karbo and K Virk (eds), *The Palgrave Handbook of Peacebuilding in Africa* (Cham, Springer, 2018).
Ntanda Nsereko, D, 'Article 18' in O Triffterer (ed), *Commentary on the Rome Statute of the International Criminal Court*, 2nd edn (Munich, Beck, 2008).
Ohlin, JD, 'Peace, Security, and Prosecutorial Discretion' in C Stahn and G Sluiter (eds), *The Emerging Practice of the International Criminal Court* (Leiden, Martinus Nijhoff, 2009).
Rashid, F, '"The Interests of Justice" under the ICC Prosecutor Power: Escaping Forward' in E Cigdem et al (eds), *Crossing Conceptual Boundaries V* (University of East London, School of Law and Social Sciences, 2013).
Raustiala, K and Slaughter, A-M, 'International Law, International Relations and Compliance' in W Carlsnaes, T Risse and B Simmons (eds), *The Handbook of International Relations* (Thousand Oaks, CA, Sage Publications, 2002).
Reydams, L and Odermatt, J, 'Mandates' in L Reydams, J Wouters and C Ryngaert (eds), *International Prosecutors* (Oxford, Oxford University Press, 2012).
Schabas, W, 'Selecting Situations and Cases' in C Stahn (ed), *The Law and Practice of the International Criminal Court* (Oxford, Oxford University Press, 2015).
Scheffer, D, 'A Review of the Experience of the Pre-Trial and Appeals Chambers of the International Criminal Court Regarding the Disclosure of Evidence' in C Stahn and G Sluiter (eds), *The Emerging Practice of the International Criminal Court* (Leiden, Martinus Nijhoff, 2009).
—— 'False Alarm about the Proprio Motu Prosecutor' in M Minow, C True-Frost and A Whiting (eds), *The First Global Prosecutor: Promise and Constraints* (Ann Arbor, MI, University of Michigan Press, 2015).
Schneider, CE, 'Discretion and Rules, A Lawyer's View' in K Hawkins (ed), *The Uses of Discretion* (Oxford, Clarendon Press, 1992).
Seils, P, 'Putting Complementarity in its Place' in C Stahn (ed), *The Law and Practice of the International Criminal Court* (Oxford, Oxford University Press, 2015).
Stahn, C, 'Judicial Review of Prosecutorial Discretion: Five Years On' in C Stahn and G Sluiter (eds), *The Emerging Practice of the International Criminal Court* (Leiden, Martinus Nijhoff, 2009).
Stahn, C, 'Bridge Over Troubled Waters?' in C Stahn and M El Zeidy (eds), *The International Criminal Court and Complementarity: From Theory to Practice* (Cambridge, Cambridge University Press, 2011).
Stahn, C, Bergsmo, M and Chan H, 'On the Magic, Mystery and Mayhem of Preliminary Examinations' in M Bergsmo and C Stahn (eds), *Quality Control on Preliminary Examinations, Vol I* (Brussels, TOAEP, 2018).
Stegmiller, I, 'Confirmation of Charges' in C Stahn (ed), *The Law and Practice of the International Criminal Court* (Oxford, Oxford University Press, 2015).
Stiglitz, J, 'On Liberty, the Right to Know, and Public Discourse: The Role of Transparency in Public Life' in MJ Gibney (ed), *Globalizing Rights, The Oxford Amnesty Lectures* (Oxford, Oxford University Press, 1999).
Stone, C, 'Widening the Impact of the International Criminal Court' in M Minow, C True-Frost and A Whiting (eds), *The First Global Prosecutor: Promise and Constraints* (Ann Arbor, MI, University of Michigan Press, 2015).
Stuckenberg, C-F, 'Cumulative Charges and Cumulative Convictions' in C Stahn (ed), *The Law and Practice of the International Criminal Court* (Oxford, Oxford University Press, 2015).
Tochilovsky, V, 'Charging in the ICC and Relevant Jurisprudence of the Ad Hoc Tribunals' in J Doria, H-P Gasser and M Cherif Bassiouni (eds), *The Legal Regime of the International Criminal Court* (Leiden, Martinus Nijhoff, 2009).
Turone, G, 'Powers and Duties of the Prosecutor' in A Cassesse, P Gaeta and J Jones (eds), *The Rome Statute of the International Criminal Court: A Commentary, Vol II* (Oxford, Oxford University Press, 2002).
Tyler, T and Jackson, J, 'Future Challenges in the Study of Legitimacy and Criminal Justice' in J Tankebe and A Liebling (eds), *Legitimacy and Criminal Justice: An International Exploration* (Oxford, Oxford University Press, 2013).

van der Wilt, H, 'Self-Referrals as an Indication of the Inability of States to Cope with Non-State Actors' in C Stahn (ed), *The Law and Practice of the International Criminal Court* (Oxford, Oxford University Press, 2015).

Vinjamuri, L, 'The ICC and the Politics of Peace and Justice' in C Stahn (ed), *The Law and Practice of the International Criminal Court* (Oxford, Oxford University Press, 2015).

JOURNAL ARTICLES

Ambach, P and Rackwitz, KU, 'A Model of International Judicial Administration? The Evolution of Managerial Practices at the International Criminal Court' (2013) 76 *Law & Contemporary Problems* 119.

Ambos, K and Stegmiller, I, 'Prosecuting International Crimes at the International Criminal Court: Is there a Coherent and Comprehensive Prosecution Strategy?' (2013) 59 *Crime, Law and Social Change* 415.

Appel, B, 'In the Shadow of the International Criminal Court: Does the ICC Deter Human Rights Violations ?' (2018) 62 *Journal of Conflict Resolution* 3.

Aptel, C, 'Prosecutorial Discretion at the ICC and Victims' Right to Remedy' (2012) 10 *Journal of International Criminal Justice* 1357.

Bensouda, F, 'Children and International Criminal Justice' (2015) 43 *Georgia Journal of International and Comparative Law* 591.

Blome, K and Markad, N, '"Contested Collisions": Conditions for a Successful Collision Management – The Example of Article 16 of the Rome Statute' (2016) 29 *Leiden Journal of International Law* 551.

Bone, R, 'Who Decides? A Critical Look at Procedural Discretion' (2007) 28 *Cardozo Law Review* 1962.

Bosco, D, 'Putting the Prosecutor on a Clock? Responding to Variance in the Length of Preliminary Examinations' (2018) 112 *AJIL Unbound* 158.

Bovens, M, 'Analysing and Assessing Accountability: A Conceptual Framework' (2007) 13 *European Law Journal* 447.

Branch, A, 'Uganda's Civil War and the Politics of ICC Intervention' (2007) 21 *Ethics & International Affairs* 179.

Brubacher, M, 'Prosecutorial Discretion within the International Criminal Court' (2004) 2 *Journal of International Criminal Justice* 71.

Buisman, C, 'The Prosecutor's Obligation to Investigate Incriminating and Exonerating Circumstances Equally: Illusion or Reality?' (2014) 27 *Leiden Journal of International Law* 205.

Carnero Rojo, E, 'Standard of Proof Required to Issue an Arrest Warrant for Genocide' (2010) 27 *Utrecht Journal of International and European Law* 61.

Cassese, A, 'The Legitimacy of International Criminal Tribunals and the Current Prospects of International Criminal Justice' (2012) 25 *Leiden Journal of International Law* 491.

Chaikin, D, 'Network Investigations of Cyber Attacks: The Limits of Digital Evidence' (2006) 46 *Crime, Law and Social Change* 239.

Chevalier-Watts, J, 'Effective Investigations under Article 2 of the European Convention on Human Rights: Securing the Right to Life or an Onerous Burden on a State?' (2010) 21 *European Journal of International Law* 701.

Cimiotta, E, 'The Relevance of *Erga Omnes* Obligations in Prosecuting International Crimes' (2016) 76 *Zeitschrift für ausländisches öffentliches Recht und Völkerrecht* 687.

Clark, JN, 'Plea Bargaining at the ICTY: Guilty Pleas and Reconciliation' (2009) 20 *European Journal of International Law* 415.

Covey, R, 'Plea-Bargaining Law after Lafler and Frye' (2013) 51 *Duquesne University Law Review* 595.

Cronin-Furman, K, 'Managing Expectations: International Criminal Trials and the Prospects for Deterrence of Mass Atrocity' (2013) 7 *International Journal of Transitional Justice* 434.

Damaška, M, 'Negotiated Justice in International Criminal Courts' (2004) 2 *Journal of International Criminal Justice* 1018.

Dancy, G and Montal, F, 'Unintended Positive Complementarity: Why International Criminal Court Investigations May Increase Domestic Human Rights Prosecutions' (2017) 111 *American Journal of International Law* 689.

Dancy, G and Wiebelhaus-Brahm, E, 'The Impact of Criminal Prosecutions during Intrastate Conflict' (2018) 55 *Journal of Peace Research* 47.

Dastugue, M, 'The Faults in "Fair" Trials : An Evaluation of Regulation 55 at the International Criminal' (2015) 48 *Vanderbilt Journal of Transnational Law* 273.

Davis, C, 'Political Considerations in Prosecutorial Discretion at the International Criminal Court' (2015) 15 *International Criminal Law Review* 170.

deGuzman, M, 'Gravity and the Legitimacy of the International Criminal Court' (2008) 32 *Fordham International Law Journal* 1400.

—— 'Choosing to Prosecute: Expressive Selection at the International Criminal Court' (2012) 33 *Michigan Journal of International Law* 265.

—— 'How Serious Are International Crimes? The Gravity Problem in International Criminal Law' (2012) 51 *Columbia Journal of Transnational Law* 1.

—— 'The International Criminal Court's Gravity Jurisprudence at Ten' (2013) 12 *Washington University's Global Studies Law Review* 475.

Del Ponte, C, 'Prosecuting the Individuals Bearing the Highest Level of Responsibility' (2004) 2 *Journal of International Criminal Justice* 516.

de Vleming, F, 'Selection of Defendants' in L Reydams, J Wouters and C Ryngaert (eds), *International Prosecutors* (Oxford, Oxford University Press, 2012).

Drumbl, M, 'Collective Violence and Individual Punishment: The Criminality of Mass Atrocity' (2005) 99 *Northwestern University Law Review* 101.

—— 'The Effects of the Lubanga Case on Understanding and Preventing Child Soldiering' (2012) 15 *Yearbook of International Humanitarian Law* 87.

Dutton, Y and Alleblas, T, 'Unpacking the Deterrent Effect of the International Criminal Court : Lessons From Kenya' (2017) 91 *St John's Law Review* 105.

Dworkin, R, 'Judicial Discretion' (1963) 60 *Journal of Philosophy* 624.

El Zeidy, M, 'The Gravity Threshold under the Statute of the International Criminal Court' (2008) 19 *Criminal Law Forum* 35.

Engle, K, 'Anti-Impunity and the Turn to Criminal Law in Human Rights' (2015) 100 *Cornell Law Review* 1069.

Ferstman, C, 'Limited Charges and Limited Judgments by the International Criminal Court – Who Bears the Greatest Responsibility?' (2012) 16 *International Journal of Human Rights* 796.

Franceschet, A, 'The International Criminal Court's Authority Crisis and Kant's Political Ethics' (2016) 16 *International Criminal Law Review* 201.

Franck, T, 'Legitimacy in the International System' (1988) 82 *American Journal of International Law* 705.

Glasius, M, 'Do International Criminal Courts Require Democratic Legitimacy?' (2012) 23 *European Journal of International Law* 43.

Goldston, J, 'More Candour about Criteria: The Exercise of Discretion by the Prosecutor of the International Criminal Court' (2010) 8 *Journal of International Criminal Justice* 383.

Green, L, 'First-Class Crimes, Second-Class Justice: Cumulative Charges for Gender-Based Crimes at the International Criminal Court' (2011) 11 *International Criminal Law Review* 529.

Greenawalt, A, 'Justice without Politics? Prosecutorial Discretion and the International Criminal Court' (2007) 39 *New York University Journal of International Law and Politics* 584.

—— 'Complementarity in Crisis: Uganda, Alternative Justice, and the International Criminal Court' (2009) 50 *Virginia Journal of International Law* 108.

Hamilton, R, 'The ICC's Exit Problem' (2015) 47 *New York University Journal of International Law and Politics* 1.

Hansen, TO, 'Reflections on the ICC Prosecutor's recent "Selection Decisions"' (2013) 17 *Max Planck Yearbook of United Nations Law* 125.

Hanlon, K, 'Peace or Justice: Now That Peace is Being Negotiated in Uganda, Will the ICC Still Pursue Justice?' (2007) 14 *Tulsa Journal of Comparative & International Law* 295.

Harmon, M and Gaynor, F, 'Prosecuting Massive Crimes with Primitive Tools: Three Difficulties Encountered by Prosecutors in International Criminal Proceedings' (2004) 2 *Journal of International Criminal Justice* 403.

Hart, HLA, 'Discretion' (2013) 127 *Harvard Law Review* 652.

Hashimoto, E, 'Towards Ethical Plea Bargaining' (2008) 30 *Cardozo Law Review* 949.

Heller, KJ, 'Radical Complementarity' (2016) 14 *Journal of International Criminal Justice* 637.

Henham, R, 'The Ethics of Plea Bargaining in International Criminal Trials' (2005) 26 *Liverpool Law Review* 209.

Henham, R and Drumbl, M, 'Plea Bargaining at the International Criminal Tribunal for the Former Yugoslavia' (2005) 16 *Criminal Law Forum* 49.

Hill, T, 'Kant on Punishment: A Coherent Mix of Deterrence and Retribution?' (1997) 5 *Jahrbuch fuer Ethik und Recht* 291.

Hoffer, P, 'Principled Discretion: Concealment, Conscience, and Chancellors' (1991) 3 *Yale Journal of Law & the Humanities* 53.

Hola, B, Smeulers, A and Weerdesteijn, M, 'The Selection of Situations by the ICC: An Empirically Based Evaluation of the OTP's Performance' (2015) 15 *International Criminal Law Review* 1.

Isanga, J, 'The International Criminal Court Ten Years Later: Appraisal and Prospects' (2013) 21 *Cardozo Journal of International & Comparative Law* 235.

Jain, N, 'Interpretive Divergence' (2017) 57 *Virginia Journal of International Law* 45.

Jalloh, C, 'Regionalizing International Criminal Law?' (2009) 9 *International Criminal Law Review* 445.

Jo, H and Simmons, B, 'Can the International Criminal Court Deter Atrocity?' (2016) 70 *International Organization* 443.

Jørgensen, N, 'The Genocide Acquittal in the Sikirica Case Before the International Criminal Tribunal for the Former Yugoslavia and the Coming of Age of the Guilty Plea' (2002) 15 *Leiden Journal of International Law* 389.

Keith, KJ, 'The International Rule of Law' (2015) 28 *Leiden Journal of International Law* 403.

Keller, LM, 'Achieving Peace with Justice: The International Criminal Court and Alternative Ugandan Mechanisms' (2008) 23 *Connecticut Journal of International Law* 209.

—— 'Comparing the "Interests of Justice": What the International Criminal Court Can Learn from New York Law' (2013) 12 *Washington University Global Studies Law Review* 1.

Kennedy, KC, 'Equitable Remedies and Principled Discretion: The Michigan Experience' (1997) 74 *University of Detroit Mercy Law Review* 609.

Kirsch, P, 'The Role of the International Criminal Court in Enforcing International Criminal Law' (2007) 22 *American University International Law Review* 539.

Klabbers, J, 'Towards a Culture of Formalism? Martti Koskenniemi and the Virtues' (2013) 27 *Temple International and Comparative Law Journal* 417.

Klabbers, J, 'Friedrich Kratochwil. The Status of Law in World Society: Meditations on the Role and Rule of Law' (2015) 25 *European Journal of International Law* 1195.

Knoops, G-JA, 'The Legitimacy of Initiating Contemporary International Criminal Proceedings: Rethinking Prosecutorial Discretionary Powers from a Legal, Ethical and Political Perspective' (2004) 1 *International Studies Journal* 365.

Knoops, G-JA and Zwart, T, 'The Flotilla Case before the ICC: The Need to Do Justice While Keeping Heaven Intact' (2015) 15 *International Criminal Law Review* 1069.

Koh, HH, 'Why Do Nations Obey International Law?' (1997) 106 *Yale Law Journal* 2599.

Krauss, R, 'The Theory of Prosecutorial Discretion in Federal Law: Origins and Developments Prosecutorial Discretion Today' (2009) 6 *Seton Hall Circuit Review* 1.

Kumm, M, 'The Legitimacy of International Law: A Constitutionalist Framework of Analysis' (2004) 15 *European Journal of International Law* 907.

Lacey, N, 'The Path Not Taken: HLA Hart's Harvard Essay on Discretion' (2013) 127 *Harvard Law Review* 636.

Langer, M, 'From Legal Transplants to Legal Translations: The Globalization of Plea Bargaining and the Americanization Thesis in Criminal Procedure' (2004) 45 *Harvard International Law Journal* 1.

Langobardo, M, 'Everything is Relative, Even Gravity' (2016) 14 *Journal of International Criminal Justice* 1011.

Lawrie, L et al, 'The Use of Population-Based Surveys for Prosecutions at the International Criminal Court' (2014) 24 *International Criminal Justice Review* 5.

Lepard, B, 'How Should the ICC Prosecutor Exercise His or Her Discretion: The Role of Fundamental Ethical Principles' (2009) 43 *John Marshall Law Review* 553.

Lockhart, N and Sheargold, E, 'In Search of Relevant Discretion: The Role of the Mandatory/Discretionary Distinction in WTO Law' (2010) 13 *Journal of International Economic Law* 379.

Ludwin King, EB, 'Does Justice Always Require Prosecution? The International Criminal Court and Transitional Justice Measures' (2013) 45 *George Washington International Law Review* 85.

Macdonald, A, '"In the Interests of Justice?" The International Criminal Court, Peace Talks and the Failed Quest for War Crimes Accountability in Northern Uganda' (2017) 11 *Journal of Eastern African Studies* 628.

—— 'Somehow This Whole Process Became so Artificial: Exploring the Transitional Justice Implementation Gap in Uganda' (2019) 13 *International Journal of Transitional Justice* 225.

Marston Danner, A, 'Enhancing the Legitimacy and Accountability of Prosecutorial Discretion at the International Criminal Court' (2003) 97 *American Journal of International Law* 510.

Mcmillan, N and Mickler, D, 'From Sudan to Syria: Locating "Regime Change" in R2P and the ICC' (2013) 5 *Global Responsibility to Protect* 283.

McKnight, J, 'Accountability in Northern Uganda: Understanding the Conflict, the Parties and the False Dichotomies in International Criminal Law and Transitional Justice' (2015) 59 *Journal of African Law* 193.

Mégret, F, 'Beyond "Gravity": For a Politics of International Criminal Prosecutions' (2013) 107 *Proceedings of the Annual Meeting (American Society of International Law)* 428.

—— 'The Anxieties of International Criminal Justice' (2016) 29 *Leiden Journal of International Law* 197.

Meloni, C, 'The ICC Preliminary Examinatin of the Flotilla Situation: An Opportunity to Contextualise Gravity' (2016) 33 *Questions of International Law* 3.

Mennecke, M, 'Punishing Genocidaires: A Deterrent Effect or Not?' (2007) 8 *Human Rights Review* 319.

Meron, T, 'Judicial Independence and Impartiality in International Criminal Tribunals' (2005) 99 *American Journal of International Law* 359.

Minow, M, 'Do Alternative Justice Mechanisms Deserve Recognition in International Criminal Law?: Truth Commissions, Amnesties, and Complementarity at the International Criminal Court' (2019) 60 *Harvard International Law Journal* 1.

Moreno-Ocampo, L, 'Keynote Address: Integrating the Work of the ICC into Local Justice Initiatives' (2005) 21 *American University International Law Review* 497.

Mullins, C and Rothe, D, 'The Ability of the International Criminal Court to Deter Violations of International Criminal Law: A Theoretical Assessment' (2010) 10 *International Criminal Law Review* 771.

Murphy, R, 'Gravity Issues and the International Criminal Court' (2006) 17 *Criminal Law Forum* 282.

Mylonas, A et al, 'Smartphone Sensor Data as Digital Evidence' (2013) 38 *Computers & Security* 51.

Nerlich, V, 'The Confirmation of Charges Procedure at the International Criminal Court: Advance or Failure?' (2012) 10 *Journal of International Criminal Justice* 1339.

Niemann, G, 'The Life and Times of a Senior Trial Attorney at the ICTY from 1994–2000' (2004) 2 *Journal of International Criminal Justice* 435.

Olásolo, H, 'The Prosecutor of the ICC before the Inititation of Investigations: A Quasi-Judicial or a Political Body?' (2003) 3 *International Criminal Law Review* 87.

Paulson, S, 'Formalism, "Free Law", and the "Cognition" Quandary: Hans Kelsen's Approaches to Legal Interpretation' (2008) 27 *University of Queensland Law Journal* 7.

Portilla, JC, 'A Forgiveness Law: The Path to Solve the Peace versus Justice Dilemma' (2015) 1 *Boston College Journal of Law & Social Justice* 193.

Pues, A, 'Discretion and the Gravity of Situations at the International Criminal Court' (2017) 17 *International Criminal Law Review* 960.

—— 'Towards the "Golden Hour"? A Critical Exploration of the Length of Preliminary Examinations' (2017) 15 *Journal of International Criminal Justice* 435.

Rauxloh, R, 'Negotiated History: The Historical Record in International Criminal Law and Plea Bargaining' (2010) 10 *International Criminal Law Review* 739.

Robinson, D, 'Serving the Interests of Justice: Amnesties, Truth Commissions and the International Criminal Court' (2003) 14 *European Journal of International Law* 481.

—— 'A Cosmopolitan Liberal Account of International Criminal Law' (2013) 26 *Leiden Journal of International Law* 127.

—— 'Inescapable Dyads: Why the ICC Cannot Win' (2015) 28 *Leiden Journal of International Law* 323.

Robinson, D and, MacNeil, G, 'The Tribunals and the Renaissance of International Criminal Law: Three Themes' (2016) 110 *American Journal of International Law* 191.

Rodman, K, 'Is Peace in the Interests of Justice? The Case for Broad Prosecutorial Discretion at the International Criminal Court' (2009) 22 *Leiden Journal of International Law* 99.

—— 'Justice as a Dialogue Between Law and Politics: Embedding the International Criminal Court within Conflict Management and Peacebuilding' (2014) 12 *Journal of International Criminal Justice* 437.

Sácouto, S and Cleary, K, 'The Gravity Threshold of the International Criminal Court' (2008) 5 *American Journal of International Law* 807.

—— 'Importance of Effective Investigation of Sexual Violence and Gender-Based Crimes at the International Criminal Court' (2009) 17 *American University Journal of Gender, Social Policy & the Law* 337.

Sanchez Leon, NC, 'Could the Colombian Peace Accord Trigger an ICC Investigaton on Colombia?' [2016] *AJIL Unbound* 172.

Schabas, W, 'Prosecutorial Discretion versus Judicial Activism at the International Criminal Court' (2008) 6 *Journal of International Criminal Justice* 731.

—— 'Victor's Justice: Selecting "Situations" at the International Criminal Court' (2010) 43 *John Marshall Law Review* 535.

Scharf, M, 'The Amnesty Exception to the Jurisdiction of the International Criminal Court' (1999) 32 *Cornell International Law Journal* 507.

—— 'Trading Justice for Efficiency' (2004) 2 *Journal of International Criminal Justice* 1070.

Schrag, M, 'Lessons Learned from the ICTY Experience' (2004) 2 *Journal of International Criminal Justice* 427.

Shaw, GC, 'HLA Hart's Lost Essay: Discretion and the Legal Process School' (2013) 127 *Harvard Law Review* 666.

Shoamanesh, S, 'Institution Building: Perspective from within the Office of the Prosecutor of the International Criminal Court' (2018) 18 *International Criminal Law Review* 489.

Sloane, R, 'The Expressive Capacity of International Punishment: The Limits of the National Law Analogy and the Potential of International Criminal Law' (2007) 43 *Stanford Journal of International Law* 39.

Smeulers, A, Weerdesteijn, M and Hola, B, 'The Selection of Situations by the ICC: An Empirically Based Evaluation of the OTP's performance' (2015) 15 *International Criminal Law Review* 1.
Snyder, J and Vinjamuri, L, 'Trials and Errors' (2003) 28 *International Security* 5.
Stahn, C, 'Complementarity, Amnesties and Alternative Forms of Justice: Some Interpretative Guidelines for the International Criminal Court' (2005) 3 *Journal of International Criminal Justice* 695.
—— 'Modification of the Legal Characterization of Facts in the ICC System: A Portrayal of Regulation 55' (2005) 16 *Criminal Law Forum 1.*
—— 'Justice Delivered or Justice Denied?: The Legacy of the Katanga Judgment' (2014) 12 *Journal of International Criminal Justice* 809.
Studzinsky, S, 'Sexualstraftaten im ersten Völkerstrafrechtsprozess – ein Kommentar' (2017) 2 *Streit – Feministische Rechtszeitschrift* 51.
Tallgren, I, 'The Sensibility and Sense of International Criminal Law' (2002) 13 *European Journal of International Law* 561.
Tiemessen, A, 'The International Criminal Court and the Politics of Prosecutions' (2014) 18 *International Journal of Human Rights* 444.
Turner, J, 'Plea Bargaining and International Criminal Justice' (2017) 48 *The University of the Pacific Law Review* 219.
Vaid, K, 'Discretion Operationalized Through Law: Proprio Motu Decision-Making at the International Criminal Court' (2013) 25 *Florida Journal of International Law* 359.
Varaki, M, 'Effectiveness Considerations Between Legitimacy and Prosecutorial Discretion' (2014) 108 *Proceedings of the Annual Meeting (American Society of International Law)* 304.
—— 'Introducing a Fairness-Based Theory of Prosecutorial Legitimacy before the International Criminal Court' (2016) 27 *European Journal of International Law* 769.
Ventura, M, 'The "Reasonable Basis to Proceed" Threshold in the Kenya and Côte d'Ivoire *Proprio Motu* Investigation Decisions: The International Criminal Court's Lowest Evidentiary Standard?' (2013) 12 *The Law & Practice of International Courts and Tribunals* 49.
Webb, P, 'The ICC Prosecutor's Discretion Not to Proceed in the "Interests of Justice"' (2005) 50 *Criminal Law Quarterly* 305.
Wippman, D, 'Atrocities, Deterrence, and the Limits of International Justice' (1999) 23 *Fordham International Law Journal* 473.
Zakerhossein, MH, 'To Bury a Situation Alive: A Critical Reading of the ICC Prosecutor's Statement on the ISIS Situation' (2016) 16 *International Criminal Law Review* 613.
Zaum, D, 'The Norms and Politics of Exit: Ending Postconflict Transitional Administrations' (2009) 23 *Ethics & International Affairs* 189.

OTHER REPORTS AND DOCUMENTS

Aksenova, M, 'The Al Mahdi Judgment and Sentence at the ICC: A Source of Cautious Optimism for International Criminal Justice', 13 October 2016, available at: EJILTalk.org.
Avocat Sans Frontières, *A Beggar has no Choice: Victims' Perspectives on a Reparations Framework for Uganda* (2017), available at: www.asf.be.
Bitti, G, 'The Interests of Justice – where does that come from? Part I, 13 August 2019, available at: ejiltalk.org.
—— 'The Interests of Justice – where does that come from? Part II', 14 August 2019, available at: ejiltalk.org.
FIDH, 'Enhancing Victims' Rights Before the ICC: A View from Situation Countries on Victims' Rights Before the ICC' (2013), available at: www.fidh.org/IMG/pdf/fidh_victimsrights_621a_nov2013_ld.pdf.
Guilfoyle, D, 'A Tale of Two Cases: Lessons for the Prosecutor of the International Criminal Court (Part III)', 30 August 2019, ejiltalk.org.

—— 'Reforming the International Criminal Court: Is it Time for the Assembly of State Parties to be the adults in the room?' 8 May 2019, available at: ejiltalk.org.

Hamilton, R, 'Closing ICC Investigations: A Second Bite at the Cherry for Complementarity?' (2012) Harvard University Human Rights Program, Research Working Paper Series HRP 12-001, May 2012.

Heller, KJ, 'The Pre-Trial Chamber's Dangerous Comoros Review Decision' (*Opinio Juris*, 2015), available at: opiniojuris.org/2015/07/17/the-pre-trial-chambers-problematic-comoros-review-decision.

—— 'Can the PTC Review the Interests of Justice?', 12 April 2019, available at: opiniojuris.org.

Human Rights Watch, 'Making Justice Count, Lessons from the ICC's Work in Côte D'Ivoire', 4 August 2015, available at: www.hrw.org.

—— 'Agreeing to Impunity', 22 December 2015, available at: www.hrw.org.

—— 'Human Rights Watch Comments on the ICC Office of the Prosecutor Draft Policy Paper on Case Selection and Prioritisation', 3 May 2016, available at: www.hrw.org.

—— 'Côte d'Ivoire: Simone Gbagbo Acquitted After Flawed War Crimes Trial', 29 March 2017, available at: www.hrw.org.

—— *Pressure Point: The ICC's Impact on National Justice* (2018).

IACH, *Report on Measures Aimed at Reducing the Use of Pre-Trial Detention in the Americas* OEA/Ser.L/V/II.163, 3 July 2017.

International Law Commission (ILC), 'Draft Statute for an International Criminal Court with Commentaries' article 51, 1994, available at: legal.un.org/ilc/texts/instruments/english/draft articles/7_4_1994.pdf.

Jacobs, D, 'Shifting Scale of Power: Who is in Charge of the Charges at the International Criminal Court and the Uses of Regulation 55 ?' (2013) Grotius Centre Working Paper 2013/004-ICL, available at: papers.ssrn.com.

—— 'ICC Pre-Trial Chamber rejects OTP request to open an investigation in Afghanistan: some preliminary thoughts on an ultra vires decision', 12 April 2019, available at: dovjacobs.com.

Karnavas, M, 'Al Mahdi Culturecide Judgment: A watershed moment for plea agreements', 30 September 2016, available at: michaelgkarnavas.net.

Keppler, E, 'AU's "ICC Withdrawal Strategy" Less Than Meets the Eye', 1 February 2017, available at: www.hrw.org.

Lomo, Z and Hovil, L, 'Whose Justice? Perceptions of Uganda's Amnesty Act 2000: The Potential for Conflict Resolution and Long-Term Reconciliation', (2005) Refugee Law Project Working Paper No 15, 15 February 2005.

Mégret, F and Jurdi, NN, 'The International Criminal Court, the "Arab Spring" and its Aftermath' [2016] Diritto umani e diritto internazionale 1, available at: papers.ssrn.com/sol3/papers.cfm?abstract_id=2793884.

Mcdonald, A and Haveman, R, 'Prosecutorial Discretion: Some Thoughts on "Objectifying" the Exercise of Prosecutorial Discretion by the Prosecutor of the ICC' [Expert Consultation Process on General Issues Relevant to the ICC Office of the Prosecutor] (2003), available at: www.issafrica.org/anicj/uploads/McDonald-Haveman_issues_relevant.pdf.

Miles, T, 'ICC Prosecutor vows to investigate both sides in Ivory Coast' (*Reuters*, 3 June 2016), available at: af.reuters.com/article/topNews/idAFKCN0YP251.

Office of the United Nations High Commissioner for Human Rights, *Rule-of-Law Tools for Post-Conflict States*, HR/PUB/06/4, New York, Geneva, 2006.

Popovski, V and Turner, N, 'Legality and Legitimacy in the International Order' *Policy Brief No 5* (United Nations University, 2008).

Rubin, A 'France hands ISIS suspects to Iraq, which sentences them to hang' *New York Times* (29 May 2019), available at: nytimes.com.

Sácouto, S and Cleary, K, 'The Practice of Cumulative Charging at the International Criminal Court' (War Crimes Research Office, 2010), available at: www.wcl.american.edu/warcrimes/icc/documents/WCRO_Report_May2010.pdf.

—— Stewart, J, Public Lecture, 'Transitional Justice in Colombia and the Role of the International Criminal Court', Bogota, 13 May 2015, available at: www.icc-cpi.int.

—— Speech 'The Role of the ICC in the Transitional Justice Process in Colombia', Bogota, 30 May 2018.
Shubert, A and Schmidt, N, 'German ISIS member faces war crime trial over Yazidi girl's murder' (CNN, 9 April 2019), available at: edition.cnn.com.
UK Discussion Paper, 'International Criminal Court Complementarity', 1996, available at: www.iccnow.org/documents/UKPaperComplementarity.pdf.
United Nations, ICTR Office of the Prosecutor, *Complementarity in Action: Lessons Learned from the ICTR's Prosecutor's Referral of International Criminal Cases to National Jurisdictions for Trial*, February 2015.
Uprimny, R and Sanchez, NC, 'The ICC and Negotiated Peace: Reflections from Columbia', 11 February 2015, available at: www.opendemocracy.net.
Vasiliev, S, 'Not just another "crisis": Could the blocking of the Afghanistan investigation spell the end of the ICC? (Part I)', 19 April 2019, available at: ejiltalk.org.
Whiting, A, 'The ICC's End Days? Not so Fast' (*Spreading the jam* Blog, 2014), available at: dovjacobs.com/2014/03/20/guest-post-the-iccs-end-days-not-so-fast.
—— 'The ICC Prosecutor should Reject Judges' Decision in Mavi Marmara' (*Just Security* Blog, 20 July 2015) available at: www.justsecurity.org/24778/icc-prosecutor-reject-judges-decision-mavi-marmara/.
—— 'Encouraging the Acceptance of Guilty Pleas at the ICC' (Blog post, 11 February 2015), available at: postconflictjustice.com.

International Criminal Court

Paper on some policy issues before the Office of the Prosecutor, Annex: Referrals and Communications, September 2003.
Policy on Children, November 2016.
Policy Paper on Case Selection and Prioritisation, 15 September 2016.
Policy Paper on Preliminary Examinations, November 2013.
Policy Paper on Sexual and Gender-Based Crimes, June 2014.
Policy Paper on the Interests of Justice, September 2007.
Policy Paper on Victims' Participation, April 2010.
Pre-Trial Practice Manual, September 2015.
Prosecutorial Strategy 2009–2012, 1 February 2010.
Report of the Bureau on Complementarity, ICC-ASP/16/33, 22 November 2017.
Report of the Court on the Basic Size of the Office of the Prosecutor, ICC-ASP/14/21, 7 August 2015.
Report on Preliminary Examination Activities 2011, 13 December 2011.
Report on Preliminary Examination Activities 2012, November 2012.
Report on Preliminary Examination Activities 2013, November 2013.
Report on Preliminary Examination Activities 2014, 2 December 2014.
Report on Preliminary Examination Activities 2015, 12 November 2015.
Report on Preliminary Examination Activities 2016, 14 November 2016.
Report on Preliminary Examination Activities 2018, 5 December 2018.
Report on the Activities Performed during the First Three Years, June 2003–June 2006, 12 September 2006.
Report on activities and programme performance of the International Criminal Court for the year 2017, ICC-ASP/17/2
Second report of the Prosecutor to the Security Council pursuant to UN SC Res 1593(2005), 13 December 2005, S/PV.5321.
Situation in Colombia, Interim Report, November 2012.
Situation in the Central African Republic, Background Factsheet ICC-OTP-BN-20070522-220-A_EN, 22 May 2007.

Statement of the Prosecutor to the Security Council, 7 November 2012, UN Doc S.PV/6855.
Strategic Plan 2012–2015, 11 October 2013.
Strategic Plan 2016–2018, 6 July 2015.
Strategic Plan 2019–2021, 17 July 2019.

ICC Press Releases

'ICC Office of the Prosecutor participates in training initiative in Uganda: Collaboration is key to closing the impunity gap', ICC-CPI-20180313-PRPR1368, 13 March 2018, available at: www.icc-cpi.int/Pages/item.aspx?name=pr1368.
'ICC Prosecutor, Fatou Bensouda, issues Draft Policy Paper on Case Selection and Prioritisation, for comment', ICC-CPI-20160229-PR1192, 29 February 2016, available at: www.icc-cpi.int/Pages/item.aspx?name=pr1192&ln=en.
'Message from the Prosecutor of the International Criminal Court, Fatou Bensouda, calling for defection by LRA fighters', 1 April 2016, available at: www.icc-cpi.int/Pages/item.aspx?name=160401-otp-stat.
'Statement of ICC Prosecutor, Fatouh Bensouda, on the Conclusion of the Peace Negotitations between the Government of Colombia and the Revolutionary Armed Forces of Colombia – People's Army' (1 September 2016), available at: www.icc-cpi.int//Pages/item.aspx?name=160901-otp-stat-colombia.
'Statement of the Prosecutor of the International Crimimnal Court, Fatou Bensouda, on the Alleged Crimes Committed by ISIS', 8 April 2015, available at: www.icc-cpi.int/en_menus/icc/press and media/press releases/Pages/otp-stat-08-04-2015-1.aspx.
'The determination of the Office of the Prosecutor on the communication received in relation to Egypt', ICC-OTP-20140508-PR1003, 8 May 2014, available at: www.icc-cpi.int/Pages/item.aspx?name=pr1003.

ICC Assembly of State Parties

Assembly of States Parties to the Rome Statute of the International Criminal Court 14th Session, Official Records, Vol II, ICC-ASP/14/20, 2015.
Resolution on the Programme budget for 2016, the Working Capital Fund and the Contingency Fund for 2016, scale of assessments for the apportionment of expenses of the International Criminal Court and financing appropriations for 2016, Resolution ICC-ASP/14/1, 26 November 2015.
Strengthening the International Criminal Court and the Assembly of States Parties, Resolution ICC-ASP/15/Res.5, 24 November 2016.

TREATIES, CONVENTIONS AND OTHER INTERNATIONAL LEGAL MATERIALS

Legislation

Charter of the United Nations 1945
Council of Europe Convention on Access to Official Documents, Council of Europe Treaty Series – No 205, 18 June 2009 (not entered into force yet), available at: www.coe.int/en/web/conventions/full-list/-/conventions/rms/0900001680084826
European Convention on Extradition 1957

Regulations of the Office of the Prosecutor, ICC-BD/05-01-09
Rome Statute of the International Criminal Court 1998
Rules of Procedure and Evidence of the International Criminal Court ICC-ASP/1/3 and Corr.1 2002, as amended
Vienna Convention on the Law of Treaties 1969

United Nations

Declaration on Principles of International Law concerning Relations and Co-operation among States in Accordance with the Charter of the United Nations, UN GA Resolution 2625, 24 October 1970
Declaratory Statement by the Republic of South Africa on the Decision to Withdraw from the Rome Statute of the International Criminal Court, United Nations C.N.786.20, 19 October 2016
General Comment No 32: Article 14 'Right to Equality before Courts and Tribunals and to a Fair Trial', Human Rights Committee CCPR/C/GC/32, 2007
Official Records of the United Nations Diplomatic Conference of Plenipotentiaries on the Establishment of an International Criminal Court (Volume II) A/CONF.183/13, 2002
South Africa: Withdrawal of Notification of Withdrawal, UN Doc C/N/121.2017.TREATIES-XVIII.10, 7 March 2017
Transforming our world: the 2030 Agenda for Sustainable Development, UN GA Resolution A/RES/70/1, 21 October 2015
United Nations Diplomatic Conference of Plenipotentiaries on the Establishment of an International Criminal Court, Report of the Preparatory Committee on the Establishment of an International Criminal Court, Vol III (1998) A/CONF.183/2
United Nations, 'Letter dated 15 November 2018 from the Special Adviser and Head of the United Nations Investigative Team to Promote Accountability for Crimes Committed by Da'esh/Islamic State in Iraq and the Levant addressed to the President of the Security Council', S/2018/1031, 16 November 2018
UNGA Res 70/1 (2015) Transforming our world: the 2030 Agenda for Sustainable Development, 21 October 2015, A/RES/70/1
UNSC Res 1593 (2005), 31 March 2005, S/RES/1593(2005)
Security Council Resolution 1593 (2003), 31 March 2005
Security Council Resolution 1970 (2011), 26 February 2011
Uniting for peace, UN GA Resolution 377, 3 November 1950
UNSC Res 1970 (2011), 26 February 2011, S/RES/1970(2011)

Index

Lightning Source UK Ltd.
Milton Keynes UK
UKHW020030170720
366664UK00003B/97

9 781509 928682